Mary-Ann Gallagher Sadakat Kadri

Gardner

D0808601

VIENNA PRAGUE
BUDAPEST

CADOGANguides

Contents

Budapest

07

08

Reference

Authors' acknowledgements

Mary-Ann Gallagher: Grateful thanks to all at Vienna Apartments, and to the taxi drivers, museum curators and coffee shop staff for their wonderful stories and insights.

Sadakat Kadri would like to thank the many people who have helped with information for this guide, and James Alexander for his thorough update of the Cadogan city guide to Prague, which was the inspiration for this text.

Matthew Gardner would like to thank Judit Mihalcsik at the Tourism Office of Budapest; and Alison and Theo for being such flexible and inspiring travel companions. He, and Cadogan Guides, would also like to credit and thank Marietta Pritchard for the Budapest history and Edwin Heathcote for the Budapest Art and Architecture sections.

About the authors

Mary-Ann Gallagher (Vienna) has written, and contributed to, more than a dozen Cadogan guides, including *Dublin*, *Flying Visits Ireland* and, most recently, *Flying Visits Mediterranean* and *Flying Visits Central and Eastern Europe*. Her travels have taken her everywhere from Japanese hill villages to glossy European capitals. Born in the UK, she is constantly on the move, but recently settled under the blue skies of Barcelona.

Sadakat Kadri (Prague) was born in Fulham in 1964 of a Pakistani father and a Finnish mother. He studied history and law at Trinity College, Cambridge, and took a Masters degree at Harvard Law School. He is a qualified New York attorney and a practising London barrister. His hobbies include cooking chicken.

Matthew Gardner (Budapest) is an unrepentant hedonist who loves travel almost as much as football, jazz, food and Shiraz. Though raised in outer London, he lives in a remote valley in Western Canada with his wife Alison, their rumbustious two-year-old son Theo, Lola and Frankie the dogs, Aspen the cat, occasional itinerant packrats, and baby no.2, a formidable kicker whose arrival is imminent.

Cadogan Guides
Network House, 1 Ariel Way
London W12 7SL
info@cadoganguides.co.uk
www.cadoganguides.com

The Globe Pequot Press
246 Goose Lane, PO Box 480, Guilford,
Connecticut 06437–0480

Copyright © Mary-Ann Gallagher, Sadakat Kadri
and Matthew Gardner 2005

Cover design by Sarah Gardner
Book design by Andrew Barker
Cover photographs: (front) © Celestial Panoramas
Ltd/Alamy; alan copson/jonarnoldimages; jon
arnold/jonarnoldimages; (back) © Peter Adams/
jonarnoldimages
Maps © Cadogan Guides, drawn by Maidenhead
Cartographic Services Ltd
Managing Editor: Natalie Pomier
Editorial Assistant: Nicola Jessop
Editors: Linda McQueen, Dominique Shead
Proofreading: Ali Qassim
Indexing: Isobel McLean
Production: Navigator Guides Ltd

Printed in the USA by Versa
A catalogue record for this book is available
from the British Library
ISBN 1-86011-187-4

Introduction

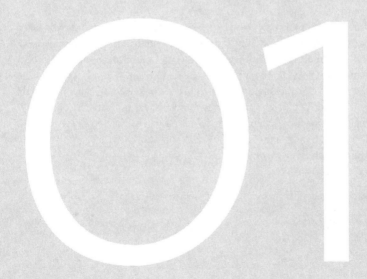

The great central European cities of Vienna, Prague and Budapest are often combined into a single trip. This is partly because of their physical proximity, and partly also because of their shared histories and cultures, which make the experience of visiting them similar in some ways, and certainly worthwhile for comparison. Lovers of café life, sticky cakes, classical music, Baroque or Gothic architecture, Art Nouveau, Jewish history or antiques shopping will find something of interest in each; each has a palimpsest of a castle whose layers tell the story of the city's past; each has a labyrinthine warren of an old town at its heart, with lanes and passages to wander and get lost in.

Not surprisingly, however, each city has its own distinct character, supported by different languages that are a matter for fierce national pride even as they whole-heartedly enter today's Europe; and each is compact, with a modern, clean, efficient transport system that make getting around easy for native and visitor alike.

A Guide to the Guide

For many with little time to spare, combining visits to two or three cities is the best option; indeed many tour operators (including those listed on pp.9–10) offer such holidays tailor-made. If you prefer to draw up your own itinerary and choose your own accommodation, the **Travel** chapter will help you get there by air or by train or coach, travel between cities, and make sure you have the correct kind of passport or visa.

Each of the three cities has its own separate **Practical A–Z** chapter, giving you all the background you will need, from electricity and money to telephones, tipping and toilets. This is also where you will find an explanation of the **price categories** used for the hotel and restaurant listings for each city – because there is a difference in cost between the cities, each has its own range.

The three **city chapters** open with extensive listings, and this is where you will find information on city transport, tourist information, hotels, restaurants, cafés, festivals, shopping and entertainments. They all have a box on **food and drink**, giving you a flavour of the local specialities and wines you might want to look out for, and a brief run-down of the city's **history, art and architecture** before embarking on the **sight-seeing**. At the end of each city are suggestions for **day trips** further afield, often upriver or into forests or up mountains, to make a real contrast to city streets.

Finally there is a **Language** chapter, including pronunciation advice and some basic useful phrases, and a menu reader.

Travel

02

Many people visiting all three cities will find it easiest to book on a tour operator trip that conveys you between them (*see* pp.9–10). However, their proximity to one another makes it easy for the independent traveller to fly to one of the three and take a train to the others. Many airlines offer single fares, so you can fly into one place and out of another.

Getting There

By Air

All three cities have a nearby airport. Thanks to no-frills airlines in the UK, prices are becoming more competitive. Budget flights are usually cheaper if booked early and on-line – last-minute bookings don't tend to be much less expensive than flights by major carriers. Shop around and book ahead.

In the UK, for flights and price comparisons on the Internet, see *www.skyscanner.net*, *www.whichbudget.com* (claims to include all routes flown by budget UK airlines on a single site), *www.traveljungle.co.uk*, *www.opodo.co.uk*, *www.travelocity.co.uk*, *www.expedia.co.uk* or *www.aboutflights.co.uk* (t 0870 330 7311).

From North America, it's marginally easier to find flights to Prague than Budapest or Vienna; however, most flights will involve a stopover in another European city. For fares, schedules and price comparisons on the Internet see *www.traveljungle.us*, *www.lastminute.com*, *www.expedia.com*, *www.orbitz.com*, *www.travelocity.com* and *www.flyaow.com* (discounted fares and schedules on 500 worldwide airlines, also car hire and hotels).

Airline Carriers

UK and Ireland

British Airways (BA), t 0870 850 9850, *www.ba.com*. To Vienna from London Heathrow, Birmingham and Manchester. To Prague from London Heathrow and Dublin. To Budapest from London Heathrow.

Austrian Airlines, t 020 (020) 7766 0300, *www.aua.com*. To Vienna from London Heathrow and London Gatwick. To Budapest via Vienna.

ČSA Czech Airlines, t 0870 444 3747, *www.czechairlines.com*. To Prague from London Heathrow, London Stansted, London Gatwick, Manchester, Birmingham, Edinburgh, Glasgow and Dublin.

Malév Hungarian Airlines, t 0870 909 0577, *www.malev.com*. To Budapest from London Gatwick, London Heathrow and Dublin. To Prague (and on to Budapest) from Edinburgh, Birmingham, Glasgow and Manchester.

Air Berlin, t 08707 388 880 (8p/min), *www.airberlin.com*. To Vienna and Budapest from London Stansted.

British Midland (BMI), t 08706 070 555, *www.flybmi.com*. London Heathrow to Vienna.

bmibaby, t 08702 642 229, *www.bmibaby.com*. To Prague from Cardiff, Manchester, Nottingham EMA, Durham Tees Valley, Birmingham and Edinburgh.

easyJet, t 0905 821 0905 (65p/min), *www.easyjet.com*. To Prague from Bristol, London Gatwick, London Stansted, Newcastle and Nottingham EMA. To Budapest from Bristol, London Gatwick, Luton and Newcastle.

EU Jet, t 0870 414 1414, *www.eujet.com*. To Prague from Kent International Airport.

Flyglobespan.com, t 08705 561 522, *www.flyglobespan.com*. To Prague from Glasgow.

Jet 2, t 0870 737 8282, *www.jet2.com*. To Prague from Belfast International and Leeds-Bradford. To Budapest from Manchester.

Ryanair, t 0871 246 0000, *www.ryanair.com*. Flies from London Stansted to Graz (90 miles from Vienna – about a 2½hrs away by car or 1hr by train).

SkyEurope, t (020) 7365 0365, *www.skyeurope.com*. To Budapest from London Stansted. To Bratislava from Manchester and London Stansted (a SkyShuttle bus takes passengers on the 50km ride from Bratislava to Vienna).

Thomsonfly, t 0870 1900 737, *www.thomsonfly.com*. To Prague from Doncaster/Sheffield.

Wizz Air, t (00 36) 1470 9499, *www.wizzair.com*. To Budapest from London Luton and Liverpool.

USA and Canada

Austrian Airlines, USA **t** 800 843 0002, Canada **t** 888 817 4444, *www.aua.com*. Direct to Vienna from New York (JFK) and Toronto. To Budapest and Prague via Vienna.

By Train

You can take the train all the way; connections are complicated and it's a good idea to book ahead (reservations can only be made a maximum of two months in advance).

For **London Waterloo–Prague**, there are two main options, the first taking Eurostar, sleeper and EuroCity trains via Brussels and Berlin. The journey takes 23hrs: travel by Eurostar from London Waterloo to Brussels early evening, then take the sleeping car from Brussels to Berlin, then a EuroCity train from Berlin to Prague the next day, arriving Prague Holešovice station early afternoon. Or travel by day to Brussels and Frankfurt, leaving London Waterloo on the Eurostar for Brussels, taking a train from Brussels to Frankfurt, and then the Frankfurt–Prague sleeper.

For **London Waterloo–Vienna**, the best option is to take a Eurostar and sleeper train via Paris (an emasculated version of the original 1856 'Orient Express', now reduced to Paris–Vienna only). The journey takes 21hrs: take an early afternoon Eurostar to Paris Gare du Nord, go across town to the Gare de l'Est, and take the late-afternoon 'Orient Express' sleeper train to Vienna. Alternatively take the morning Eurostar to Brussels, a teatime high-speed 'ICE' train from Brussels to Cologne, then catch the 'CityNightLine' overnight hotel train, arriving at breakfast-time in Vienna. Another option is to take the Eurostar to Paris, an overnight sleeper from Paris to Munich and then a day train to Vienna.

For **London Waterloo–Budapest**, the journey takes 24hrs: take the Eurostar to Paris Gare du Nord, go to the Gare de l'Est, and take the

---

ČSA Czech Airlines, t 800 223 2365, *www.czechairlines.com*. To Prague direct from New York (JFK and Newark) and Toronto.

Malév Hungarian Airlines, t (212) 566 9944, *www.malev.com*. To Budapest direct from New York (JFK) and Toronto.

American Airlines, t 800 433 7300, t 800 543 1586 (TDD), *www.aa.com*. To Prague, Vienna and Budapest via London.

British Airways, t 800 AIRWAYS, *www.ba.com*. To Prague, Vienna and Budapest via London and other European cities.

Air Canada, t 1 888 567 4160 (Canada), t 800 268 0024 (USA), *www.aircanada.ca*. Flies (in conjunction with Austrian Airlines) direct to Vienna from Toronto. To Prague via London, Vienna and Frankfurt. To Budapest via Frankfurt.

Continental, USA and Canada t 800 231 0856, *www.continental.com*. To Budapest, Prague and Vienna via Amsterdam.

Delta, USA and Canada t 800 241 4141, t 800 831 4488 (TDD), *www.delta.com*. To Prague directly from New York (JFK and Newark) and via Amsterdam, Brussels, Helsinki, Paris, Riga and Vienna. To Budapest from Paris and Prague. To Vienna from Prague, Paris, Milan.

Northwest Airlines, t 800 447 4747 (24hr), *www.nwa.com*. To Prague, Vienna and Budapest via Amsterdam.

United Airlines, t 800 538 2929, t 800 323 0170 (TDD), *www.united.com*. Direct to Vienna from New York JFK and Washington DC. To Budapest via Frankfurt.

Charters, Discounts, Students and Special Deals

UK and Ireland

Besides saving 25% on regular flights, people under the age of 26 have the choice of flying on special discount charters. Students with ID cards are eligible for considerable reductions, not only on flights but also on trains and admission fees to museums, concerts and more. Agencies specializing in student and youth travel can supply ISICs (International Student Identity Cards).

Check websites including: *www.travellersweb.ws* (t 0870 922 0145, cheap flights, car hire and holidays); *www.cheapflights.co.uk*; *www.lastminute.com*; *www.expedia.co.uk*; *www.skydeals.co.uk*; *www.sky-tours.co.uk*; *www.aboutflights.co.uk* (t 0870 330 7311); *www.travelocity.com*; *www.travelselect.com*.

Budget Travel, 134 Lower Baggot St, Dublin 2, t (01) 631 1111, *www.budgettravel.ie*.

Club Travel, 30 Lower Abbey St, Dublin 1, t (01) 435 0016 within Eire, *www.clubtravel.ie*.

Europe Student Travel, 6 Campden St, London W8, t (020) 7727 7647. A small travel agent catering to non-students too.

original 'Orient Express' sleeper (*see* 'Vienna', previous page) to Vienna, arriving early morning. Then take an 'Avala' InterCity train, arriving at Budapest Keleti station at lunchtime. Alternatively you could take the Brussels–Cologne–Vienna route (*see* 'Vienna'): from Vienna it takes just under 2½ hours to Budapest, *see* opposite.

Train Operators, Booking Agencies and Other Useful Websites

Eurostar, t 08705 186 186, *www.eurostar.com*.
Deutsche Bahn UK, t 0870 243 5363, *www. deutsche-bahn.co.uk*; trains to Austria via Brussels and Germany; website features timetables for all journeys within Europe.
Rail Europe: UK: 178 Piccadilly, London W1, **t** 08705 848 848, *www.raileurope.co.uk*; USA and Canada: *www.raileurope.com*.

Ffestiniog Travel, t 01766 512400, *www.fest travel.co.uk*. Can book Eurostars, intercity trains throughout Europe, rail-sea-rail journeys and every kind of railpass.
Trains Europe, *www.trainseurope.co.uk*.
The Man in Seat Sixty-One, *www.seat61.com*. Excellent website featuring lyrical descriptions and meticulously researched details on every conceivable aspect of train travel.

Rail Passes

If you're planning to make more than one journey between the cities, it's well worth investing in a rail pass. The excellent-value **Eurodomino** or **'Freedom' Pass** entitles European citizens of at least 6 months' duration to unlimited rail travel within one country for one month. Prices vary slightly according to the agency you use, but passes are available

---

STA, 6 Wright's Lane, London W8 7RG, *www. statravel.co.uk*, **t** 08701 600 599, with 65 branches throughout the UK.
Trailfinders, 194 Kensington High St, London W8, **t** (020) 7937 1234, *www.trailfinders.co.uk*.
United Travel, 2 Old Dublin Rd, Stillorgan, County Dublin, **t** (01) 215 9300, *www. unitedtravel.ie*.

USA and Canada

If you're resilient, flexible and/or youthful and prepared to shop around for budget deals on stand-bys or even courier flights (you can usually only take hand luggage on the latter), you should be able to get yourself some rock-bottom prices. Check the *Yellow Pages* for courier companies. For discounted flights, try the small ads in newspaper travel pages (for example, *San Francisco Chronicle*, *New York Times*, *Chicago Tribune*, and *Toronto Globe and Mail*). Numerous travel clubs and agencies also specialize in discount fares, but they may require you to pay an annual membership fee.

Check websites including: *www.justfares. com* (**t** 800 766 3601); *www.flyaow.com* (discounted tickets on 500 airlines), *www. air-fare.com*; *www.cheapflights.com*; *www. expedia.us*; *www.travelocity.com*; *www.orbitz. com*; *www.priceline.com* (bid for low-cost airline tickets); *www.travellersweb.ws* (**t** 866 888 2192); *www.smartertravel.com*. Airlines update their websites late-night, so check for

special deals after midnight, before they've been advertised in that morning's papers.
Airhitch, t 877 247 4482, *www.airhitch.org*. Last-minute discount tickets to Europe.
Last Minute Travel Club, USA/Canada **t** 800 442 0568, *www.lastminutetravel.com*. Annual membership entitles you to cheap stand-by deals, special car rental rates in Europe and Europass train tickets.
New Frontiers, 5757 West Century Bd, Suite 650, Los Angeles, CA 90045, **t** 800 677 0720, *www.newfrontiers.com*. Low-cost scheduled transatlantic flights, also package holidays, hotels, discount rail passes, car rental, etc.
STA, **t** 800 777 0112 *www.statravel.com*, with branches at most universities and at 10 Downing St, New York, NY 10014, **t** (212) 627 3111, and ASUC Travel Center, Martin Luther King Jr Building, 2nd Floor, University of California, Berkeley, CA, **t** (510) 642 3000.
Travel Avenue, **t** 800 333 3335, *www.travel avenue.com*. The oldest rebate travel agency.
TFI, 34 West 32nd St, New York, NY 10001, **t** 800 745 8000, *www.lowestairprice.com*. Low-cost negotiated fares; discounts of up to 80%.
Travel Cuts, 187 College St, Toronto, Ontario ON M5T 1P7, **t** 866 246 9762 or **t** 800 592 CUTS from the USA, *www.travelcuts.com*. Canada's largest student travel specialists, with branches in most provinces, plus 14 branches in the USA, including Portland, San Francisco, Stanford, LA, San Diego, New York, Seattle.

for 3–8-day periods, so that an adult travelling via Brussels and Berlin to Prague, Vienna and Budapest might invest in passes to Belgium, Germany, the Czech Republic, Austria and Hungary for around £43, £138, £78, £35 and £59 respectively (less for under 26s). Alternatively you might consider a one-month **All Zone Inter-Rail Pass**, offering one month's unlimited travel through Zone E (France, Belgium, the Netherlands and Luxembourg), Zone C (Austria, Germany, Switzerland and Denmark) and Zone D (Czech and Slovak Republics, Hungary, Croatia and Poland), available from £295 (under-26s) or £415 (26 or over). Passes include discounted fares on some ferries plus reduced fares on Eurostars.

The equivalent North American **Eurail Pass** takes in first class travel through 17 countries including France, Germany, Austria and Hungary, but not the Czech Republic, so you'll have to buy separate tickets to Prague. Eurail passes are valid for 15, 21, 30, 60 or 90 days (prices range from $588–$1,654 for adults travelling 1st class or from $382–$1,075 for under 26s travelling 2nd class). Cards are also not valid for travel on trains in the UK; however, all include discounts on Eurostar, plus free or discounted travel on selected ferries, lake steamers, boats and buses.

Rail Passes for UK and Europe Residents
www.raileurope.co.uk/railpasses. Rail pass enquiry line **t** 08707 30 44 95.
www.railchoice.co.uk.
www.seat61.com/Railpass.htm; extensive information on every kind of rail pass.

Rail Passes for US/Canadian Residents
www.raileurope.com, USA **t** 877 257 2887; Canada *www.raileurope.com/canada*, **t** 800 361 RAIL.
www.europeonrail.com, **t** (201) 255 2898: rail passes, rail and drive, car rental, timetables.
www.railconnection.com, **t** 888 RAILPASS.
www.railpass.com, **t** 800 722 7151.
www.eurorailways.com, **t** 866 768 8927: rail passes, rail 'n' drive passes, senior and youth passes, car rental, air tickets.
www.europrail.net, **t** 888 667 9734.

By Train Between the Three Cities
There are frequent direct train connections between all three cities.

Prague to Budapest is 276 miles/444km; the journey takes around 7hrs, or 9hrs overnight, and costs around £45 one way or £90 return. Up to four trains a day leave from Prague hl.n. or Prague Holešovice for Budapest Nyugati pu and Budapest Keleti pu, and vice versa.

Vienna to Prague is 156 miles/251km; the journey by train takes 4½ hrs or 7hrs overnight and costs around £35 one way or £70 return. Up to five trains a day leave from Vienna Südbahnhof for Prague hl.n. and Prague Holešovice, and vice versa.

Budapest to Vienna is 134 miles/215km; the journey takes just under 3hrs and costs around £27 one way or £55 return. Up to four trains a day leave from Budapest Keleti Pu for Vienna Südbahnhof and Vienna Westbahnhof, and vice versa.

You can book tickets via the Rail Europe or Deutsche Bahn websites a maximum of 60 days ahead. To check timetables see Deutsche Bahn *http://bahn.hafas. de/english.html*, or for travel from Vienna see *http://fahrplan.oebb. at/bin/oebb.wo2/query.exe/en*.
Hungary international rail information, **t** (+36 1) 461 5500, *www.elvira.hu*.
Vienna rail information, **t** (+43 0) 5 1717, *www.oebb.at*.

By Coach

Travelling by coach is tiring but cheap. It takes 25hrs on **Eurolines** to Vienna, and return tickets booked 30 days in advance cost £66. It takes 23hrs to Prague, costing £59 return. It takes 28hrs to Budapest, costing £69 return.

An excellent cost-cutting option for travelling between cities is a **Busabout** pass, allowing flexible travel on coaches used exclusively by independent travellers. Unlimited passes span from 2 weeks (£259 or £229 for under 26s) to 6 months; flexipasses start at £299 or £259 for under 26s and are valid for 8, 12, 16 or 20 days, with each additional day costing £35. Eurolines also offer a pass ranging from 15, 30 to 60 days.
Busabout, 258 Vauxhall Bridge Rd, London SW1V 1B7, **t** (020) 7950 1661, *www.busabout.com*.
Eurolines, **t** 08705 808080, *www.eurolines.com*.

By Car

Driving to Prague, Vienna or Budapest is no picnic: it takes almost two days of solid driving via Belgium and Germany. Drivers will need to ensure that they have proof of ownership of the car, or a letter from the owner giving permission to drive the car (smuggling of stolen cars is a common crime). All vehicles must be roadworthy, registered and insured, at least third party; you'll need a 'green card' international insurance form. UK and the Republic of Ireland driving licences are accepted, so long as they carry a photograph. If yours doesn't, either trade your old one in for a new-style photocard, or get an International Driving Permit (IDP). Canadian and American drivers also need an IDP.

Crossing the channel is cheapest by ferry from Dover, quickest via the Channel Tunnel. For ferries, check out *www.ferrybooker.com*.

Eurotunnel, t 08705 35 35 35, *www.eurotunnel. com*. Operates the shuttle through the Channel Tunnel, Folkestone to Calais.

Hoverspeed, t 0870 240 8070, *www.hover speed.co.uk*. Dover to Calais and Ostende.

P&O Ferries, t 08705 20 2020, *www.poferries. com*. Dover to Calais and Zeebrugge.

Seafrance, t 08705 711 711, *www.seafrance. co.uk*. Dover to Calais.

Car Hire

UK
Avis, t 08700 100287, *www.avis.co.uk*.
Budget, t 08701 539170, *www.budget.com*.
easyCar, t 09063 33 33 33 (60p/min), *www.easycar.com*.
Europcar, t 08706 075000, *www.europcar.com*.
Hertz, t 08708 448844, *www.hertz.co.uk*.
Thrifty, t (01494) 751600, *www.thrifty.co.uk*.

USA and Canada
Auto Europe, t 888 223 5555, *www.autoeurope.com*.
Avis Rent a Car, t (USA) 800 230 4898, t (Canada) 800 272 5871, *www.avis.com*.
Europe by Car, t 800 223 1516, *www.europebycar.com*.
Europcar, t 877 940 6900, *www.europcar.com*.
Hertz, t (USA) 800 654 3131, t 800 854 3001 (international toll free), *www.hertz.com*.

Belgian and German motorways are free but you must buy a **pass** for Austrian, Czech and most Hungarian motorways, available at border crossings, post offices and petrol stations, valid for 10 days, a month or a year.

Motoring organizations can provide more information on routes and petrol prices.

AAA (USA), t (407) 444 4000.
AA (UK), t 08706 000 371, *www.theaa.com*.
RAC (UK), t 08705 722 722, *www.rac.co.uk*.
Moto Europa, (Europe), *www.ideamerge.com/ motoeuropa*. Driving-abroad website.

You could also consider **hiring a car** when you get there. To save money, look into air and holiday package deals. Car hire firms are also listed under the three cities in this book. It's often cheaper to book through car hire companies in your own country before you go. For an instant online price comparison, log on to *www.autosabroad.com*, t 08700 66 77 88.

By Hydrofoil from Budapest to Vienna

From April to September, the Hungarian shipping company Mahart PassNave runs a daily hydrofoil service up the Danube from Budapest to Vienna via Bratislava; fares cost €99 return or €79 one way, €84 return or €67 one way for students with ISIC cards.

Entry Formalities

Passports and Visas

All three countries are EU members.

Vienna: UK and Irish citizens need a passport valid for at least 6 months; visas are not required and visitors may stay for an unlimited period provided their passports remain in date. US and Canadian citizens need a passport valid for at least 6 months: visas are not required for US and Canadian citizens staying less than 90 days; visas are required for a stay exceeding 90 days.

UK Embassy, 18 Belgrave Mews West, London SW1X 9HU, t (020) 7235 3731, *www.austria. org.uk*.

US Embassy, 3524 International Ct NW, Washington DC 20008, t (202) 895 6767, *www.austria.org*.

Tour Operators and Special-interest Holidays

There are hundreds of 'multicentre' package tours to all three capitals to choose from.

From the UK

Abercrombie & Kent, St George's House, Ambrose St, Cheltenham, Glos GL50 3LG, t 0845 070 0610, *www.abercrombiekent. co.uk*. Luxurious city breaks in each of the three capitals, staying in four-star hotels.

Ace Study Tours, Babraham, Cambridge, CB2 4AP, t (01223) 835 055, *www.study-tours.org*. In-depth cultural tours led by writers, art and architectural historians: includes 'Art Treasures of Vienna and Budapest', exploring the shared Habsburg inheritance, 'Splendours of Prague' and 'Baroque Vienna'.

Archers Direct, t 0870 460 3894, *www.archers direct.co.uk*. A low-cost 2-week 'Bohemian Rhapsody' music coach holiday visiting all three capitals, plus Munich and Salzburg.

Brompton Travel, 3 Hinchley Way, Hinchley Wood, Esher, Surrey KT10 0BD, t (020) 8398 3672, *www.bromptontravel.co.uk*. Opera tours covering entire opera seasons.

Čedok, Suite 22–23, 5th Floor, Morley House, 314–22 Regent St, London W1B 3BG, t (020) 7580 3778, *www.cedok.co.uk*. Former Czech national tourist agency and a reliable source of information on city breaks in Prague.

Cox and Kings, 4th Floor, Gordon House, 10 Greencoat Place, London SW1P 1PH, t (020) 7873 5027, *www.coxandkings.co.uk*. Luxurious city breaks in all three cities.

Crystal Holidays, King's Place, Wood St, Kingston, Surrey KT1 1JY, t 0870 166 4951. Weekend breaks in all three cities.

Equity Total Travel, 47 Middle St, Brighton BN1 1AL, t (01273) 277 377, *www.equityweekends. co.uk*. Group tours by coach, also tailor-made short breaks.

Group Travel Connection, 40 Gay Street, Bath BA1 2NT, t (01225) 466620, *www.group travel.co.uk*. Tailor-made tours (art, history, architecture, garden design, etc, including exclusive visits to museums).

Inghams Eurobreak, 10-18 Putney Hill, London SW15 6AX, t (020) 8780 7700, *www.euro break.com*. Hotels and flights to all cities.

Kirker Holidays, 4 Waterloo Court, Theed Street, London SE1 8ST, t 0870 112 3333, *www.kirkerholidays.com*. Short breaks staying at upmarket hotels in Prague, Vienna and Budapest; multicentre breaks.

Leger Holidays, t 0800 018 9898, *www. leger.co.uk*. Offers the 'Grand Imperial Explorer' – an 8 day multicentre air tour visiting Prague, Vienna and Budapest.

Martin Randall, 10 Barley Mow Passage, London W4 4GF, t (020) 8742 3355, *www. martinrandall.com*. Superb cultural tours led by lecturers: includes 'The Habsburg Empire', an intensive 18-day tour taking in Vienna, Budapest, Slovakia and Prague via private coach; the Austro-Hungarian Music Festival; Budapest Spring Music Festival.

Orient Express, Sea Containers House, 20 Upper Ground, London, SE1 9PF, t (020) 86042242, *www.orient-express.com*. From Venice to London, stopping off for two nights at Prague, Vienna or Budapest.

Page and Moy, 135–140 London Road, Leicester, LE2 1EN, t 0870 833 4012, *www.page-moy.co. uk*. 'Prague, Vienna & Budapest': modestly priced three-centre escorted tours with sightseeing, concerts, cruises, excursions.

Prospect Tours, PO Box 4972, London W1A 7FL, t (020) 7486 5704, *www.prospecttours.com*. Music and cultural tours: includes Budapest Spring Festival and Budapest at Christmas.

Prague: As Vienna.

UK Embassy, 29 Kensington Park Gardens, London W8 4QY, t (020) 7235 3731, *www. czechembassy.org.uk*.

US Embassy, 3900 Spring of Freedom St, NW, Washington DC 20008, t (202) 274 9123, *www.mzv.cz/washington*.

Budapest: UK citizens need a passport valid for at least 6 months; visas are not required for UK citizens staying less than 6 months.

US, Canadian and Irish citizens, as US and Canadian citizens in Vienna. All visitors staying more than 30 days must register with the police or local government office within 48hrs of arrival.

UK Embassy, 35 Eaton Pl, London SW1X 8BY, t (020) 7235 2664, *www.huemblon.org.uk*.

US Embassy, 3910 Shoemaker St, NW, Washington DC 20008, t (202) 362 6730, *www.huembwas.org*.

Titan Hitours, Crossoak Lane, Redhill, Surrey RH1 5EX, t (01293) 455 345. Fully escorted 10-day multicentre coach tours.

Travel for the Arts, 12–15 Hanger Grn, London W5 3EL, t (020) 8799 8350, *www.travelforthearts.co.uk*. Tailor-made opera tours and weekends based on performances.

Travelsphere, Compass House, Rockingham Road, Market Harborough, Leics, LE16 7QD, t 0870 240 2426, *www.travelsphere.co.uk*. Wide choice including an 8-day tour of all three cities, plus a value for money 12-day 'Eastern Explorer' tour.

United Travel, 2 Old Dublin Road, Stillorgan, Co. Dublin, t (01) 215 9300, *www.unitedtravel.ie*. City breaks in Prague, Budapest and Vienna.

Voyages Jules Verne, 21 Dorset Square, London, NW1 6QG, t (020) 7616 1010, *www.vjv.co.uk*. Special tours: the Habsburgs, along the Elbe, Vienna, Budapest and Bratislava.

Wallace Arnold, Lowfields Rd, Leeds, West Yorkshire LS12 6DN, t (0113) 263 4234, *www.wallacearnold.com*. 12-day coach tours taking in each of the three cities.

In the USA and Canada

Check *www.affordabletours.com*, t 800 935 2620, for thousands of discounted escorted tours by established operators including Contiki, Maupin, Trafalgar, etc.

Abercrombie and Kent, 1520 Kensington Road, Oak Brook, IL 60523, t 800 554 7016, *www.abercrombiekent.com*. Escorted tours including a 10-day 'Tale of Three Cities', featuring guest speaker, behind the scenes tours of Budapest and Prague opera houses, private concert, vintage tram ride and top of the range dining and hotels.

Contiki Travels, 801 Katella Avenue, Anaheim, CA 92805, t (714) 935 0808, *www.contiki.com*. Coach tours for 18–35-year-olds.

Dailey-Thorp Travel, PO Box 670, Big Horn, Wyoming, 82833, t 800 998 4677, *www.daileythorp.com*. Luxury escorted tour taking in opera houses in all three cities.

Europe Train Tours, 2485 Jennings Rd, Olin, NC 28660, t 800 551 2085, *www.etttours.com*. Escorted and non-escorted tours by train and coach.

Globus, t 866 755 8581, *www.globusjourneys.com*. 11-day tour of Vienna, Budapest and Prague travelling by hydrofoil and train.

Go Ahead Vacations, 1 Education St, Cambridge MA 02141, t 800 590 1170, *www.goaheadvacations.com*. A reasonably priced 11-day tour of the three capitals.

Go-Today.com, t 800 227 3235, *www.go-today.com*. Hugely discounted last minute packages and vacations from the US. You can also book ahead for discount holidays (e.g. biking from Vienna to Prague or Budapest).

Kesher Kosher Tours, 347 Fifth Ave. Ste. 706, New York, N.Y. 10016, t (212) 481 3721, t 800 847 0700, *www.keshertours.com*. Intensive 12-day Jewish heritage tour taking in Vienna, Budapest, Bratislava and Prague.

International Curtain Call, 3313 Patricia Ave, Los Angeles, CA 90064, t 800 669 9070, *www.iccoperatours.com*. Opera tours focusing on the Vienna and Prague Festivals.

Maupintours, t 800 255 4266, *www.maupintour.com*. Three-night city getaways: half-day sightseeing, transfers by private car, American breakfasts.

Trafalgar Tours, 11 East 26th Street, New York, NY 10010, t (866) 247 9880, *www.trafalgartours.com*. 10-day tours to Prague, Vienna and Budapest.

Worldwide Classroom, PO Box 1166, Milwaukee, WI 53201, t (414) 351 6311, t 800 276 8712, *www.worldwide.edu*. From language schools to university exchanges.

Customs

Those arriving from another EU country do not have to declare goods imported into Austria, Hungary or the Czech Republic for personal use if they have paid duty on them in the country of origin. In theory, you can buy as much as you like, provided you can prove the purchase is for your own use. In practice, Customs will be more likely to ask questions if you buy in bulk.

Travellers from the USA are allowed to bring home, duty-free, goods to the value of $800, including 250 cigarettes or 50 cigars, plus one litre of alcohol. For more information, call the US Customs Service.

UK Customs, t 0845 010 9000, *www.hmce.gov.uk*.

US Customs, t (202) 354 1000, *www.customs.gov*; see the pamphlet *Know Before You Go*.

Austria: Practical A–Z

Climate and When to Go

Austria has mild summers and cold winters, with temperatures dropping considerably the higher you go. The cities are perhaps best visited from April to October, when the weather is pleasantly warm, but cosy cafés and a wealth of excellent museums and sights make them good options all year round.

Christmas markets and the famous ball season in Vienna draw plenty of visitors in December and January.

If you are travelling further afield, note that resorts in rural areas have two distinct seasons: a summer season for those interested in hiking, fishing or other outdoor activities, and a winter season when skiing and snowboarding take over. Transport is often reduced and many hotels and restaurants may close during the quiet periods (April–May and Oct–Nov) in these regions.

Disabled Travellers

For Vienna, go to *www.vienna.info* and click on Specials and 'Vienna for visitors with disabilities', where you will find 120 pages for downloading, with information on hotels, transport, restaurants, cinemas and theatres and sightseeing, regularly updated.

The UK charity Holiday Care offers a wealth of information for disabled travellers. They provide fact sheets on many destinations, including Austria (available online at *www. holidaycare.org.uk/datasheets/Austria.html*).

Driving

You need a special pass (called a '*vignette*') to drive on Austrian motorways. These are available at post offices, larger petrol stations and are valid for 10 days, two months or one year. A 10-day pass currently costs around €8. You will be fined if you are caught driving without this pass. More information (in German only) at *www.vignette.at*.

Electricity

The current used in Austria is 220v, which is fine for British applicances (240v). Visitors from North America, with 110v appliances, will need to use a transformer.

Plugs have two pins in Austria, but adaptors are easily available in department stores or shops selling electrical goods.

Embassies and Consulates

In Vienna
UK: Jaurèsgasse 12, **t** (01) 716130, *www.britishembassy.at*.
USA: Boltzmanngasse 16, **t** (01) 31339, *www.usembassy.at*.
Canada: Laurenzerberg 2, **t** (01) 531 383 000, *www.dfait-maeci.gc.ca*.
Australia: Winterthur House, Mattiellistrasse 2, **t** (01) 50674, *www.australian-embassy.at*.

Austrian Embassies Abroad
UK: 45 Princes Gate, Exhibition Road, London SW7 2QA, **t** (020) 7584 4411, *london@wko.at*.
USA: 3524 International Court NW, Washington DC, **t** (202) 895 6700, *www.austro.org*.
Canada: 445 Wilbrod St, Ottowa, K1N 6M7, **t** 613 789 1444, *www.austro.org*.
Australia: 12 Talbot St, Farrest Act 2603, Canberra, **t** 02 6295 1533.

Health and Emergencies

EU-citizens are entitled to emergency health care though reciprocal health-care agreements, but you'll need to bring a stamped form E111 with you (available from post offices in the UK). In practice, this is a time-consuming and painfully bureaucratic process and visitors (both from the EU and other countries) are advised to take out travel insurance which covers health emergencies.

Local **pharmacies** are well-equipped to deal with minor ailments, and are usually open Mon–Fri 8am–noon and 2–6pm, Sat 8am–noon. Lists of duty pharmacies and 24hr pharmacies are posted outside all pharmacies. In an emergency head for the nearest *Ambulanz* (emergency room) at any hospital.

The helpful **Vienna Medical Association Service for Foreign Patients**, 1 Weighburgasse 10/12, **t** (01) 5150 1213, 24-hour hotline **t** (01) 513 95 95 (U1, U3 to Stephansplatz), is open

Mon–Wed 8–4, and Thurs–Fri 8–6. It provides information on English-speaking doctors and local hospitals.

Emergency Numbers
t 112 (pan-European emergency number, for all services)
t 122 (fire brigade)
t 133 (police)
t 144 (ambulance)
t 120 (motorway breakdown)

Money

Austria's unit of currency is the **euro**, available in coins (1, 2, 5, 10, 20 and 50 cents, and 1 and 2 euros) and notes (5, 10, 20, 50, 100, 200 and 500).

ATMs (*bankomats*) are found on virtually every street corner, and almost all accept foreign credit cards and have instructions in English. Some central banks also have automatic money-changing machines which accept foreign banknotes. Banks usually offer a better rate of exchange than the various *bureaux de change* clustered in the city centre, although it is often cheaper to withdraw money using your credit card from an ATM (check rates before you leave home).

Banks are usually open Mon-Fri 8–12.30 and 1.30–3, until 5.30 on Thurs, although some city centre banks don't close at lunchtimes.

All major travellers' cheques are widely accepted, and those issued by AmEx, Thomas Cook and Visa are instantly replaced in case of loss of theft.

National Holidays

The following are all public holidays, when many places will be closed.

1 Jan New Year's Day
6 Jan Epiphany
Easter Sunday
Easter Monday
1 May Labour Day
Whit Monday (6th Mon after Easter Sun)
Ascension Day (6th Thurs after Easter Sun)
2 June Corpus Christi
15 Aug *Maria Himmelfahrt*
26 Oct National Holiday

1 Nov *Allerheiligen*
8 Dec *Maria Empfängnis*
25 Dec Christmas Day
26 Dec *Stefanitag*

Post and Post Offices (*Post- und Telegrafen*)

Post offices (*see* **Vienna**, p.21, for the address of the central office) have yellow signs, and the postboxes are also yellow. Those with an orange strip have weekend post collections. Postcards sent to destinations within Europe will take 3–4 days, and cost 52 cents; those sent outside Europe take around 5 days and stamps are 1.10 cents.

More information can be found at *www.post.at* (some information in English).

Stamps can also be bought from newsagents, and most post offices also have stamp-vending machines.

Price Categories

The hotels and restaurants in this section of the guide have been grouped into price categories according to the following rates:

Hotels
Average price for a double room with bath/shower and WC in high season.

luxury over €200
expensive €150–200
moderate €100–150
inexpensive under €100

Restaurants
Prices for a three course meal for one person with wine:

luxury €60 to astronomical
expensive €40–60
moderate €25–40
inexpensive under €25

Telephones

There are plenty of public telephones scattered around, most of which have instructions in English. They accept coins or phonecards (available from post offices or newsagents).

Post offices have phone booths, which are usually cheaper for long-distance calls. Rates are high, but are cheaper after 6pm on weekdays and all day at weekends.

To **call abroad** from Austria, dial 00 plus the country code (1 for the USA and Canada, 44 for the UK, 353 for Ireland, 61 for Australia, and 64 for New Zealand).

For **directory enquiries** relating to Austria or the EU call 118877, or **international directory enquiries** on t 0900 118877 (both usually have English-speaking operators).

The **international country code** for Austria is t (00) 43, and the **city code** for Vienna is 01, which you don't need to dial from within the city. Drop the first 0 of the city code if phoning Vienna from abroad.

Phone numbers vary in length, and some of them include direct dial extensions, which are tacked on to the end of the main number, sometimes with a dash, sometimes not.

Time

Austria is on Central European Time, which is one hour ahead of GMT. Clocks go forward one hour on the last Sunday of March, and go back on the last Sunday of October.

Tipping

In restaurants, add about 10% to the bill, or round it up to the nearest euro in cheaper places. Taxis usually expect around 10%. Hotel porters usually expect a euro for each piece of baggage, and hotel cleaning staff (in the smarter hotels at least) and anyone else who provides a service.

Toilets

There are public toilets scattered around the city centre, many of which are open 24 hours. Those with attendants usually charge 50 cents. Underground (U-Bahn) stations also have toilets, in varying states of cleanliness.

Tourist Information

www.austria-tourism.at has local sites for most countries; start on the home page and then choose your country of origin.
UK: 14 Cork Street, London W1, t (020) 7629 0461, t 0845 101 1818.
USA: PO Box 1142, New York, NY 10108-1142, t (212) 944 6880; 11601 Wilshire Bd, Suite 2480, Los Angeles CA 90025, t (310) 477 2038.
Canada: 2 Bloor St East, Suite 3330, Toronto, ON M4W 1A8, t (416) 967 3381.

Austria: Vienna

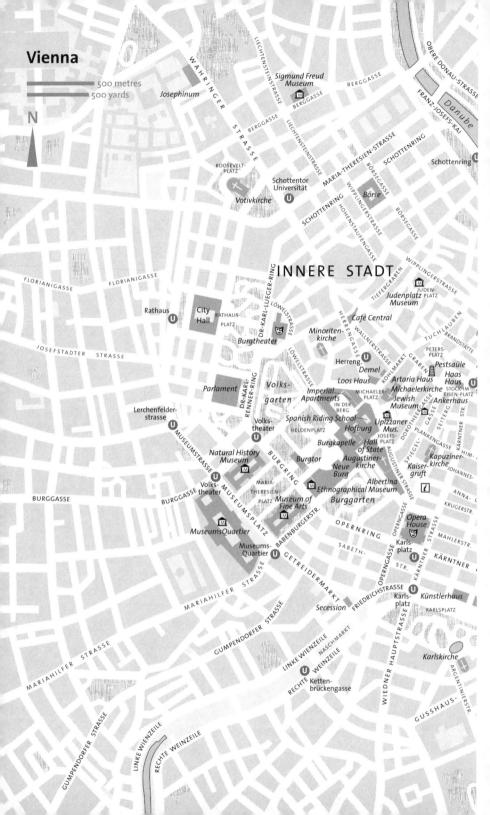

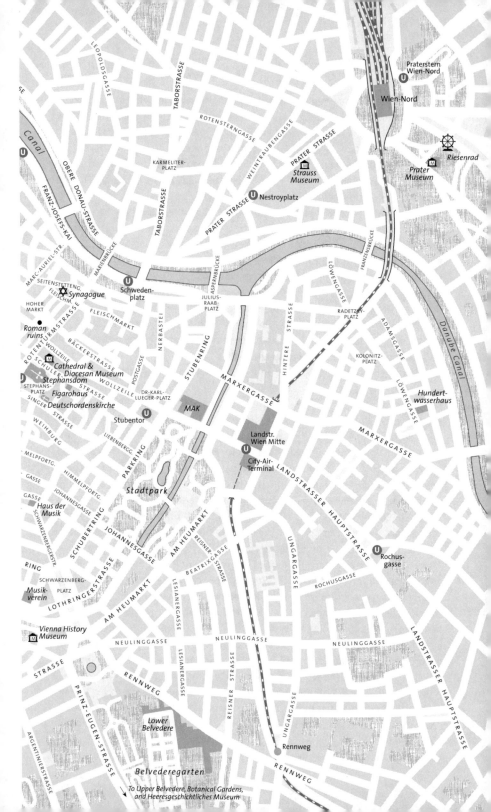

The streets of Vienna are paved with culture, the streets of other cities with asphalt.
Karl Kraus (Austrian writer, 1874–1936)

Vienna, long the glittering capital of a vast empire, oozes Imperial magnificence: from its opulent palaces and glorious gardens to the equestrian ballets at the Spanish Riding School, the city gorgeously evokes the splendour of the Habsburg court during the Baroque age. The Habsburgs have been gone for almost a century, but they left behind their splendid art collections and priceless jewels in extraordinary, world-class museums – as well as their hearts and entrails in the city's macabre catacombs and burial crypts.

As Habsburg influence began to wane in the mid-19th century, the increasingly powerful burghers of Vienna were flaunting their wealth by erecting the showcase monuments which still line the Ringstrasse. In the lavish new Opera House, they whirled to the strains of Strauss waltzes as far-flung territories were shorn from the Empire. *Fin-de-siècle* Vienna was explosive: its coffee houses were brimming with writers, artists and philosophers; the Secessionists, led by Gustav Klimt, had electrified the art world; and Jugendstil architecture was blooming across the city. The decadent, hothouse atmosphere of turn-of-the-20th-century Vienna has long vanished, but its memory is still evoked in the city's legendary coffee houses, or when a street musician breaks into a poignant waltz.

The 20th century was a whole different story: two world wars and their aftermath put an end to the party. The last Habsburg emperor abdicated in 1918, when the Republic of Austria was declared, and the Reds took over the capital. Red Vienna erected the vast public housing projects which still stand on the fringes of the city, but Austria was on its knees. Rich, neighbouring Germany seemed to provide the only solution, and in 1938 Hitler declared the incorporation of Austria into the German Reich from a balcony of the former Imperial palace. The once-thriving Jewish community was virtually wiped out, and the city was destroyed by bombs. After a decade of Allied Occupation, Vienna began to repair its monuments and its relationship with the rest of Europe. But the country has found it difficult to shake off its reputation for xenophobia and anti-Semitism and the recent antics of Jörg Haider, the extremist right-wing populist, have brought sanctions and unwelcome international attention. However, with the awarding of the 2004 Nobel prize for literature to Elfriede Jelinek, whose works bitterly condemn her homeland, the spotlight is now on those who oppose the ugly prejudice which has long blighted the country.

For decades, Vienna has clung to the splendour and romance of its Imperial heritage. The first major sign that things were changing was the erection of Hans Hollein's curving glass-and-steel Haas Haus right opposite the Viennese holy-of-holies, the Stephansdom cathedral. Baroque riding stables have been glamorously converted into one of the world's largest cultural complexes, with a string of excellent museums and a wealth of cafés where fashionable Viennese lounge on terraces in summer. The Albertina has had a futuristic new make-over and the city's culinary scene has never been so creative. The palaces, cafés and opera houses still provide Vienna with its alluring old world charm, but the recent injection of 21st-century confidence and optimism have given the city a welcome new dynamism.

Addresses

Vienna is divided into 23 numbered districts or *Bezirke*. Addresses are commonly prefixed with a number indicating the district, and the street number follows the street name (for example, 1 Dorotheergasse 11 means No.11 Dorotheergasse, in the First District). The Innere Stadt (Inner City) is the 1st district, with the other districts spiralling outwards from here. Post codes incorporate the district number, so the post code for the 1st district is A-1010, and for the 15th district it's A-1150, etc.

Getting There

Many airlines fly direct to Vienna from London and other UK airports (*see* **Travel**, p.4), and from the USA and Canada (p.5). You can also travel by train or coach, *see* pp.5–7.

Getting from the Airport

Vienna international airport, Flughafen Wien-Schwechat, **t** (01) 7007 222 33, *www. viennaairport.com*, is 20km southeast of the city. There are three **bus** services to the city centre: one for Schwedenplatz, one for UNO City, and another for the train stations at Südtiroler Platz, Südbahnhof and Wesbahnhof. They leave every 30mins (between 5am–11.30pm) and cost €6.

A faster option is the **city–airport train**, which departs at least every half-hour between 5.05am and 11.35pm and costs €15 (return); *www.cityairporttrain.at*. There is also an **S-bahn** (commuter train), line S7, to Wien Nord, Mitte and Rennweg stations, which costs €3 (single) and departs every 30mins.

There is a **taxi** rank outside the arrivals hall. Journeys to the city centre cost €25–35.

Getting Around

You can get information, plans and tickets for the U-Bahn, tram and bus systems, at the **transport information offices** located at U-Bahn stations across the city, including Stephansplatz, Karlsplatz, Volkstheater and Westbahnhof (*open Mon–Fri 6.30am–6.30pm, Sat–Sun 6.30am–4pm*).

Also see *www.wienerlinien.at*.

Tickets

Tickets, available from ticket machines at tram and bus stops and in U-Bahn stations, or at newsagents, are valid for all forms of public transport. A **single ticket** costs €1.50; a **24hr Rover ticket** costs €5 and offers unlimited use of the public transport for 24 hours; a **72hr Rover ticket** is €12; and an 8-day **strip ticket** or *Streifenkarte* (which can be shared – just date-stamp a strip for each person using it) costs €24. Other **passes** include weekly, monthly and student passes (visit the information offices). The **Vienna Card** (*see* p.20) offers concessions on public transport.

By U-Bahn

Vienna has a clean, efficient and inexpensive underground metro system which is easy to use. There are five colour-coded numbered lines (U1, U2, U3, U4, and U6), and plans are available in all U-Bahn ticket offices. Date-stamp your ticket in the orange machines at the entrance to the underground before getting on the train. *See* p.284 for a map.

By Tram (Strassenbahn)

Vienna's older trams – snub-nosed, rickety and endearingly old-fashioned – are gradually being replaced by a sleek, 21st-century version designed by Porsche. The excellent tram system doesn't penetrate the old city, but is useful for getting around the surrounding neighbourhoods.

Trams 1 and 2, which circle the Ringstrasse around the old city, are the most useful for visitors, but tram stops have maps showing the vast network of lines. Date-stamp your ticket in the machines by the doors.

By Bus

Most places on a visitor's itinerary will be served by metro or tram, but, for those that aren't, there are buses. Bus stops have useful bus maps and you should date-stamp your ticket in the machines by the doors.

Night buses run every 30mins from around 12.30am to 5am, and the standard public transport tickets are valid.

By Taxi

Vienna's taxis have a 'taxi' sign on the roof, illuminated when they are free. They can be found at numerous taxi ranks (but not hailed on the street), or call **t** 40100 or **t** 60160. **Fares** are reasonable (a short trip in the centre costs between €5–10), but more expensive after 10pm and at weekends, and there are supplements for luggage. A small tip is expected.

By Car

A car is virtually useless in Vienna's city centre, and parking can be hard to find. Public transport is clean, efficient and inexpensive. However, your own transport can be very useful for visiting sights outside the centre. That said, Austria's national public transport system is excellent, and most places are easily accessible by train or bus.

There are several car hire offices at the airport, with branches in the city centre. **Avis, t** (01) 7007 32700 (airport), **t** (01) 587 6241 (city centre), *www.avis.com.*
Europcar, t (01) 7007 32699 (airport), **t** (01) 512 8677 (city centre), *www.europcar.com.*
Hertz, t (01) 7007 32661 (airport), **t** (01) 714 6565 (city centre), *www.hertz.com.*
Budget, t (01) 7007 32711, **t** (01) 714 6717 (city centre), *www.budget.com.*

On Foot

The old heart of Vienna is perfect for strolling – small and compact with cobbled alleys and secret passages beckoning at every turn. The Ringstrasse and access to the many attractions just off it are plagued by traffic, but most of the main sights are within easy walking distance of each other.

Tourist Information

Vienna: Main tourist office (Wien Tourismus) is at 1 Albertinaplatz, **t** (01) 211 14, hotel booking **t** (01) 24 555, *www.vienna.info. Open daily 9–7, U1, U2, U4 to Karlsplatz.* The helpful staff have lots of glossy maps and leaflets, offer a hotel-booking service, a ticketing service for major (and many minor) venues, a *bureau de change*, and sell the **Vienna Card** (a discount pass, *see* below). There are smaller branches at the airport and at the Westbahnhof train station. There's a special youth information service at 1 Babenbergerstrasse 1, *www. jugendinfowien.at.*

Rest of Austria: Austrian tourist information office, 4 Margaretenstrasse 1, **t** (01) 587 20 00, *www.austria.info.*

The **Vienna Card** offers discounts of between 10% and 35% at museums and attractions, shops and restaurants plus 72hrs' unlimited use of public transport. It costs €16.90, and can be bought at the tourist information office, main train stations, some hotels, or by credit card on **t** (01) 798 44 00-148. Each card allows you to take a child under 15 along for free.

Guided Tours

The tourist office produces a monthly booklet listing the various **walking tours** offered by official guides in Vienna. Themes include Jewish Vienna, Art Nouveau Vienna, Vienna in the footsteps of *The Third Man,* Freud's Vienna, Red Vienna, and the Homes of Mozart, Beethoven and Schubert. Tours usually last 1½–2hrs, and cost €11 (€10 with the Vienna Card), or €6 for under-18s. Visit *www.wienguide.at* for more information, or call **t** (01) 774 89 01.

Pedal Power, 2 Ausstellungsrasse 3, **t** (01) 729 72 34, *www.pedal power.at*, offer **cycling tours** of the city, which begin from the Prater. They also rent out bikes.

During the summer, **boat excursions** along the Danube and the Danube Canal are offered by **DDSG Shipping Co.**, Handelskai 265, **t** (01) 726 8123/588 80-0, *www.ddsg.blue-danube.at,* and **Pyringer-Zopper Danube Shipping, t** (01) 715 15 25-20, *www.donauschiffahrtwien.at.*

The **Vienna Sightseeing Bus** makes a tour of the city's main sights, and is a 'Hop-on Hop-off' service with multilingual audioguides. Tickets are available for 1, 2 or 24hrs, and prices start at €12. The starting point is outside the Staatsoper. Info from **Vienna Sightseeing**, 14 Graf Starhemberg Gasse 25, **t** (01) 712 46 830, *www.viennasightseeing.at.*

Horse-drawn carriages (*fiaker*) clatter around the cobbled streets and are available from outside Stephansdom and the Hofburg. It costs around €50 for a 30min tour of the city, but agree the terms before you get in.

Internet Access

There are plenty of places to pick up e-mails or surf the Net in Vienna, including several coin-operated terminals in some of the cafés. The easiest option is to head for one of the three branches of **Bignet**, which have several computer terminals, booths to make cheap international calls, and also offer fax, scanning and printing services. All have cafés:

6 Mariahilferstrasse 27, **t** (01) 20506, *open daily 10am–2am.*

1 Kärntner Strasse 61, **t** (01) 503 9844, *open daily 10am–midnight.*

1 Hoher Markt 8, **t** (01) 533 2939, *open daily 10am–midnight.*

Post Offices

The main post office is at Fleischmarkt 19, **t** 0800 100 100, U-Bahn to Schwedenplatz, open daily 24hrs, with several branches scattered around the city.

Festivals and Events

31 Dec and 1 Jan: New Year's Eve concerts by the Vienna Philharmonic at the Musikverein (*see* p.32); Beethoven's Ninth Symphony at the Konzerthaus (*see* p.32).

6 Jan–Ash Wed: *Fasching* (Carnival). All kinds of events, including lavish balls (the most glamorous is the Opera Ball, held the last Thursday before Shrove Tuesday), and the traditional meal of *Heringschmaus* (herring and pickled fish) on Ash Wednesday.

Jan (usually 2nd and 3rd weeks): *Resonanzen*, a festival of medieval music held at the Konzerthaus.

Late Feb–mid-Mar: Dance Festival, classic and contemporary dance at various venues across the city; *Haydn Tage*, celebrating the works of Haydn at the Konzerthaus.

Mar: Easter Market at the Freytung, with arts and crafts and traditional foods.

April–May: *Frühlingsfestival*, a festival of classical music, hosted in alternate years by either the Musikverein (*www.musikverein.at*) or the Konzerthaus (*www.konzerthaus.at*).

1 May: *Tag der Arbeit*, Labour Day, is marked with parades and processions on the Rathausplatz and Ringstrasse; *Maifest*, concerts and funfairs in the Prater.

Mid-May–mid-June: Vienna *Festwochen*, excellent festival of the performing arts at venues across the city. Info at **t** (01) 589 22 22, *www.festwochen.at*.

June–July: *Jazzfest Wien*, city-wide jazz festival, with concerts held in venues across the city. *www.viennajazz.org*.

July–Aug: Free concerts in the parks; hugely popular outdoor film screenings (free) in front of the Rathausplatz and in the Augarten Park (*www.kinountersternen.at*).

Oct: *Viennale*. Long-established international film festival, *www.viennale.at*.

Nov: *Wien Modern* – the Konzerthaus hosts this excellent festival of contemporary music, *www.konzerthaus.at*.

Dec: Christmas markets (*Christkindlmärkte*) spring up across the city, including the Rathausplatz, Karlplatz, Schönbrunn, and Spittelberg, with arts and crafts, traditional food and drink, and lots of special activities for children.

Shopping

Traditional Viennese and Austrian specialities include cut glass, embroidered lace, typical Austrian clothes like dirndls and *lederhosen*, the ubiquitous chocolate 'Mozart Balls' from Salzburg and a wonderful range of cakes including the celebrated *Sachertorte* (which can be expensively packed up and even posted by the Hotel Sacher shop, *see* p.24).

The main shopping streets are **Kärntner Strasse** (1st district) and **Mariahilfer Strasse** (6th district), with department stores, all the major fashion chains (including H&M, Zara, Mango and Benetton), and a couple of shopping malls. Along **Graben** and **Kohlmarkt** (both 1st district), you'll find chi chi designer fashion (Chanel, Louis Vuitton, etc.), and the fancy *pâtisserie*-cum-café Demel (*see* 'Cafés'). **Dorotheergasse** and **Josefstädter Strasse** (both 1st district) are lined with smart antique dealers. The narrow streets and passages of the **old town** are wonderful for a stroll, with tiny shops selling everything from religious objects to slick designer household goods.

Many of the **museum shops** are excellent, especially the original, contemporary household goods, accessories and *objets d'art* on sale at the MAK shop (*see* p.72) and the MuseumsQuartier shop (*see* p.68).

Shops are usually **open** from Monday to Saturday from 9 or 10am to 6 or 7pm, although many close earlier (around 5pm) on Saturdays. Few shops are open late, and even fewer are open on Sundays.

Vienna t (01) –

See 'Addresses', p.19.

Antiques

Dorotheum, 1 Dorotheergasse 14, **t** 5156 0280, *www.dorotheum.com*. Set up as a pawn shop more than 200 years ago, this is now the oldest and most prestigious auction house in Central Europe. You can pick up cheaper items in the Glashof.

Herbert Asenbaum, 1 Kärntner Strasse 28, **t** 512 2847. A sparkling range of antique jewellery and silverware, along with other antiques.

Books and Maps

Freytag & Berndt, 1 Kohlmarkt 9, **t** 533 86 56, *www.freytagberndt.at*. An enormous range of maps and travel books in several different languages are on offer at the renowned map-makers' flagship store.

Shakespeare and Co., 1 Sterngasse 2, **t** 535 50 53. This friendly little shop has a good range of books in English, including a small travel section, plenty of books on Vienna, and lots of English-language teaching materials. They also sell some second-hand books, and host readings and other events.

Department Stores and Malls

Gasometer, 11 Guglgasse, *www.g-town.at*. A stunning architectural *tour de force*, this shopping centre (and apartment complex) is housed in four former gas containers. Unfortunately the shopping doesn't live up to the dramatic setting, with the usual very ordinary chain stores, a supermarket, bars and cafés and a cinema. *U-Bahn Gasometer*.

Ringstrassen Gallerien, 1 Kärntner Ring 11–13. A big, upmarket shopping centre spread over two adjoining buildings, with expensive boutiques, a good supermarket, and lots of cafés and restaurants. *Open Mon–Sat 7.30am–10pm*.

Steffl, 1 Kärntner Strasse 19, **t** 514 310. This convenient department store has several floors of fashion, an electrical goods department (if you need a plug-adaptor in a hurry), and a panoramic bar on the top floor.

Fashion and Accessories

Humanic, 1 Kärntner Strasse 1, **t** 413 89 22, *www.humanic.at*. This chain of shoe stores has all kinds of styles for men, women and children, from the practical to the funky.

Helmut Lang, 1 Seilergasse, **t** 513 25 88, *www.helmutlang.com*. Austrian-born designer Helmut Lang's flagship store in Vienna, with a full range of his pared-down and ultra-stylish clothes, accessories and fragrances for men and women.

Loden-Plankl, 1 Michaelerplatz 6, **t** 533 80 32, *www.loden-plankl.at*. One of the oldest and most famous stores dedicated to traditional Austrian clothing, this sells a full range of dirndls, *lederhosen*, and feathered hats.

Food and Drink

Altmann & Kühne, 1 Graben 30, **t** 533 09 27. A divine little shop selling exquisite, hand-made chocolates in pretty boxes. They're expensive, but worth every penny.

Bäckerei Grimm, 1 Kurrentgasse 10, **t** 533 13 84. It's worth making a trip to this excellent bakery for the smell alone – although once inside you won't be able to resist purchasing one of their delicious loaves. *Open Mon–Fri 10–6; closed Sat and Sun.*

Meinl am Graben, 1 Graben 19, **t** 532 33 34. Vienna's premier gourmet supermarket, with three floors stocked with all kinds of delicious produce and an excellent restaurant (*see* 'Eating Out', p.27) upstairs. *Open Mon–Fri 8–8, Sat 8.30–8*.

Zum Schwarzen Kameel, 1 Bognergasse 5, **t** 533 81 25, *www.kameel.at*. This classic café-restaurant has an excellent deli and wine shop attached, with all kinds of delectable goodies from Austria and abroad. *Open Mon–Sat 8.30am–midnight*.

Glass and Porcelain

J&L Lobmeyr, 1 Kärntner Strasse 26, **t** 512 05 08. If you've admired the cut-glass chandeliers at the Vienna Opera House, you can pick some up at this world-famous store. As well as exquisite glassware, there's also a small museum and a selection of porcelain.

Rasper & Söhne, 1 Graben 15, **t** 534 330. This elegant shop stocks a wide range of Austrian glassware and porcelain, along with other household goods.

Kids' Stuff

Dohnal, 1 Kärntner Strasse 12, **t** 512 73 11. Austrian children's clothing for under-16s.

Kober, 1 Graben 14–15, **t** 533 60 19. A big, expensive toy emporium, with the latest electronic gadgets and sturdy wooden toys.

Markets

Naschmarkt, 4 Naschmarkt. The city's famous open-air food market is a fabulous riot of colour and smells, with all kinds of stalls selling wonderfully fresh produce. *Open Mon–Fri 6am–6.30pm, Sat 6am–2pm.*

Kettenbrückengasse (5th district): Saturday flea market.

Kunst und Antikmarkt, Donaukanal-Promenade. Art, antiques, bric-a-brac and plain old junk are laid out in heaps at this summer market by the Danube Canal. *Open May–Sept Sat 2–8, Sun 10–8. U-Bahn to Schwedenplatz.*

Music

Arcadia, 1 Kärntner Strasse 40, **t** 513 95 68. Arcadia has an excellent selection of classical recordings, which often (but not always) feature Austrian performers.

EMI, 1 Kärntner Strasse 30, **t** 512 36 75. This massive emporium stocks a huge selection of classical and pop CDs.

Sports and Activities

Vienna **t** (01) –

Football

Hanappi Stadium, 14 Kaisslergasse 6, **t** 914 55 19. This stadium is home to Rapid Vienna, the biggest Austrian team. (The national team play at the huge **Ernst Happel Stadium**, 2 Meierstrasse 7, **t** 7280 8540).

Franz Horr Stadium, 10 Fischonhofgasse 10–12, **t** 710 4528, *www.fk-austria.at*. The home of Rapid Vienna's only rivals, Austria Memphis.

Ice-skating

Eislaufanlage Engelmann, Syringasse 6–8, **t** 405 14 25. A popular outdoor ice-rink. *Open late Oct–Mar.*

Rathausplatz, 1 Rathausplatz. The square in front of the City Hall becomes an outdoor ice-rink in winter. *Open late Jan–early Mar.*

Weiner Eislaufverein, 3 Lotheringasse 22, **t** 713 63 53. Another good outdoor ice-rink. *Open late-Oct–Mar.*

Horse-Racing

Freudenau Prater, 2 Freudenau 65, **t** 728 95 17. Flat-racing is held at the eastern end of the Prater from spring to autumn.

Kreieau Stadium, 2 Nordportalstrasse 247, **t** 728 00 46. An elegant trotting stadium, built in 1913, which hosts international trotting races from September to June.

Skiing

Many Vienna-based travel agencies offer one-day ski packages, including transport and lift-pass. These usually head for the slopes at Semmering (about 60 miles/90km from the city). For more info, contact Semmering tourist office, **t** (02664) 20025, *www.semmering.at*, or look at *www.tiscover.com/noe-sued*.

Swimming

Krapfenwaldbad, 19 Krapfenwaldgasse 65–73, **t** 320 1501. Perhaps the loveliest of Vienna's many outdoor municipal swimming pools (the tourist office has a complete list), with original 1920s fittings and beautiful views over the city. *Open May–Sept.*

Donauinsel (*see* p.78). The Danube canal is lined with beaches.

Watersports

To mess about in boats, head for the Alte Donau (*see* p.78), where there are sailing schools and boat-rental outlets.

Where to Stay

Vienna **t** (01) –

Vienna offers a wide range of accommodation, from aristocratic palaces and opulent 19th-century hotels to family-run pensions and youth hostels. It's surprisingly expensive to stay in this city, and many hotels are often busy with tour groups. The tourist office has a hotel booking service, and can provide lists of rooms available in private houses (usually outside the centre, but inexpensive and quiet). Check websites for special deals, particularly at the chain hotels and those geared towards business travellers. Prices include breakfast at most hotels, but it's worth checking before you arrive. Within the Inner City is more expensive; prices drop outside the Ringstrasse.

Innere Stadt

Ambassador, 1 Neuer Markt, **t** 96161, **f** 513 29 99, *www.ambassador.at* (*luxury*). This regal, five-star hotel is crammed with gilt, marble pillars, chandeliers and statues. Popular with visiting dignitaries, the rooms are formal and elegant, with heavy drapes and sturdy dark wooden furniture, and the finest have adjoining sitting rooms.

Astoria, 1 Kärntnergasse 32–4, **t** 515 770, **f** 515 77 82, *www.austria-trend.at* (*luxury*). This is a classic old-fashioned hotel, which still manages to ooze turn-of-the-20th-century opulence while its facilities are bang up-to-date. The spacious rooms are well equipped, and there's a smart restaurant and bar.

Hotel Sacher, 1 Philharmonikerstrasse 4, **t** 514 560, **f** 514 56 810, *www.sacher.com* (*luxury*). The *grande dame* of the Viennese hotel scene boasts splendid rooms filled with extraordinary art and antiques, a fabulous restaurant (where Emperor Franz Josef once tucked into his daily *Tafelspitz* – boiled beef), and a legendary café (*see* p.31). The hotel is justly famous for the magnificent service offered by its staff. To push the boat out, book one of their stunning suites.

Mailberger Hof, 1 Annagasse 7, **t** 5120 6410, **f** 5120 64110, *www.mailbergerhof.at* (*luxury*). This is one of the prettiest hotels in central Vienna, set in a an elegant former palace overlooking a graceful stone courtyard. The rooms and suites are traditionally decorated with floral prints and burnished antiques, and there's a fine restaurant in the cellar.

Kaiserin Elisabeth, 1 Weihburgasse 3, **t** 51526, **f** 515267, *info@kaiserinelisabeth.at* (*expensive*). This delightful hotel retains much of its grandiose 19th-century opulence, and guests are greeted with a swirl of velvet and glittering crystal in the lobby. The rooms are equally plush, and most have been sympathetically modernized.

König von Ungarn, 1 Schulerstrasse 10, **t** 515 840, **f** 515 848, *www.kvu.at* (*expensive*). The framed signatures of famous guests line the walls at this charming, good-value hotel which shares the same 16th-century building as the Figarohaus (*see* p.49). Passages lead to the bedrooms, all individually decorated with a tasteful mixture of traditional and modern styles, there's a wonderful glassy atrium to relax in, and a good restaurant in the vaulted cellar. Unsurprisingly, this is one of the most sought-after hotels in the city and you'll need to book well in advance.

Pension Pertschy, 1 Habsburgergasse 5, **t** 534 49 49, **f** 534 490, *www.pertschy.com* (*moderate*). The Pertschy is an excellent modestly priced choice in a prime location off the swish Graben. The building has seen better days, but it overlooks a stone courtyard and most of the comfortable rooms have been newly renovated in a slightly flashy faux-Baroque style. Some have retained attractive period touches like old-fashioned ceramic heaters, and there's a cosy, wood-panelled breakfast room.

Nossek, 1 Graben 17, **t** 5337 0410, **f** 535 36 46, *www.pension-nossek.at* (*moderate*). This modest, family-run hotel offers attractive rooms (the best have balconies overlooking the chic boutiques of the Graben), with basic bathrooms, but otherwise tastefully furnished with Persian rugs and antiques.

Wandl, 1 Petersplatz 9, **t** 534 550, **f** 534 55 77, *www.hotel-wandl.com* (*moderate*). This slightly ramshackle, family-run hotel has been going for almost two centuries, and the venerable old building still has hints of its former grandeur. Rooms vary widely; some boast original fittings while others are much plainer, but most are spacious and have polished wooden floors.

Zur Wiener Staatsotper, 1 Krugerstrasse 11, **t** 513 12 74, *office@zurweinerstaastoper.at* (*moderate*). Tucked down a pedestrian street off Kärntner Strasse, this welcoming hotel is squeezed into a tall, narrow 19th-century townhouse. The rooms are smallish, but good value for the location.

Hotel Orient, 1 Tiefer Graben 30, **t** 533 73 07, **f** 535 03 40, *www.hotelorient.at* (*inexpensive*). Taking the Japanese 'love hotels' as inspiration, the Orient has themed rooms and suites available by the hour, or by the night. *Fin-de-siècle* detailing and brisk service ensure that it's all more tongue-in-cheek than tacky.

Pension Suzanne, 1 Walfischgasse 4, **t** 513 25 07, **f** 513 25 00, *www.pension-suzanne.at* (*inexpensive*). Possibly the best city-centre budget option, the simple little Suzanne is always booked out months in advance. Tucked away in unprepossessing surroundings just off Kärntner Strasse, its old-fashioned charming rooms, some with little kitchenettes, get friendly service from the Strafinger family. The best rooms look out on to the street – interior rooms face a dowdy courtyard.

Schweizer Pension Solderer, 1 Heinrichgasse 2, **t** 533 81 56, **f** 533 64 69, *schweizer.pension@cello.at* (*inexpensive*). A pristine little pension, run by Swiss sisters, this offers budget rooms with or without bathrooms. Some still have their original ceramic heaters, and most have cable TV.

Around the Ringstrasse

Bristol, 1 Kärntner Ring 1, **t** 515 160, **f** 16 550, *www.westin.com/bristol* (*luxury*). Possibly the most luxurious hotel in the city, the Bristol is a Viennese institution, and the interior is a glorious whirl of gilt, polished marble and glittering crystal. There's a splendidly formal restaurant, an elegant drawing room for afternoon tea, and the gorgeous rooms and suites are kitted out with every imaginable creature comfort.

Das Triest, 4 Wiedner Hauptsrasse 12, **t** 589 180, **f** 589 18 18, *www.dastriest.at* (*luxury*). This sleekly designed modern hotel is slotted behind an elegant old façade. With its pared down minimalism and light-filled public spaces, it's the antithesis of most of Vienna's traditional luxury accommodation. The top floor suites have private roof gardens, and there's an elegant Italian restaurant and glossy cocktail bar.

Im Palais Schwarzenberg, 3 Schwarzenbergplatz 9, **t** 798 45 15, **f** 798 47 14, *www.palais-schwarzenberg.com* (*luxury*). This beautiful Baroque palace is surrounded by ornamental gardens, and has been elegantly converted into a chic and wonderfully intimate hotel with just 44 magnificent rooms. Those in the main building are full of grandiose finery, but there is also a handful of stylish, contemporary rooms in the converted stable block. Exquisite paintings and sculpture are scattered around the

spectacular public *salons*, and there's a romantic restaurant in the conservatory.

Imperial, 1 Kärntner Ring 16, **t** 501 100, **f** 501 10 410, *www.luxurycollection.com/imperial* (*luxury*). The Imperial combines the best of traditional Vienna with crisp modern design in its sumptuous and spacious rooms, which are filled with heavy drapes and crystal chandeliers yet boast huge, modern bathrooms. There's a beauty centre and fitness room, and service is polished and attentive.

Marriott Hotel, 1 Parkring 12a, **t** 515 180, **f** 515 18 6736, *www.marriott.com* (*luxury*). This huge, glassy hotel has a superb location, and offers every imaginable comfort (including indoor pool, sauna, and gym) yet remains rather soulless. There is a plant-filled atrium with waterfalls and fairy lights, which has plenty of shops and cafés. Exterior rooms look out over rooftops and the nearby Stadtpark, but can be noisy.

Le Meridien, 1 Opernring 13, **t** 588 900, **f** 588 90 90 90, *http://vienna.lemeridien.com* (luxury). Near the Opera House, with a historic façade hiding minimalist modern 'design' style, all glass and cool colours. Pool, fitness centre, restaurant and bar, and the rooms all have hi-tech flat screen TVs and Internet access.

Hotel-Mercure Secession, 6 Getreidemarkt 5, **t** 588 380, **f** 588 38 212 (*expensive*). A modern, glassy hotel in the Mercure chain, this is geared towards business clientele, but offers crisp, well-equipped rooms at reasonable prices. Look out for special weekend deals.

Hotel Regina, 9 Rooseveltplatz 15, **t** 404 460, **f** 408 8392, *www.kremlehnerhotels.at* (*expensive*). This grand old pile next to the Votivkirche has been going for more than a century, and is awash with velvet drapes and oversized statuary. The rooms are large and reasonably comfortable, although the facilities are dated, The location is excellent, but this hotel is best avoided in high season when it fills up with tour groups.

Rathauspark, 1 Rathausstrasse 17, **t** 404 120, **f** 404 12 761, *www.austria-trend-at.rhw* (*expensive*). This elegant hotel is set in the former home of author Stefan Zweig, and retains some of its pretty period details including ornamental ceilings in some of the rooms and suites.

Hotel am Schubertring, 1 Schubertring 11, **t** 717 020, **f** 713 99 66, *hotel.amschubertring@ chello.at* (*moderate*). Housed in a graceful Jugendstil building, this is a charming hotel filled with Art Nouveau-style lamps, murals and furniture. The rooms are spacious and comfortable, and the staff are welcoming and attentive. Room rates drop considerably during the winter months.

Josefshof, 8 Josefsgasse 4–6, **t** 40419, **f** 4041 9150, *www.josefshof.com* (*moderate*). This pretty 19th-century hotel is painted a sunny primrose-yellow, and has a delightful little garden courtyard. The rooms, with parquet floors and wooden furniture, are plainer and less charming than the exterior suggests, and a little over-priced in high season.

Hotel Baltic, 9 Skodagasse 15, **t** 405 62660 (*inexpensive*). A faded, but still charming, pension located in a battered Jugendstil building. Most of the rooms are spacious, all are crammed with a rickety mix of antique and 70s furniture, and the best have balconies. Bathrooms are old-fashioned, but it is still a great deal for its location. Note that the Baltic operates a cash-only policy.

Quisiana, 6 Windmühlgasse 6, **t** 587 71 55, **f** 587 71 56, *office@quisiana.com* (*inexpensive*). The Quisiana is a good-value budget choice, offering spartan but adequate rooms with and without bathrooms. It's close to the centre and the buzzy shopping street of Mariahilfer Strasse.

Pension Wild, 8 Langegasse 10, **t** 406 51 74, **f** 402 21 68, *www.pension-wild.com* (*inexpensive*). Run by the Wild family, a deservedly popular *pension* which books up far in advance. The rooms are basic, but pristine, and the owners are utterly charming. It's located close to the MuseumsQuartier, a short walk to the Ringstrasse.

Further Afield

Dorint Biedermeier, 3 Landstrasse Hauptstrasse 28, **t** 716 71 0, **f** 716 71 503, *www. dorint.com/wien* (*expensive*). Charmingly set around a cobbled Beidermeier passage courtyard, this elegant hotel offers spacious and blissfully quiet rooms prettily decorated in traditional Viennese style. It's just a short walk from the Belvedere palaces and the Ringstrasse, but, if you can't tear yourself

away, there's also a traditional restaurant, coffee house and wine cellar.

Parkhotel Schönbrunn, **t** 87 804, **f** 87 804 3220, *parkhotel.schoenbrunn@austria-trend.at* (*expensive*). This plush hotel is on the Schönbrunn estate (*see* pp.74–6), and was partly financed by Emperor Franz Josef who used it as a guest house. It's set in gorgeous gardens, where you can sprawl on a sun lounger or take a dip in the pool. It's a short and easy U-Bahn journey to the city centre.

Alla Lenz, 7 Halbagasse 3–5, **t** 523 69 89, **f** 523 69 89-55, *alla-lenz@magnet.at* (*moderate*). This upmarket *pension* offers all kinds of unexpected extras, including a rooftop swimming pool. The rooms are crisply furnished and there are also self-catering apartments available.

Altstadt Vienna, 7 Kirchengasse 41, **t** 522 66 66, **f** 523 49 01, *www.aldstadt.at* (*moderate*). This delightful, rather smart *pension* offers traditional rooms and suites, each individually decorated, and many with superb views over the city. Service is personal and friendly, and there are buses to the city centre.

Altweinerhof, 15 Herkotglasse 6, **t** 892 60 00, **f** 892 60 08, *www.altweinerhof.at* (*inexpensive*). This family-run hotel offers a range of simple rooms and more luxurious suites (which are in the *moderate* price range) but the big draw here is the fabulous - restaurant. Dine elegantly on traditional Austrian fare in the wood-panelled dining room, relax in the conservatory or out in the shady courtyard.

Hotel Pension Franz, 9 Währingerstrasse 12, **t** 310 40 40 (*inexpensive*). Packed with weathered Baroque flummery, this is an excellent choice right opposite the imposing Votivkirche (the best rooms overlook the church). It's crammed with battered furniture, including lots of antiques, and, although it's been decades since any modernization took place, it's still an excellent budget choice.

Lauria, 3 Kaiserstrasse 77, **t** 522 25 55, *lauria_ vienna@hotmail.com* (*inexpensive*). A very welcoming budget hostel, with dorm accommodation or rooms for 2–4 travellers, and communal kitchen facilities. They also have self-catering apartments. It's close to the Berghaus Stadthalle U-Bahn station.

Student Residences (*Saisonhotels*)

Between July and September, student residences around the city rent out rooms and apartments. Reserve well in advance.

Academia Hotels, t 401 76 55, *www.academia-hotels.co.at.*
Rosenhotels Austria, t 911 49 10, *www.rosenhotels.com.*

Apartment Rental

There are dozens of companies offering apartments for rent in Vienna. These are generally better value than hotels, and are particularly good for families, or anyone staying for a week or more. As with hotels, prices drop outside the Innere Stadt.

Sacher Apartments, 1 Roternturmstrasse 1, **t** 533 32 38. Slap bang in the city centre, these affordable apartments have little in the way of charm but plenty of mod-cons, and an unbeatable location.

Vienna Apartments, t 493 32 57, *http://vienna.apartments.at.* A very friendly, helpful family-run business with an excellent website which allows you to see the various properties available. Most are outside the centre, but all are close to public transport. Highly recommended.

Eating Out

Vienna t (01) –

Innere Stadt

Do & Co, 6th floor, Haas-Haus, 1 Stephansplatz 12, **t** 535 39 69, *www.doco.com* (*luxury*). The most famous restaurant in the Haas-Haus building, this serves elaborate and award-winning international cuisine to a well-heeled crowd who come to admire each other and the stunning views of the Stephansdom. *Booking essential.*

Meinl am Graben, 1 Graben 19, **t** 532 33 34 (*luxury*). This relaxed restaurant above the excellent Meinl gourmet supermarket (*see* 'Shopping', p.22) serves some of the best cuisine in the city. Celebrity chef Christian Petz may have left, but his legacy lives on, and you'll find beautifully prepared food using the freshest ingredients accompanied by a fabulous selection of wines. The best tables have cushioned benches set into the windows, and offer great views of the Graben. Highly recommended. *Open till midnight; closed Sun.*

Cantinetta Antinori, 1 Jasormigottstrasse 3–5, **t** 533 77 22, *www.antinori.it* (*expensive*). One of the chicest Italian restaurants in the city, this serves delicious, ultra-fresh cuisine in a flamboyant red setting lit with chandeliers. Sister restaurant to the Antinori brothers' celebrated Florentine establishment, it serves the excellent range of Antinori wines. It's still a place to see and be seen; *book*.

fabios, 1 Tuchlauben 6, **t** 532 22 22, *www.fabios.at* (*expensive*). Currently one of the hottest restaurants in town, ultra-stylish fabios produces some of the finest and most imaginative Italian cuisine in Vienna. The seafood is particularly good – beautifully fresh and exquisitely prepared, and it's worth saving room for the melt-in-the-mouth desserts. Book weeks in advance.

Zum Schwarzen Kameel, 1 Bognergasse 5, **t** 533 81 25, *www.kameel.at* (*expensive*). A stunningly beautiful Jugendstil restaurant, 'The Black Camel' dining room is formal and elegant, serving spectacularly good Austrian fare, but many stand at the bar and tuck into delectable hams and other nibbles. There's also a fabulous deli. *Closed Sun.*

Aioli, 3rd floor, Haas-Haus, 1 Stephansplatz 12, **t** 535 39 69, *www.doco.com* (*moderate*). One of several restaurants in the emblematic Haas-Haus building, this fashionable brasserie-cum-*tapas* bar offers exquisitely prepared Catalan dishes in a cool chrome setting. You'll need to book weeks in advance for one of the tables in the curved window overlooking Stephansdom. Service, can be erratic. *Open till 2am; closed Sun.*

Kiang, 1 Rotgasse 8, **t** 533 08 56 (*moderate*). One of the pioneers of Asian fusion cuisine in Vienna, Kiang has been serving up spicy delights in a dramatically modern setting for almost two decades. *Closed Sun.*

Novelli, 1 Bräunerstrasse 11, **t** 513 42 00, *www.novelli.at* (*moderate*). Also run by the Antinori brothers (*see* 'Cantinetta Antinori'), this is another haunt of Vienna's beautiful people. Deftly prepared Italian cuisine, stylish décor and a plant-filled summer terrace have ensured its popularity. At the top end of this price category. *Closed Sun.*

Palmenhaus, 1 Burggarten, **t** 533 10 33 (*moderate*). This glorious Jugendstil palmhouse has been spectacularly converted into a bar-cum-brasserie, where you can dine amid the foliage on Mediterranean fare accompanied by an excellent selection of wines. In summer, there's an outdoor barbecue and the celebrated terrace is packed all year round.

Wiebels Wirthaus, 1 Kumpfgasse 2, **t** 512 39 86 (*moderate*). This elegant, romantic Viennese eaterie serves some of the best traditional dishes in the city, including delicious game in season. The wine list features the finest Austrian wines, and the service is impeccable. *Closed Sun.*

Yohm, 1 Petersplatz 1, **t** 533 29 00, *www.yohm. com* (*moderate*). A trendy Asian restaurant popular with Vienna's fashionable youth, Yohm serves fabulous, delicately spiced fusion cuisine in a vibrant setting.

Toko Ri, 1 Salztorgasse 4, **t** 532 77 77 (*moderate*). One of the oddest designer restaurants in the city, this aqua-green sushi bar features curious walls of floating fish (there are several other branches across the city). Tasty sushi at reasonable prices, too.

Bodega Marqués, 1 Parisergasse 1, **t** 533 91 70, *www.marques.at* (*inexpensive*). This cool, vaulted cellar tapas bar offers a delicious range of Spanish tapas made with fresh and authentic ingredients, accompanied by an excellent – and lengthy – wine list. Unsurprisingly, it's always packed. *Closed Sun.*

Expedit, 1 Wiesingerstrasse 6, **t** 512 33 13, *www.expedit.net* (*inexpensive*). A young, relaxed clientele pack themselves into this former warehouse to enjoy tasty Italian specialities in a laid-back setting (complete with noisy TV in the corner). *Closed Sun.*

Fino, 1 Tuchlauben 7, **t** 535 28 88 (*inexpensive*). A super-stylish wine bar, serving a range of tiny but delicious morsels to accompany the huge wine list. *Closed Sun.*

Hoher Markt sausage stand, 1 Hoher Markt, no tel (*inexpensive*). There are dozens of *Würstelstanden* all around the city, but this one is perfectly placed for when the munchies hit after a night in the bars of the Bermuda Triangle (*see* 'Bars and Clubs'). *Open daily 7am–5am.*

Kern's Beisl, 1 Kleeblattgasse 4, **t** 533 91 88 (*inexpensive*). This delightful, crowded and atmospheric *Beisl* (*see* p.45) serves up stews and other sturdy Austrian dishes to a mixed group of budget-minded locals, business people and students. Cash only.

Nationalbibliothek, 1 Josefsplatz 1, **t** 532 85 66 (*inexpensive*). This is one of the best public canteens in the city, offering delicious lunchtime specials at bargain prices. It's hidden away in the National Library, but is open to all. *Open Mon–Fri 10–4; closed Aug.*

Wrenkh, 1 Bauernmarkt 10, **t** 533 15 26, *www.wrenkh.at* (*inexpensive*). Christian Wrenkh's flagship restaurant is glassy and modern, and the (mostly) vegetarian cuisine is inspired and delicious. Some organic meat and fish dishes have been added to the once strictly veggie menu, and it's popular with fashionable locals.

Zum Finsteren Stern 2, 1 Schulhof 8, **t** 535 21 00 (*inexpensive*). The original Zum Finistern Stern (at Sterngasse 2, **t** 535 81 52) is a fabulous wine bar selling delicious snacks, but owner Ella de Silva's newest venture is more of a bistro. In the cool, cream-painted, vaulted cellar, you'll find a tasty daily menu and a range of snacks, all prepared according to what's in season. *Closed Mon–Sat lunch and all day Sun.*

Around the Ringstrasse

Do & Co Albertina, 1 Albertinaplatz 1, **t** 532 96 69, *www.doco.com* (*luxury*). The indefatigable team behind Do & Co are also responsible for the elegant Asian fusion cuisine at the light-filled restaurant in the newly revamped Albertina gallery (*see* p.58).

Steirereck, Meierei im Stadtpark, **t** 713 31 68, *www.steirereck.at* (*luxury*). One of the most lauded restaurants in Vienna, this is beautifully set in the Stadtpark. The menu reinvents classic Austrian dishes with spectacular success, and they are presented with aplomb by the theatrical staff. The outstanding food is accompanied by an equally stellar wine list. It also offers a more affordable lunchtime menu. *Closed Sat and Sun.*

Indochine 21, 1 Stubenring 18, **t** 513 76 60, *www.indochine.at* (*expensive*). Lazy paddle fans, potted palms, and dazzling yellow walls provide a sleek backdrop for the superb French-Vietnamese cuisine at this fashionable restaurant. The adjoining bar is a good place for a cocktail, too.

Café Florianihof, 8 Florianigasse 45, **t** 402 48 42, *www.florianhof.at* (*moderate*). The beautiful original Jugendstil décor has been preserved at this elegant café-restaurant, where light streams in through the huge windows. It serves delicious breakfasts as well as a more extensive brasserie-style menu, and you can linger over newspapers.

Gasthaus Wild, 3 Radetzkyplatz 1, **t** 920 94 77 (*moderate*). One of the best of the new breed of neo-*Beisln* which have sprung up in Vienna over the past few years, the Wild serves authentic Austrian recipes prepared with the finest local ingredients. *Restaurant closed Mon.*

Zu ebener Erde und erster Stock, 7 Burggasse 13, **t** 523 65 24 (*moderate*). This traditional pub in a Beidermeier building in the pretty Spittelburg quarter has a charming restaurant on the first floor, where you can dine on good Austrian fare under the beams. *Closed Sat lunch. Sun and Mon.*

Das Moebel, 7 Burgasse 10, **t** 524 94 97, *www.dasmoebel.at* (*inexpensive*). This bright funky café does reasonable breakfasts, cakes and snacks – and if you like the décor, you can buy it, as the café functions as a gallery for young furniture designers. It's also a good place to come for a drink in the evenings.

Ra'mien, 6 Gumpendorfer Strasse 9, **t** 585 47 98 (*inexpensive*). With fabulous, perfectly spiced Asian food upstairs, and DJs and cocktails in the cool-but-kitsch bar downstairs, it's easy to see why Ra'mien is one of the hottest restaurants in town. Prices go up a category in the evenings. *Open Tues–Sun 11am–midnight, bar open till 2am, until 4am Thurs–Sat; closed Mon.*

Tunnel, 8 Lederergasse 39, **t** 947 57 20, *www.tunnel-vienna-live.at* (*inexpensive*). A big student favourite, the Tunnel is a spacious, wood-panelled pub with simple dishes – pizza, pasta, couscous, all in big portions – along with good breakfasts on the menu. There's live music in the evenings.

Una, 7 Museumsplatz 1, **t** 523 65 66 (*inexpensive*). The stunning blue and gold mosaic ceiling isn't the only thing that sets Una apart from other restaurants in the trendy MuseumsQuartier: the assured bistro cuisine at reasonable prices, including delicious grilled fish and meat dishes, make it a better option than many of the flashier restaurants clustered here. *Closed Sun eve.*

Further Afield

Altwienerhof, Herklotzgasse 6, **t** 892 60 00 (*luxury*). This splendid restaurant is a wonderful place for a splurge, with stunning French and modern European cuisine served in a pretty cobbled Beidermeier courtyard. The legendary wine list features the finest French wines, and the desserts are heavenly.

Steirer Stub'n, 5 Wiedner Hauptstrasse 111, **t** 544 43 49 (*expensive*). A firm favourite with Viennese gourmets, you'll find delicious Austrian cuisine at this traditional restaurant, where classic recipes are not tampered with but prepared with ultra-fresh seasonal ingredients. Austrian wines are available by the glass, and the service is impeccable.

Stadtwirt, 3 Untere Viaduktgasse, **t** 713 38 28 (*moderate*). Great Austrian food, prepared without fuss and served up in hearty portions. Big, bustling and unpretentious, it's usually packed out.

Ubl, 4 Pressgasse 26, **t** 587 64 37 (*inexpensive*). A classic Viennese *Beisl*, with authentic 1920s décor and wood panelling, the Ubl offers tasty Austrian dishes, including stews and *Schnitzel*, at very reasonable prices.

Heurigen

The wine-growing areas which ring Vienna are famous for their *Heurigen*, traditional taverns selling local wines. According to custom, *Heurigen* serve the new vintage, or *Heuriger*, wines (after a year, they become *Alte* wines) from their own wineries, usually accompanied by a buffet of hot and cold snacks. Some traditions, such as the custom of hanging a pine branch over the door, survive, but many *Heurigen* have developed over the years to become much slicker establishments, open year-round and geared towards tourists. It's worth seeking out the surviving old-style places which can't accommodate large tour groups, and enjoy the beautiful views from their outdoor terraces in peace. Always call in advance to check opening times, or contact the tourist information office for a full list.

Heuriger Göbel, 21 Stammersdorger Kellergasse 151, **t** 294 84 20. This elegant, glassy *Heuriger* was designed by architect Hans-Peter Göbel, whose wines are among the best produced in Vienna.

Hirt, 19 Eiserhandgasse 16, **t** 318 96 41. A delightful rustic little *Heuriger* which serves simple snacks on two panoramic terraces.

Reinprecht, 19 Cobenzlgasse 22, **t** 320 14 71 or 320 13 89. One of the largest of the *Heurigen* in Cobenzlgasse, the Reinprecht is set in a handsome former monastery. It's enormously popular with tourist groups, but the menu is more substantial than most.

Sirbu, 19 Kahlenberger Strasse 210, **t** 320 59 28. This traditional spot offers fabulous views over the Danube, along with all the popular *Heuriger* snacks at the buffet.

Wiengut Heuriger Wieninger, 21 Stammersdorfer Strasse 78, **t** 292 41 06. Franz Wieninger produces some of the top Viennese wines, available to taste along with a tasty selection of traditional dishes.

Cafés and Coffee Houses

Innere Stadt

Aida, 1 Stock-im-Eisen-Platz 2, **t** 512 29 77, *www.aida.at*. The much-loved chain of Aida café-*pâtisseries* are famous for its sublimely kitsch 1950s styling and low prices. The coffee is by no means the best in town, but the cakes are good and the people-watching – Aida attracts all kinds – is fabulous. Look out for the trademark hot pink neon sign on other branches throughout the city. The first floor of this branch has great views.

Café Alt Wien, 1 Bäckerstrasse 9, **t** 512 522. This dimly lit café is almost completely papered over with posters, and is best in winter when it feels cosy rather than gloomy. *Open Mon–Thurs 10am–2am, Fri–Sat 10am–4am; closed Sun.*

Café Bräunerhof, 1 Stallburggasse 2, **t** 512 38 93. One of the loveliest, if least flamboyant, and most authentic of Vienna's coffee houses, the Bräunerhof has faded Jugendstil décor, smoke-yellowed walls, and wood-panelled seating areas. Linger over the coffee and delicious cakes, or tuck into old-fashioned Viennese specialities for lunch.

On Saturday afternoons, a string trio provide the background music. *Open Mon–Fri 8am–9pm, Sat 8am–7pm; closed Sun.*

Café Central, 1 Herengasse 1, **t** 533 37 64 26. Inextricably linked with giants of the literary and artistic world at the turn-of-the-20th-century, the Café Central reopened its doors in 1986. Some of its original fittings have been preserved intact, but it's largely the preserve of tourists nowadays. *Open Mon–Sat 8am–10pm, Sun 10am–6pm.*

Demel, 1 Kohlmarkt 14, **t** 535 171, *www.demel.at*. Demel and the Hotel Sacher claim to be the only establishments with the authentic recipe for *Sachertorte*. You can do a taste test here – although you will be tempted by the whole fabulous array of exquisite *pâtisserie* on offer. This is perhaps the grandest *Konditorei* in the city, with prices to match. *Open daily 10am–7pm.*

Café de l'Europe, 1 Graben 31, **t** 532 14 69. This café has suffered unsympathetic remodelling in recent years, but it remains a classic on the chic Graben. The upstairs tea room has wonderful views. *Open till midnight.*

Café Frauenhuber, 1 Himmelpfortgasse 6, **t** 512 83 83. This is the oldest café in Vienna, with an opulent interior of plush red banquettes and crystal chandeliers. Nowadays it's popular with shoppers and tourists alike and is always full. *Closed Sun.*

Café Griensteidl, 1 Michaelerplatz 2, **t** 535 26 92. The original Griensteidl café was a legendary meeting place for writers, architects and artists at the end of the 19th century, but it was demolished in 1897. This new version was opened in 1990, and has a perfect people-watching terrace on the vast Michaelerplatz . Perhaps inevitably, given its location at the meeting point of the chic Kohlmarkt shopping street and the Hofburg palace, it's always packed with tourists.

Café Hawelka, 1 Dorotheergasse 6, **t** 512 82 30, *www.hawelka.at*. This famous, old-fashioned coffee house was long renowned as a meeting place for intellectuals and artists. Nowadays, the arty crowd have moved on, but the Hawelka remains a much-loved institution, partly thanks to the presence of the redoubtable and delightful Hawelkas themselves. *Closed Sun lunch and Tues.*

Café Kleines, 1 Franziskerplatz 3. This sweet, old-fashioned coffee house is tucked away on a pretty square where tables are laid out in summer. Simple, charming and as tiny as the name suggests, it attracts a laid-back crowd of thespians and artists.

Café Sacher, 1 Philharmonikerstrasse 4, t 514 56 661, *www.sacher.com*. A bastion of tradition and place of sweet temptation, elegant origin of *Sachertorte*. Try the chocolate Sacher liqueur with a hint of apricot.

Segafredo, 1 Graben 29, t 533 50 25. This sleek red and black café is still the place to see and be seen, with Vienna's most self-consciously beautiful people posing on the terrace. One of the best cups of coffee in town.

Triolaa, 1 Bognergasse 4, t 533 84 90, *www. triolaawien.at*. This popular espresso café offers cool minimalist design to go with the good coffee, and delicious Italian-influenced food. *Closed Sun*.

Around the Ringstrasse

Café Prückel, 1 Stubenring 24, t 512 61 15. This huge, light-filled café sits right opposite MAK (*see* p.72) and is popular with local artists and designers, plus a hardcore crowd of regular bridge players who huddle in a back room. The original turn-of-the-20th-century building has completely overhauled, when the cool, retro 1950s-style banquettes were added. It's the perfect spot to linger with the newspapers after a hard morning's sightseeing.

Café Landtmann, 1 Dr Karl-Lueger-Ring 4, 241 000, *www.landtmann.at*. Once a favourite haunt of Sigmund Freud, the Landtmann remains one of Vienna's foremost classic coffee houses, with a grand interior, and formal service. It's popular with politicians from the nearby Rathaus, along with actors from the Burgtheater, who add to the feel of a smart gentleman's club. *Open daily 8am–midnight*.

Café Sperl, 6 Gumpendorfer Strasse 11, t 586 41 58, *www.cafesperl.at*. This giant on the Vienna coffee house scene has appeared in countless films, thanks to its beautifully untouched, if now rather threadbare, original décor. A visit is still a theatrical experience, with its plush velvet booths and tuxedoed waiters.

Halle, 7 Museumsplatz 1, t 523 70 01. One of the most fashionable cafés on the fashionable Museumsplatz in the heart of the MuseumsQuartier, the light, bright, ultra-modern Halle serves good coffee and snacks to a crowd of arty regulars. Posing on the so-called 'Spanish Steps' is *de rigueur*.

High Tea, 4 Paniglgasse 17, t 504 15 08, *www. hightea.at*. A relaxed, laid-back mixture of shop, tea room and café, this is furnished with a mixture of flea-market finds and cool modern details. There's a wide range of teas to choose from, plus excellent light meals and snacks. *Closed Sat eve and Sun*.

MAK Café, 1 Stubenring 3–5, t 714 01 21. The sublimely minimalist café at the Museum of Applied Arts (MAK, *see* p.72) is one of the best-known museum cafés in the city, thanks to its elegant design and good food. Breakfast out on the terrace is an institution at the weekends, when you'll have to fight for a table. *Open till 2am; closed Mon*.

Further Afield

Café Anzengruber, 4 Schleifmühlgasse 19, t 587 82 97. This is a great neighbourhood café, with formica tables, faux-leather booths and bold paintings. There's a good selection of Italian food, including pasta dishes at reasonable prices. *Closed Sun*.

Café Westend, 7 Mariahilfer Strasse 128, t 523 31 83. This old-fashioned coffee house, complete with marble-topped tables and enormous chandeliers, is perfect for a break from shopping along Mariahilfer Strasse, or if you have time to kill at the Westbahnhof train station.

Entertainment

The weekly *Falter* magazine (in German) has the most comprehensive listings section and is available at news stands throughout the city. The monthly *Wien Magazin*, available free from the tourist office, has listings for theatre, opera, and cinema with some information in English. The tourist office and many hotels (particularly at the top end of the scale) have ticketing services, but it's usually best to buy directly from the box offices. **Austria Ticket Online**, *www.austria-ticket.com*, sells tickets for major theatres and opera houses, plus the biggest pop and rock concerts and sports events. Tickets for the major theatres and opera houses usually go on sale one month before the date of performance and are available through the **Österreichischer Bundestheaterkassen**, 1 Hanuschgasse 3, **t** 514 44 7880, or online at *www.burgtheater.at*. The **Wien-Ticket Pavilion**, next to the Staatsoper (*open daily 10am–7pm*), has tickets for all venues and its commission rates are reasonable compared to many of the ludicrously priced agencies around the city.

Theatre and Dance

Burgtheater (National Theatre), 1 Dr. Karl-Lueger-Ring 2, **t** 514 444140, *www.burg theater.at*. This magnificent 19th-century theatre (*see p.61*) is Austria's most prestigious, with an internationally recognized ensemble of actors. The Burgtheater also manages the **Akademietheater**, 3 Liszt-strasse 1, *www.akademietheater.at*, which is a more intimate space for classical theatre, and the **Kasino am Schwarzenburgplatz**, 3 Schwarzenburgplatz 1, which showcases up-and-coming talent.

English Theatre, 8 Josefsgasse 12, **t** 402 126012, *www.englishtheatre.at*. Established in the 1960s; its performances regularly feature famous actors and directors.

Josefstadt Theater, 6 Josefstädter Strasse 26, **t** 4270 000, *www.josefstadt.org*. This delightful theatre in the Josefstadt district was established in 1788, and Beethoven composed and conducted his overture *The Consecration of the House* for its reopening in 1822 after major renovation. It currently hosts traditional performances of drama, comedies and occasional musicals. The Josefstadt also manages the **Kammerspiele**, 1 Rotenturmstrasse 20, a smaller space which offers a similar programme.

International Theatre, 9 Porzellang 8, **t** 319 62 72. Another English-language theatre.

Kaberett Simpl, 1 Wolzelle 36, **t** 512 47 42. Fluent German-speakers will enjoy the satirical *Kabaretts*, a long Viennese tradition.

Tanzquartier Wien, **t** 581 359160, *www.tqw.at*. Vienna's only dedicated dance-space, with studios and performance halls, offers excellent contemporary dance. It's located in the MuseumsQuartier complex (*see pp.68–9*).

Volkstheater, 7 Neustiftgasse 1, **t** 524 72 63, *www.volkstheater.at*. Another grand institution in Vienna, this venerable 19th-century theatre performs classical drama.

Opera, Ballet and Classical Music

Konzerthaus, Lothringerstrasse 20, **t** 242 02 00, *www.konzerthaus.at*. An extravagant Ringstrasse building, the Konzerthaus offers a programme which isn't afraid to stray from purely classical music (although this features most prominently), and has a new hall largely dedicated to contemporary music. It hosts several prestigious music festivals, including the *Frühlingsfestival* (classical music) and *Wien Modern*, Vienna's best festival of modern music.

Musikverein, Karlsplatz 6, **t** 505 81 90, *www.musikverein.at*. Another pompous Ringstrasse edifice, the Musikverein is the setting for the annual New Year's Day concerts performed by the Vienna Philharmonic. Resolutely traditional, it is famous for its amazing acoustics, achieved with a floating ceiling and a chamber beneath the floor.

Staatsoper, 1 Opernring 2, **t** 514 442 250, *www.wiener-staatsoper.at*. Vienna's legendary opera house (*see p.66*) provides an opulent setting for some of the finest opera performances in the world. It's also the home of the Staatsoper Ballet.

Wiener Volksoper, 9 Währinger Strasse 78, **t** 514 443 670, *www.volksoper.at*. Traditionally, the Volksoper hosted performances of light opera, but this is now fleshed out with musicals and some operas. It's easier to get tickets for the Volksoper than for the Staatsoper, even though many of the singers perform at both.

Wiener Kammeroper, 1 Fleischmarkt 24, **t** 512 01 0077, *www.wienkammeroper.at*. A Jugendstil gem is the permanent home of this opera company, which has performances on a smaller scale and includes many less well known operas in its repertoire.

Cinemas

Burg, 1 Opernring 19, **t** 587 84 06, *www.burgkino.at*. This cinema shows a combination of Hollywood blockbusters and cult classics, and famously screens *The Third Man* (in English) most Friday, Saturday and Sunday nights (check times in *Falter*).

English Cinema Haydn, 6 Mariahilfer Strasse, **t** 587 22 63, *www.haydnkino.at*. All the latest English-language blockbusters.

Österreiches Filmmuseum, 1 Augustiner-strasse 1, **t** 533 70 54, *www.filmmuseum.at*. Housed in the Albertina, this shows classic and cult screenings, and hosts retrospectives and film festivals. Films are always in the original language.

Votiv Kino, 9 Währinger Strasse 12, **t** 317 35 71, *www.votivkino.at*. Excellent art house cinema showing films in their original language, and with a great Sunday morning film-plus-breakfast deal.

Nightlife

Innere Stadt

American Bar, 1 Kärntner Strasse 10, **t** 512 32 83. Adolf Loos designed this sleek modernist bar in 1908, and it still serves impeccable, if pricey, cocktails. *Open daily 12pm–4am*.

Broadway Piano Bar, 1 Bauernmarkt 21, **t** 533 28 49. A mellow music bar, where the owner will tinkle away on the ivories as you sip your drink. Regular live music performances. *Open Mon–Sat 9pm–3am*.

Flex Halle, 1 Donaukanal/Augartenbrücke, **t** 533 75 25. Still one of the hottest clubs in town, with resident and guest DJs from around the world spinning the latest dance and electronic music. *Open from 11pm*.

Krah Krah, 1 Rabensteig 8, **t** 533 81 93, *www. krah-krah.at*. One of the first bars to appear in the so-called 'Bermuda Triangle', a cluster of late-night bars, big, noisy Krah Krah remains enduringly popular. *Open Mon–Sat 11am–2am, Sun and hols 11am–1am*.

Oswald & Kalb, Bäckerstrasse 14, **t** 512 13 71. A sleek vaulted bar, where the wines are good and the clientele relaxed and well-heeled. *Open daily 6pm–2am*.

Vis à Vis, Wollzeile 5, **t** 512 93 50, *www.weibel. at*. A must for all wine-enthusiasts, this is a great place to try a wide range of Austrian wines, perfectly accompanied by delicious little snacks. *Open daily 3pm–10.30pm*.

Zwölf-Apostelkeller, Sonnenfelsgasse 3, **t** 512 67 77. An old-fashioned brick cellar, with wooden tables, sturdy wines and traditional grub, this is a raucous but fun student hang-out. *Open daily 4.30pm–midnight*.

Around the Ringstrasse

Aux Gazelles, 6 Rahlgasse 5, **t** 585 66 45. A sumptuous North African-themed restaurant-bar-club, where you can slurp some oysters at the oyster bar, and chill out in the beautiful cocktail bar and lounge, where DJs provide a soothing ethno-beat soundtrack. *Open Mon–Thurs 10am–2am, Fri–Sat 10am–4am, Sun 10am–9pm*.

Castillo Comida y Ron, Stubenring 20, **t** 512 4 04, *www.castillo-comida.at*. A very chic drinking hole, where you can try an incredible range of rums, either in an impeccably mixed cocktail, or straight up. *Open Mon–Fri 11–3 and 6–1, Sat–Sun 6–1*.

Club-U, 1 Otto Wagner Pavilion, Karlsplatz, **t** 505 99 04. The location is the draw here – underneath one of Otto Wagner's twin frothy U-Bahn station pavilions (*see* p.66). It's a café by day (*9am–7pm*). *Open nightly from 9pm*.

Volksgarten, Volksgarten/Burgring, **t** 533 05 18. One of the most popular and over-the-top clubs in Vienna, with a huge dance floor which opens up on summer nights, and a pavilion called the 'Banana' with its own garden and outdoor dance floor. *Open Wed–Sat from 11pm*.

Further Afield

B72, 8 Hernalser Gürtel, Bogen 72, **t** 409 21 28, *www.b72.at*. Open nightly from 9pm. A great two-storey music bar in one of the vaulted arches under the U6 underground line, with excellent DJs and regular live music events.

Titanic Bar, 6 Theobaldgasse 11, **t** 587 47 58, *www.titanic.at*. Tucked behind the MuseumsQuartier complex, the Titanic Bar is an achingly cool spot for a cocktail and some elegant snacks, and you can head downstairs to the club afterwards. *Open Tues–Thurs 7pm–2am, Fri–Sat 7pm–4am*.

U4, 12 Schonbrünner Strasse 222, **t** 815 83 07, *www.u4club.at*. An institution, U4 has been going for years and still packs in a young, studenty crowd. Lots of live music, regular DJs and themed events.

History

Romans and Babenburgs

Vienna began humbly, with a small Celtic settlement on the banks of the Danube. In the 1st century BC the **Romans** established the garrison town of Vindobona (you can still see some remnants under the Hoher Markt, see p.53), but it was merely an outpost of the provincial capital at Carnuntum, about 25 miles west. Continually beset by attacks from troublesome German and Hungarian tribes, the exhausted Romans finally withdrew and handed over the settlement to the Huns in the 4th century.

It wasn't until the 10th century, when the **Babenburg dukes** acquired the territory, that the town began to expand. The name **Wenia**, which would transmute into **Wien** (Vienna), came into use during the 9th century, and the town became an important trading centre thanks to its strategic location at the crossroads between East and West. In 1156, **Heinrich II 'Josomirgott'** (who acquired his nickname from his favourite oath, 'So help me God!') moved his court to Vienna, and, under his successors, **Leopold V** and **Leopold VI**, the town flourished economically and culturally.

In the mid-13th century, **Freidrich II**, who had no heir, fell in battle against the Magyars, ending three centuries of Babenburg rule, and **Ottokar II** of Bohemia took advantage of the power vacuum to take possession of Vienna. In order to cement his position, he astutely married Friedrich's widow, and sought election to the vacant German throne. However, the Electors were wary of his ambition and increasing power, and chose the little-known **Count Rudolf of Habsburg** as King-Emperor in 1273, under the mistaken assumption that he would be easier to control.

The Rise of the Habsburg Dynasty

But Rudolf easily matched Ottokar for boldness, cunning and ambition: the Bishop of Basel, hearing of Rudolf's elevation, is said to have muttered wryly, 'Sit fast, Lord God, or Rudolf will occupy thy throne.' By 1276, Rudolf had taken Vienna from Ottokar, beginning more than six centuries of Habsburg rule. His son, universally known as **Albrecht the One-Eyed** owing to a disfiguring battle injury, was as power-hungry as his father, but his merciless cruelty angered the Viennese, who revolted in the late 13th century. The 14th century began badly, with plagues of locusts that ravaged the surrounding countryside and the arrival of the **Black Death**, which decimated the city's population. Things improved under **Rudolf IV 'the Founder'**, who expanded what would become the Stephansdom cathedral and established Vienna's university.

In 1438, **Albrecht V** was elected Holy Roman Emperor, a title which would become virtually synonymous with the Habsburgs for almost four hundred years. A year later, Albrecht was killed fighting against the Ottomans (who would remain a thorn in the side of the Habsburg rulers until the late 17th century). The accession of Albrecht's grandson, **Maximilian I** (1493–1519) marked the beginning of a Golden Age in the fortunes of both the Habsburgs and Vienna, which was developing into a major European city with a strong reputation for learning and the arts. Through the astute marriages and dynastic alliances which always characterized the Habsburg dynasty, Maximilian managed to acquire vast swaths of land, including Burgundy, Flanders,

Bohemia, and much of Spain, including the rich Spanish territories of South America. His grandson, **Charles V** (1519–1558), acceded to an Empire on which the 'sun never set', although he ceded the Austrian possessions to his brother, Ferdinand, in 1521.

The **Ottomans** continued to batter at the gates of Vienna, and, in 1529, laid siege to the city. Ottoman victory seemed assured, and yet the besieging forces – mystifyingly – withdrew back to Hungary. Vienna's defences were immediately reinforced. The Ottomans were not the only problem facing the Viennese: the **Reformation** pitted Catholics against Protestants, and tensions regularly erupted into conflict. The **Jewish community** also suffered: restrictions on the owning of property and the plying of certain trades were imposed, and all Jews were required to identify themselves with a yellow ring. Although more than three quarters of the population was Protestant, the Habsburg rulers vigorously championed the Catholic faith by persecuting 'heretics' and inviting the Jesuits, zealous leaders of the **Counter-Reformation**, to the city in 1551. Churches and monasteries proliferated, the University and other major institutions were purged of Protestantism, and laws were passed ensuring that only Catholics could become burghers of the city.

Baroque Vienna

Despite the simmering religious tensions, Vienna was blossoming into a major centre of the arts, particularly under **Leopold I** (1658–1705), who was determined to outshine his cousin Louis XIV of France. Vienna saw more than four hundred theatrical spectacles under his reign, many featuring the emperor himself, who was a gifted composer and performer (his extraordinary ugliness, the talk of courts across Europe, proved no impediment). Painting, architecture, music and dance flourished, and a slew of new theatres were established. Patron of the arts he may have been, but Leopold was also a religious bigot. The Habsburgs had thrown their considerable weight behind the cause of the Counter Reformation, and the establishment of the Imperial Burial Vault in the Capuchin church (Kaisergruft; see p.49) was a flamboyant outward symbol of their commitment to the cause. In 1699, Leopold, who harboured all kinds of ludicrous notions about the Jews (including that they were responsible for his wife's failure to conceive), expelled them from their enclave in what is now the Second District, stripped them of their property (which was given to Christians) and renamed the area Leopoldstadt. But, although Jews and Protestants were persecuted, the threat of Islam was perceived as even more dangerous. In a famous sermon, court preacher Abraham a Sancta Clara answered his own question, 'What is a Turk?' with a list of blistering insults which began with 'he is a replica of the Anti-Christ'. In 1683, the Ottomans besieged the city for the last time. Leopold fled, but the Viennese held out for two months, and were finally saved by the arrival of relief forces led by the Polish king. Victory was claimed by Leopold on his return, and the city gates were festooned with inscriptions celebrating Austria's triumph 'with the help of Jesus Christ'. With the restoration of peace, Vienna began a building spree, particularly under **Karl VI** (1711–40), who commissioned the beautiful Court Library (Hofbibliotek; see p.54), the Winter Riding School (see p.57), and the Karlskirche (see p.66) among many other landmark edifices.

The Golden Years

Karl VI had no male heir, but under the terms of the Pragmatic Sanction of 1713 his daughter, **Maria Theresia** (1748–80) inherited the throne. Despite the wars which ravaged Europe during the 18th century, Austria under Maria Theresia would enjoy hitherto unimagined peace and affluence. The young queen – who bore 16 children – astutely characterized herself as 'Mother of the Nation' and was adored by her people, whom she treated with a bossy familiarity, much as she dealt with her own children (her daughter Marie-Antoinette, once wrote, 'I love the Empress, but I am afraid of her'). She shrewdly surrounded herself with capable advisors, and ushered in a new, enlightened period of government. When her adored husband **Franz Stephan** died in 1765, she ruled jointly with her son, **Josef II** (1765–90), who would take her enlightened reforms further, although his earnest, well-meaning manner failed to captivate the Viennese. Josef II worked ceaselessly: he abolished serfdom, reduced censorship, introduced an administrative system to carry out the reforms, and curtailed the power of the nobility, as well as opening up Imperial parks, including the Prater (*see* p.78) to the people. Probably his greatest legacy was the institution of **freedom of worship**, to Protestants and Orthodox Christians in 1781 and to Jews in 1782.

The 19th Century

Josef II was succeeded briefly by his son, **Leopold II**, who died after reigning for only two years. By the time **Franz II** came to the throne in 1792, revolution was sweeping Europe, and his great-aunt, Marie-Antoinette, was guillotined in Paris the following year. A decade later, **Napoleon** was sweeping across the continent and his armies occupied Vienna in 1805 and again in 1809. In 1804, Napoleon declared himself Emperor and Franz II retaliated by declaring himself Emperor of Austria, although this new title made little difference to his beleaguered land in the face of Napoleon's incursions. The following year, he was forced to relinquish the title of Emperor of the Holy Roman Empire, and great swaths of Austrian territories, including the Low Countries and parts of Italy, were ceded to the French. Napoleon was finally defeated in 1814, and the allied powers (Austria, Britain, Russia and Prussia among others) came for the **Congress of Vienna** to discuss how Europe should be carved up in the wake of Napoleon's fall. Franz II's gifted chief minister **Clemenz Metternich** ensured that Austria emerged from the Congress with substantial territories, but the enormous cost of hosting and entertaining the foreign representatives – more than 50,000 florins – was wrung from the protesting populace in the form of taxes. But the end of the wars brought relative prosperity, and Vienna was to enjoy thirty years of relative peace and stability. This, however, was largely achieved through the repressive government of Franz II and Metternich, whose secret police ensured that any lingering revolutionary fervour was immediately quashed. The city's population exploded, as peasants driven from the war-ravaged countryside poured into Vienna to seek work at the newly industrialized factories which were springing up. Their living conditions were squalid, and there was at least one major cholera epidemic. In 1835, **Ferdinand I**, who suffered from epilepsy, ascended to the throne, shored up by a **Great Council** which counted Metternich among its members.

1848 was the year of **revolution** across Europe: the French king was deposed and revolutionary fervour once again swept the continent. Vienna was no exception: simmering discontent from the poor and the politically frustrated middle classes finally boiled over in March of that year. Metternich, who was hated by the people, was forced to flee (apparently disguised as a washerwoman), and the remaining ministers were forced to grant some concessions including a new constitution and the lifting of the repressive censorship laws which had long stifled artistic and intellectual life. In October, the Habsburg family including **Ferdinand I** (who acceded to the throne in 1835) abandoned the Hofburg and made for a new, temporary home in Moravia, as troops were massed around the city under Marshal Windischgraetz. The city was finally subdued, but more than 2,000 Viennese were killed and another 2,000 were arrested. In the new post-Revolution Habsburg order, Ferdinand I was forced to abdicate by senior family members in favour of his 18-year-old nephew, **Franz Josef** (1848–1916) who would rule for 68 years. Once the ringleaders of the Revolution had been executed, his next task was to bring the rebellious Hungarians, who refused to recognize his legitimacy, to heel. This was finally achieved in 1867, with the *Ausgliech* (**Compromise**) with Hungary, which established dual monarchy. Franz Josef was crowned King of Hungary, and the Hungarians were granted their own parliament with responsibility for everything except defence and foreign affairs. Peace may have been made with the Hungarians, but the increasing demands of the myriad other ethnic groups which came under Austrian rule would remain a thorn in the side of the emperor throughout his long reign.

In Vienna, the last decades of the 19th century were marked by a building frenzy which began with the destruction of the city walls in 1857. The broad, boulevard of the Ringstrasse, which still circles the old city, was constructed and lined with resplendent museums and theatres (*see* 'Art and Architecture', p.41) which ranked with some of the finest in Europe. Financially, the city was thriving, although there were some major upsets, including a terrible crash in 1873 which bankrupted over one hundred banks and companies. The anti-Semitism which had long smouldered in the city was fanned again by rumours that the crash was engineered by Jewish financiers, not least by **Karl Lueger**. Leader of the Christian Social Party and mayor of the city from 1897, he was virulently anti-Semitic but his exposure of corruption within the upper echelons of the government and his socialist policies made him hugely popular with the Viennese (although Franz Josef, unhappy with his anti-Jewish stance, blocked his election three times before finally bowing to public opinion). In response to these attacks, **Theodor Herzl** developed his highly controversial ideas for a Jewish state, arguing that Jews were not safe in Central Europe. This notion outraged the Viennese Jews, but was the seed for the eventual creation of Israel. Vast numbers of immigrants, particularly Czechs and Jews from the eastern borders of the Empire, increased tensions further. Despite this ugly backdrop, the artistic and intellectual creativity in *fin-de-siècle* Vienna was extraordinary: Gustav Mahler was presiding over the Staatsoper; Klimt had led the Secession movement away from the turgid Eclecticism of the Künstlerhaus; and Freud published *On the Interpretation of Dreams* and coined the term 'psychoanalysis'.

The Early 20th Century: Red Vienna

The farthest-flung corners of the Empire were clamouring for independence as Austria entered the 20th century. In 1908, Austria annexed Bosnia-Herzegovina, a disastrous move which almost completely destroyed relations with the Slavs. In 1914, Archduke **Franz Ferdinand** was assassinated in Sarajevo. The Austrians declared war, without consulting their powerful neighbours, triggering a chain of events which culminated in the outbreak of the **First World War**. Franz Josef died in 1916, and was succeeded by **Karl I**, whose clandestine and unsuccessful attempt to sue for peace with the western powers in 1917 was humiliatingly made public the following year. When the war finally ended, Karl I was forced to resign the throne, although he refused to offically abdicate. He, his family and their entourage packed their bags and left the Hofburg, never to return. The Austrian Empire was in shreds, shorn of all its non-German speaking territories, and its population decimated.

The **Republic of German Austria** was declared in 1918. The people were starving and desperate, and saw annexation by Germany as their only hope, but this was firmly denied by the Allied powers, who refused to countenance a more powerful Germany. In 1919, the Social Democrats (founded in the 1880s by the Prague-born Jew **Viktor Adler**) swept to power in the Vienna City Council, and the city gained its nickname '*Rotes Wien*', meaning 'Red Vienna'. The rest of Lower Austria was dominated by the conservative Christian Socials, which caused considerable tension, but, when Vienna became a *Bundesland* (Federal Province) in its own right, the Social Democrats embarked on a staggeringly ambitious social programme which (among many other social and cultural initiatives) saw the creation of new housing and the development of the welfare system. However, tensions between the Church-backed Christian Socials who held the balance of power in the national government and the Social Democrats who controlled Vienna grew throughout the 1920s, flaring into conflict on several occasions (both parties had private armies).

The worldwide economic depression of the 1930s exacerbated the situation, and in 1934 a three-day battle between the two forces ended Social Democrat rule in the city. Meanwhile, Adolf Hitler had won an absolute majority in the German parliament, and began to put pressure on Austria by insisting on the appointment of Nazis to key Austrian political posts. The Austrian Chancellor, Kurt Schuschnigg, decided to hold a plebiscite, believing that the country would vote against the **Anschluss** (Union) with Germany, but Hitler was enraged by this and insisted on Schuschnigg's resignation. Schuschnigg's replacement, the Nazi Seys-Inquart, immediately invited German troops across the border, ostensibly to prevent civil war. Hitler followed, and was greeted by a rapturous crowd on the Heldenplatz.

The Jews were hounded mercilessly, and on the infamous night of 9 November 1938 ('*Kristallnacht*'), synagogues, prayer houses, homes and business across the city were torched, and tens of thousands sent to concentration camps. During the **Second World War**, the city was repeatedly bombed, and few of its monuments were spared. Finally, the Soviets reached the city in spring 1945 and it was declared independent again on 27 April 1945.

Post-war Vienna

Post-war Vienna was divided into four zones, each controlled by one of the occu-pying powers. The occupation dragged on until 1955, when the Allied forces finally withdrew and the **Austrian State Treaty** was ratified. During the Cold War years, Vienna, as capital of a neutral country bordering the Warsaw Pact countries, was chosen for high-level political and diplomatic discussions, including the meetings between Kennedy and Khrushchev in 1961 and between Carter and Brezhnev in 1979. Austria established a free trade treaty with the European Economic Community (now the **European Union**) in 1972, and applied for full membership in July 1989. The country formally joined the European Union in 1995. Scandal rocked the country in 1986, when it was revealed that newly elected president **Kurt Waldheim** had served in a German Wehrmacht unit implicated in war crimes. He was shunned by most of the international community, and Austria was put on a watch list. Waldheim did not run for office again, and was replaced in 1992 by **Thomas Klestil**. In 1998, the Austrians raised their international standing once again by promising to restore artworks belonging to Jewish families who had fled the city in 1938. Unfortunately, this noble gesture was soon overshadowed by another political scandal: in 2000 the far-right **Freedom Party** (FPÖ) under the xenophobic **Jörg Haider** formed a coalition govern-ment with the conservative **People's Party** (ÖVP) led by **Wolfgang Schuessel**. The international community responded by freezing all high-level diplomatic contacts and briefly imposed sanctions. Protest against the new government erupted across the city, with marches and demonstrations on the Heldenplatz and elsewhere. In the fiercely fought 2002 elections the ÖVP had its biggest electoral success, but they still had too few votes to form a government alone. Talks with other parties broke down, and they once again formed a coalition government with the FPÖ (although without Haider, who had become embroiled in political scandal and was forced to withdraw). Chancellor Schuessel's policies have swung to the right during his party's alliance with the FPÖ, and immigration and asylum issues remain political hot potatoes.

Art and Architecture

Early Vienna

The Romans left nothing interesting behind when they abandoned their small garrison town in the 5th century: the **Vienna History Museum** (*see* p.67) contains a few pot shards and coins, and there are minor ruins (featuring little more than heating conduits, and the sparse walls of the guardhouse) thinly scattered around the city, most notably under the **Hoher Markt** (*see* p.53). The origins of the great cathedral of **Stephansdom** are still shadowy: the oldest surviving section of the present building, the massive Giant's Doorway, dates back to the first half of the 12th century, but recent excavations have unearthed what may be the ruins of a pagan temple erected on the site several centuries earlier. The church contains beautiful examples of Gothic craftsmanship, including the celebrated **Pilgram's Pulpit** (*see* p.47). The city's other great landmark, the vast **Hofburg** palace (*see* pp.53–60), also contains a medieval kernel, the Alte Burg (old fortress), although little is visible today underneath the embellishments and extensions of succeeding centuries. The web of crooked streets splintering east of Stephansdom are the hub of the medieval city (even Stephansdom, now the literal and spiritual heart of modern Vienna, once stood outside the old city walls), and still retain their appealingly haphazard medieval aspect. Here you'll find the simple Gothic church of St Rupert (**Rupertskirche**), originally founded in 711 but first documented in 1161, its sturdy tower peering above the huddled rooftops. The 14th-century **Minoritenkirche** (on Minoritenplatz) is altogether grander, although the tip of its tower was blown off during a Turkish bombardment and replaced with a curious pointy cap. The **Augustinerkirche** (where the Habsburg hearts are gruesomely stored in their silver urns), also dates from the 14th century (*see* p.58), and the 13th-century church of **Maria am Gestade** contains some delicate Gothic tracery. One of the most recent and poignant discoveries in Vienna are the sparse remains of a 15th-century **synagogue** (*see* pp.52–3), now buried beneath Judenplatz but accessible through the Judenplatz Museum. Close by, the oldest secular frescoes in the city, the **Neidhart Frescoes** (*see* p.52), are jolly depictions of popular scenes, painted around 1400. The **Museum of Medieval Art** (in the Orangerie of the Lower Belvedere, *see* p.71) displays fine altarpieces and statuary from the 14th and 15th centuries, including the extraordinary Altar of Znaim.

Baroque Vienna

With the Turks battering at the gates of Vienna during much of the 16th and 17th centuries, the city was more concerned with defences than art and the city boasts little Renaissance architecture. However, once the Turks were finally defeated, extravagant Baroque palaces and buildings began to bloom across the city. The sumptuous **Belvedere Palace** (*see* pp.69–71), the Imperial lodge at **Schönbrunn** (*see* pp.74–6), the magnificent **Karlskirche** (*see* p.66), and the dazzling **Prunksaal** and **Winter Riding School** (both in the Hofburg, *see* pp.58 and 57), are among the most spectacular of the new constructions, many designed by the indefatigable Johann Bernhard Fischer von Erlach.

The decorative arts flourished (there's an excellent collection of furniture and ceramics at **MAK**, *see* p.72) and both the **Kunsthistoriches Museum** (*see* pp.62–5) and the **Lower Belvedere** contain fine 18th-century statuary and paintings in their Baroque collections. The Imperial Apartments at Schönbrunn, a whirl of gilt, marble and crystal, eloquently convey the wealth and extravagance of Baroque Vienna.

The Habsburgs staunchly allied themselves with the Counter-Reformation, and lavish new churches – the **Jesuitenkirche**, the **Franziskanerkirche**, and **Peterskirche** among them – were erected, their statue-festooned façades and dazzling interiors a magnificent testament to the wealth and power of the Catholic Church, and a deliberate rejection of the stark simplicity promoted by the Protestants. Equally florid public statuary, such as the **Plague Column** (Pestsäule) in Graben (*see* p.51), and the **Marriage Fountain** (Vermählungsbrunnen) in Hoher Markt (*see* p.53), were also designed to convey the twin spiritual threats of Protestantism and Islam.

19th-century Vienna

After the defeat of Napoleon in 1814, Vienna enjoyed a period of peace and affluence. However, the upper middle classes found themselves excluded from the
political process under the restrictive rule of Emperor Franz II and Chancellor
Metternich. As a result, they began to look to their homes to provide a showcase for
their newly acquired wealth, and domestic architecture and the decorative arts
flourished. The elegant, simple lines which characterized this style of furniture and
design became known as **Beidermeier** ('Beider' means plain and 'Meier' was a
common surname, but the name came from a popular German cartoon of the age
depicting smug *nouveau riche* burghers). The movement was deliberately anti-French,
and rejected the lavish ornamentation of the earlier French Empire style. Despite the
matter-of-fact name, the costly materials and fine craftsmanship meant that only the
very wealthy could afford to commission the new designs. There is a wealth of
Beidermeier design at MAK, and the rather dull idealised versions of upper class
domestic life which characterized the painting and sculpture of the period can be
found at the Upper Belvedere and at the Kunsthistoriches Museum. The **birthplace of
Franz Schubert** (*see* 'Music', p.42) boasts an elegant Beidermeier courtyard.

In 1857, the walls which had contained the old city for centuries were finally demolished. In their place, a grand circular boulevard, the **Ringstrasse**, grew up, lined with a
slew of lavish museums, theatres and public buildings. By now, architectural fashion
had swung away from the elegant simplicity of the Beidermeier age towards monumental Eclectic Historicism. From the lavish neo-Renaissance Kunsthistoriches
Museum to the Greek Revival **Parlament** and the spiky towers of the neo-Gothic
Rathaus, late 19th-century architects like **Gottfried Semper** (responsible for the
Staatsoper) and **Karl von Hasenauer** (who collaborated with Hasenauer on the
Kunsthistoriches Museum) plundered myriad historical periods for their inspiration.
The fine arts followed the same monumental course, with massive canvases
depicting major historical events, and can be seen in the collection of 19th-century art
in the Upper Belvedere as well as at the Kunsthistoriches Museum.

As the 19th century drew to a close, a new and dynamic aesthetic was emerging in
Vienna's artistic community: in 1897, Gustav Klimt, Josef Hofmann, Josef Maria
Olfbrich and Kolo Moser withdrew from the conservative Society of Artists at the
Künstlerhaus and formed the **Association of Visual Artists Secession**. The
Secessionists vehemently rejected the turgid, backward-looking values of the
Historicists, and the rigid traditionalism of the art establishment in favour of an
idealised, quasi-religious quest for beauty which emphasised the natural and functional. It was the specifically Viennese expression of the Jugendstil movement, and
the stunning **Secession Building** (*see* pp.67–8) was a physical embodiment of their
beliefs, which eschewed elaborate ornament and embraced modern techniques and
materials. Viennese Secessionism owed more to the restrained forms of architects like
Charles Rennie Macintosh (whose work was featured in an enormously successful
exhibition in 1902) than to the flowing curves of French Art Nouveau, and its main
exponent in the capital was **Otto Wagner** (1841–1918). His delicate buildings (which
include the frothy pavilions created for the new underground network on Karlsplatz,

Music in Vienna

Vienna resonates with music. Since the late 18th century, some of the world's greatest musicians and composers have flourished here, and the city is liberally strewn with monuments to titans of the musical world, from Mozart to Mahler. The following short list of celebrated musicians associated with the city incorporates details of memorials, museums and burial places.

The young **Franz Josef Haydn** (1732–1809) first came to Vienna aged eight, and was a choirboy at Stephansdom. Under the patronage of the wealthy Esterházy family (*see* Eisenstadt, p.86), he would become one of the most creative and influential composers in the history of music. The Haydn Museum (6 Haydngasse 19, t (01) 596 1307, *www.wienmusem.at*) is where he lived for the last years of life, and created some of his most celebrated works, including *The Creation* and *The Seasons*.

Wolfgang Amadeus Mozart (1756–1791), child prodigy, and later friend and admirer of Haydn, was born in Salzburg but regularly performed for the Imperial family in Vienna. He moved to the city in 1781, and was engaged as court composer in 1787, a year after the presentation of *The Marriage of Figaro*, his most successful work. His uncoventional beliefs made him unpopular at court, and he died a pauper in 1791. He was buried (like all non-aristocratic Viennese of the period) in an unmarked grave in St Marx Cemetery (*see* p.77), where a memorial has been erected. You can also visit his home, the Figarohaus (*see* p.49). There will be city-wide celebrations in 2006.

Ludwig van Beethoven (1770–1827) was born in Germany, but came to Vienna in the mid 1790s where he was taught by Haydn and created his most enduring works. Notoriously restless, he moved 69 times in thirty years, and three of his former residences are memorials to the great composer. These include the Pasqualiti House (1 Mölker Bastei 8, t 535 8905); the Heiligenstädt Testament House (19 Probusgasse 6, t (01) 370 5408), and the Eroica House (19 Döbliner Hauptstrasse 92, t (01) 369 1424). Although his music intitially failed to capture a popular audience, his funeral was attended by more than 10,000 people. His body was removed to the Central Cemetery (*see* p.77) in 1899, where it remains a place of pilgrimage. There's also a small museum dedicated to his life and work at Baden (*see* p.81), where he regularly spent his summers.

Franz Peter Schubert (1797–1828) was born in Vienna (Schubert Birthplace, 9 Nussdorferstrasse 54, t (01) 317 3601, *www.wienmuseum.at*) and produced an extraordinary number of intensely lyrical works in his short life. It was only after his death that his music began to attract widespread recognition and his body, like

see pp.67–8) emphasised the use of new materials like concrete and iron, and were exquisitely decorated with floral motifs and gilding. Wagner would later dispense with ornamentation altogether as his work moved towards Modernism, most notably in the remarkable **Post Office Savings Bank** (near MAK, at Georg-Coch-Platz 2).

Early 20th-century Vienna

Gustav Klimt (1862–1918) is the most celebrated Austrian artist of the late 19th and early 20th centuries: his early work was in the Historicist tradition (you can see his

Beethoven's, was transferred to the Central Cemetery (*see* p.77) in 1899. Schubert's last residence (4 Kettenbrückengasse, **t** (01) 5816730, *www.vienmuseum.at*) is also a small museum.

The Viennese waltzes which still haunt the city streets are the legacy of the extraordinary Strauss family. **Johann Strauss II** (1825–1899), known as 'The Waltz King', composed almost 400 waltzes, cluding the celebrated operetta *Der Fledermaus*, but his father **Johann Strauss I** (1804–1849) had already composed the Radetsky March, and brothers **Josef** (1827–1870) and **Eduard** (1835–1916) made their own contributions to this quintessentially Viennese musical style. They are all buried in the Central Cemetery, *see* p.77.

German-born **Johannes Brahms** (1833–1897) made his home in Vienna from 1868, where he took several positions as a choral and orchestral conductor and performed as a soloist. His songs (which often incorporated popular musical styles), symphonies and concertos were enormously popular in late 19th-century Vienna. He is also buried in the Central Cemetery, *see* p.77.

If the music of Brahms responded to the *Zeitgeist* of pleasure-loving Vienna at the end of the 19th century, his contemporary, the devout **Anton Brückner** (1824–1896), was its antithesis. Brückner's sublime, elegiac symphonies, deeply influenced by Wagner and Beethoven, earned him the nickname 'God's musician'. There are no major memorials to this composer in Vienna, who is buried near Linz.

Gustav Mahler (1860–1911) studied at the Vienna Conservatory of Music, and later became director of the Staatsoper (*see* p.66), where he is commemorated with a memorial plaque. As a conductor, Mahler gained his greatest fame with opera, but his creative energies were directed towards symphony and song. He was forced to undergo Christian baptism to take the post of director, but anti-Semitism dogged his career in Vienna and he eventually left for the United States. He was laid to rest in an austere Jugendstil tomb designed by Josef Hoffmann in Grinzing Cemetery (Grinzinger Friedhof) in the 19th district.

While director of the Staatsoper, Mahler championed young composers including **Arnold Schönberg** (1874–1951), who fled Nazi persecution and emigrated to the United States in 1933. Among Schöberg's early pupils were **Anton van Webern** (1883–1945), and **Alban Berg** (1885–1935) who both developed Schönberg's ground-breaking twelve-tone composition technique. Schönberg is remembered in Vienna's Arnold Schönberg Center (3 Zaunergasse 1–3, **t** (01) 712 1888, *www.schoenberg.at*), a music school and archive dedicated to his life and work.

early mural decorations on the staircase of the Kunsthistoriches Museum), but his mature works are characterized by a highly decorative style which reached its apotheosis with the famous *The Kiss* (in the Upper Belvedere). The haunting *Beethoven Frieze* is on view in the basement of the Secession Building. Klimt and the other leaders of the Secession movement were determined to open up the inward-looking art world of Vienna, and mounted major exhibitions dedicated to the Symbolists, Impressionists and other international art movements, which deeply affected young Viennese artists. **Egon Schiele** (1890–1918), a student at the Vienna Academy of Fine Art, was greatly influenced by Klimt's ornamental elegance but his paintings are imbued with a dramatic Expressionist intensity and made bold new use of colour. There's a superb collection of his work at the Leopold Museum, *see* p.68. Other key innovators in the early years of Austrian Expressionism were **Richard Gerstl** (1883–1908), **Oskar Kokoshka** (1886–1980) and **Herbert Boeckl** (1894–1966).

The Secessionists believed in the *Gesamtkunstwerk* (total work of art), and every detail, from the façade to the light fittings, was subject to the same rigorous principles of design. In 1903, the architect **Josef Hofmann** and designer **Kolo Moser** took this theory to its logical conclusion and formed the **Wiener Werkstätte** (Vienna Workshops), an arts and crafts co-operative which produced everything from furniture to postage stamps (a gallery at MAK illustrates the extraordinary variety of their output). Not everyone approved of this approach, and detractors included architect **Adolf Loos** (1870–1933) who championed a simple, functional approach to interiors rather than the lavish, hand-crafted décor of the Secessionists. Loos, whose writings (particularly *Ornament and Crime*, published in 1908) attracted more fame during his lifetime than his buildings, believed that the absence of decoration generated spiritual power, and sought to purge his buildings of all ornament. The **Loos House** is the most representative of his works in the city centre, and its uncompromising severity famously got him in trouble with the emperor (*see* p.52). One of the earliest Modernists, Loos' rigorous pursuit of pure forms was a model for later architects.

After the First World War, Vienna became increasingly politicised, and new buildings reflected the principles of the ruling Social Democrat Party. The enormous **Karl Marx Hof**, a huge public housing complex containing 1600 apartments, was built between 1927–30 and reflected the ideals of 'Red Vienna'. In the years leading up to the Second World War, the city was to lose many of its most promising artists and architects, with thousands more incarcerated or exterminated under the Nazi regime. The city suffered terribly during bombardments, when many of its most beautiful buildings were damaged or destroyed. Many have been restored, but some are lost for ever.

Modern Vienna

From the late 1950s, a group of architects known collectively as the '**Austrian Phenomenon**' (which included Hans Hollein, Walter Pichler and groups such as HausRucker Co, Coop Himmelb(l)lau and Missing Link) began to attract international attention with their visionary projects and installations, usually small-scale and often temporary (the Architekturzentrum, p.69, regularly hosts exhibitions featuring their work). At the same time, the **Viennese Actionists**, among them Günter Bros, Otto Muehl and Hermann Nitsch (*see* Museum moderner Kunst, p.69), sought to shatter traditional conceptions of art with their violent and shocking public performances (Hermann Nitsch, for example, regularly enacted fake crucifixions). Art met architecture in the colourful, playful paintings and buildings designed by **Friedensreich Hundertwasser** (1928–2000), who famously declared himself an 'enemy of the straight line' (*see* Hundertwasserhaus, p.77, and KunstHausWien, p.78). Hundertwasser fans should make the trek out to the the city's rubbish incinerator (the Fernwärme, 9 Spittelauer Lande 45), topped with his trademark gilded onion dome,

Food and Drink

Vienna, like most major capitals, has a wide range of restaurants serving everything from sturdy local dishes to chic fusion cuisine (although the latter is a relative new-comer to Vienna's culinary scene). The traditional *Beisln* – simple inn-like places – have been going upmarket in recent years, and, in the best, classic Austrian recipes have been given a new lease of life. This reflects what's happening to Viennese palates: food, a long ignored facet of Austrian culture, is now sexy, and the city's gourmets have an ever-growing number of excellent restaurants.

Traditional Austrian cooking is simple and hearty, and always good for keeping out the cold: meat features heavily, particularly pork and veal, along with game, goose and duck in winter. The classic dish is *Wiener Schnitzel*, a breaded veal escalope, and delicious soups, like *Leberknödelsuppe* (a herby beef broth with dumplings) are also common. An excellent local dish which appears on menus in winter is *Martinigansl*, roast goose served with red cabbage and potato dumplings, Another favourite is Hungarian goulash, well seasoned with paprika, or local variations made with pota-toes or frankfurters. For a quick snack, the city is liberally sprinkled with *Würstelstands*, simple outdoor booths selling hot sausages (best eaten doused in mustard). In late spring, try the delicious fresh asparagus, and in summer, juicy fruits like local strawberries and apricots are piled high at market stands. In autumn, the Viennese collect pungent wild mushrooms, particularly chanterelle and porcini mushrooms, which are delicious simply sautéed.

Vienna's fabulous **cafés** are legendary, many oozing *fin-de-siècle* grandeur, and all serving a dazzling array of cakes and pastries. The most famous is the *Sachertorte*, a moist chocolate cake with an apricot filling hidden beneath a thick chocolate topping: the Hotel Sacher and the fancy pâtisserie Demel both claim the original recipe (although when these claims led to the courts, it was the Hotel Sacher that was finally granted rights to the term 'the original *Sachertorte*').

The pause for afternoon coffee and cake is called the *Jause*. Don't miss sweet delights like the delectable *Topfenknödel*, dumplings made of curd cheese with a crispy, nutty coating which come served with a fruit compote, the delicately spiced apple strudel, or the rich, chocolatey *Mohr im Hemd*, a steamed pudding with a thick chocolate sauce and vanilla-scented cream.

Viennese coffee is taken very, very seriously: the most common is the *melange*, a coffee with milk, but if you want it black, ask for a *Schwarzer*. With whipped cream and rum, it's a *Fiaker*, and with an egg yolk and brandy, it's a *Kaisermelange*. Strong, syrupy Turkish coffee, made in a special long-handled copper pot, is also common.

Vienna is almost completely circled by **vineyards**, many with restaurants to sample the new vintages along with simple (and, in some cases, more elaborate) Austrian specialities. A visit to a local *Heurigen* is a pleasure that shouldn't be missed (see below). The most famous local grape is the grüner veltliner, which produces a fruity white wine, but there are also some excellent rieslings, and pinot blancs. Red wines are generally soft and fruity, but there are some robust reds made with the blaufränkisch grape.

which he strikingly remodelled in 1989. In 1995 **Hans Hollein** was commissioned to create a new building opposite the venerable Stephansdom, but his glassy modern Haas Haus (*see* pp.48–9) caused a furore with many Viennese, who felt it had no place on the square. The most successful contemporary architecture in the city has taken older buildings and remodelled them, such as the Baroque Imperial Riding Stables which were expanded in 2001 to create one of Europe's largest cultural complexes, the **MuseumsQuartier** (*see* pp.68–9).

Around the City

Innere Stadt (Inner City)

The historic core of Vienna is a compact maze of narrow passages and cobbled squares, where ancient churches, Baroque mansions and modern shopping streets jostle cheek-by-jowl. It's dominated by the glittering tiled roof and jagged spires of Stephansdom, Vienna's magnificent Gothic cathedral, which is both the literal and metaphorical heart of the city. A great swath of the old city centre is taken up by the Hofburg or Imperial Palace, a sprawling complex built over 800 years, which is home to the celebrated Winter Riding School, the spectacular Secular and Sacred Treasury, and the Imperial apartments once inhabited by Franz Josef and Empress Sisi. Horse-drawn carriages clatter romantically across the cobbles, and coffee houses beckon cosily from every street corner.

Stephansdom

1 Stephansplatz, t 5155 23526. Open daily 6am–10pm. Guided tours (times vary, but usually 3.45pm in English) €4/children €1.50.

The spiky towers and steeple of St Stephen's Cathedral soar theatrically above the huddled streets of the Inner City, much as they have for almost 800 years. The original church was begun in the 12th century, but gained its colossal proportions in 1359 when Rudolf IV of Habsburg ordered its complete reconstruction in the Gothic style and had it raised to the status of cathedral. Friedrich III enlarged it further a century later, making Stephansdom one of the largest and most magnificent cathedrals in Europe – and the Habsburg name, as the ambitious rulers intended, was on everyone's lips. Rudolf IV, Friedrich III and other prominent members of the Imperial family are interred here, and the cathedral's shimmering tiled roof, added in the early 19th century, depicts the double-headed eagle, symbol of the Habsburg dynasty. The **roof** was badly damaged by bombs during the Second World War, but meticulous post-war restoration ensured that its magnificent gold and green chevron design glitters beautifully once again (*you can admire it at close quarters during the summer, when roof walks are held daily at 7pm in July and Aug; adm*). These bombs were just the latest in a long line of attacks (twice by the Turks, again by Napoleonic armies) which damaged but failed to destroy the cathedral, and its remarkable endurance has earned it a special place in Viennese hearts, who call one tower *Steffl*, 'little Stephen'.

The main entrance is through the '**Giant's Doorway**', one of the few surviving sections of the original Romanesque church. No one really knows how it got its intriguing name, but it is said that early builders discovered some enormous mammoth bones and believed they belonged to giants. The '**Heathen Towers**' which flank the imposing portal date back to the late 13th century, and are a reminder of a pagan shrine which was believed to have existed here long before the cathedral's construction. To the right of the doorway, the letters 'O5', the symbol of the Austrian Resistance (capital O and the 5th letter, E, the first two letters of Oesterreich), were carved into the stone in 1945. The symbol is now protected behind a glass panel, after it was repeatedly coated in chalk to make it stand out whenever Kurt Waldheim, former Austrian President and Nazi-collaborator, attended Mass. On the left of the doorway, a worn alcove was used to measure the size of a loaf of bread by medieval customers who suspected they'd been diddled by local bakers.

The vast, dim interior, with its lofty vaulted ceiling and ranks of slender columns, is crammed with masterpieces of Gothic craftsmanship. The most celebrated is the beautiful **Pilgram's Pulpit** (1515), carved with such delicacy that the stone appears as insubstantial as foam. A staircase winds around the pillar to the main pulpit, with a rank of salamanders and toads (good and evil) creeping up the balustrade towards a perfectly wrought dog, yapping furiously at the intruders. Portraits of the four Fathers of the Church (Augustine, Ambrose, Gregory and Jerome) are sculpted with astonishing naturalism, and Anton Pilgram himself (the master craftsman who created the pulpit) peers out of a window below to admire his handiwork. (He pops up again, in another self-portrait, beneath the corbel of the original organ in the north aisle.)

To the right of the main entrance, a canopy protects the 17th-century statue of the **Pötschen Madonna**, which supposedly wept tears during the Battle of Zenta against the Turks in 1697, and assured victory to the Habsburg armies under Prince Eugene of Savoy. The Prince's elaborate tomb is tucked away behind a massive grille in the **Tirna Chapel** off the north aisle. There are several other miraculous statues, including the 14th-century **Servant's Madonna** in the south aisle, which apparently proved a wrongly accused maid innocent of thievery, and the **Lord of Tooth Ache**, now in a small chamber of the north aisle, which once stood in the graveyard and is claimed to have stricken non-believers with toothache.

The black-marble **High Altar** is dark and gloomy, with overblown Baroque sculpture and a grisly depiction of the martyrdom of St Stephen. To the left, is the exquisite **Wiener Neustadt** altarpiece, with painted panels which open out to reveal scenes of the life of the Virgin Mary, which was commissioned in 1447 by Friedrich III. Friedrich himself is buried in an opulent red marble **tomb** on the other side of the High Altar, thickly encrusted with sculpted saints, fabulous creatures and inscribed with his famously enigmatic 'AEIOU' motto. This acronym was emblazoned everywhere during the Emperor's lifetime, but it wasn't until just before his death that Friedrich finally revealed its meaning: *Alles Erdreich Ist Österreich Untertan* ('The whole world is subject to Austria'). The **Donor's Tomb**, topped with effigies of Rudolf IV and his wife Catherine of Luxemburg, sits close to the High Altar, but their remains are actually buried in the catacombs.

Off the north aisle, stairs lead up to the **North Tower** (*open Nov–Mar 8.30–5; April–Oct 8.30–5.30; July–Aug 8.30–6, adm*) which was originally meant to be as tall as the main steeple, or South Tower, but which remained unfinished – the mundane explanation is that the builders ran out of funds and that the Gothic style had gone out of fashion, but the more romantic tale has it that work was stopped after a young architect threw himself off the tower because of an unrequited love affair. Now capped with a copper dome, it houses the huge **Pummerin** ('Boomer') bell, originally made from melted-down cannons taken from the Turks after they were defeated in 1683. The original *Pummerin* plummeted through the roof in 1945, and the present bell – even larger than the first – was made from its remains and dates from 1952. The South Tower, or steeple, fondly known as '*Steffl*', can also be climbed (*open daily 9–5.30; adm*). If you make it up the 343 steps, you'll be rewarded with spectacular views across the old city rooftops from a tiny platform.

Further down the north aisle, is the entrance to the **Catacombs** (Katakomen; *guided visits only, every 15–30mins, Mon–Sat 10–11.30 and 1.30–4, Sun and hols 1.30–4.30; adm*) which contains the remains of the principal members of the Habsburg family. The earlier rulers were left intact, but by the 17th century Habsburg burial customs had been formalized in macabre fashion: their hearts were presented to the Augustinerkirche (*see* below), and their entrails (considered the seat of the emotions) were given to the Stephansdom. What was left was entombed in elaborate sarcophagi in the Kapuzinerkirche (*see* pp.49–50). After vigorous and antiseptic renovations in the 1960s, the Stephansdom catacombs are at first disappointingly lacking in Gothic creepiness, but then the small chamber housing the bronze urns of Imperial entrails gives way to the 18th-century tunnels and chambers piled high with the bones and skulls of more than 16,000 cadavers.

The cathedral treasures are kept on display in the **Cathedral and Diocesan Museum** (Erzbischöfliches Dom- und Diözesanmuseum; *1 Stephansplatz 6, t 512 52 3569, www.dommuseum.at; open Tues–Sat 10am–5pm; adm*), up a narrow staircase in a Baroque townhouse on the northern side of the square. There are ranks of 14th- and 15th-century saints (including one bizarre Madonna whose cloak opens to reveal God the Father being worshipped by a crowd of saints), several paintings, including two by Luis Cranach, and a delicate 16th-century *Pietà* by Luís Morales. There is a host of ornamental church plate, mainly from the 16th century, and the burnished gold burial cloth of Duke Rudolf IV 'The Founder', who first enlarged the cathedral and established Vienna's prestigious university. The most valuable treasures are kept in a low-lit chamber, and include a jewel-studded 16th-century reliquary containing the bones of St Leopold, some exquisitely illuminated manuscripts, and an embroidered cassock.

Stephansplatz and Around

Opposite the Giant's Doorway of the Stephansdom, the curving steel-and-glass **Haas Haus** (*Stephansplatz 12; open daily 6am–2am. U-Bahn to Stephansplatz*) by celebrated architect Hans Hollein, was erected in 1990 amid huge controversy – 'carbuncle' was the least offensive of the descriptions it elicited. If traditionalists were appalled by its proximity to Stephansdom, enthusiasts of contemporary architecture were disappointed by its blandness. This is emphasised by its use as a mini-shopping centre, but the three bars and restaurants on the upper floors, all with beautiful views of Stephansdom, remain among the most sought-after in the city.

The narrow, medieval lanes to the east of Stephansplatz are perfect for an aimless stroll, each corner throwing up a delightful cobbled courtyard, or elaborate Renaissance doorway. **Blutgasse** – 'Blood Street' – is one of the prettiest, despite its grim name. According to local legend, a group of Templar knights were attacked with such viciousness here in 1312 that the street flowed with blood. **Singerstrasse** is also crammed with noble mansions, many still bearing elaborate stone carvings, as well as the elegant little church, the **Deutschordenskirche** (*1 Singerstrasse 7, t 512 1065; church open daily 7–6; free; treasury open Mon and Thurs 10–12, Wed and Fri 3–5, Sat 10–12 and 3–5; adm*). This was commissioned by the Brotherhood of Teutonic Knights, an ancient order established during 12th-century crusades and still active. The church was originally Gothic, but it's hard to discern beneath the flurry of Baroque gilding which was added later. The Order's **treasury** (*Schatzkammer*; through the courtyard and up the staircase) contains a vast and eclectic collection spanning almost nine centuries and encompassing everything from medals, seals and coins to weapons, reliquaries and jewels. Look out for the curious Welcome Cups in Room 2, including one in the form of a dog (made for a member of the Hund family) and another in the form of a stag sporting bright orange coral antlers. The collection of weaponry includes intricately decorated Persian and Turkish swords and sabres, studded with jewels and covered in delicate gold filigree. Room 4 contains some strange devices for self-mortification, including a deceptively handsome 17th-century scourge.

Domgasse (stroll up Blutgasse from Singerstrasse) is another elegant street, with graceful cobbled courtyards and palaces adorned with swirling Baroque façades. Mozart lived with his young wife Constanze and their son at No.5 between 1784 and 1787, now known as the **Figarohaus** (*1 Domgasse 5, t 513 6294; open daily Tues–Sun 9–6; adm*) and is said to have spent some of his happiest and most productive years here.

He created some of his greatest works during this period, including *The Marriage of Figaro* after which the building is named. Unfortunately, as Mozart died impoverished, there's almost nothing to see inside, and only true aficionados will appreciate the copies of his annotated sheet music and the music available on the headphones.

Kärntner Strasse, a broad, pedestrianized thoroughfare, sweeps down from Stephansplatz to the Staatsoper, and is the main shopping street of central Vienna. What it lacks in charm it makes up for in buzz and bustle – almost every major chain store, from H&M to EMI, is represented here. When shopping palls, you can stop for cocktails at the sleek American Bar, designed by Adolf Loos, or sink into a plush velvet bench at the venerable Café Frauenhuber.

Just west of Kärntner Strasse (walk down Marco d'Aviano Gasse) the small Neuer Markt square contains one of Vienna's most popular sights: the **Imperial Burial Vault** (Kaisergruft; *1 Neuer Markt/Tegetthoffstrasse, t 512 68 53 12, www.kaisergruft.at; open daily 9.30–4*). In 1618, the church of the Capuchins was selected as the last burial place of the Habsburg rulers – at least, what was left of them after their hearts were taken to Augustinerkirche and their entrails to Stephansdom. By choosing the **Kapuzinerkirche**, the church of the zealous and ascetic Capuchin Order, the Habsburgs under Ferdinand III (the first Habsburg Emperor to be buried here, in 1633) proclaimed themselves at the forefront of the Counter Reformation. The modern entrance is to the right of the church, and a blank modern passage leads down to the vaults. All Habsburgs have the right to be buried here, and a wall in the first and oldest chamber is filled with the tiny tombs of a dozen Habsburg children. Ranks of incredibly elaborate Imperial tombs follow, of which possibly the most opulent is that of Karl VI (1685–1740), surmounted with grimacing skulls and etched with a gory battle scene. The next chamber contains the famous double tomb of the redoubtable Maria Theresia (1717–1780) and Franz Stephan (1708-65). Maria Theresia was heart-broken at the death of her husband: she insisted on sewing his shroud, preserved his apartments in the Hofburg palace just as he had left them, and seriously considered entering a convent. The tomb she had designed for them both is an enormous, frilly affair, which stands over three metres high and is thickly covered in rococo flounces. It's topped with effigies of the royal couple looking deliciously like a pair of lovers disturbed in their half-made bed. Next to this Baroque extravagance is the pointedly plain and unadorned coffin of their eldest son, Josef II (1741–1790), whose rule was characterised by earnest, well-meaning reforms but who – unlike his domineering mother – failed to win the hearts of the people. The Neue Graft (New Vault) is dark and chilly, with a curious jagged modern roof. Napoleon's second wife, the Habsburg princess Marie Louise, lies here, along with Maximilian I, whose brief rule as Emperor of Mexico was cut short when he was tried and shot by his subjects in 1867. The following vault, with elegant Secession detailing, contains the coffins of Franz Josef I (1830–1916) and his wife Elisabeth of Bavaria (1854–1898), better known as Sisi, both covered with drapes and always surrounded by a sea of fresh flowers. Franz Josef, mild, kind and hard-working, was greatly loved and admired by his people, and Sisi's unconventional life (see p.56) and dramatic death at the hands of an assassin are legendary. Near their coffins lies the tomb of their son, the Crown Prince Rudolf, who committed suicide in 1889 (see pp.80–81). The final vault contains the tomb of Empress Zita, who died in exile in 1989 and was buried here with elaborate pomp and ceremony. She was the wife of the last Austrian emperor, Karl I, who died and was buried in Madeira in 1922, but is commemorated here with a bust.

On the other side of Kärntner Strasse (take Krugerstrasse), you'll reach one of the city's newest and most high-tech museums, the fantastic **Haus der Musik** (1 Sielerstätte 30, t 51648, www.hdm.at; open daily 10–10), a vast emporium of sound housed in an elegant former palace. Most of the excellent exhibits are interactive – you can compose your own waltz, or conduct the Vienna Philharmonic. The futuristic second-floor Sonosphere throbs with the sound of the heartbeat in the womb, or myriad sounds from beneath the oceans. A series of galleries are dedicated to Austria's major composers – Schubert, Beethoven, Mozart, Haydn, Strauss, and Mahler – and you can catch a re-run of the New Year's Day Vienna Philharmonic concerts. The top-floor café has fabulous views over the rooftops to Stephansdom.

West of Stephansplatz

The **Graben** leads west of Stephansplatz. Although the name translates as 'ditches' (after a moat which lay outside the old city walls), this street is one of the most chi-chi in central Vienna, lined with expensive boutiques (many bearing the royal appointment device 'k.u.k', denoting *kaiserlich und köninglich*, or 'imperial and royal'). It's dominated by an elaborate Baroque pillar in the centre, covered in puffs of angels, which was commissioned by Emperor Leopold I after the city was delivered from the plague in 1679; the **Plague Column** (Pestsäule) was designed by the Jesuits and features the Plague, in the guise of an old crone, being killed off by an angel, while the emperor, resplendent in a wig, prays earnestly. The subliminal message, incorporated by the canny Jesuits, was the deliverance of the city from the twin spiritual plagues of the infidel Turks and Protestantism. Among the regal early 19th-century buildings which line the Graben, look out for No.13 (now the upmarket clothing store Knize) designed by Loos, and the **Ankerhaus**, at No.10, designed by Otto Wagner. Austria's hottest contemporary architect, Hans Hollein, designed the shop front at No.26.

Leading off Graben, smart **Dorotheergasse** reeks of old money, with its elegant antique shops and legendary auction house, the **Dorotheum** (*see* 'Shopping').

The Palais Eskelles at No.11 is now home to the fascinating **Jewish Museum of the City of Vienna** (Jüdisches Museum der Stadt Wien; *1 Dorotheergasse 11, t 535 04 31, www.jmw.at; open Sun–Wed and Fri 10–6, Thurs 10–8; closed Mon; adm, combined ticket with Judenplatz Museum and Synagogue available*), which outlines the history of the Jewish community in the city through imaginative permanent and temporary exhibitions. At the end of the 19th century, the Jewish community was flourishing in Vienna, and had become the third-largest in Europe. A Jewish Museum, Europe's first, was founded in 1895 but forcibly closed by the Nazis on the eve of the Second World War. The visit begins on the top floor with a stark reminder of the pogrom of November 1938, the infamous *Kristallnacht* ('Crystal Night'), when synagogues and prayer houses were torched, and thousands of Austrian Jews arrested and many sent to Dachau. Ranks of glass cabinets are crammed with charred and blackened Torah crowns, lamps, plates, and other ritual objects saved from the fires. The first and second floors house temporary exhibitions dedicated to different aspects of Jewish life in the city. Squeezed behind the temporary exhibition space on the second floor, look out for the *21 Holograms*, a permanent installation created by projecting random episodes from the history of the Jews in Vienna as holograms. The picture changes, depending on the viewer's position, reflecting the uncertainty of memory. Beneath each hologram is a quotation, such as this from Berthold Viertel: 'There are only six Jews in this town. Can you imagine the cultural standards in a town where you can count the Jews on your fingers?' The installation would be much more successful if it were possible to see it properly – the low light makes it frustratingly difficult to make out the images. On the ground floor, the glassed-over courtyard has become an attractive, light-filled auditorium. The whitewashed walls are studded with stamped block prints by the American artist Nancy Spero depicting a medieval matzoh bakery and the smoky ruins of a synagogue in the wake of the Nazi destruction. Dedicated to 'Remembrance and Renewal', they try to capture the fragmentary nature of memory.

A glass cabinet spanning an entire wall contains valuable ritual objects collected by Max Berger, whose family were wiped out by the Nazis.

Even snootier than Graben, adjoining **Kohlmarkt** is lined with top international fashion boutiques, but it's most famous for the legendary *Konditorei* **Demel** (*see* 'Cafés', p.30). In opulent 19th-century surroundings, ladies-who-lunch and footsore tourists from the nearby Hofburg gather over sublime, frothy cakes and cream-topped hot chocolate. Adolf Loos designed the sleek, Modernist portal of the **Manz bookstore** at No.12, and Otto Wagner's student, Max Fabiani, was responsible for the elegant **Artaria Haus** (now home to the Freydt & Bernt map shop) at No.9.

Kohlmarkt opens up on to **Michaelerplatz**, overlooked by one of the grandest gate-ways to the Hofburg Palace (*see* opposite). This pompous neo-Baroque archway is thickly covered with heavy-handed sculptures, and was begun in the 1720s but only completed in the 1890s. In stark contrast, the **Loos Haus**, facing it across the square, is resolutely unadorned. Designed by Adolf Loos for the prestigious men's tailor's Goldman and Salatsch, it was built between 1909 and 1911 and caused a furore while still in the planning stages. The Imperial family apparently despised the 'house without eyebrows', a reflection of Loos' decision not to add the customary Viennese window boxes, and planning permission was only finally given once he promised to add some. Roman ruins have been discovered at the centre of the square, and are partly visible from a viewing platform, but there's not much to see. The **Michaelerkirche** (*open daily 6.30–6; adm*) was once the Imperial church and gives the square its name. It was originally built in the 13th century, but the interior is over-whelmingly Baroque, and an extravagant neoclassical façade was tacked on in 1792. A small fee grants admission to the small, macabre crypt, where the desiccated remnants of former parishioners can be glimpsed in their open coffins.

Heading back down Kohlmarkt, the street name changes to Tuchlauben. At No.19, the **Neidhart Frescoes** (*t 535 9065, www.wienmuseum.at; open Tues–Sun 9–12, adm*) are the oldest secular frescoes in Vienna, discovered by chance during building work in 1979. They were commissioned around 1400 by a wealthy cloth merchant, and illus-trate the stories of Neidhart von Ruental, a 12th-century aristocratic minstrel, depicting rosy-cheeked figures dancing, playing ball games and pelting each other with snowballs.

Little Schultergasse winds from Tuchlauben to the **Judenplatz**, dominated by Rachel Whiteread's *Memorial to Austrian Holocaust Victims*, a boxy concrete sculpture remi-niscent of a library with locked doors and shelves full of books facing the wrong way. This represents the truncated lives of the 65,000 Austrian Jews who were killed by the Nazis. The **Judenplatz Museum** (Museum Judenplatz Wien; *1 Judenplatz 8, t 535 04 31, www.jmw.at; open Sun–Fri 10–6, Thurs 10–8; adm, combined ticket with Jewish Museum and synagogue available*) opened in 2000, and is dedicated to the history of medieval Jewish Vienna. In a stark, uncompromisingly modern space, visitors are given special headphones which are linked to sensitive computer screens giving futuristic audio-visual descriptions of medieval Jewish Viennese life. Traditional exhibits are limited to a few stones, and a model of the city around 1420. A subter-ranean passage leads to the sparse ruins of the medieval synagogue, the oldest in the city, where it is just possible to trace the original outlines of the walls, with a small section of tiled floor, and the barely visible mound of the bimah, a special platform from which the Torah was read. The combined ticket also allows admission to the only Jewish **synagogue** to survive the fires of *Kristallnacht* (*a 10min walk from the Judenplatz at 1 Seitenstettengasse 4, admission by guided visit only, bring ID*). This elegant Beidermeier construction dates from 1824 and is now Vienna's main synagogue.

On the other side of Tuchlauben, you'll find **Hoher Markt**, Vienna's oldest square. It's now an unappealing car park, surrounded by banal buildings from the 1960s and 70s, but endowed with a very good *Würstelstand*. At the centre, the flamboyant Baroque **Marriage Fountain** (Vermählungsbrunnen) with its sickly-sweet depiction of the marriage of Mary and Joseph by the High Priest, is a reminder of the square's former glory. At the northern end of the square, a delightful and extravagantly gilded Jugendstil **clock** on the Anker insurance building, draws a crowd each day at noon, when twelve little figures from Viennese history shuffle across the clock-face to the accompaniment of tinny organ music. If you miss the noon performance, you can catch at least one figure strutting its stuff every hour. Beneath the Hoher Markt, scant **remains of Roman Vindobona**, dating from around AD 1, have been discovered (Römishe Ruinen unter dem Hoher Markt; *t 535 5606, open Mon 1–4.30, Tues–Sun 9–12.15; adm*), and interesting displays recount life in the former Roman garrison.

The Imperial Palace (Hofburg)

U-Bahn to Stephansplatz, Herrengasse or Volktheater; tram 46, 49, 48A to Dr Karl-Renner Ring; tram D, J, 1, 2, 57A to Burgring.

*There are various **combination tickets** available for some of the attractions of the Hofburg Palace and the Kunsthistoriches Museum: **Gold Pass** (€23): Kunsthistoriches Museum, Lipizzaner Museum, Neue Burg (Collection of Ancient Musical Instruments, Collection of Arms and Armour and the Ephesus Museum), Austrian Theatre Museum, Schatzkammer (Imperial Treasury), and the Wagenburg (Carriage Museum, at Schönbrunn). **Silver Pass** (€21): Kunsthistoriches Museum, Neue Burg, Austrian Theatre Museum, Schatzkammer (Imperial Treasury). **Bronze Pass** (€19): Kunsthistoriches Museum, Neue Burg, Treasury. **Sisi Ticket** (€19): offers a Grand Tour of Schönbrunn Palace, plus admission to the Sisi Museum and Kaiserappartements, and entrance to the Imperial Furniture collection.*

The spectacular Imperial Palace which dominates the Inner City is a sprawling, confusing maze, built over more than six centuries in a dizzying array of architectural styles. The earliest fortress was built here in 1275 by Ottokar II of Bohemia, a protective bastion designed to withstand attacks from the Ottomans and the Hungarians. In the mid-16th century it became the official residence of the Habsburg rulers under Ferdinand I (1503–1564), who remodelled the **Alte Burg** (Old Castle) in the Renaissance style, beginning a trend which was continued with increasing relish under succeeding rulers. Most chose to build new apartments in the latest fashions, rather than take over those of their predecessors, with the result that the palace grew in all directions – a wing added here, a courtyard there – with a complete disregard for uniformity. The most extravagant builder was Karl VI (1711–1740), whose additions include the sumptuous Hofbibliotek, or **Court Library**, while the **gardens** (the Volksgarten and the Burggarten) were laid out in the 19th century. It now contains more than 2,600 rooms, 19 courtyards and 18 wings – but even this wasn't enough, and, right up until the abdication of Karl I in 1918, plans were under way for yet more building work. Now one wing contains the apartments of the Austrian president, and the rest has been converted into a string of museums dedicated to everything from weaponry to Esperanto.

For a taste of the magnificent Habsburg lifestyle, you can visit the Imperial apartments, or gaze at the jewels in the glittering Treasury, but the two most celebrated attractions of the Hofburg Palace remain the delicate ballets performed by the Lipizzaner horses at the Spanish Riding School, and the Vienna Boys' Choir, who sing Sunday Mass at the Burgkapelle (chapel). Tickets for either of these are notoriously hard to come by, so organize them months in advance if possible.

Negotiating the confusing layout of the palace is difficult, but the attractions are generally arranged around four access points: the Burgkapelle and the Schatzkammer are on the **Schweizerhof** (Swiss Courtyard); the entrance to the Kaiserappartements is on the **In der Burg** courtyard; the Spanish Riding School is on **Josefsplatz**, along with the Prunksaal (in the National Library); and the collection of museums held in the Neue Burg is accessed from **Heldenplatz** (Heroes' Square).

The oldest surviving part of the palace complex is the **Schweizerhof**, a courtyard dominated by a handsome 16th-century blue and red Renaissance archway dedicated to the Swiss guards who attended Empress Maria Theresia. A staircase leads up to the Gothic **Imperial Chapel**, the Burgkapelle (*1 Schweizerhof, t 533 99 27; open for guided tours only Mon–Thurs 11–3, Fri 11–1; adm*) built in the mid 15th-century, and much restored since, although the lofty Gothic vaults and some statues have survived. The world-famous Vienna Boys' Choir sing Sunday mass here, an unforgettable experience, but tickets should be booked months in advance if possible (*Sun at 9.15am Jan–June and mid-Sept–end Dec; reservations hmk@aon.at, or t (+42) 1 533 99 27-75*).

The dimly lit chambers of the **Secular and Ecclesiastical Treasuries** (Weltliche und Geistliche Schatzkammer; *entrance below the Burgkapelle, t 525 24 448; open Wed–Mon 10–6; adm, English audioguide*) contain a dazzling array of jewel-studded crowns, Imperial robes and regalia, and magnificent religious objects, attesting to the extraordinary wealth and power of the Habsburg dynasty over 800 years.

One of the first and most magnificent exhibits is the late-16th-century crown of Emperor Rudolf II, sparkling with emeralds, rubies and sapphires and encrusted with pearls. There's also a gorgeous selection of coronation robes, including a brilliant blue velvet mantle edged with ermine, commissioned in 1838. Tiny christening garments belonging to the princes and princesses (who were baptised on the day of their birth according to Imperial custom) are laid out complete with miniature lace-edged caps, and (in a lugubrious touch) a cabinet in the same gallery contains the hefty keys to the 139 Habsburg coffins in the Kaisergruft. In Room 5, a huge, overblown cradle, groaning with allegorical figures, was donated by the City of Paris to Napoleon (who married Marie Louise of Austria in 1810) on the occasion of the birth of their son, quickly proclaimed King of Rome by the proud father. The Habsburg family took their private jewel collection with them into exile in 1918, but the state jewels they left behind are spectacular: among them are brilliant gems carved into extraordinary forms, such as the enormous 17th-century emerald which has been hollowed out to contain potions; diamond-studded ceremonial swords; and a glowing ruby set in enamel. Room 8 contains two of the most important treasures in the entire collection: a lustrous agate bowl, once believed to be the Holy Grail, which was made around the 4th century AD in Constantinople, and the so-called 'Unicorn's Horn', in fact a narwhal (a kind of whale) tusk more than 2 metres long. Rooms 9–12 exhibit the treasures of the Holy Roman Empire, including the magnificent 10th-century Byzantine crown, the 8th-century Holy Lance which contains a nail said to have come from the cross on which Christ was crucified, and faded coronation robes, exquisitely embroidered on silk, dating back over a thousand years. Room 12 contains a huge collection of gory reliquaries, mostly gathered by Karl IV of Bohemia, with the desiccated bones, hair and fingernails of scores of saints presented in costly caskets.

The Ecclesiastical Treasures are laid out in elaborate cabinets of burnished wood and gilt. There are shimmering crucifixes, sumptuously embroidered vestments glittering with gold and silver thread, medieval altarpieces, silver reliquaries and religious sculpture. Look out for a golden copy of the Column of the Virgin Mary encrusted with precious stones in Room 1, and the beautifully embroidered Pouch of King Stephen of Hungary, the oldest piece in the collection, which dates back to the late 11th century (Room 2). There's a spectacular and much-venerated reliquary in Room IV, studded with enormous gems, which supposedly contains one of the nails used to crucify Christ.

Walk through the Swiss Gate to the grand **In der Burg** courtyard, where you'll see the entrance to the **Imperial Apartments** (Kaiserappartements; *t 533 75 70, www. hofburg-wien.at; open Wed–Mon 10–6; closed Tues; adm*). The Apartments are surprisingly dull, but they have recently been pepped up for visitors with the addition of the new **Sisi Museum**, dedicated to the Empress Sisi, whose tragic life and death (often compared to that of Princess Diana) continue to fascinate millions. The new galleries contain a thin collection of personal mementoes, fleshed out with flashy displays and gossipy information panels. There are copies of her ballgowns, quotations from her letters and poetry, and photographs of the grieving crowds who attended her funeral in 1898. Her obsession with her appearance made Sisi one of the earliest fitness freaks, and some of her massive collection of gym equipment is also here.

Beyond the Sisi Museum, the Imperial Apartments where the Empress and her uxorious husband Franz Josef I lived have been preserved virtually intact. Although this section of the palace was built in the 18th century, they are mostly decorated in the flamboyant style of the 19th century, with red brocade walls, plenty of swirling gilt, and enormous chandeliers. Franz Josef gave audiences twice a week to his subjects: all were welcome (much to the annoyance of the Austrian aristocracy), but they were required to wear either uniform, a dark dress with a train, or national costume, displayed here on mannequins. The emperor was a stickler for form, and once famously berated an officer at the dinner table for not having the requisite

Sisi, the Reluctant Empress

Elisabeth of Bavaria, better known as Sisi, was never meant to be Empress of Austria. Franz Josef's mother, the indomitable Archduchess Sophie (whose own marriage had been arranged according to Habsburg custom), had picked out Sisi's elder sister, Hélène, and arranged for the pair to meet in the spa town of Bad Ischl. But the young prince was instantly smitten with 16-year-old Sisi, and the pair were engaged within three days. Their whirlwind romance captured the hearts of everyone in the empire, and the demand for souvenirs commemorating their engagement and marriage was insatiable. But, despite appearances, the relationship quickly fell into difficulties. While Franz Josef adored Sisi, his new wife was quickly disillusioned with court life. She fought bitterly with her strong-willed mother-in-law, chafed under Franz Josef's overly protective affection, and found the constraints of the Habsburg court unbearable. She was devoted to her children – Sophie, Gisela, Rupert and Marie Valerie – but she never fully recovered from the death of Sophie aged only two. In 1860 she spent several months in Madeira, ostensibly for health reasons, although the Imperial physician could find nothing wrong with her. She had barely returned to court when she set off again, this time to Crete. Her absences grew longer – she would leave for months or even years, sailing around the Mediterranean, reading, writing poetry and painting – and Franz Josef, who remained dazzled by her until the day he died, indulged her every whim. She was obsessed with her appearance, particularly the luxuriant ankle-length hair which had so captivated her husband, and refused to be photographed or painted after the age of 40. She was particularly concerned for her weight (which she never allowed to top 50kg, though she was 5ft 7" tall), and had gyms installed in all the Imperial residences. In 1867, Hungary's historic rights were restored with the *Ausgleich* (Compromise) and Sisi developed an obsession with all things Magyar, learning the language and engaging Hungarian servants. While this made her enormously popular with the Hungarians, the Viennese deeply resented her sentiments. Tragedy struck in 1890, when Crown Prince Rupert committed suicide in mysterious circumstances in Mayerling (*see* p.80) and Sisi withdrew completely. She wore black until her untimely death in 1898, when she was assassinated by an Italian anarchist on Lake Geneva.

number of buttons on his uniform sleeves, a dereliction he considered 'monstrous'. One corner of the chamber is dominated by a vast golden ceramic stove, one of several throughout the palace, which were tended by a team of Imperial Stove Stokers - once a specific job in the palace. Beyond the audience chamber is a conference room, decorated in pale eau-de-nil brocade, and behind it is Franz Josef's study, which is more personal and interesting than the other *salons*. Franz Josef, who took the Habsburg creed of 'First Servant' very seriously, was astonishingly industrious: after a cold bath and a frugal breakfast, he was at his desk by 3.30 every morning. The room is still filled with photographs of his children and grandchildren, and the famous portrait of his 'Angel Sisi', her long hair falling to her waist, sits directly opposite his desk. After Sisi withdrew to her own apartments (the emperor had to ring a bell if he wanted to enter), he slept on a simple iron bedstead in a modest room adjoining his study.

The Smoking Room, off a large *salon* used for family visits, is now dedicated to Franz Josef's younger brother, Maximilian, who accepted the crown of Mexico (against his brother's advice), but was tried and executed by revolutionaries in 1867. Next come Sisi's apartments, beginning with her extravagantly decorated bedroom and drawing room, decorated with dreamy tropical friezes which echo her overwhelming desire to escape the stifling court life. Her obsessive concern for her appearance is reflected in the lavish bathroom and a fitness room crammed with equipment. A long series of empty *salons* follows, which were famously used by the Tsar of Russia during the Congress of Russia in 1814–5, and are known as the Alexander Apartments. These culminate with the Dining Room, where the table has been set for a family dinner. Even in this intimate setting, it was impossible to escape court ceremony which dictated exactly how the table should be laid on such an occasion. For grand occasions, the Habsburgs dug out the best china, in this case a spectacular collection of porcelain and silverware (the Silberkammer) displayed on the ground floor. It includes an 18th-century Sèvres dining service, and a staggering 100ft-long gilded bronze centrepiece and candelabrum from the turn of the 19th century.

The next swath of the Hofburg's attractions are off **Josefsplatz**, dominated by a pompous equestrian monument to Emperor Josef II. This square is home to the Hofburg's most celebrated attraction, the **Spanish Riding School** (Spanische Hofreitschule; *1 Josefsplatz 1, t 533 90 31, www.srs.at; performances and morning work Feb–June and end Aug–beginning of Nov; detailed programme on website, or available in a booklet from the tourist office; adm exp*). Entering the Baroque **Winter Riding School** is like stepping inside a wedding cake: creamy stuccowork swirls across the ceiling, hung with massive chandeliers, and makes frothy puffs around the entrance arches. The origins of the legendary Spanish Riding School date back to the end of the 16th century, when the elegant horses were first bred from Spanish, Italian and North African stallions at the Imperial Stud in Lipizzaner, near Trieste. It was Emperor Karl VI (1685–1740), born and brought up in Spain, who gave it its current form and commissioned the lavish Winter Riding School from Josef Emanuel Fisher von Erlach (who also created the Prunksaal). The graceful manoeuvres performed today date back to this period, although they are based on steps developed during the Renaissance by cavalrymen who needed nimble mounts in battle. An equestrian portrait of the emperor hangs over the entrance to the ring, and the riders salute it by raising their hats as they enter. There are two galleries, where lucky spectators who booked their tickets well in advance can view the beautiful Lipizzaner horses perform their intricate ballets. Tickets to performances are very expensive, but it's possible to see the horses rehearsing their moves during the morning training sessions for a relatively reasonable fee (*€12, available on the day at Gate No.2, on Josefsplatz*). These are for committed fans only, as they can be dull, but just watching the horses being led across from their stables to the Winter Riding School is a romantic sight.

Opposite the Winter Riding School is the **Lipizzaner Museum** (*1 Reitschulgasse 2, t 533 78 11, www.khm.at; open daily 9–6; adm*), set in the stables, where once, but sadly no longer, you could peek at the stars of the show in their stalls. The museum gives an exhaustive account of the history of the Spanish Riding School, culminating with a video which describes the training of the Lipizzaners. They are born dark, but gradually whiten, and the finest animals begin their rigorous training at the age of three. The museum contains few exhibits, mainly old prints and riders' uniforms, plus portraits of famous horses. Short videos detail the intricate moves, including the extraordinary Courbette, in which the horse bounds kangaroo-like on its back legs, and the Capriole, a balletic leap in which the back legs are kicked out.

Back on Josefsplatz proper, the **Austrian National Library** (Nationalbibliothek) contains the dazzling **Hall of State** (Prunksaal; *1 Josefsplatz 1, t 534 10 0, www.onb.ac.at; open Jan–April and Nov–Dec Fri–Wed 10–2, Thurs 10–7; May–Oct Fri–Wed 10–4, Thurs 10–7; adm*), the largest Baroque library in Europe, a giddy whirl of columns, gilt, statuary and heavily allegorical frescoes. The work of Johann Bernhard Fischer von Erlach, who also designed the Karlskirche, it's one of the masterpieces of the late 18th century. Frescoes span each archway, but the hall is dominated by a huge domed allegory depicting the Apotheosis of Karl IV, painted by Daniel Gran. Delicate spiral staircases twirl up gracefully between the gilded wooden shelves, which contain more than two and a half million leather-covered books, including the 15,000-volume personal collection belonging to Prince Eugene of Savoy, much fêted hero of the Turkish campaign around the turn of the 18th century. There are several statues and busts, including one of Karl VI, who commissioned the hall, and the handful of ancient globes are just a harbinger of what's to come in the **Globe Museum** (*t 534 10 297, www.onb.ac.at/sammlungen/globen; open Mon–Wed and Fri 11–12, Thurs 2–3; adm*) on the third floor. There are two other museums, one dedicated to **Esperanto** (*open Oct–June Mon–Wed 9–4; July–Sept Fri 9–1; adm*) and the other containing a collection of **papyrus** (*www.onb,ac,at/sammlungen/papyrus; open Mon–Wed and Fri 10–4; adm*). In late 2005 the Globe and Esperanto Museums are to move to a new home in the Palais Mollard-Clary, 1 Herrengasse 9.

Overlooking Josefsplatz, the 14th-century **Augustinerkirche** (*1 Augustinerstrasse 3; t 533 7099; open daily 8–5; free, adm to Loreto Chapel*) is one of the oldest surviving churches in Vienna, although its stone walls have been plastered over in an ugly institutional grey. The lofty, vaulted interior is dominated by Antonio Canova's sentimental memorial to Maria Theresia's favourite daughter, Maria Christina, which was commissioned by her husband in 1805. Weeping angels and distraught mourners cluster around the entrance to the tomb, although Maria Christina is actually buried in the Imperial burial vault in the Kapuzinerkirche. But dead Habsburgs are still the main draw in this church: while their bodies lie in the Imperial vault and their entrails in Stephansdom, their hearts are arranged in silver caskets in the tiny **Loreto Chapel** to the right of the main altar. The church is famous for the Sunday masses by Haydn and Schubert, but get there early to be sure of a place.

Augustinerstrasse leads to the **Albertina** (*1 Albertinaplatz 3, t 534 830, www.albertina.at; open Thurs–Tues 10–6, Wed 10–9; adm*), which contains one of the finest collections of graphic art in the world. This southern wing of the Hofburg palace gets its name from Duke Albert of Sachsen-Teschen, who married Maria Theresia's favourite daughter, Maria Christina, and thereby came into a fortune. He was able to fund his passion for art with Habsburg money, and founded this extraordinary collection in 1768, when he was given a thousand artworks from the Genoese art expert and ambassador to Austria, Comte Durasso. The holdings have grown to include almost 70,000 drawings and over a million graphic prints, with works by Raphael, Leonardo da Vinci, Michelangelo, Rembrandt, Picasso, Matisse, Schiele and Klimt among others. However, the star of the Albertina is undoubtedly the enormous number of works by Albrecht Dürer. The building emerged from a glossy and daring €100million expansion in 2003, which repaired the war damage to the Imperial Apartments and installed brand-new underground exhibition and storage spaces. But even its newly extended facilities are now match for the sheer wealth of material held by the gallery, which is shown in a series of temporary exhibitions highlighting a particular artist or period. Those with a penchant for Imperial interior design can visit the Imperial Apartments, which have been painstakingly restored to look much as they would have in 1822, and include a dazzling 100m-long ballroom and a Wedgwood Chamber which boasts some of the oldest English porcelain reliefs.

Wriggle back through the palace courtyards to emerge on **Heldenplatz** (Heroes' Square), where the splendid curve of the **Neue Burg** (New Castle) was built between 1881–1913 under Emperor Franz Josef I. It was part of an ambitious plan for a Kaiser Forum (Emperor's Forum) which was originally intended to be the crowning glory of the development of the Ringstrasse, but the breathtakingly grandiose plans were never fully realized. At the turn of the 20th century, the Habsburg Empire was unravelling as its diverse peoples – Hungarians, Czechs, Slovaks, Poles, Slovenes and Croats – demanded their independence, and this florid piece of bombast served only to paper over the cracks. Just five years after the completion of the Neue Burg, the last Habsburg Emperor (Karl I) abdicated and went into exile. The Neue Burg made the history books again in 1938, when Adolf Hitler proclaimed the incorporation of Austria into the Third Reich (the *Anschluss*) from one of its balconies. Now the castle houses several **museums**, all accessible with a single ticket (*t 525 24 0, www.khm.at; all museums open Wed–Mon 10–6; adm*).

The interior of the Neue Burg is every bit as florid and pompous as the exterior, with monumental staircases, ranks of marble columns, and elaborate stucco ceilings providing a splendid backdrop to the museums' collections. The **Collection of Arms and Armour** (Hofjagd-und Rüstkammer) is vast and surprisingly engrossing, with prancing horses decked out in full jousting gear, fanciful costume armour which would have been worn at court rather than on the battle field (including a set with strange duck-shaped feet which was commissioned for a wedding), and a whole gallery dedicated to exquisitely decorated Turkish armour and weaponry. There's a set of tiny child's dress armour, created for the future Charles V, and some extraordinary horse armour, including a beautifully embossed set commissioned by Friedrich III, in which a dragon seems to erupt from the rear of the saddle.

The **Collection of Ancient Musical Instruments** (Sammlung alter Musik-instrumente) is altogether more soothing – quite literally, as the audioguide provides a gentle musical background to the exhibits. It's another enormous collection, spreading across several vast galleries, and encompassing one of the most remarkable collections of Renaissance instruments in the world. Exhibits range from prehistoric rattles and early chimes and bells, to glowing 17th- and 18th-century violas, cellos and violins, and elegant pianos. Some of the most curious pieces include a strange double guitar made in Paris in the late 15th century, and a late-Gothic bass lute which is absolutely unique. There's also a glass harmonica, in which the bowls are set humming when touched with damp fingers (making a sound like that produced by running a wet finger around a wine glass). Mozart even wrote for this instrument, which has a surprisingly delicate sound (you can hear a piece on the audioguide).

The lower galleries contain the archaeological fragments discovered at **Ephesus**, one of the most important cities of Classical Antiquity and site of the Temple of Artemis, once of the Seven Wonders of the World. Almost nothing remains of the temple, but a model of the monumental altar is dotted with a few surviving sculptures, including the delicate torso of an Amazon (who were said to amputate a breast to fight better, although this figure survives intact). The most striking exhibit is the massive Parthian Monument, a series of exquisitely wrought relief panels which may have been part of an altar. They were erected to commemorate the Roman victory over the Parthians, and are considered the finest such monument in Asia Minor. An earlier frieze of a cavalry battle celebrates a Greek victory over the Galaceans, and is one of the earliest known depictions of an historic battle in the world.

The **Ethnographical Museum** (Völkerkundermuseum; *open Wed–Mon 10–6; adm*) has a separate admission fee. It is housed in what was originally intended to be the Imperial guest house, and has a separate entrance on the Heldenplatz. Its holdings span every continent, and the enjoyably diverse and curious collection has all kinds of oddities, including some fetching fashion made from reeds in rural Japan, or from seal intestine in the Arctic. The star of the Africa section is the striking series of bronze sculptures from Benin, but the most famous piece in the whole collection is the 16th-century feathered head-dress which belonged to the Aztec king Montezuma, who was stoned to death by his own people for failing to resist the Spanish conquistadors.

Around the Ringstrasse

When the city walls were finally demolished in 1857, work began on this spectacular circular boulevard, designed to outshine anything Paris or London had to offer. It was soon lined with some of Vienna's most emblematic buildings – the legendary Opera House (Staatsoper), the magnificent Fine Arts Museum (Kunsthistoriches Museum), and the National Theatre among them – which cemented Vienna's reputation as a leading centre of the arts. Nearby, the pure lines of the beautiful Secession Building highlights the revolution which the Viennese art world underwent at the turn-of-the-20th century (*see* p.43). The sublime Baroque palace of the Belvedere displays Austrian art from the last millennium, and the fashionable new Museumsquartier shows the most exciting 20th-century and contemporary Austrian art.

The Rathaus and Around

The spiky, neo-Gothic **City Hall** (Rathaus; *1 Friedrich-Schmidt-Platz 1*, *t 525 50*, *www. wien.gv.at/ma55/fuehrungen; guided tours 1pm Mon, Wed, Fri except when in session* *and hols; adm*) was built between 1872 and 1883 to replace the rambling old Rathaus on Schwedenplatz. It symbolizes the wealth and influence of the burghers, and its position opposite the Hofburg was no accident: the Imperial court was left in no doubt as to who really held the reigns of power. The design deliberately echoes the Hôtel de Ville in Brussels, another city built on the wealth of its burghers, and the architect, Friedrich Schmidt, drew heavily on the Flemish Gothic style. The courtyards are open to the public, but the lavish interior can only be visited by guided tour. Right at the top of the clocktower in the main façade, a statue of a knight in armour brandishing a lance known as the 'Rathausman' gazes out across the city. Outdoor film performances take place in summer, and the square is flooded and frozen in winter to create a popular ice rink.

It might come as a bit of a shock to see a Greek temple on the Ringstrasse, but the **Parliament building** (*Dr Karl-Renner-Ring 3, t 40 110 2570, www.parlament.gv.at; guided tours except when in session and hols, July–Aug Mon–Fri 9, 10, 11,1, 2, 3; Sept–June Mon and Wed 10, 11, Tues and Thurs 2, 3, Fri 11, 1, 2, 3; free*) does a very good imitation. The Danish-born architect, Theophil von Hansen, studied in Athens and was deeply influenced by classical Greek architecture. A pediment frieze above the columned portico depicts Franz Josef I begrudgingly granting the 17 peoples of the nation a limited constitution, and graceful caryatids, modelled on those of the Erechtheion on the Acropolis, support the porticoes along the flanks of the building. The whole complex is liberally strewn with marble sculptures, busts and chariots, and an enormous statue of Pallas Athene, Goddess of Wisdom, rises seductively above the fountain which dominates the main square. The Parlament was bombed during the Second World War and took almost a decade to rebuild. Restoration work, begun in 1990, is still continuing (much of the main square is a building site), but you can visit the interior on one of the free guided tours.

Across the Ringstrasse from the venerable political institutions is the city's most prestigious theatre, the **National Theatre** (Burgtheater; *1 Dr. Karl-Lueger-Ring 2, t 514 44 4140, www.burgtheater.at; guided tours Mon–Sat 3pm, Sun and hols 11am, July and Aug daily at 2 and 3*). It's housed in another of the grand Ringstrasse buildings, erected in 1888, only for it to be discovered that there was no view of the stage from much of the auditorium and that the acoustics were appalling. The problems were fixed, but the theatre suffered serious bomb damage during the Second World War, although extensive restoration has returned it to its former opulence. The original Burgtheater was created by Maria Theresia in 1741, but it was Josef II who raised it to the status of a national theatre in 1776. It may be one of the most celebrated theatres in Europe, but it has refused to rest on its laurels, and continues to stage some of the most exciting and innovative performances in the German-speaking world.

Next to the Burgtheater, the **Volksgarten** (*entrances on Heldenplatz and Dr Karl Renner-Ring; open daily winter 6am–8pm, summer 6am–10pm*), once the preferred strolling ground of Vienna's aristocrats, is now a welcome stretch of green on the hectic Ringstrasse. Manicured gardens unfold elegantly, and the statue of the Empress Sisi remains a pilgrimage site for her legions of fans. The glass pavilion is now one of the city's best-known clubs (*see p.33*).

Museum of Fine Arts (Kunsthistoriches Museum)

1 Maria-Theresien-Platz, t 525 24 0, www.khm.at. Hauptgebäude (Main Building). Open Tues, Wed and Fri–Sun 10–6, Thurs 10–9; closed Mon; Coin Cabinet Tues–Sun 10–6; Collection of Greek and Roman antiquities and Collection of Sculpture and Decorative Arts closed for renovation.

The vast, grandiose Kunsthistoriches Museum, across the Ringstrasse from the Hofburg, contains one of the finest and largest art collections in Europe, the legacy of several Habsburg rulers and spanning every corner of their once-vast empire. Built in overblown neo-Renaissance style at the end of the 19th century, the museum bristles with marble columns, statuary and gilded murals (some by Gustav Klimt), and the spectacular central staircase is dominated by Antonio Canova's enormous, powerful sculpture of Theseus defeating the Centaur, commissioned by Napoleon. The overwhelming setting and the sheer size of the collection may leave you breathless before you've even begun: this is definitely a museum to see in bite-sized chunks. When museum fever sets in, you can retire to the elegant (if over-priced) restaurant and café under the lofty cupola.

The collection is divided into several parts, which share the same ticket: the **Ground Floor** contains the **Collection of Sculpture and Decorative Art**, the **Collection of Greek and Roman Antiquities** and the **Egyptian and Near Eastern Collection** (parts of which are closed for restoration). The **First Floor** houses the **Picture Gallery (Gemäldegalerie)**, which is what everyone mainly comes to see: to the right (the West Wing) is the collection of Italian, Spanish and French paintings, and to the left (the East Wing) is the German, Dutch and Flemish collection. The galleries are rather confusing: a connecting series of inner galleries in both wings are numbered with Roman numerals, while a second, outer ring of smaller rooms are given standard numbers. A floor plan (available at the information desk at the entrance) is essential.

The **Second Floor** is devoted to the **Coin Cabinet**.

Gemäldegalerie East Wing: German, Dutch and Flemish Collection

Dominating **Room IX** is a gory depiction of Heaven and Hell, in which demons subject sinners to imaginative if horrible torments while saints and angels look on. **Room X** is easily the most popular gallery in the entire museum, with a spectacular and virtually unrivalled collection of the works of Pieter Brueghel the Elder, including a sublime series of paintings depicting the seasons which mark the apotheosis of 16th-century landscape composition. There are three of the original six paintings here: *The Gloomy Day*, *The Return of the Herd*, and the celebrated *Hunters in the Snow*, in which you can almost hear the crunch of the tired hunters' boots. Also here are the *Peasant Wedding* and *Peasant Dance*, full of colour, vigour and movement, yet strangely joyless – Brueghel gained his nickname 'The Peasant Painter' with the first of these, but he never sentimentalized the subjects of his paintings, nor forgot the hardship of their daily lives. **Room XI** has monumental Baroque canvases by Jordaens and Snyders, and **Room XII** contains several delicate portraits by Van Dyck, and a compelling *Samson and Delilah*. **Rooms XIII and XIV** are devoted to the museum's extensive collection of the works of Rubens, mainly panels from altarpieces, including a masterful series from the Ildefonso Altar painted towards the end of his life. There's also an intimate portrait (*The Little Fur*) of his second wife Hélène Fourment, whom he married at the age of 53 when she was only 16. The adjoining gallery, **Room 20**, has Rubens' sketches for larger paintings, including a frightening *Head of Medusa* in murky blues and greens. **Room 14** has two tiny, exquisite portraits by Van Eyck, and a panel from a small altarpiece by Bosch, depicting Christ carrying the Cross through a jeering, prodding crowd. Rembrandt dominates **Room XV**, with several portraits, including three self-portraits, and boldly painted landscapes. **Rooms 16–19** contain a mesmerizing collection of German paintings from the Danube School, including Dürer's tender, and startlingly intimate *Virgin and Child with a Pear*, and a vivid *Adoration of the Trinity* from the Landauer Altar. There's a gory *Crucifixion* by Lucas Cranach the Elder, with a battered Christ coughing up blood, and several versions of *Judith with the Head of Holofernes*, a theme he clearly found deeply seductive. Also here is Bernhard Striegel's idealized portrait of the family of Maximilian I, which, although commissioned for the emperor's private use, is clearly intended to emphasise the far-reaching dynastic alliances of the Habsburg family: his much-loved wife and son appear (although they were both dead when it was painted), along with his young grandson whom he had never even seen. **Room 18** contains portraits by Hans Holbein, court painter to Henry VIII, including a demure portrait of Lady Jane Seymour, and an unforgivingly realistic portrait of the king's personal physican, Dr John Chambers, clearly worn out by the demands of his capricious sovereign. The most curious paintings in **Room 19** are the surreal works of Arcimboldo, who served three emperors but was a particular favourite at the court of Rudolf II. (Rudolf enjoyed Arcimboldo's quirky portraits formed of inanimate objects so much that he commissioned a whole series, one of every member of his court including the cook.) Here, Arcimboldo's evocations of the seasons and the elements (two of each survive, *Summer* and *Winter*, and *Fire* and *Water*) are formed of all manner of strange objects, from starfish to rifles. Also here are Spranger's sensuous canvases, with acres of pale, gleaming flesh and cavorting nymphs. **Room 24** contains a breezy Suffolk landscape by Gainsborough, a charming, domestic scene by Pieter de Hooch of a woman suckling her baby by an open fire, and Vermeer's magnificent *The Artist's Studio*, one of his most important works.

Gemäldegalerie West Wing: Italian, Spanish and French Collection

This collection begins with a bang with a whole room full of the works of Titian, court painter to Karl V, including a blazing, dramatic *Ecce Homo* and a seductive portrait of a woman semi-clad in fur (*Mädchen im Pelz*). There are more Italian Mannerists in **Rooms II and III**, with a vivid *Judith with the Head of Holofernes* by Veronese, and Tintoretto's exquisite, light-drenched *Susannah Bathing*. **Room 4** contains Raphael's serene *Madonna im Grünen*, and Pietro Perugino's moving painting of the Virgin surrounded by children, which has just emerged from restoration and glows. There's a sensuous *Jupiter and Io* by Coreggio in **Room 3**, in which the nymph abandons herself voluptuously to Jupiter in the form of a grey cloud. **Room V** contains Caravaggio's masterpiece *Madonna of the Rosary Feast*, sharp, shadowy and unsettling, and in **Room VII** you can see huge views of Vienna and the Imperial palaces by Bernardo Belloto, commissioned by Maria Theresia. Bellota was trained by his uncle, Canaletto, whose influence is clearly apparent. Look out for the fabulous Habsburg portraits by Velázquez in **Room 10**, including one of Philip IV with the characteristic Habsburg overbite, and another of Charles III, who was spectacularly ugly.

Collection of Sculpture and Decorative Art

This wing is undergoing major restoration and won't open to the public until at least 2006. In the meantime, many of the works are displayed around the Picture Gallery.

The collection is quirkier than its name suggests, and includes all kinds of curiosities acquired by Rudolf II and Archduke Ferdinand, for their *Kunskammern*, or Chambers of Art and Marvels. Among the sculptures are several handsome bronzes by Giambologna, busts of the Imperial family, including a pensive *Charles V* by Leone Leoni (1555), and Gregor Erhart's oddly unsettling *Allegory of Vanity*, in which a beautiful youthful couple are contrasted with a hideous old crone. The shimmering colours of the paintwork have been attributed to Hans Holbein the Elder. Among the oddities are a 16th-century musical clock in the shape of a galleon in full sail, and a clockwork globe designed to demonstrate the cosmos. George Roll presented two such globes to Rudolf II and his brother, Archduke Ernst, but when the Emperor's globe broke he had Roll thrown in prison for he 'had presented him with foul fish'. There are playing cards and games boards, a table decoration made with 'Adders' Tongues' (actually sharks' teeth) which were believed to neutralise poisons, and a tankard made from Unicorn Horn (really a whale tusk) which is studded with precious jewels. Among the beautiful tapestries is a handsome 18th-century hanging from the Gobelins factory in Paris, which recreates Raphael's frescoes for the Vatican.

Collection of Greek and Roman Antiquities

Closed for restoration, but due to open in spring 2005.

These galleries are stuffed full of ancient treasures, from Etruscan art and vases to ancient Greek and Cypriot sculpture. The main gallery resembles a Roman villa, complete with a vast mosaic of Theseus and the Minotaur, and several busts. Also here is an extraordinary horde of 9th-century gold plate and vessels, discovered in 1799 in Romania.

Egyptian and Near Eastern Collection

Partly closed for restoration.

The entrance to these galleries, in the West Wing on the Ground Floor, is guarded by two solemn statues of the Egyptian goddess Sekhmet, a sphinx-like creature with a leonine face. **Room 1** contains ancient sarcophagi, a single mummy tightly wrapped in papyrus leaves, mummy cases covered with symbols and hieroglyphs, mummified animals, and canopic jars which contained the entrails removed during the mummifi-cation process. **Room 2** contains the reconstructed tomb chapel of Ka-ni-nisut, which dates back five millennia, and **Room 5** has scores of Egyptian *Books of the Dead*, the papyrus scrolls containing instructions for life in the hereafter which were placed in ancient tombs. There is a whole menagerie of fantastical gods, found in tombs, along with votive figures and amulets, and a beautiful, lapus-lazuli-blue ceramic hippo-potamus. These were often found in Middle Kingdom tombs and denoted a favourite of the king, who granted hippopotamus-hunting rights to his most beloved courtiers.

Coin Cabinet

One of the largest and most comprehensive coin collections in the world, on the Second Floor, this contains early coins from Ancient Greece and Rome, Egyptian, Celtic and Byzantine currency, and a vast array of medieval and Renaissance coins. **Rooms 2 and 3** are dedicated to 19th and 20th century medals, including one cast to commem-orate the birth of Napoleon's son.

Natural History Museum (Naturhistoriches Museum)

1 Maria-Theresien-Platz, t 521 77, www.nhm-wien.acc.at; open Thurs–Mon 10–6, Wed 10–9; adm; roof tours Wed at 5 and 6.30, Sun 2 and 4; adm.

Erected at the same time as the Kunsthistoriches Museum across the square, Vienna's Natural History Museum is equally sumptuous, and was conceived as a scientific complement to the artistic treasures held in the Museum of Fine Arts. In the mid-18th century, Emperor Franz Stephen I acquired what was then the world's largest and most celebrated natural history collection from a Florentine scholar, and these objects form the nucleus of the current holdings. Little has changed since the museum opened in 1889, and the elegant wooden cabinets are crammed with every imaginable stuffed creature from around the world, many displayed in delightfully old-fashioned dioramas.

The dinosaur skeletons in **Rooms IV and V** on the upper ground floor are the big draw, and include a spectacular 17-million-year-old tusked mammoth-like creature excavated in the Czech Republic, and the well-preserved skeleton of the Austrian Rhino. On the first floor, you enter **Room XXXIV** through the enormous lower jawbone of a whale, and the gallery itself is almost filled by a huge, floating whale skeleton. There's also a model of the sea cow, a gentle, cumbersome creature which was discovered in the Pacific by shipwrecked sailors in 1741, who passed on the news to hide-hunters. By 1768, the harmless sea cow was extinct. The skeleton of the most famous extinct species, the dodo, can also be found here (in **Room XXXI**), one of the most complete in the world. In the last room on this floor, you can see Honzo, the beer-swilling, cigarette-smoking, fight-picking chimpanzee who lived in the Vienna zoo in the 1950s. The ground floor contains the enormous mineral collection, and **Room IV** boasts opulent Jugendstil decoration with wispy nymphs erupting from the walls. It's a suitably gorgeous setting for the **Gem Collection**, of which the highlight is the 'Bouquet of Gems', which Maria Theresia apparently gave to her husband Franz

Stephan over breakfast, and which contains a staggering 3,000 precious stones, mainly diamonds.

Staatsoper to Karlsplatz

Vienna's extravagant **Opera House** (Staatsoper; *1 Opernring 2, t 514 44 2606, www. wiener-staatsoper.at; guided visits available; adm; but check times posted under the arcades on the Kärntnerstrasse side of the Opera House; for booking information, see 'Entertainment', p.32*) was the first of the grand buildings along the Ringstrasse to be completed, and opened with a performance of Mozart's *Don Giovanni* in 1869. Built in a heavy-handed neo-Renaissance style, complete with loggias to shelter carriages, the splendid main entrance is topped with bronze statues depicting Heroism, Drama, Fantasy, Humour and Love. The interior is even more opulent, and the glittering marble, gilt and profusion of allegorical frescoes provide a spectacular backdrop for the annual Vienna Opera Ball, one of the most exclusive balls on the Viennese social calendar. The main auditorium suffered extensive damage during the Second World War but has been restored with all the latest technological equipment, losing much of its original flamboyance in the process. Still, there are enough grand staircases and opulent salons to flounce around for a visit to the Opera to remain a heady and romantic experience.

Kärntner Strasse leads to **Karlsplatz**, once an elegant park on the fringe of the Ringstrasse, but which has been mercilessly chopped up and hemmed in by busy roads which often require steely nerves to cross. It's still strewn with elegant monuments but parts of its are distinctly shady, and it's best avoided at night. Almost lost in the whirl of traffic, a pair of frothy **Secessionist pavilions** were erected by Otto Wagner in 1898–9 for Karlsplatz underground station, although they have long lost their original function. Wagner used a metal frame with marble slabs to create the pavilions, which are delicately decorated with gold detailing and wrought-iron flourishes. They were almost demolished in the 1960s, but were reconstructed here after students protested, and one has become a café-club (*see* 'Nightlife', p.33), while the other occasionally hosts art exhibitions.

Across the busy main road, the **Künstlerhaus** (*1 Karlsplatz 5, t 587 9663, www. k-haus.at; open Mon–Wed and Fri 10–6, Thurs 10–9; adm*), a florid late 19th-century building, is home to Vienna's Society of Artists, against whom the Secessionists rebelled in 1897. It has shed its stuffy reputation, and hosts dynamic, resolutely modern temporary art exhibitions as well as showing the work of its members. Next door is the equally opulent **Musikverein**, doyenne of Vienna's classical music scene.

The lofty **Karlskirche** (*4 Karlsplatz, www.karlskirche.at; open Mon–Sat 9–12.30 and 1–6, Sun 1–6; last lift up to the dome 5.30; adm to dome*) dominates the southern (and more salubrious) end of Karlsplatz. One of the most extravagant expressions of European Baroque, it was commissioned by Emperor Karl VI in thanks for Vienna's delivery from the plague in 1713. Johann Bernhard Fischer von Erlach began work on the church in 1714, and it was completed by his son around 1739. The church was dedicated to St Charles Borromeo, the 16th-century Archbishop of Milan who worked tirelessly for plague victims in his city. His statue floats above the main entrance, which is carved with grim scenes of Viennese suffering during the plague. Two slender towers, reminiscent of minarets, flank the main portal, and are topped with an elegant dome. The towers were inspired by Trajan's Column in Rome, and are decorated with a spiralling series of reliefs describing the life of St Charles Borromeo. But it was no accident that the saint shared a name with the emperor, and the heavy symbolism on the towers and throughout the church can also be read as a glorification of the Habsburg dynasty. The interior is surprisingly airy, and a lift up to the ethereal dome allows close-up views of Johann Michael Rottmayer's vast fresco depicting *The Apotheosis of St Charles*, currently being restored. The church is beautifully reflected in a shallow ornamental pond, with a strange sculpture by Henry Moore which looks like an eyeball. The pool is a favourite with Viennese dogs, who come to chase sticks and cool off in summer,

A blank modern building across the square from the Karlskirche contains the **Vienna History Museum** (Wien Museum; *4 Karlsplatz, t 505 87 47, www.wienmuseum. at; open Tues–Sun 9–6; adm*) which documents the city's history from prehistoric times until the 20th century. A series of models, one on each floor (each corresponds to a particular period), show the development of the city over the centuries. On the ground floor, fragments of Roman pots, statuary and tools rub shoulders with medieval religious sculpture and the remains of the original stained glass windows of Stephansdom, which depict the stoning of St Stephen. There are some curious funerary helmets, decorated with enormous figures – dragons, angels, lions – which would have signified the religion and status of the deceased and been buried with them. On the first floor, which covers the 16th–18th centuries, Vienna's transformation from a city at war to an affluent and peaceful capital is charted with the aid of a random assortment of maps, paintings, armour, gilded house signs, and fancy wigs. The top floor is the most rewarding, and contains a reconstructed interior designed by Adolf Loos, an exquisite chair inlaid with mother-of-pearl designed by Otto Wagner, and fascinating photographs of the major buildings erected at the turn of the 20th century. But the real highlight is the collection of early 20th-century art, including several pieces by Klimt (paintings of the interior of the Opera House which were carried out before he abandoned the solemn Historicism of his contemporaries, as well as later works) and some characteristically bleak portraits by Egon Schiele.

At the other end of Karlsplatz, stranded between major roads, you can't miss the glistening golden dome of the beautiful **Secession Building** (*1 Friedriechstrasse 12, t 587 5307, www.secession.at; open Tues, Wed and Fri–Sun 10–6, Thurs 10–8; adm*). In 1897, a group of young artists, including Gustav Klimt, Josef Hofmann, Josef Maria Olfbrich and Kolo Moser, withdrew from the conservative Society of Artists at the Künstlerhaus and formed the Association of Visual Artists Secession (*see p.43*). They built this elegant, sparkling white building (completed in 1898) as a physical embodiment of the new movement's fundamental tenets, which were encapsulated in its very structure. Rejecting the weighty historicism of their predecessors, they emblazoned their motto over the main entrance: *Der Zeit ihre Kunst, der Kunst ihre Freiheit* ('To the Age its Art, to Art its Freedom'). The Secessionists viewed art as mystical, even sacred, and Olbrich's original designs describe it as a 'Temple of Art'.

References to sacred temples abound, from the inscription *Ver Sacrum* ('Holy Spring') on the façade to the stylized laurel trees which flank the doorway, which are themselves echoed in the glittering golden cupola of interlocking laurel leaves. Above the main entrance, the snakes of the *aegis* of Pallas Athene are entwined around masks representing the three arts (painting, architecture and sculpture). The spaces are deliberately divided into the ornamental entrance area, and the purely functional galleries – sleek, white, unadorned. The building was unlike anything ever seen in Vienna and critics lambasted it as 'a cross between a greenhouse and a blast furnace', ' a temple for bullfrogs' and even 'a bastard begot of temple and warehouse'. The original building was completely destroyed in 1945, when the retreating German army torched it, but it was finally renovated in 1980 and remains one of the most exquisite buildings in the city. Unfortunately, it's now stranded between busy main roads, which make it impossible to see as a whole without taking your life in your hands.

Contemporary exhibitions are held in the main galleries, and the association runs interesting tours and lecture programmes. Bizarrely, the only permanent exhibit was intended to be temporary: Klimt's unearthly *Beethoven Frieze*, painted for the 9th exhibition of the Viennese Secessionists in 1902. It was supposed to be destroyed after the exhibition, but, luckily, it was bought by a collector, and finally acquired by the Austrian government who had it placed here in a specially built gallery. The 34m-long frieze takes Richard Wagner's interpretation of Beethoven's *Ninth Symphony* as its inspiration, from the 'Yearning for Happiness' to its eventual fulfilment through the arts. Dreamy nymphs sway across the early panels, meeting terrifying monsters and wild-eyed gorgons along the way, finally discovering poetry, music and the arts and culminating in an erotic embrace amid a choir of angels on the final panel.

MuseumsQuartier

U-Bahn to MuseumsQuartier.

The former Imperial riding stables, designed by the indefatigable Johann Fischer von Erlach at the end of the 18th century, were in 2001 dramatically and expensively converted into the MuseumsQuartier, one of the world's largest cultural complexes. Bold contemporary buildings have been slotted into the spacious central courtyard, now called the **Museumplatz**, which is full of terrace cafés where Vienna's young and fashionable come to lounge on summer weekends. There's an information office-cum-shop (*open daily 10am–7pm, www.mqw.at*) at the main entrance, which is a good first port-of-call to find out what's on when – the complex hosts several one-off events to complement the offerings of its array of cultural institutions.

The pale, gleaming cube inserted into the main square of the MuseumsQuartier houses the **Leopold Museum** (*t 525 70, www.leopoldmuseum.org; open Wed, Thurs and Sat–Mon 10–7, Fri 10–9; closed Tues; adm*), with a superb collection of the works of Austrian expressionist Egon Schiele. The collection was amassed by Rudolf Leopold in the 1950s, and now comprises more than 5,000 works. The second floor is dedicated to Schiele, but there is plenty of art by other late-19th-century and 20th-century Expressionist and Modernist artists, including pieces by Klimt, Gerstl and Kokoschka.

Jutting out at an awkward angle on the other side of Museumsplatz is the unrelentingly contemporary **Museum of Modern Art** (Museum moderner Kunst) known as **MUMOK** (*t 525 00, www. mumok.at; open Tues, Wed and Fri–Sun 10–6, Thurs 10–9; closed Mon; adm*), a sleek, if forbidding, slate-grey block. It's an uncomfortable, oppressive space, with lots of steel and smoky glass but almost no natural light, but it does have an excellent collection spanning most of the major 20th-century art movements. Many of the holdings can be seen as part of changing themed exhibitions (usually on the top three floors), but some highlights are on permanent view, and cover everything from Pop Art (of which there's an excellent selection) to Arte Povera. The basement is devoted to Viennese Actionism, a deliberately provocative performance art movement whose proponents (Günter Bros, Otto Muehl and Hermann Nitsch among others) outdid each other with a succession of shocking public displays – blood, offal, and faeces feature heavily. They were active during the 1960s, and sought to change the world and challenge 'bourgeois' conceptions of art through their shocking performances.

The former Winter Riding School of the Imperial stables has been converted into a vast, contemporary exhibition space and performance hall, the **Kunsthalle Wien** (*t 521 89 33, www.kunsthallewien.at; open Fri–Wed 10–7, Thurs 10–10; adm*). It has an excellent, audience-grabbing programme of temporary exhibitions, which draw on Austrian and international artists, and remains deservedly one of the most popular art institutions in the city.

The **Architecture Centre** (Architekturzentrum Wien; *t 522 31 1530, www.azw.at; open Thurs–Tues 10–7, Wed 10–9; adm*), is an archive and exhibition space, with an excellent permanent display detailing the major developments in architecture around the world, neatly complemented by thematic changing exhibitions. They also run architecture-themed walking tours around the city, usually held on Sundays.

The **Zoom Children's Museum** (ZOOM Kindermuseum; *t 524 79 08, www.kinder museum.at; open Mon–Fri 8.30–5, Sat–Sun 10–5.30; adm; sessions must be pre-booked in advance, particularly for weekend visits*) is a must for kids, who will be having too much fun to mind the language barrier, Vienna's dedicated children's museum runs hugely popular workshops for kids of all ages. There's an ocean-themed space for babies and toddlers, while older children can mess about with video cameras and sound recordings in the ZoomLab. Note that you have to pre-book sessions in advance, particularly for weekend visits.

One of the few remaining European cities where the smoker can still light up at ease, Vienna even has its own museum dedicated to smoking, the **Tabakmuseum** (*t 526 171 760; open Tues, Wed and Fri 10–5, Thurs 10–7, Sat 10–2; closed Sun and Mon; adm*). It's run by the state tobacco monopoly, but even passionate anti-smokers will enjoy the displays of snuff boxes and pipes.

Belvedere Palace and Botanic Gardens

The glorious Baroque Belvedere Palace was built by Johann Lukas von Hildebrandt, arch-rival of Fishcher von Erlach, for Prince Eugene of Savoy, the most celebrated military general of his day. Once the Turks were subdued and the War of Succession finally came to an end, Vienna was struck with building fever and began to expand beyond the old city walls. The elegant Lower Belvedere, a summer palace, was built first in 1714–16, and surrounded with expansive landscaped gardens. However, the prince required something even grander and more prestigious and commissioned the magnificent Upper Belvedere in 1721 – which functioned essentially as an extravagant party pavilion for Prince Eugene's spectacular firework shows and other festivities. The palaces are linked by graceful formal **gardens** (*open daily 6am–dusk*), designed in the French style by Dominque Girard, and liberally strewn with fountains and statuary. Some years after the prince's death, the palaces were eventually sold to Maria Theresia in 1752, when they became known as the Belvedere. Emperor Josef II moved the Imperial Art Gallery here, and opened the grounds to the public as a pleasure garden. The art collection was rehoused when the Kunsthistoriches Museum was built, and the palace became the residence of Archduke Franz Ferdinand.

Both palaces were severely damaged during the Second World War, but were immaculately restored and now contain the **Austrian Gallery collection**: the Upper Belvedere is home to 19th and 20th-century art, including a stunning collection of works by Klimt, Schiele and Kokoshka, and the Lower Belvedere contains art from the medieval to the Baroque periods.

In the **Upper Belvedere** (Oberes Belvedere; *3 Prinz-Eugen-Strasse 27, t 79557, www.belvedere.at; open Tues–Sun 10–6; closed Mon; adm; combined ticket to all the Belvedere collections available; guided tours or audioguide*), a vast stone staircase guarded by a fleet of chubby cherubs affords stunning views of the ornamental lake and gardens, and leads to the palace's most extravagant chamber, the Marble Hall. The red marble panels and Baroque frescoes by Carlo Carlone are under wraps for restoration at the moment (due to be unveiled in 2005), but you can still enter and admire the breathtaking views over Vienna, dominated by the spire of Stephansdom. To see the collection chronologically, head up to the second floor, which contains the early 19th-century and Biedermayer collection. There are several portraits, including Gérard's portrait of the Viennese banker, Moritz Christian Fries, and massive, idealized landscapes. The Biedermayer period is represented with cosy family scenes of wealthy burghers, plenty of still lifes, and sentimental peasant scenes, which were very popular during the period.

Returning to the first floor, the late 19th-century collection includes several fine views of Vienna, such as Carl Kuger's smoky *Arrival of a Train at Westbahnhof*, and a throng of sentimentalized portraits. There is a wonderful self-portrait by Gustave Courbet, *The Wounded Man*, who had just been separated from his lover, and several scenes depicting the newly built Ringstrasse. The collection picks up steam with some Impressionist gems, including Renoir's dewy *Bather with Loose Blonde Hair* and *After the Bath*, and Van Gogh's clear, luminous *Plain at Anvers*, painted only weeks before his death. Carl Moll's *Dusk* is hauntingly lovely, and hangs close to two works by Munch: *Men in the Sea*, bright, joyful and confident, and a wonderful *Seascape* which features the Nordic midnight sun. There's an early portrait by Klimt, of a sour-faced miss in a pink, frilly dress, but the following gallery contains the real star of the Belvedere: Klimt's famous *Kiss*. This was virtually the last of his golden paintings, which had been inspired by Italian mosaics, and his later work (in the next gallery) is bolder, more colourful and entirely free of elaborate gilding. (Just off this room, take a peek into the extravagantly Baroque double-storey chapel, built so that the prince could attend mass from the gallery.) The following galleries are devoted to the Viennese Expressionists, and include a whole room full of works by Egon Schiele, including the characteristically grim *Death and Girl*, and a sublime, pearly autumnal scene, with bare trees silhouetted against a rosy sky. Oscar Kokoshka's deliberately provocative paintings include the gory *Still Life with Dead Mutton*, a gleaming sheep's head paired with a blood-red tomato.

Stroll down the elegant gardens, under the gaze of inscrutable Sphinxes, and past ornamental ponds with lavish fountains, to the prince's first palace, the **Lower Belvedere** (Unteres Belvedere; *3 Rennweg 6, t 79557; see Upper Belvedere*). The Baroque collection is housed in the main building, perfectly at home in the lavish marble-and-gilt halls. You may be greeted with a line of grimacing, leering, sobbing, laughing busts, a series of unintentionally hilarious character studies by Franz Xaver Messerschmidt (usually kept in the Grotesques' Gallery, but recently brought to the front of the museum as a teaser). In the adjoining gallery, admire the same sculptor's regal busts of Maria Theresia and Franz Stephan I. There are several domestic and courtly scenes by Franz Christoph Janneck from the first half of the 18th century, followed by monumental landscape and genre scenes, and an array of ecstatic late-Baroque religious paintings. The centrepiece of the Lower Belvedere is the lavish Marble Hall, a double-decker extravaganza of red marble walls, white marble angels and *trompe l'œil* frescoes, with depictions of triumphs from the Prince's legendary military career. These culminate in a vast ceiling fresco in which the Prince is transformed into Apollo. At the centre of the chamber is Georg Raphael Donner's lead sculpture from the fountain at Neue Markt, in which four river deities are grouped around 'Providentia', in a flattering allegory praising the city of Vienna's good government. The Hall of Grotesques is thickly covered with mythical beasts, dragons and Sphinxes among others, and allegories of the four season and four elements stretch across the ceiling. Another opulent marble gallery follows, specially commissioned to house the prince's collection of classical statuary acquired from Herculaneum, and off it is the glittering Cabinet of Gold, in which every service gleams with gold and mirrors.

Take the path outside to the **medieval collection**, housed in the former **Orangerie**. There are early 14th-century paintings, with intricate gold-leaf decoration, several excellent altarpieces including a fine triptych commissioned by Albrecht V. There are some brutal scenes from the Passion from the Salzburg painter Rueland Frueaf the Elder, and several pieces from the accomplished Michael Pacher, who was clearly influenced by Flemish and northern Italian art and strove to achieve perspective.

The palace gardens link with Vienna's extensive **Botanical Gardens** (*main entrance Rennweg 14, t 4277 54190; open daily 9am–dusk, closed during bad weather*) created by Maria Theresia in 1754 for the cultivations of medicinal plants. They were expanded and given their current form in the 19th century, and are now part of Vienna University's Botanical Institute. The tranquil, extensive gardens and shady paths are a welcome relief from the hubbub of the city, and perfect for a picnic lunch.

MAK

1 Stubenring 5, t 711 36 0, www.mak.at. Open Wed–Sun 10–6; Tues 10am–midnight; closed Mon.

The Austrian **Museum of Applied Arts and Contemporary Art**, better known simply as MAK, may be housed in a monumental, 19th-century Ringstrasse building, but its displays are anything but stuffy: in 1993, the curators invited celebrated artists to redesign the exhibition halls and the results (while sometimes annoyingly pretentious) have been a huge success. Add to that a fantastic shop full of stylish goodies and an excellent café, and it's easy to see why MAK has become the fashionistas' museum of choice.

The exhibits are laid out chronologically, beginning with the **Romanesque and Gothic galleries**, which contain sumptuously embroidered liturgical vestments, covered with fabulous creatures, which are among the finest pieces in the museum's textile collection. Beyond it is a collection of **glass and lacework**, largely Venetian, from the 16th and 17th centuries. The **Baroque gallery** is suitably monumental, and contains the painstakingly recreated early 18th-century **Dubsky Porcelain Room**, which came from the Dubsky Palace in the Czech Republic and gets its name from the heavy use of ceramics on every surface. The delicate Far Eastern porcelain which had recently been introduced was much in fashion, and the Oriental theme is echoed in the huge tapestries. The **19th-century galleries** begin with monumental cabinets, intricate glassware, and lavish dinner services including one commissioned by Napoleon on the occasion of the birth of his son, the Duc de Reischstadt. In the following gallery, there's a selection of exquisite Oriental rugs and fabrics, including a unique 16th-century silk rug from Egypt, The most ingenious and enchanting presentation is in the **Historismus, Jugendstil, Art Deco room**, where the chair collection (arranged by Barbara Bloom) is beautifully back-lit and visible in silhouette through white screens, the forms emerging like shadow-puppets, enabling visitors to see the changing styles across the years.

Upstairs, a gallery is dedicated to the **Wiener Werkstätte** (Vienna Workshops), an arts and crafts co-operative founded in 1903 by architect Josef Hofmann and designer Kolo Moser. They actively promoted design in all its forms, from the humble (ashtrays and postage stamps) to the classic (furniture and ceramics). There's an astonishing array of pieces here, from cigarette boxes to a gorgeous silver and ebony tea service studded with coral. The main highlight of the **Art Nouveau and Art Deco gallery** is a series of drawings by Klimt for a nine-panelled frieze, commissioned for the Palais Stoclet in Brussels, but look out for an elegant writing cabinet by Mackintosh, and a luminous collection of vivid Bohemian glass. Photographs and models of major modern and contemporary buildings introduce a gallery dedicated to **20th- and 21st architecture**, and includes Kiesler's curious *Endless House* (1959), a curvaceous concrete sphere on pillars, and Liebeskind's design for the Jewish Museum in Berlin. From here, stairs lead up to a loft-like space with spiky examples of contemporary art.

The perfect antidote to museum overload, the **Stadtpark** (*open 24hrs*) stretches leafily to the south of MAK. The main entrance is flanked by a pair of Jugendstil columns, and small pavilions and statues of musical greats from Schubert to Strauss are scattered across the lawns.

Outside the Centre

Strung out around the edge of the city centre are a host of sights, from the Baroque pomp and splendour of the Imperial lodge in Schönbrunn to the dreamy expanse of the Prater gardens. Linger in Freud's consulting room, or check out the gruesome anatomical models in the Josephinum; go boating on the Danube, or take in the city views on the Reisenbad, the ferris wheel immortalized in the film of *The Third Man*.

Sigmund Freud Museum

9 Berggasse 19, t 319 1596, www.freud-museum.at; tram D to Schlickgasse, tram 37, 38, 40, 41 to Schwarzspanierstrasse, or bus 40 A to Berggasse. Open daily July–Sept 9–6; Oct–June 9–5; adm. Audioguide; guided tours by appt.

Tucked away in this leafy, residential district, the Sigmund Freud museum is discreetly signposted and hard to find (take the stairs up from the entrance hall). Freud lived, practised and studied here from 1891 until the Nazis forced him to emigrate in 1938, and in 1971 it was opened as a museum by his daughter Anna.

The waiting room is the only room which has been restored to look just as it did in Freud's time, and the rest of the apartment is now an exhibition space and study centre. One small room contains multilingual video screens showing black and white films of the Freud family, narrated by Anna, and there's a temporary exhibition gallery and a reference library. The waiting room contains a cabinet of antiques and curiosities, and the walls are lined with diplomas, certificates, and photographs, including one of the participants of the International Psychoanalytical Congress in Weimar in 1911. The consulting room contains copies of early photographs and documents, from the young Sigmund's school report (in which his 'moral conduct' is praised as 'exemplary') to the romantic letters exchanged between Freud and his fiancée, Martha Bernays. (In one he describes the effects of cocaine on German soldiers' endurance, and announces his intention to give it a go.) The former study contains excerpts from his books, more photographs, including one of Jung, and a few personal trinkets such as his hat and cane. There are deeply disturbing photographs depicting the burning of Freud's books in Vienna in 1933, and another of Hitler addressing a vast throng of rapt Viennese in May 1931. 2006 celebrates the 150th centenary of Freud's birth.

Josephinum

9 Währinger Strasse 25, t 4277 63401; tram 37, 38, 40, 41 to Schwarzspanierstrasse. Open Mon–Fri 9–3; adm.

In 1785, Josef II established the Josephinum as an institute for military surgery after seeing at first hand the crude techniques employed on the battlefield. The Institute was closed in the late 19th century, and now contains a small museum of medical history with cabinets full of alarming ancient instruments and gory diagrams. The main draw is a series of 18th-century anatomical models, commissioned by Josef II around 1780 and built in Florence. The eerily realistic wax figures expose the heart, brain, lungs and other internal organs, and are displayed in the original burnished rosewood cabinets. Bizarrely, in the centre of all this lies a Barbie-like creature, complete with pearl necklace and fluffy blonde hair, smiling above her gaping chest cavity.

Schönbrunn

*13 Schönbrunner Schloss Strasse 47, t 811 3239, www.schoenbrunn.at;
U-Bahn to Schönbrunn, tram 10, 58, bus 10a to Schloss Schönbrunn.
See below for opening times of attractions within palace complex.*

*Admission tickets: **Imperial Tour**: 22 rooms in the palace, €8 with audioguide.
Grand Tour: 40 rooms, including the ornate 18th-century audience rooms,
€10.50 with audioguide, guided tour €13. **Classic Pass**: Grand Tour, plus
admission to Privy Garden, Gloriette, Maze and Labyrinth, and Schönbrunn
Bakery, €14.90. **Gold Pass**: Classic Pass plus admission to Schönbrunn Zoo,
Palm House, Desert Experience House, Carriage Museum, €36. See also
Sisi Pass (under Hofburg, p.53).*

Schönbrunn, an enormous, frilly Baroque palace on the southwestern outskirts of Vienna, was the summer residence of the Imperial family. The original hunting lodge was destroyed by the Turks in 1683, and a replacement was commissioned from Johann Fischer von Erlach in 1695. He planned a gigantic palace on a fabulous scale, one which would outshine Versailles, but finally the Imperial family were forced to make do with a mere 1,441 rooms in the final design by Nikolaus Pacassi. The palace was completed under Maria Theresia in the mid-18th century, and became the empress's favourite residence. It's possible to tour the extravagant interior, but be warned that Schönbrunn Palace is one of the biggest attractions in the whole of Austria, and the experience can be daunting: tour buses disgorge endless streams of visitors, and the tour of the apartments is a slow shuffle through the crowds. It's possible to escape the hordes in the beautiful gardens, which extend for miles and are scattered with other attractions including a puzzling maze and labyrinth, an exotic 19th-century palm house, the splendid Imperial carriage museum, and a zoo.

Imperial Apartments

*Open Nov–Mar daily 8.30–4.30; April–June and Sept–Oct daily 8.30–5;
July–Aug daily 8.30–6; tickets are marked with an entrance time; adm exp.*

The tour of the palace begins in the West Wing with the humdrum **apartments** belonging to Franz Josef and Sisi. In the main audience chamber, a stuffy, walnut-panelled hall, the dutiful emperor would receive up to a hundred people in a morning, and the adjoining waiting room was kitted out with a billiard table for bored peti-tioners. Franz Josef's office is next, followed by his spartan bedroom which contains the simple iron bedstead on which he died in 1916. Sisi's dressing room had plenty of space for her endless array of beauty products, and connects with the marital bedroom – where the empress is said to have kept her new husband waiting for two days after her wedding day before finally succumbing. Passing through a lavish neo-rococo **reception room**, decked out in white and gold silk, there's a family **dining room**, with portraits of Maria Theresia's daughters, including the young Marie Antoinette who was famously guillotined during the French Revolution. The **Mirror Room** was used for family concerts, including one given by the six-year-old Mozart and his sister, and legend has it that the child prodigy smothered the empress with kisses – no doubt a tale put about to enhance her reputation as 'Mother of the Empire'. The magnificent **Great Gallery** was used for balls, including during the Congress of Vienna in 1815 ('the congress danced but didn't advance'), and is a whirl of gilded stucco, crystal chandeliers (which held 70 candles each before the introduction of electricity) and enormous frescoes praising the Habsburg reign. Maria Theresia and her husband Franz Stephan are enthroned in the centre of the enormous ceiling fresco, and the hall was used for a celebrated meeting between Kennedy and Khrushchev in 1961. There is a pair of exquisite circular chambers off the **Small Gallery**, extravagantly decorated in the popular late-Baroque Orientalist style with glossy lacquer panels and porcelain, and used by the Empress Maria Theresia for secret meetings with her advisers. The **Carousel Room**, in which the indomitable empress appears riding a Lipizzaner at the Winter Riding School in 1743, and the **Ceremonial Hall**, with a vast painting of Josef II's wedding to Isabella of Palma, follow, and mark the culmination of the Grand Tour.

If you've opted for the Imperial Tour, the best is yet to come: the following *salons* are the most opulent of the entire palace. The **Blue Chinese Salon**, covered in delicately hand-painted wallpaper inset with pretty panels, is where negotiations were held which finally led to Karl I's abdication in November 1918 – to the outrage of his wife, the Empress Zita, who said. 'A sovereign can never abdicate...never, never, never. I would rather fall here at your side.' Nearby is the **Napoleon Room**, which was origi-nally Maria Theresia's bedroom but was taken over by the diminutive Frenchman after his marriage to the Princess Marie Louise. Maria Theresia's pale-blue and green study is covered with graceful drawings and a medallion of her favourite daughter, Maria Christina, and leads into the splendid, if overwhelming, **Millions Room**, covered in fabulously expensive, rare rosewood panelling inset with Indo-Persian etchings. In the **bedroom**, the only surviving State Bed, built for the marriage of Maria Theresia and Franz Stephan, is barely discernible under the weight of its ornate decoration and richly embroidered hangings. The final rooms were used by Archduke Franz Karl, father of Franz Josef: more lavish than his son's plain quarters, they are still a disap-pointment after the eye-popping Baroque extravagance of Maria Theresia's apartments and are now filled with Habsburg family portraits.

Carriage Museum (Wagenburg)

t (01) 877 32 44, www.khm.at. Open April–Oct daily 9–6; Nov–Mar 10–4; adm.

The former stables now house the Imperial Coach Museum, where glittering Baroque carriages and sleighs, monumental funerary carriages, and sleek early automobiles eloquently convey the dazzling opulence of the Habsburg court. Possibly the most lavish is the Grand Carosse, an Imperial carriage built around 1763 but used right up until 1916: oozing gilded flourishes, its windows are made of Venetian glass and painted allegorical panels praise the sovereign's virtues. There's a sleek two-seater sleigh with a natty leopardskin interior, and a special hunting carriage made for Prince Leopold of Bourbon-Salerno, specially fitted with a revolving seat so that the plump prince could turn and take his shot. There are some wonderful children's carriages, every bit as opulent as the full-size versions, including an extravagant one built for Napoleon's son, the King of Rome, which was pulled by two specially trained merino sheep. A grim, black 19th-century funerary carriage was most recently used for the burial of the former Empress Zita in 1989. Just one of the Imperial court's fleet of automobiles, designed by Gräf and Stift, has survived, and still bears the Imperial Crown instead of a licence plate.

Schlösspark

Open daily 10am–dusk.

Schönbrunn's gorgeous gardens stretch for miles, formally laid out in the French style in the 18th century, and scattered with statuary and fountains. For fabulous views over the whole park, make for the **Gloriette** (*access above the café, open April–June and Sept daily 9–6; July and Aug 9–7; Oct 9–5; adm*), a huge, florid victory arch surmounted with the Imperial eagle, which was erected in 1775. Kids will enjoy the **maze** and **labyrinth** (*same opening times as Gloriette; adm*), near the exuberant Baroque Neptune fountain. A huge swath of the park is taken up with the **Vienna Zoo** (Tiergarten; *t* 877 9294-0, *www.zoovienna.at; open daily Nov–Jan 9–4.30; Feb 9–5; Mar and Oct 9–5.30; April 9–6; May–Sept 9–6.30; adm*), successor to Franz Stephan's Imperial Menagerie, which still contains some of the original Baroque cages. It's the oldest zoo in the world, and houses more than 750 species, including pandas, elephants, and lions. Near the entrance to the zoo, the 19th-century **Palm House** (Palmenhaus; *open May–Sept daily 9.30–5.30; Oct–April daily 9.30–4.30; adm*) is a graceful wrought iron and glass pavilion based on the famous greenhouses of Kew, with luxuriant palms flourishing in the tropical heat.

Heeresgeschichtliches Museum

3 Arsenal, Objekt 18, t 79 5610, www.bmlv.gv.at/hgm; U-Bahn Südtirolerplatz, tram D, O 18 to Südbahnhof or Fasangasse, bus 69A to Arsenal. Open Sat–Thurs 9–5; closed Fri; adm.

Behind the Belvedere palaces, and to the east of Südbahnhof, stands the forbidding military Arsenal, built to curb unrest after revolution erupted across Europe in 1848. The entrance area is dominated by statues of famous generals, and the rear courtyard is crammed with tanks and other military vehicles. The first floor contains booty from the Turkish campaigns, including a tent belonging to the Grand Vizier. On the ground floor, there's a fine collection of uniforms (the Austrian army won a prize for most

Death in Vienna

The Viennese take death very seriously: to see the full pomp and ceremony which attends burials, visit the **Burial Museum** (Bestattungsmuseum; *4 Goldegasse 19, t 50 195; open by appointment only Mon–Fri 12–3*). The **Zentralfriedhof** is the biggest and most atmospheric cemetery, *see* below, but you can make a pilgrimage to the tombs of some of Vienna's most illustrious citizens in the following other graveyards:

St Marx Cemetery (Friedhof St Marxer; *3 Leberstrasse 6–8; tram 18, 71 to St Marx, or bus 74A to Hofmannsthalgasse; open 7am–dusk*). Tucked away in a bleak district bounded by motorways, this tree-lined 18th-century cemetery is where Mozart was buried in a pauper's grave in 1791.

Heitzinger Cemetery (Heitzinger Friedhof; *13 Maxingstrasse 15; U-Bahn Heitzinger*). The most atmospheric cemetery in Vienna, with the graves of Gustav Klimt, Otto Wagner, Franz Gillparzer and Katharina Schratt, actress and mistress of Franz Josef. It's close to Schönbrunn Palace.

elegant uniform at the 1900 Paris Exhibition), and a fascinating display on the shocking assassination of Archduke Franz Ferdinand in Sarajevo on 28 June 1914, which precipitated the events leading up the First World War. Among the exhibits is the car in which the archduke and his wife were shot, and the sofa on which he bled to death.

Central Cemetery (Zentralfriedhof)

11 Simmeringer Hauptstrasse 234, t 760 41; tram 6, 71 to Zentralfriedhof. Open winter 8am–dusk, summer 7am-dusk.

This vast cemetery, one of the largest in Europe, was opened in 1875, and contains more than 2.5 million graves and memorials. The plan, available at the entrance, is essential. The Tombs of Honour are grouped in section 32A, and include a memorial to Mozart (whose remains are lost in a mass paupers' grave in the Friedhof St Marxer, *see* box above), and the graves of Beethoven and Schubert, who were disinterred and reburied here in 1899, Brahms, along with most of the Strauss family. The most atmospheric section is the huge Jewish area, with its crumbling, overgrown graves, many horrifically desecrated in the pre-war years. Behind the church are graves belonging to members of the Austrian Resistance, and the Soviet soldiers who died during the liberation of Vienna.

Hundertwasserhaus

On the corner of Löwengasse with Kegelgasse; U-Bahn, tram to Landstrasse or Hetzgasse. Closed to the public.

Slap bang in the middle of an otherwise unremarkable residential street, architect Friedensreich Hundertwasser's playful, multi-coloured apartment building (1985) appears to have been transported from another planet. Hundertwasser was an enemy of the straight line, and there isn't one in sight – even the floors undulate dreamily. Trees and shrubs peer down from the communal roof terrace, and onion domes appear to float above the roof. The flats are private and not open to the public, but Hundertwasser's equally quirky shopping complex, the **Kalke Village**, is just across the street. Here, you can pick up all kinds of tacky memorabilia or have a drink in the (wobbly-floored) café. Committed fans of Hundertwasser can head around the corner to the fairytale **KunstHausWien** (*3 Untere Weissgerberstrasse 13, t 712 0495, www. kunsthauswien.at; open daily 10–7, guided tours Sun and hols 12 and 3; adm*), another wacky blend of styles and bold colours. Inside are galleries displaying his paintings, temporary modern art exhibitions and a café.

The Prater

U-Bahn, tram 5, 21, O to Praterstern.

This fabulous stretch of green parkland has been the city's most celebrated playground since Josef II opened it to the public in 1766. The chestnut-shaded avenue of the Hauptallee extends for 5km through the centre of the park and is a long-standing favourite for a Sunday stroll. The **Volksprater funfair** (*open daily 10am–11pm*), at the northwest end, is the most popular section of the park, dominated by the giant **Reisenrad** or ferris wheel (*open daily May–Sept 9am–midnight, Mar–April and Oct 10–10; Nov–Feb 10–8; adm*), immortalized in *The Third Man*. The Reisenrad was built over a century ago, and continues to make its panoramic, if sedate, journey high above the treetops.

The Old Danube and Donauinsel

After centuries of unpredictable flooding, the Viennese finally dug a new, deep causeway for the Danube river at the end of the 19th century, which now runs a smooth, dead-straight course across the northeast of the city. A single undulation remains of its original course, known as the **Alte Donau** (Old Danube; *U-Bahn Alte Donau*). This curving crook of water is prettily fringed with weeping willows and bathing areas, and there's a smattering of restaurants and bars. It's the best place for sailing and other watersports, with plenty of boat-hire locations.

The **Donauinsel** is an island caught between the Danube river and the Danube Canal, and is lined with little beaches and shady picnic areas. The wide paths make it good for biking and roller skating (*there's a rental place right next to the Donauinsel U-Bahn station*). A tacky but fun collection of bars and restaurants are clustered next to the U-Bahn stop, popular on balmy summer nights.

Stift Klosterneuburg

t (02) 243 4110, www.Klosterneuburg.com; S-bahn from Franz-Josefs-Bahnhof to Klosterneuberg-Keyerling. Open daily 10–12 and 1.30–4.30; adm; guided tours (call in advance to arrange an English tour).

Set high above the river Danube, 8 miles from the centre of Vienna, this massive fortified abbey was built in the 12th century to house the last remains of St Leopold. The saint, originally a margrave of the Babenburg dynasty, was later boldly, if entirely unconvincingly, claimed by the Habsburgs, and the abbey became an important pilgrimage location. Karl VI, who was obsessed with his ancestry, determined to expand the original complex in the 18th century, envisaging a massive complex on the scale of the Escorial near Madrid. Although the abbey was unfinished at his death in 1740, enough Baroque finery survives to give visitors a sense of what it might have looked like had Karl VI lived to complete it (you can visit the buildings as part of a guided tour).

The abbey is now most famous for the celebrated 12th-century *Verduner Altar*, housed in a chapel off the main church. This magnificent altarpiece is one of the most extraordinary examples of medieval craftsmanship, and is made up of 51 scenes from the Bible, each exquisitely wrought in enamel. The abbey has also long been known for its wines, which you can taste (and buy) in the brick-vaulted *vinothek*.

Day Trips from Vienna

It doesn't take long to escape the hubbub in Vienna: the glorious expanse of the Vienna Woods creeps up to the fringes of the city, sprinkled with wine villages and perfect for hiking and picnicking.

To the north, the Danube meanders through some of the most exquisite countryside in Austria, guarded by ancient castles and monasteries, and a paradise for gourmets and cyclists. The flat lands of Burgenland to the southwest offer more wine, a curious inland sea, and whitewashed Hungarian-style villages topped with untidy storks' nests. One of Europe's most panoramic railways clunks up to the extraordinary peaks of the Semmering range, where the Viennese come for summer hiking or winter sports.

Austria's efficient train system will whisk you in style to most destinations mentioned below, but a car is useful for exploring at leisure.

The Vienna Woods (Wienerwald)

Vienna is blessed with the leafy Wienerwald right on its doorstep, a gently undulating region of forests and hills which almost completely encircles the city and extends for more than 400 square miles. Much of it is protected forest, criss-crossed with excellent walking and cycling trails, but it's also peppered with elegant spa towns and unassuming wine villages full of excellent *Heurigen*.

Mödling

Mödling, 10 miles from Vienna, has a tiny but appealing old quarter, with 16th- and 17th-century houses clustered around cobbled squares, and a miniature Rathaus with a graceful loggia. Beethoven spent the summer of 1819 in Mödling, and rented rooms at Hauptstrasse 79, which have been converted into a **museum** (*t (02236) 26726; open Tues–Sun 9–12*). He hoped to return the following summer, but was refused accommodation on account of his unpredictable and eccentric behaviour. If sightseeing begins to pall, you can take a dip in the town's Jugendstil swimming pool, the **Stadtbad**, or head for the numerous walking trails which penetrate the forest from here (*maps and more information from the tourist office*). On the western fringe of the town, the **Seegrotte Hinterbrühl** (*t (02235) 26364; open daily 9–12 and 1–3.30; adm, includes boat ride*) is a former gypsum mine, which was flooded in 1912, and then drained and used by the Nazis to build jets during the Second World War. Tours (*in several languages*) culminate with a fun underground boat ride.

Mayerling

West of Mödling, the unassuming hamlet of Mayerling is set in one of the most beautiful valleys in the Vienna Woods, with craggy hills, swift-flowing rivers and dense forests. The village has become inextricably linked with the tragic suicide of Prince Rupert in 1889. The Imperial hunting lodge in which Rupert and his 17-year-old lover, Maria Vetsera, shot themselves was subsequently demolished by Emperor Franz Josef. A Carmelite **convent** was erected in its place, which now contains a few sticks of furniture and photographs of the tragic pair.

Maria Vetsera was buried at **Stift Heiligenkreuz**, a beautiful Cistercian abbey lost in a peaceful expanse of woods a few miles from Meyerling. The original abbey was built during the Middle Ages as a burial chapel for the Babenburg dukes, and although it was substantially rebuilt after Turkish attacks in the 1690s, it still contains some lovely Romanesque and Gothic elements, particularly in the church which was begun in 1135.

Getting There

There are frequent **trains** (every half-hour) to Mödling, Baden and Gumpoldskirchen from Vienna Südbahnhof. An infrequent **bus** service links Baden with Mayerling, but, to explore the woods properly, it is best to have your own transport.

You can download **cycling** maps showing the enormous network of cycling trails from *www.mtbwienerwald.at*.

Tourist Information

Mödling: K Elizabetherstrasse 2, t (02236) 26727, *www.moedling.at*. Open Mon–Fri 9–5.
Heiligenkreuz: Heiligenkreuz 15, t (02258) 8720, *www.heiligenkreuz.at*. Open Mon–Fri 8–4.
Baden: Brusattiplatz 3, t (02252) 22600-600, *www.baden.at*. Open summer Mon–Sat 9–5, Sun 10–12; winter Mon–Fri 9–5.
Gumpoldskirchen: Schrannenplatz 5, t (02252) 63536, *www.gumpoldskirchen.at*.

Eating Out

Mödling
Babenbergerhof, Babenbergergasse 6, t (02236) 22246 405 (*moderate*). Smart hotel-restaurant in the heart of Mödling.

Meyerling
Buchner, Hauptstrasse 54, t (02236) 41415 (*inexpensive*). A traditional *Heuriger* with tasty Austrian specialities to accompany the local wine.

Baden
Badner Stübel, Gutenbrunnerstrasse 19, t (02252) 41232 (*moderate*). An old-fashioned, family-run restaurant serving good local dishes in a delightful, 19th-century house.

Gumpoldskirchen
Heuriger Bruckberger, Wienerstrasse, t (02252) 62230 (*inexpensive*). One of several traditional *Heurigen* clustered along Wienerstrasse and Neustiftsgasse, this one is particularly friendly and serves great food.

Mystery at Mayerling

No one knows why the prince and his lover chose to kill themselves in the early hours of January 29 1889. Romantics insist it was for love, but Rupert was a notorious womanizer, and Maria Vetsera was merely the latest in a long line of pretty young mistresses. Some have suggested that he was frustrated with his lack of a real political role at court, and others that he had contracted a venereal disease which he believed to be fatal. Empress Zita was one of many who suspected he had been assassinated by political enemies. The real reason behind the suicide pact was buried with the prince, who was entombed with full Habsburg pomp and ceremony in the Kaisergruft (*see* pp.49–50), despite his wish to be buried simply next to his mistress.

The adjoining chapter house contains the oldest ducal tomb. Come for mass if you can, movingly sung by the community of monks.

Baden

Southwest of Mayerling, the delightful spa town of Baden still oozes a slightly battered turn-of-the-20th-century charm. The Romans discovered the curative effects of its natural springs, and the town reached the height of its fame in the 19th century when celebrated artists, musicians and even the Imperial family would summer here and take the waters. The old centre is a higgledy-piggledy maze of 16th-and 17th-century mansions spiralling out from the Hauptplatz, which is dominated by a florid Baroque plague column. The **Kurpark**, a formal garden which merges into the surrounding forest, is a delightful place for a stroll or a picnic. You can still take the waters at one of the numerous **spas** (*the tourist office provides a leaflet listing them all*), or explore some of the numerous *Heurigen* in the area.

Gumpoldskirchen

With its redolent fairytale name, this is the most celebrated wine village in these parts. The town erupts twice a year with a fabulous wine festival (in June and August), and the countless excellent *Heurigen* produce the world-famous Gumpoldskirchner wines. Local tourist offices have an annual guide (*free*) listing all the best *Heurigen* throughout this region (*see also* 'Eating Out').

Up the Danube

The slow-moving river meanders gently through the verdant Danube Valley, past medieval villages, orchard-covered hills which blaze with blossom in spring, and snaking vines. The massive fortresses and monasteries which glower from the hills attest to the valley's strategic location at the crossroads of East and West, a reminder of hotly contested territorial battles which once ravaged the now-idyllic countryside.

The most beautiful section of the Danube Valley is the **Wachau**, the stretch of river which winds between Krem and Melks, a paradise for gourmets thanks to its abundance of excellent restaurants and vineyards, and for cyclists, who potter along the

Getting There

Tulln (25 mins) and Krems (one hour) are served by **suburban trains** (S-Bahn) from Franz-Josef Bahn. Trains for Melk (75 mins) depart from Vienna's Westbahnhof station, but there is also a single-line railway connecting Krems and Melk, which is slow but picturesque.

The Wachau is a popular destination for excursion companies, who run **bus or boat tours** of the region. There are countless **river cruises** along the Danube with stops at all the main towns and villages.

Tourist Information

Tulln: Minoritenplatz 2, **t** (02272) 67555, *www.tulln.info.*
Krems: Undtrasse 6, **t** (02732) 82676, *www.krems.info.*
Melk: Babenbergerstrasse, **t** (02752) 523 07410, *www.niederoserreich.at/melk.*

Eating Out

Tulln

Der Floh, Tullnerstrasse 1, Langenbarn, near Tulln, **t** (02272) 62809, *www.derfloh.at* (*expensive–moderate*). This welcoming, stylish, wood-panelled restaurant and guest house serves delicious gourmet Austrian cuisine from an award-winning young chef.

Krems

Hagmann, Landstrasse 8, **t** (02732) 83167 (*inexpensive*). There are countless fabulous *Heurigen* in the Krems area, or you could stop at this wonderful *Konditorei* for coffee and cakes.

Melk

Stadt Melk, Hauptplatz 1, **t** (02752) 525 47 (*moderate*). Excellent Austrian fare and an extensive wine list.

gentle riverside cycling paths. The area's stunning natural beauty and historical importance were recognised in 2000, when the Wachau was granted World Heritage Site status by UNESCO.

Tulln

Heading northwest from Vienna, the first major town is Tulln (about 20 miles from Vienna), which likes to call itself 'the Cradle of Austria'. The Romans established a garrison town here (a magnificent Roman watchtower survives), and it was effectively Austria's first capital under the Babenburgs. But Tulln was quickly eclipsed by Vienna, and is now a sleepy, provincial town scattered with ancient churches including the magnificent **Minoritenkirche**. This has been lovingly restored, and the adjacent buildings contain a quirky museum with an eccentric collection of archaeological artefacts and historic fire engines. Nowadays, Tulln is best known as the birthplace of Egon Schiele, Austria's original *enfant terrible*, who was born above the train station (his father was station master) in 1890. The **Egon-Schiele Museum** (*Donaulände 28, t (02272) 64570, http://egonshiele.museum.com; open Tues–Sun 1–6; adm*) dedicated to his life and work is located in the prison where he was briefly incarcerated in 1912 for corrupting minors with erotic drawings.

Krems an der Donau

Thirty miles west of Tulln, Krems an der Donau is a picture-postcard town at the start of the Wachau proper, enchantingly set in a sea of vines. Medieval Krems and Renaissance Stein, once separate settlements, have merged over the years, and the cobbled streets are lined with pretty ice-cream coloured houses and a smattering of ancient mansions, many with elegant stone courtyards. Krems has been producing excellent wines for centuries and there are several wonderful *Heurigen* in the area: the tourist office, located in a former Capuchin monastery, has full details along with a wine museum. From the top of the town, you can see the romantic onion-domed spires of **Stift Göttweig** (**t** *(02732) 85581; open Mar–Nov daily 10–5; adm by guided tour only*), an 11th-century abbey which was rebuilt in the 18th century after a devastating fire. You can visit the flamboyant Baroque interior as part of a guided tour, but they are given in German only.

Dürnstein and Beyond

About five miles upstream of Krems, medieval Dürnstein is piled winsomely on the river bank, dominated by the stony ruins of a battered castle. Richard the Lionheart was kept prisoner here by the Babenburg Duke Leopold V in the 12th century: according to legend, Lionheart was discovered by his faithful minstrel, Blondel, who searched the countryside looking for his master and finally found him by playing a song known only to the two of them beneath his window. Lionheart was eventually released after the payment of a huge ransom. The castle is now in ruins, although some efforts have been made to restore it recently, but it's worth the climb for the staggering views over the surrounding countryside.

The river continues to wind sinuously past medieval villages like delightful **Weissenkirchen**, with its charming cobbled streets and terraced vineyards, and its larger neighbour **Spitz an der Donau**. Just beyond **Aggstein**, the fairytale castle of **Aggsbachdorf** is perched vertiginously on a rocky outcrop, and offers more gorgeous views. Legend recounts that the castle's 13th-century owner, Georg Sheck von Wald, would force his enemies to leap to their deaths from the rock at the summit of the castle.

Melk

The little Renaissance town of Melk huddles in the shadow of the extravagant **Stift Melk** (**t** *(02752) 5550; open Palm Sunday–first Sunday after All Souls daily 9–5; May–Sept 9–6; guided visits at 11am and 2pm in German only; adm to abbey, church free*), one of the most sumptuous Baroque monasteries in Austria and a huge tourist attraction. Once the site of a Babenburg fortress, the building was given to the Benedictines in 1089, and became a renowned centre of scholarship during the Middle Ages (described in Umberto Eco's *The Name of the Rose*, which is partly set here). The original monastery was destroyed by the Turks in 1683, but subsequently rebuilt and expanded in flamboyant Baroque style. It still houses a community of monks, who run one of Austria's most prestigious schools.

The highlights of the abbey museum are, frustratingly, only sporadically on view, but include the *Melker Kreuz*, a 14th-century gem-studded reliquary containing a fragment of the True Cross, an exquisite 11th-century portable altar, and a much venerated 13th-century reliquary containing the jawbone of St Kolomain (*see* over). The magnificent library is crammed with leather-covered tomes – there are more than 2,000 volumes from the 9th to the 15th centuries alone. A cloud of *putti* fly pudgily across the ceiling, in Paul Troger's lavish ceiling fresco allegorizing Faith.

The monastery was long a centre of pilgrimage thanks to its numerous relics, none more famous than the body of St Kolomain, an Irish saint with a gift for healing. His body (minus the jawbone, presumably) is hidden from view in the opulent church, topped with a vast dome, and oozing elaborately gilded stuccowork. There are plenty of other gruesome relics on view in the church's side chapels, with everything from glittering receptacles containing nails and hair to full skeletons leering from glass coffins.

The Southern Alps

Less than 80 miles from Vienna, the Alps make their last thrust before levelling out into the Hungarian steppes. The dramatic scenery and famously clean air drew wealthy 19th-century excursionists, and a spectacular railway was constructed through the Semmering Pass in 1854. This, along with a delightfully old-fashioned cog-wheel steam engine at Puchberg-am-Schneeberg, are still much-loved by the Viennese, who come to this region in droves to walk in summer, and ski in winter.

Semmering, an elegant mountain town sprinkled with Jugenstil villas, is the largest of the Southern Alpine resorts. It sprawls across a hillside overlooking the Semmering Pass, and is liberally strewn with upmarket hotels (including the Imperial family's favourite, the Grand Hotel Panhans) and restaurants. In winter it's a popular skiing centre, with plenty of facilities (travel agents in Vienna sell special packages for a day or a weekend trip). The extraordinary mountain railway, built in the mid-19th century, has been granted UNESCO World Heritage status, and is one of the most dramatic and beautiful train journeys in Europe, particularly the last section between Payerbach and Semmering. To the north of the resort, the **Höllental** (Valley of Hell) is a staggeringly beautiful, narrow gorge, carved out by the River Schwarza.

Scheeberg, at 2,076m, is the highest mountain range close to Vienna and another hugely popular destination for winter sports. In 1897, a cog-wheel steam engine was

Getting There

The most spectacular way to get to Semmering is on the **train** from Vienna Südbahnhof (hourly trains).

By **car**, it's an easy journey straight down the S6 motorway from Vienna.

Tourist Information

Semmering: Passhöhe 248, **t** (02664) 20025, *www.semmering.at*.

Puchberg: Sticklergasse 3, **t** (02636) 2256, *www.tiscover.at/puchberg-am-schneeberg*.

Eating Out

Semmering

Restaurant Wintergarten, Hotel Panhans, Hochstrasse 32, **t** 02664 8181 (*expensive*). Dine in style in the sumptuous restaurant of the beautiful Jugendstil Hotel Panhans.

Zum Stoasteirer, Zaubergasse 2, **t** 02664 2498 (*moderate*). This chalet-style restaurant offers excellent Austrian cuisine, which changes with the season, along with a good list of regional wines. There are welcoming staff and fabulous views.

completed, which still makes a dramatic ascent up the mountain from Puchberg-am-Schneeberg to the small station at Hochschneeberg (with a hotel-restaurant). From here, you can linger over lunch or strike out into the surrounding peaks: the highest, Klosterwappen, is about an hour's hike.

Around the Neusiedler See

The northern tip of Austria's easternmost province, **Burgenland**, is dominated by the vast, reed-fringed lake of the **Neusiedler See**. Thanks to its unusual microclimate, the lake attracts a wealth of bird and animal life and is now a National Park. The baking heat of summer has made it a popular excursion for the beach-starved Viennese, who come to sunbathe and swim, while in winter it freezes to become an enormous ice-rink. Close by, Eisenstadt, the charming, tiny capital of Burgenland, retains vestiges of its Hungarian heritage (the region only became part of Austria after the First World War) and delightful Rust, the smallest town in the country, is famous for its wines.

Eisenstadt has long been linked with Haydn, who lived here for much of his life under the patronage of the powerful Hungarian Esterházy family. Their castle still dominates the town, an immense medieval fortress which has undergone numerous facelifts and is now primarily Baroque and neoclassical. The otherwise dull guided tours of the **castle** (still owned by the wealthy Esterházy family), include a visit to the lavishly frescoed Haydnsaal, where the composer once conducted his own works and where concerts still regularly take place. Close by, Eisenstadt's medieval Jewish quarter, the **Unterberg**, remains astonishingly intact, although its small community were sent to the death camps by the Nazis during the Second World War. The history

Getting There

There are direct **trains** to Neusiedl am See from Vienna Südbahnhof at least every hour, with **bus** links to villages and towns around the lake including Rust and Mörbisch. There is one daily direct train to Eisenstadt from Vienna, but otherwise you will have to change at Neusiedl.

This area is perfect for exploring on two wheels and there are scores of **bicycle** rental outlets in every town and hamlet.

Tourist Information

Eisentadt: Schloss Esterházy, t (00800) 2837, *www.tiscover.at/eisenstadt*.
Rust: Rathaus, Conradplatz 1, t (02685) 502, *www.rust.or.at*.
Neusiedl am See: Obere Haupstrasse 24, t (02167) 8600, *www.neusiedlersee.com*.

Eating Out

Eisenstadt
Im Esterházy, Schloss Esterházy, t (02682) 62819 (*moderate–inexpensive*). This is a handsome restaurant in the castle itself, where you can linger over the papers in the café, or dine substantially on excellent modern Austrian cuisine.

Rust
Inamera, Oggauerstrasse 29, t (02685) 6473 (*moderate*). A stylish whitewashed restaurant serving sophisticated local cuisine.

Neusiedl am See
Am Nyikokspark, Landgasthaus, t (02167) 40222 (*moderate*). An elegant restaurant in the magnificent surroundings of the former Langasthaus, with creative Austrian cuisine.

of the Jews in Eisenstadt is recounted in the small **Jüdisches Museum** at Unterbergasse 6, which contains one of the only synagogues in the area to have survived the horrors of *Kristallnacht*. Most of Eisenstadt's other attractions are linked to Haydn, and include his home, the Haydnhaus, on Josef-Haydn-Gasse (only for die-hard fans), and his mausoleum, in the frilly Baroque **Bergkirche**.

Close to the shores of the Neusiedler See, **Rust** is crammed with 16th- and 17th-century houses, many sporting an untidy fringe of storks' nests. Nesting storks bring luck according to local superstition, but, if they fail to return, an unpleasant surprise is in store. The reeds from the nearby lake are used in local crafts, including basketwork and thatching, but Rust is best known for its excellent wines (try and make it for Golden Wine week at the end of July).

To the north, brash and unappealing **Neusiedl am See** is the main transport hub of the region, with train and bus connections to Vienna, but it's not worth lingering here. South of Rust, the tiny village of **Mörbisch**, a straggle of brilliantly whitewashed houses with brightly painted doors, sits on the Hungarian border and feels distinctly un-Austrian. At the end of July, the village hosts an excellent operetta festival (more information at *www.seefestpiele-morbisch.at*), with performances taking place on a floating stage. Close by is the formidable **Burg Forchenstein**, a virtually impregnable medieval fortress owned by Esterházy family, which now contains an enormous weaponry collection.

For swimming and other watersports, head for **Podersdorf am See**, on the eastern edge of the lake, which is the only village right on the water's edge (the other settlements are separated from the lake by a reedy marshes).

Czech Republic: Practical A–Z

05

Climate and When to Go

Prague's climate is not extreme. The average temperature hovers at freezing point from December to February, climbing to shirtsleeves weather in May. July and August are the hottest months, reaching the high 20s °C. The chill of autumn sets in in late September. The driest month is February and the wettest July, when warm showers of Bohemian acid rain drop lazily in the late evening.

Millions of tourists visit Prague each year, half of them in August, when the city resembles a theme park. Consider visiting in late June, early July or better still early September; Prague's buskers are still out in force, its gardens and islands are in late bloom, and the city heaves a sigh of relief at having survived the deluge.

Disabled Travellers

Even the most powerful wheelchair is likely to whine to a halt on Prague's hills, and its crowded public transport system can be inaccessible to the most able-bodied, but the city is at last addressing the problems of people with limited mobility. Olga Havel, the wife of Václav, worked tirelessly for disabled people until her death in 1996, and the foundation that she created, Výbor dobré vůle (*see* below), is the capital's most useful information source for visual, auditory or dietary problems, and for wheelchair users.

The capital is starting to provide for blind people. Metro entrances bleep; train and tram stops are announced, and opening and closing of doors signalled; traffic lights click or squeak when it is safe to cross.

The Czech Republic's thermal springs and spas are said to alleviate scores of medical conditions, from cerebral palsy to psoriasis.

Czech Organizations
Czech Association of Disabled People
(Sdruženi zdravotné postižených), Karlinské nám. 12, **t** 224 816 997. Helpful advice.
PIS (Prague Information Service), Old Town Hall, Staroměstské nám., Prague 1, **t** 224 482 202 or **t** 12444 (general info), *www.pis.cz*. Can provide information for visitors on accessibility.

Prague Wheelchair Users Association (Pražská organizace vozíčkářů), Benediktská 6, **t** 224 827 210, **f** 224 826 079, *www.pov.cz*. Offers some assistance for disabled visitors to Prague, but its 'Accessible Prague' guide is more useful.
Výbor dobré vůle (Committee of Good Will), Senovážné nám. 2, **t** 800 110 010, *www.rdv.cz*. The foundation set up by Olga Havel.

Electricity

The Czech Republic's voltage is 220v, but you'll need a plug with two round prongs before anything will fire up. Get a universal adaptor before leaving that can deal with the earthing prong that sticks out of some sockets. The voltage in older parts of town may be 110v, although this is now rare. It is fine for US equipment, but UK hairdryers will work at half speed, while your laptop and fax will not work at all. If in doubt, pack a transformer.

Embassies and Consulates

Foreign Embassies in Prague
Canada: Mickiewiczova 6, **t** 272 101 800, **f** 272 101 890, *www.dfait-maeci.gc.ca*.
UK: Thunovská 14, **t** 257 402 111, **f** 257 402 296, *www.britain.cz*.
USA: Tržiště 15, **t** 257 530 663, **f** 257 530 583, *www.usembassy.cz*.

Czech Embassies Abroad
UK: 26 Kensington Palace Gardens, London W8 4QY, **t** (020) 7243 1115, **f** (020) 7727 9654, *london@embassy.mzv.cz*, *www. czechembassy.org.uk*.
USA: 3900 Spring of Freedom Street NW, Washington DC, **t** (202) 274 9100, **f** (202) 966 8540, *washington@embassy.mzv.cz*, *www.mzv.cz/washington*.

Health and Emergencies

Emergencies
In an emergency call the relevant number:
Ambulance: t 155
Fire: t 150

Municipal Police: **t** 156
National Police: **t** 158

Health and Insurance

If you hold a British or Irish passport, you're entitled to the same free emergency medical treatment as Czech citizens. You may have to pay for it upfront and get reimbursed later. E111 forms are available free from post offices in the UK and Ireland. You can fill in the form on the spot and a cashier will stamp it to validate it. You will need your national insurance number and your passport. Take the form with you when you travel.

British and Irish citizens may nonetheless consider taking out health insurance. US and Canadian travellers have no alternative. Check if your credit card covers you – many do. Some clinics in Prague do not, however, accept health insurance, or else only accept Czech health insurance policies. Take out a policy with one of the insurance providers who have their own clinics in the city (*see* below), or be sure to ask for a list of hospitals and clinics that will accept your insurance (*see* pp.95–6).

Aetna Global Healthcare, 29 Kingstone Rd, Bristol BS3 1DS, UK, **t** (0117) 966 3724, **f** (0117) 966 1186, *info@integraglobal.com*, *www.integraglobal.com/integrahealth*.

AXA PPP HealthCare, Phillips House, Crescent Rd, Tunbridge Wells, Kend TN1 2PL, UK, **t** 0870 608 0850, *www.axappphealthcare.com*.

BUPA, Perlová 1, **t** 221 66 73 59, **f** 221 66 73 87, *info@health-insurance.cz*, *www.health-insurance.cz*.

Travel insurance policies differ hugely in theft and loss coverage: check if stolen cash is reimbursed, and read the small print.

Money

The Czech currency is the **crown** (*koruna česká*, abbreviated to kč), which is made up of 100 heller (*halér*). At the time of writing, the rate of exchange is 46kčs to the pound sterling, 25kčs to the US dollar and 31kčs to the euro. Assume prices 25 per cent lower than at home, particularly in restaurants and cafés. Imported goods are expensive.

In Prague, the plastic revolution is well under way, but cash is still ubiquitous. Many shops and restaurants still insist on cash rather than credit cards, although you will find ATMs everywhere.

When changing money, don't bother with the 'black market'. *Bureaux de change* exist in every hotel and all over town, with 24-hour 'Chequepoints', including one at the top of Václavské nám., on 28 října 13. Commission is high, and you should try to change your money at a bank, for a 1–2 per cent charge.

Easiest of all is to use a credit or debit card in an **ATM machine**. Holders of **MasterCard** and **Visa** cards will probably be charged around 1.5 per cent commission, but the rates will be better than at a bank or *bureau de change*. **Debit cards** with a Maestro or Cirrus symbol can also be used in most ATMs, with a 2 per cent commission. Cash advances can also be obtained from banks and *bureaux de change* with your card, and major cards can now be used in all the swankier restaurants, shops and hotels, but are not accepted everywhere.

Few shops accept travellers' cheques in payment, but they are the safest way to carry around large sums in Prague.

Banking hours are Mon–Fri 9–5.

The four main **Czech banks** are Česka sporitelna, Československá obchodni banka (ČSOB), Komerčni banka and Živnostenská banka. Most major international banks are also represented.

Visitors from outside the Czech Republic can reclaim the **Value Added Tax** (currently 16%) for purchases of more than 1,000kčs per day and from shops with the the the Tax Free Shopping symbol in the window.

National Holidays

1 Jan New Year's Day
Easter Monday
1 May Labour Day
8 May VE Day
5 July Introduction of Christianity
6 July Death of Jan Hus
28 Oct Foundation of the Republic)
17 Nov Struggle for Freedom and Democracy Day
24 Dec Christmas Eve
25 Dec Christmas Day
26 Dec St Stephen's Day

Post

Correspondence can take anything from five days to two weeks to reach home. There is an **Express Service** that does not cost much and can halve that time. **Stamps** (*známka*) can be bought from tobacconists and card shops, as well as post-office counters.

Price Categories

Hotels

For a double room with bath in high season:

luxury over 7,500kčs
expensive 4,500–7,500kčs
moderate 3,000–4,500kčs
inexpensive 1,500–3,000kčs
cheap under 1,500kčs

Rates are 20–50 per cent lower off-season (Nov–March, except Christmas and New Year). Most expensive and moderate hotels include breakfast in the price and take credit cards, but few cheap hotels accept them.

Restaurants

You should expect to pay roughly the following for a three-course dinner, including wine or beer:

expensive over 800kčs
moderate 500–800kčs
cheap under 500kčs

Most foreign visitors will still find eating out to be good value in all but the most exclusive restaurants, but remember that for many Czechs a meal even in the moderate category is something of a luxury. All places listed take credit cards unless otherwise stated.

Telephones

Most UK **mobiles** can be used throughout the Czech Republic, assuming that you've asked your company to activate roaming. Very few of Prague's public phones take cash; to use them, invest in a phone card, available from newsagents and tobacconists, post offices, hotels, etc.

All Czech numbers now have 9 digits and there is no **area code**. The **international code for the Czech Republic** is **t** (00) 420.

Useful numbers: directory enquiries , **t** 120; international directory enquries, **t** 0149; operator, **t** 0102; international operator, **t** 0131.

International dialling codes from Prague: to Canada, **t** 00 1; to Ireland, **t** 00 353; to the UK, **t** 00 44; to the USA, **t** 00 1.

Time

The Czech Republic is on Central European Time (CET) which is one hour ahead of GMT, going forward one hour in synchronization with British Summer Time (BST).

Tipping

Praguers will round up a bill in a restaurant or a pub by a few crowns, but there is no hard and fast rule. In restaurants, leave 5–10 per cent if the service was good, and about the same to your taxi driver in the unlikely situation that you were not ripped off anyway. Tour guides in castles and at monuments outside Prague rely almost entirely on tips, so be sure to give them a few coins.

Toilets

There are toilets in every metro station, and in strategic locations across town. If you're desperate, it is acceptable to rush into the nearest café or wine bar and ask for the *záchod*, a.k.a. WC (pronounced *ve tse*). 'Men' is *muži*; 'women' is *ženy*.

Tourist Information

www.visitczechia.cz
Czech Tourist Centre (Canada), 401 Bay Street, Suite 1510, M5H2Y4 Toronto, Ontario, **t** (416) 363 9928, *ctacanada@iprimus.ca*.
Czech Tourist Centre (UK), Morley House, 320 Regent St, London W1B 3BG, **t** (020) 7631 0427, *www.visitczechia.org.uk*.
Czech Tourist Centre (USA), 1109 Madison Avenue, New York, NY 10028, **t** (212) 288 0830, *travelczech@pop.net*.

Czech Republic: Prague

06

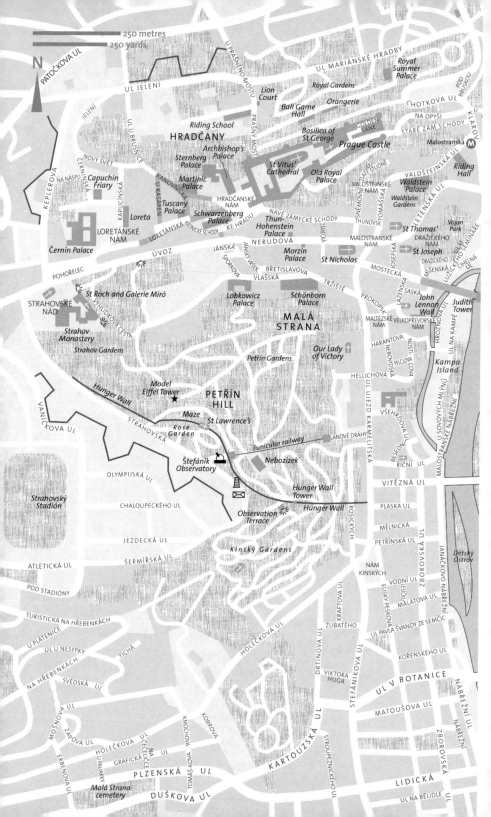

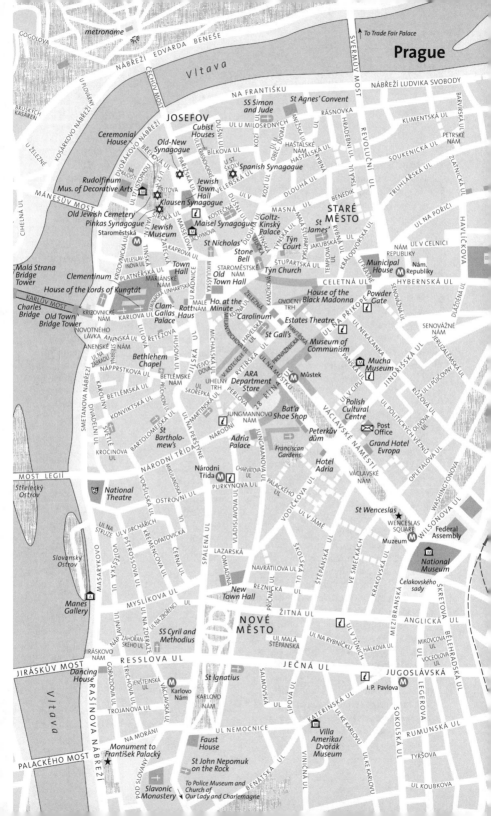

Getting There

Many airlines fly direct to Prague from London and other UK airports (*see* **Travel**, p.4), and from the USA and Canada (p.5). You can also travel by train via the Channel Tunnel or by coach, *see* pp.5–7.

Getting from the Airport

Prague's small international airport is Ruzyně, some 20km west of the city centre.

The **minibus** is the most convenient and reliable method of transport into the city. The drivers are helpful and will drop you at or very near your precise destination for approximately 300kčs per person. For a mere 90kčs, you can be dropped at Náměstí Republiky, a central square. Buses depart every 30 minutes after 6am from outside the arrivals hall; the last bus leaves at 9pm. Journey time is 20–40 minutes.

Alternatively, a regular **city bus** (no.119) leaves the airport every 10 minutes for the Dejvická **metro** station. **Taxi** fares to the city centre should be around 400–500kčs.

Getting Around

Public Transport Information, t (02) 296 191 111, *www.dp-praha.cz* (offices at Ruzyně Airport, train and bus stations and major metro interchanges) provide leaflets in English. The PIS has a free transport map. Routes of buses and trams are marked on city maps.

Tickets (*jízdenka*) are valid for metro, tram and bus. You can buy tickets from yellow machines in metro stations and on street corners, or buy them at newsagents, tobacconists (look for the '*trafika*' sign) and cafés. You cannot buy them on trams or buses, so get a few at a time. A single ticket costs 8kčs (valid for 15mins once validated), or 12kčs if you want to make a transfer (valid for 60 mins).

A **24hr pass** costs 70kčs; a **72hr pass** costs 200kčs; a **168hr (one week) pass** costs 250kčs. Validate your ticket or pass by punching it in the machines on board the tram or bus, and in the ticket hall of metro stations. **Day passes** (*celodenní jízdenka*) covering all three services can be bought from the red machines in most stations, and you can get passes of up to a week from almost any *tabák*. For a transport map, *see* the inside back cover of this guide.

By Metro

This is the easiest way to get around town. The chrome-plated Soviet-built network runs with the efficiency of totalitarianism. Its three lines and three intersections present few difficulties to even the worst sense of direction. Trains run from 5am to midnight, every few minutes at peak hours. Stops are scattered all over the centre. The junctions are at Muzeum (lines A and C), Můstek (lines A and B) and Florenc (lines B and C). Lines are colour-coded. You need to know the station at the end of the line to go in the right direction. The metro symbol is a white 'M' in a white triangle on a green square.

By Tram

These quaint beasts shudder around Prague, their cream-and-crimson livery a feature of city life. Trams run from 4.30am to midnight, every 5–10mins. You can rely on them to arrive almost to the minute at the time advertised on the stop. Night trams take over all major routes after midnight. Routes 51–58 all pass through Lazarská street in the New Town.

By Bus

There are few buses in the centre, but you may use them to reach outlying areas.

By Funicular

The funicular up Petřín Hill leaves from Újezd and stops at Nebozízek en route. The service runs from 9.15am to 8.45pm. Regular transport tickets and passes are valid.

By Taxi

Taxis are the source of much unhappiness for tourists. Many cabbies will add several hundred per cent to your fare if you let them. Always ask the price before setting off. Hailing taxis at a hotel, airport or station will double the fare. The least stressful option is to dial a cab. The following are safe, cheap and reliable: **Profi Taxi**, t 800 118 294, and **AAA Radio Taxi**, t 14014. Both firms are used to foreigners, and the controller will usually speak some English. Tipping is optional. Main taxi ranks are in Wenceslas Square; on the corner of Národní and Spálená; in Malostranské náměstí, on the Staré Město side of Charles Bridge; in Staroměstské náměstí, and next to the Powder Tower.

Car Hire

Avis, Klimentská 46, t 221 851 225,
 t (airport) 235 362 420, *www.avis.cz (open Mon–Fri 8–4.30, Sat–Sun 8–2)*.
Budget, Čistovická 100, t 224 889 995, *www. budget.cz (open daily 8–5)*.
Europcar, Pařížská 28, t 224 810 515, *www. europcar.cz (open daily 8–8)*.
Hertz, Karlovo nám. 28, t 222 231 010,
 t (airport) 220 11 42 70, *www.hertz.cz (open Mon–Fri 8–8, Sat–Sun 8–10)*.
National, (airport) t 220 114 554.
Sixt, (airport) t 220 115 346.

Bike Hire

No Czech rides a bicycle across the hills of smoggy Prague, but odd foreigners can get away with it. Rent one at **City Bike**, Králodvorská 5, t (0776) 180 284 *(open daily 9–7)*.

Tourist Information

The official dispenser of advice to tourists is the **Prague Information Service (PIS)**, with branches around the city *(see* below). Helpful bilingual staff can help you to find a hotel room, sell you a museum pass, fill you in on events and tell you about places to see in and around Prague. The website is very useful.
Prague Information Service (PIS), infoline
 t 12444 *(Mon–Fri 8am–7pm)*, t 187 for general information (Czech and English), *www.pis.cz*.
Na příkopě 20 *(open April–Oct Mon–Fri 9–7, Sat–Sun 9–5; Nov–Mar Mon–Fri 9–6, Sat–Sun 9–3)*.
Old Town Hall *(open April–Oct Mon–Fri 9–7, Sat–Sun 9–6; Nov–Mar Mon–Fri 9–6, Sat–Sun 9–5)*.
Hlavní nádraží *(open April–Oct Mon–Fri 9–7, Sat–Sun 9–4; Nov–Mar Mon–Fri 9–6, Sat–Sun 9–3)*.
Malá Strana Bridge Tower *(open April–Sept daily 10–6)*.
The **Prague Card** is a three-day pass which allows unlimited use of the public transport system and gives free entrance to the city museums and state-run galleries. It costs

790kčs for adults and 610kčs for students and is available from **Čedok**, Na příkopě 18, Staré Město, t 224 19 71 11, and other travel agencies. Most museums offer half-price tickets to students, children and the elderly.
 You'll find a dizzying array of **walking tour** leaflets at the PIS:
Prague Walks, Nezamyslova 7, t 603 271 911, *www.praguewalks.com*. Themes include Art Nouveau, Velvet Revolution, Prague's ghosts and old pubs.
City Walks, t 222 244 531, *walks@prague walkingtours.com*. Mysterious Prague, Kafka's Prague and a Revolution Walk.
Original Walking Tours, t 222 520 573, *prague travel@praguetravel.cz*. Velvet Revolution, Mysteries and Ghosts, King's Way.

Internet Access

You can connect to the Internet at cybercafés across the city.
Bohemia Bagel, Masná 2, t 224 81 25 60 *(open Mon–Fri 7am–midnight, Sat–Sun 8am–midnight)*. Cheap, fast connections, bagels and bottomless coffee.
Café.com, Na poříčí 36, t 224 81 94 35 *(open Mon–Fri 9am–midnight, Sat–Sun 11am–midnight)*. Cold beer, cocktails and computers in a basement bar.
Café Electra, Rašínovo nábřeží 62, t 224 92 28 87 *(open 8am–midnight)*.
U zlaté růže, Thunovská 21, t 257 53 39 74 *(open daily 10–8)*. Cosy café below the castle walls.

Post Offices

Main post office: Jindřišská 14, t 221 131 111. Main hall *(open Mon–Fri 7am–8pm)*. Fax, telegram, post and telephone services are available 24 hours. Other branches at Kaprova 12, Third Courtyard of Prague Castle, and Hybernská 15.

Emergencies

In an emergency call the following: ambulance t 155; fire t 150; municipal police t 156.

Hospitals and Clinics

American Medical Center, Kladenská 68, t 221 433 130, *www.amcenters.com (open 9–6)*. Branch at Janovského 48, t 220 807 756 *(open 8.30–6)*.

Nemocnice Na Homolce, Roentgenova 2, t 257 271 111, *www.homolka.cz* (*open daily 7.30–4pm*). Credit cards accepted. The best Czech hospital, used to dealing with foreigners.

Policlinic at Národní, Národní 9, t 222 075 120, 24hr line t 06 06 46 16 28 (*open Mon–Fri 8–6*). Visa and MasterCard accepted. Health insurance not accepted. Central, private health clinic with English-speaking doctors.

You can redeem prescriptions at any **pharmacy** (*lékárna*). There are 24hr pharmacies at the following addresses: Palackého 5, t 224 946 982; Belgická 37, t 222 519 731; Štefanikova 6, t 257 320 194.

Festivals and Events

Prague Spring Music Festival is the biggest number in Prague's musical calendar (May/June). Bohemia Tickets International (*see* p.102) can provide advance information and tickets by post (also box office at Hellichova 18, Malá Strana, t 257 31 25 47, *www.festival.cz*).

Dance Prague (Tanec Praha) festival in June showcases contemporary dance (Husitská 24a, Žižkov, t 222 721 531, *www.tanecpha.cz*).

Prague Autumn is a festival of classical music in September (box office at Pribenicka 20, t 222 540 484, *www.pragueautumn.cz*).

International Jazz Festival, in September (box office at Sazka Arena, t 266 121 122, *info@sazkaticket.cz*).

Musica Judaica is an international festival of music works by Jewish composers in November (box office at Nadace Musica Iudaica, Besedni 3, t 257 320 064).

Shopping

The free market has hit Prague big-time. In the city where once a crate of olive oil could attract a 20-strong queue you can now buy anything – from a mango to a MiG-50 fighter jet. While few visitors will yet be tempted to shop till they drop, Western designer goods are now ubiquitous. However, although the quality of service has improved hugely in recent years, you should be prepared to occasionally encounter a rather startling level of rudeness. Standard shopping hours are 9–6 on weekdays, and 9–1 on Saturday.

Bookshops

The following shops are the most interesting for English speakers.

Anagram, Týn 4. Friendly English-language bookshop. Ask nicely and you might get a hand-drawn bookmark.

Big Ben, Malá Stupartská 5. Small but well-stocked with a decent selection of international magazines and periodicals.

The Globe Bookstore and Coffeehouse, Pštrossova 6. A fixture on the expat scene, with a well selected collection of English-language novels and non-fiction works (secondhand and new), and a buzzing café attached.*Open till midnight*.

Shakespeare & Sons, Krymska 12, Prague 10, t 271 740 839. Popular English-language bookstore with a good range of genres and staff recommendations. *Open daily 12–12*

U knihomola (The Bookworm), Mánesova 79. An excellent collection of English books and selected works in Czech, German, French and Spanish. Downstairs is a café. *Open daily, until midnight Fri and Sat.*

Clothes and Accessories

Ivana Follová, Ungelt Týn 1. Czech chic for hip chicks. Twenty designers supply this place with everything from belts and hats to shirts and skirts. High quality, reasonable prices. *Open daily*.

Mýrnyx Týrnyx, Saská. Wacky, very cool designs from Czech designers as well as a great second-hand section. There's an excellent clubwear shop (**Devata vlna**) next door. *Open daily*.

Originál Moda, Jungmannova 13. Czech-designed fashion, jewellery, cards, hand-painted scarves and knick-knacks. A good place to pick up a present or two.

Crystal

Bohemian crystal is said to be among the finest in the world.

Bohemia Crystal, Na příkopě 17. Glittering selection of pricey crystal goods. *Open daily*.

Moser, Na příkopě 12 (first floor). A glittering treasure trove of crystal. As well as tortuously wrought goblets, coloured scent bottles and other glassy *objets*, you'll find silverware and porcelain here. *Closed Sun*.

Department Stores and Malls

Prague's department stores were once palaces of command-economy kitsch, but in recent years they have become showcases for imported Western goods. The pre-revolutionary form of Czech consumerism is still in evidence in the ornate shopping arcades that are hidden around Václavské náměstí. Try the **Lucerna complex** or the **Pasáž Rokoko**.

Shopping malls seem to spring up daily; there's a monster mall in **Smíchov** and at least half a dozen along **Na příkopě**.

Where to Stay

Staré Město

Casa Marcello, Řásnovka 783, **t** 222 310 260, **f** 222 313 323, *www.casa-marcello.cz* (*luxury*). Plush and intimate, in a former nuns' dormitory on a cobbled street near St Agnes' Convent.

The Iron Gate, Michalská 19, **t** 225 777 777, **f** 225 777 778, *www.irongate.cz* (*luxury*). A fine historic conversion, with two wings from the 14th and 16th centuries respectively. There are echoes of the past throughout, from painted ceiling beams to original 14th-century frescoes. Kitchenettes are hidden away inside antique wardrobes. Book the Tower Suite for pure romantic indulgence.

Clementin, Seminařská 4, **t** 222 22 17 98, **f** 222 22 17 68, *www.clementin.cz* (*expensive*). A pretty hotel set in the narrowest house in Prague. The rooms are bland but comfortable.

Hotel Metamorphis, Malá Štupartská 5, **t** 221 771 011, *www.metamorphis.cz* (*expensive*). Overlooking busy, touristy Týn Court, and almost too centrally placed for nightlife and sightseeing unless you come in low season. The elegant rooms have superb views of the old town. There's a restaurant, café and bar.

Hotel U Prince, Staroměstské nám., **t/f** 224 213 807, *www.hoteluprince.cz* (*expensive*). In front of the Astronomical Clock on Staroměstské náměstí, this 12th-century building offers five-star comforts, including two vaulted restaurants, a rooftop terrace, rooms and apartments stuffed full of antiques and slick service.

Cloister Inn, Konviktská 14, **t** 224 211 020, **f** 224 210 800, *www.cloister-inn.cz* (*moderate*).

The upmarket cousin of the infamous Penzion Unitas (*see* below), which sits below it, while the nuns who own it live next door. Good value, but be sure to book ahead.

U Krále Jiřího (King George's House), Liliová 10, **t** 221 466 100, **f** 221 466 166, *www.kinggeorge. cz* (*moderate*). Cosy, stylish, Baroque *pension* in the middle of the old town and a stroll away from the Charles Bridge. Excellent value; book at least two months ahead. Eight rooms and four apartments.

U staré paní (The Old Lady), Michalská 9, **t** 224 228 090, **f** 224 212 172, *www.ustarepani.cz* (*moderate*). Simple, clean and modern hotel, a very short walk from everything on the right bank of the river.

U zlaté studny (The Golden Well), Karlova 3, **t** 222 220 262, **f** 222 22 01 03, *www. uzlatestudny.cz* (*moderate*). A 16th-century building, with painted wooden ceilings; two rooms and four suites handsomely furnished with antiques.

Penzion U medvídků (The Little Bear), Na perštýně 7, **t** 224 21 19 16, **f** 224 22 09 31, *www.umedvidku.cz* (*inexpensive*). A former brewery; the old-fashioned beer hall is one of Prague's best, and there's a garden and reasonably priced restaurant. The rooms are simply decorated, but some still have Gothic rafters and painted Renaissance ceilings.

Penzion Unitas, Bartolomějská 9, **t** 224 221 802, **f** 224 217 555, *www.unitas.cz* (*inexpensive*). Cheap boarding house in a former monastery, opposite a police station that used to be the central interrogation centre of Prague's secret police. Interviewees were often held here; Václav Havel spent several nights in room P6.

Josefov

Intercontinental, Náměstí Curieových 5, **t** 296 63 11 11, **f** 224 81 00 71, *www.interconti.com* (*luxury*). Five-star facilities and comfortable rooms, located at the centre of Josefov. Terrace restaurant with views, swimming pool and fitness club. If only it did not look like an ugly piece of concrete Lego.

Hotel Josef, Rybná 20, **t** 221 700 111, **f** 221 700 999, *www.hoteljosef.com* (*expensive*). Frosted glass, curves of chrome and white walls provide a minimalist welcome at Hotel Josef. The rooms are chic but plain.

Superiors have glass-walled bathrooms, DVD-CD players, mini-bars and Internet access. Book a room with a terrace on the 7th or 8th floor.

Albatros, Nábřeží Ludvíka Svobody, **t** 224 810 541, **f** 224 811 214, *www.botelalbatros.cz* (*inexpensive*). A Prague 'boatel', moored on the Vltava. Near Staroměstské nám., but too far from Charles Bridge to be dreamy. Two long corridors of clean cabins, all with showers.

Prague Castle and Hradčany

Hotel Hoffmeister, Pod Bruskou 7, **t** 251 017 111, **f** 251 017 120, *www.hoffmeister.cz* (*luxury*). Luxurious and modern. By a main road, but close to the metro and a 10-minute walk from anywhere in old Prague. Named after Adolf Hoffmeister, caricaturist and epicure, whose portraits adorn the walls.

Pyramida, Bělohorská 24, **t** 233 102 111, **f** 233 356 159, *www.hotelpyramida.cz* (*expensive*). Vast, with well-equipped rooms and a fitness centre with a pool and sauna. It's a short walk from Prague Castle, albeit along a main road; 325 rooms, including 12 suites, and business facilities.

Romantik Hotel U raka, Černínská 10, **t** 220 511 100, **f** 220 510 511, *www.romantikhotels.com/prag* (*expensive*). A quiet stay in one of the drowsiest, most beautiful streets of Prague. The offensive log cabin extension is warmer and more comfortable than the mess of cottages around it. Just six double rooms, and no meals, but the owner can sort out your dinner reservations when you arrive.

U Krále Karla (King Charles), Úvoz 4, **t** 257 533 594, **f** 257 530 919, *www.thecharleshotel prague.com* (*moderate*). A Baroque house with modernized interior, cluttered with stained glass and furnishings a little too faux for their own good but very stylish all the same. Painted beamed ceilings and fireplaces in each of the three suites. Set on the tranquil, romantic and very steep hill leading up to Strahov Monastery.

Malá Strana

The Charles, Josefská 1, **t** 257 532 913, **f** 257 532 910, *www.hotels-of-prague.com* (*luxury*). Extremely friendly and well-appointed; a converted Baroque townhouse that's a hop, skip and jump away from Charles Bridge.

Velvet curtains, engraved furniture, wood and terracotta floors and Persian rugs beneath ceilings with painted beams.

The Golden Wheel, Nerudova 28, **t** 257 535 490, **f** 257 535 491, *www.thegoldenwheel.com* (*expensive*). This 14th-century building has been converted into Nerudova's latest and most stylish hotel, with 17 individually designed rooms. Lifts whizz guests between floors, while old photos and contemporary art adorn the walls. At the back is a tiny garden with views up to the castle.

U páva (The Peacock), U Lužického semináře 32, **t** 257 533 360, **f** 257 530 919, *www. romantichotels.cz* (*expensive*). A charming hotel, perfectly located, with courteous staff. Prices vary according to the view; pay the premium to get one of the third-floor rooms looking up to the castle over Vojan Gardens.

U tří pštrosů (The Three Ostriches), Dražického nám. 12, **t** 257 532 410, **f** 257 533 217, *www. utripstrosu.cz* (*expensive*). Perhaps the most picturesque hotel in Prague, set in a 16th-century townhouse all but built into the Charles Bridge. Rooms with views are more expensive, as are the plush suites.

Dům U velké boty (House at the Big Shoe), Vlašska 30, **t** 257 533 234, **f** 257 531 360, *www.bigboot.cz* (*moderate*). Friendly family-run *pension* in a converted 17th-century townhouse, surrounded by cobbled alleyways. Only 12 rooms, so book ahead. In-house laundry and fitness equipment. No breakfast.

Hotel Dientzenhofer, Nosticova 2, **t/f** 267 914 576, *www.vol.cz/rfk/dientzen.html* (*moderate*). Charming *pension*, in the 16th-century birthplace of Prague's greatest Baroque architect. Tucked away on a silent street and backing on to the Čertovka stream, it is so popular that you must book months ahead.

U kříže (The Cross), Újezd 20, **t** 257 313 272, **f** 257 312 542, *www.ukrize.com* (*moderate*). A modernized and unpretentious hotel in an elegant Baroque building. Rooms and suites for two or four people available.

U modrého klíce (The Blue Key), Letenská 14, **t** 257 534 361, **f** 257 534 372, *www.bluekey.cz* (*moderate*). A smartly renovated 14th-century Gothic palace, by the Waldstein Gardens. It is next to a tram line, but quiet (try to get a room on the courtyard at the back) and staff are friendly. Sauna, Jacuzzis, 22 rooms, business facilities.

Nové Město

Hotel Esplanade, Washingtonova 19, t 224 501 111, f 224 229 306, *www.esplanade.cz* (*luxury*). Traditional elegance on a grand scale. The hotel was opened in 1927 and oozes old-fashioned luxury in its dark panelling, chandeliers and drapes, and a fleet of smiling, charming staff.

Carlo IV, Senováïné nám. 13, t 224 593 111, f 224 593 000, *www.boscolohotels.com* (*expensive*). This grandiose Italianate building, formerly a bank and post office, has been masterfully converted, with a stylish bar and restaurant in the former vault. Rooms, the smallest of which may seem cramped, all have Internet access through the TV and full four-star facilities. The infinity-edge swimming pool in the basement is a delight. Year-round promotions make this great value for money.

Hotel Liberty, 28. října 11, t 224 239 598, f 224 237 694, *www.hotelliberty.cz* (*expensive*). New, plush hotel in a refurbished Art Nouveau mansion just off Václavské náměsti. Luxurious extras include a gym, sauna and Jacuzzi plus a beauty salon.

Grand Hotel Evropa, Václavské nám. 25, t 224 228 117, f 224 224 541, *www.hotelevropa.cz* (*moderate*). Prague's legendary Art Nouveau hotel. The rooms are stark (unless you manage to nab one of the suites) but the common areas are sumptuous indeed, filled with dusty *chaises longues*, mirrors, lanterns and the fronds of a hundred plants – all under a vast skylight and within the ovals, arches and wrought iron of the New Art at its most atmospheric.

Hotel Harmony, Na poříčí 31, t 222 319 807, f 222 310 009, *www.hotelharmony.cz* (*moderate*). A functionalist block on a busy street, friendly and comfortable. Sixty well-equipped rooms, some of which have disabled access and facilities, while others come with fridge and TV. Some have both.

Hotel Imperial, Na poříčí 15, t 222 316 012, f 224 816 309, *www.hotelimperial.cz* (*inexpensive*). A 1920s hotel with a stunning Art Deco café, offering faded grandeur on a budget. The

impressive staircase leads to some good-value, extremely plain rooms with high ceilings but no luxuries. A great choice.

Penzion U Suterů, Palackého, t 224 94 82 35, f 224 94 82 33, *www.usuteru.cz* (*cheap*). Tucked down a side street, this friendly pension offers elegant, whitewashed rooms, some with Baroque vaults, some with Gothic rafters. There's a fine budget restaurant which is popular with locals. Although very central, it's a great place to feel as though you have slipped off the tourist track.

Eating Out

All restaurants are open daily for lunch and dinner unless otherwise stated.

Staré Město

Bellevue, Smetanovo nábř. 18, t 222 221 443, f 222 220 453, *www.zatisigroup.cz* (*expensive*). Elegant furnishings, attentive service and excellent food in this riverside restaurant. Fabulous views up to the castle. Champagne and live jazz brunch on Sun.

Parnas, Smetanovo nábř. 2, t 224 218 521, f 224 216 244, *www.restaurantparnas.cz* (*expensive*). Walnut-panelled Art Deco interior, an expansive view over the river to the castle, and a creamy, saucy, sumptuous menu.

U modré růže (The Blue Rose), Rytířská 16, t 224 225 873, t/f 224 222 623, *www.umodreruze.cz* (*expensive*). The 14th-century vaults and tinkling piano make this far more suitable for a lingering evening meal than lunch. One of Prague's most exceptional restaurants.

Zelezná Brata, Michalská 19, t 225 777 334, *www.irongate.cz* (*expensive*). Set in the 14th-century vaults of the Iron Gate Hotel, just south of the old town square, this restaurant is a good place to sample Bohemian cuisine. The menu features pastoral favourites such as *halusky*, a form of *gnocchi* served in a sheep's cheese sauce. The highlight, though, is the live gypsy music.

Gulu Gulu, Tñská 12, t 224 827 177 (*moderate*). This new restaurant is a reincarnation of the original Gulu Gulu on Betlémské nám. Czech, French and Italian dishes are served at very reasonable prices. It's an easygoing place with candlelit tables and Miró-like doodles splashed across the walls.

Reykjavík, Karlova 20, **t** 222 221 218 (*moderate*). The prefabricated steakhouse décor of this place conceals one of Prague's better fish restaurants, serving a daily range of scaly creatures flown in fresh from Iceland. Try the fish soup, a legend in its own lunchtime.

7 Angels, Jilská 20, **t** 224 226 955 (*moderate*). A cosy Czech restaurant serving pork, goulash and dumplings to jolly accordion music (Wed–Sun).

Country Life, Melantrichova 15, **t** 224 213 366; branch at Jungmannovo 1, **t** 257 044 419 (*cheap*). Vegetarian café with great views of the old town, serving delicious sandwiches, soups, casseroles and juices. No smoking. (*Closed Fri evenings and weekends; cash only.*)

Klub Architektů, Betlémské nám. 5a, **t** 224 401 214 (*cheap*). Set in Gothic cellars, this serves satisfying portions of tasty Czech food at reasonable prices. Popular among Czech students and resident foreigners. Outdoor terrace in summer.

U vejvodů, Jilská 4, **t** 222 251 282 (*cheap*). A 14th-century beer hall, over-sanitized by renovation, but still popular. Its menu of stodgy Czech delicacies can be washed down with refreshing Pilsner lager.

Josefov

Pravda, Pařížská 17, **t** 222 326203 (*expensive*). Stylish modern sister restaurant of trendy Barock across the street. Next to the Old-New Synagogue, serving a pricey but delicious range of dishes from across the world. Outdoor seating.

King Solomon, Široká 8, **t** 224 818 752 (*moderate*). Welcoming, low-key kosher restaurant in the heart of the Jewish quarter. Dine in a cosy alcove at the front, or in the light-filled conservatory at the back. The friendly staff will help you order if you are unused to kosher food. *Reserve for Fri dinner and Sat lunch* .

Kozička, Kozi 1, **t** 224 818 308 (*moderate*). Cellar restaurant and bar, adorned with, among other things, a tin goat. The food is excellent. *Closed for lunch on Sat and Sun.*

U červeného kola (The Red Wheel), Anežská 2, **t** 224 811 118 (*moderate*). Intimate steak restaurant, tucked away in a sublime corner near St Agnes' Convent. There are a couple of cosy dining rooms decorated with a mish-mash of antiques and old clocks, and a great roof terrace.

Chez Marcel, Haštalská 12, **t** 222 315 676 (*cheap*). Large, laid-back French café with big windows perfect for idling away an afternoon. Downstairs there's a basement bistro, serving good mussels and *steak-frites*.

Orange Moon, Rámová 5, **t** 222 325 119 (*cheap*). Basement restaurant serving spicy Indian and southeast Asian cuisine. Good for vegetarians.

U Španělské Synagogy, on the corner of Široka and Dušni, **t/f** 224 813 257 (*cheap*). Colourful café-restaurant right next to the Spanish synagogue. Good for snacks and breakfast.

Prague Castle and Hradčany

Peklo (Hell), Strahovské nádvoří 1, **t** 220 516 652 (*expensive*). An extraordinary dining experience, in the 12th-century beer cellars of the Strahov Monastery. The dishes are sparse, expensive and delicious, but the décor isn't what you'd expect: fairy lights line the steps that sweep down from the entrance, and one chamber has been made into a disco.

U zlaté hrušky (The Golden Pear), Nový Svět 3, **t** 220 514 778, **t/f** 220 515 356, *www. zlatahruska.cz* (*expensive*). Wonderful Czech and French food in a cottage on the most romantic alleyway in Prague. Outdoor dining in summer; cosy wood-panelled dining rooms in winter. Unctuous service.

Lví Dvůr, U Pražského mostu 6/51, **t** 224 372 361 (*moderate*). The former zoo at the palace is now a decent restaurant, with a rustic interior, fantastic views from the terrace, and typical Czech dishes including roast suckling pig on a spit.

Oživlé Dřevo, Strahovské nádvoří I, **t/f** 220 517 274 (*moderate*). Czech specialities served up in a vaulted cellar behind the monastery; in summer, eat out on the terrace for some of the loveliest views in Prague.

Klášterní Pivovar, Strahovské nádvoří 302, **t** 233 353 155 (*cheap*). The monks once brewed beer here; now they let someone else do it for them in this cavernous restaurant and beer cellar in the monastery grounds.

Sate, Pohořelec 3, **t** 220 514 552 (*cheap*). Spicy Indonesian food and fast service. Vegetarians and non-pork eaters can have the small menu customized to their taste. *Cash only.*

Malá Strana

Circle Line, Malostranské nám. 12, **t** 257 530 021, *www.praguefinedining.cz* (*expensive*). French cuisine and seafood in swish surroundings. Undoubtedly one of Prague's best restaurants, and a favourite with diplomats and government officials.

Kampa Park, Na Kampě 8b, **t** 257 532 685, *www.kampapark.com* (*expensive*). A Swedish-run restaurant with an excellent reputation among Prague's menu-watchers. Entrées are light on the stomach and heavy on herbal themes, and the riverside location is superb on a summer evening. Children under 10 eat for free. Stunning riverside setting next to the Charles Bridge.

U modré kachničky (The Blue Duckling), Nebovidská 6, **t** 257 320 308, *www. umodrekachnicky.cz* (*expensive*). The first post-revolutionary restaurant to take Czech food seriously and be taken seriously. Extremely popular and rightly so. Game is a speciality. A quiet walk away from Charles Bridge, it is intimate, well-mannered, and cluttered with comfortable kitsch.

Bazaar, Nerudova 40, **t** 257 535 050 (*moderate*). A hotchpotch of a menu, from Mediterranean to Thai, in a glittering restaurant, which assaults your senses from the moment you enter its candle-lit vestibule and are met by a mobile-and-micro-skirt-wielding waitress. Transvestite shows and fortune-telling nights add to the bizarre mix.

U Maltézských rytířů (The Knights of Malta), Prokopská 10, **t** 257 531 324 (*moderate*). Cosy place serving a small but very tasty selection of Czech dishes to the tinkling of a pianist.

U zlatý had (The Golden Snake), Plaská 4, **t** 251 512 063 (*moderate*). A fantastic restaurant, hidden down a side street. There's a wine cellar where you can try out regional wines before deciding on one to accompany your meal. The upstairs dining area is comfortable, with wooden tables and candlelight.

Gitanes, Tržište 7, **t** 257 530 163 (*moderate*). Mediterranean meets gypsy in this brightly painted restaurant, full of quirky paintings. Mediterranean and Slavic dishes.

U Čerta (At the Devil), Nerudova 4, **t** 257 531 526 (*cheap*). Straightforward Czech dishes in a homely little restaurant on one of Malá Strana's best-known streets.

Nové Město

La Perle de Prague Dancing House (Tančící Dům), Rašínovo nabřeží 80, **t** 221 984 160, *www.laperle.cz* (*expensive*). French gourmet restaurant at the top of Frank Gehry's 'Fred and Ginger' building. The 7th-floor view is spectacular (especially if you eat on the terrace) and the food is delicious.

U šuterů, Palackého 4, **t** 224 948 235 (*moderate*). Cosy Czech restaurant, serving such stalwarts as duck with dumplings and sauerkraut. Good-value lunch menu. *Closed Sun.*

Zahrada v opeře (Opera Garden), Legerova 75, **t** 224 239 685 (*moderate*). Stunning modern restaurant designed by one of Prague's hottest young architects. Excellent fresh seafood, Czech specialities, and live piano music twice a week.

Café Universal, V Jircharich 6, **t** 224 934 416 (*moderate*). Another trendy hangout behind the National Theatre; this one has dusky pink walls with one long French poem spiralling around the room, wooden tables and chairs. Unusual salads and good French dishes (many of them vegetarian).

U provaznice (At the Rope Makers), Provanická 3, **t** 224 232 528 (*moderate*). Good pub grub (fried cheese and the like) in a friendly, jostling atmosphere. It's always packed.

Cafés

The following cafés are open every day from morning to evening.

Café Milena, Staroměstské nám. 22, Staré Město, **t** 221 632 602. One of the more civilized cafés on the square, with a menu of sandwiches, pancakes and ice cream. Named after a lover of Franz Kafka, whose bust presides over the room.

Café Montmartre, Řetězova 7, Staré Město, **t** 222 221 244. Shabby-chic café which was a famous watering hole for writers and intellectuals between the wars. Wannabe poets now lounge on the battered sofas.

Design Salon Club, Řytiřská 4, Staré Město,
t 222 873 201. Arty café-bar with changing
exhibitions, a huge video screen, and plenty
of designer furniture and knick-knacks.

Obecní Dům Kavárna, Nám. Republiky 5, Staré
Město, t 220 002 763. One of the most glamorous Art Nouveau cafés in town.

Bakeshop Praha, Kozi 1, Josefov, t 222 316 823.
Excellent bakery with a small café. Try the
delicious carrot cake.

Gourmand Au Gourmand, Dlouha 10, Josefov,
t/f 222 329 060. Wonderful cakes, quiches
and pastries from this delightful deli; pretty
tiled floors and a handful of tables and
chairs where you can enjoy good coffee.

Hogo-Fogo (Hoity-Toity), Salvatorská 4, Josefov,
t 222 317 023. Quiet and unassuming, with a
crowd of young Czechs to match.

U zavěšenýho kafe (The Hanging Coffee),
Úvoz 6, Hradčany, t 257 532 868. An intimate,
smoky café on the curve of the cobbled
stairway leading up from Nerudova.

Malostranská Kavárna, Malostranské náměstí
5, Malá Strana, t 257 532 110. This legendary
café is one of the best places in the city for
cream cakes and coffee.

U malého Glena (Little Glen's), Karmelitská
23, Malá Strana, t 257 531 717. A culinary mish-
mash of Tex-Mex, Czech food and kebabs in
a cosy, friendly and laid-back café (jazz club
by night). Deservedly popular with Czechs
and foreigners. Great weekend brunch.

U zeleného caje (Green Tea), Nerudova 19,
Malá Strana, t 257 530 027. Sort of Body Shop
for tea freaks. Brews you can choose range
from camomile to strawberry, and the food
includes pizzas and sandwiches.

Café Louvre, Národní 20, Nové Město, t 224
930 949. Founded at the turn of the 20th
century, this cavernous café has deep-pink
walls, icing-sugar stucco and chandeliers.
It was once a favourite with Kafka and
Max Brod. The food in the café is basic –
fried cheese – but tasty and reasonably
priced. Upstairs is a more upmarket
dining room, a billiard hall, and a non-
smoking room.

Kavárna Slavia, Smetanovo nábřeží 2, Nové
Město, t 221 771 651. The legendary café has
been smartly restored after a decade in
limbo. The views from the plate-glass
windows can't be beaten.

Entertainment and Nightlife

To find out what's going on, scour the
Prague Post (the weekly 'Night and Day'
supplement provides up-to-date listings and
information); *Prague Guide* (monthly English-
language freebie, available in hotel lobbies,
with some cultural listings); *Culture & Guide*
(another English-language freebie which you
can pick up in tourist offices); or at the Prague
Information Service (PIS), Betlémské nam. 2.

It is best to get event tickets from the venue.
However, if pressed for time, you can book
seats for all the major theatres and operas,
through the following agencies: **Bohemia
Tickets International**, Malé nám. 13, t 224 227
832 (*open Mon–Fri 10–7, Sat 10–5, Sun 10–3*);
Ticketpro, Klimentská 22, t 296 329 999 (*open
daily 8.30–8.30*); **Ticketstream**, Koubkova 8,
t 224 263 049 (*open Mon–Sat 9–6*).

Opera and Classical Music

Following a feud, Prague opera acrimo-
niously split into two separate companies in
1992: the neo-Renaissance **National Opera**
(Národní opera; Národní 2, Nové Město, t 224
901 448, *www.narodni-divadlo.cz*) and the
State Opera (Státní opera; Wilsonova 4, Nové
Město, t 224 227 266, *www.opera.cz*). Or you
can take in a Mozart opera at the **Estates
Theatre** (Stavovské divadlo; Ovocný trh 1, Staré
Město, t 224 215 001, *www.narodni-divadlo.cz*).
The Art Nouveau **Smetana Hall of the
Municipal House** (Smetanova síň Obecního
domu; Nám. Republiky 5, Nové Město, t 222
002 100, *www.obecnidum.cz*) houses the
Prague Symphony Orchestra, and the Czech
Philharmonic Orchestra is based at the
Rudolfinum (Alšovo nábřeží 12, Staré Město,
t 227 059 309). *See also* music festivals, p.96.

Theatre

The largest theatres are the **National
Theatre** (Národni 2, t 224 901 448, *www.
narodni-divadlo.cz*) and the neighbouring
Lanterna Magika Theatre (Národní Třída 4,
Nové Město, t 224 931 482, *www.laterna.cz*),
squatting under what looks like a very big
piece of plastic bubble wrap. The **Black Theatre**
sparked off an entire genre of gimmickry
(called 'black-light theatre') that you'll find

across the capital, on the basis of one idea: that black-clad actors can move things against a dark stage without being seen.

Prague's smaller theatres have been having a renaissance since 1989. Two interesting theatres are **Divadlo na zábradlí** (Anenské nám. 5, Staré Město, **t** 222 868 868, *www. nazabradli.cz*) and Divadlo labyrint (now called the **Svandovo divadlo**; Stefanikova 57, **t** 234 651 111, *www.svandovodivadlo.cz*), and the most innovative theatre is now to be found among the three hydraulically controlled stages of the newly modernized **Divadlo Archa** (Na poříčí 26, Nové Město, *www.archatheatre.cz*). With a strong bias towards music and dance, it is also the theatre most accessible to non-Czech speakers, and well worth investigating if experimentalism is your thing.

Dance

The National Theatre is the home of the **Czech National Ballet** (*www.balet.cz*) and most performances are held at the National Theatre or the Estates Theatre. There are also performances by visiting ballet companies at the State Opera. *See also* 'Festivals', p.96.

Bars

Château, Jakubská 2, Staré Město, **t** 222 316 328 (*open daily 4pm–5am; 4am in winter*). This maelstrom of the city's social scene used to be Chapeau Rouge and everyone still calls it that. A good place to begin the night if you have no idea where you want to end it.

U supa (The Vulture), Celetná 22, Staré Město, **t** 224 212 004 (*open daily noon–midnight*). A spacious beer hall, serving as its speciality a rich dark brew called Purkmistr 12°. It also serves steak, duck and tasty game dishes.

U zlatého tygra (The Golden Tiger), Husova 17, Staré Město, **t** 222 22 11 11 (*open daily 3pm–11pm*). Dank but lively beer hall. Václav Havel brought ex-President Clinton here for a beer.

Reduta, Národní 20, Nové Město, **t** 224 933 487, *www.redutajazzclub.cz*. Prague's longest-established jazz venue. When Bill Clinton hit the city on his 1994 European tour, it was in Reduta that he played his sax.

Alcohol Bar, Dusni 6, Josefov, **t** 224 811 744 (*open daily 7pm–2am*). Yet another posey bar in a neighbourhood packed with them; this one does cigars and cocktails for the jet set.

Kozička, Kozi 1, Josefov, **t** 224 818 308 (*open Mon–Fri noon–4am, Sat–Sun 4pm–4am*). Buzzing bar, which gets packed out with trendy regulars.

U černého vola (The Black Ox), Loretánské nám. 1, Hradčany, **t** 220 513 481 (*open daily 9am–10pm*). A very popular pub with the locals. Great atmosphere, and excellent location for post-prandial strolling.

U sv. Tomáše (St Thomas'), Letenská 12, Malá Strana, **t** 257 533 466 (*open 11.30am–midnight; music from 8*). One of Prague's best-known and oldest beer halls, with all that that entails: crooners, bassoonists, dumplings aplenty, and droves of homesick Germans. Walled garden open in summer.

Zanzibar, Lázenská 6, Malá Strana, **t** 602 780 076 (*open Mon–Sat noon–3am, Sun 5pm–3am*). Hip pink and neon cocktail bar near the Charles Bridge. One of the best late-night bars in the city.

U Fleků, Křemencova 9–11, Nové Město, **t** 224 915 118 (*open daily 9am–11pm*). Prague's best-known beer hall, which has brewed the same 14° beer on the premises since 1459. Five hundred seats and simple Czech food. Shady garden for raucous summer drinking.

Clubs

Karlovy Lázné (Charles Baths), Karlův Most, Staré Město, **t** 222 220 502 (*open 9pm–5am*). Four heaving dancefloors in the erstwhile municipal public baths of Prague. If you want to dance in a disused swimming pool, this is the club for you.

Lávka, Novotného lávka 1, Staré Město, **t** 222 222 156 (*open daily 10pm–4am*). Enticing location on an island just under Charles Bridge, with a view of river, bridge and castle that can be hallucinogenic during a hard night of outdoor dancing. It's during the long hot summers that Lávka takes off, to an unrelenting soundtrack of MTV/Europap.

Roxy, Dlouhá 33, Staré Město, **t** 224 826 296 (*open club nights 8pm–5am*). A former cinema, stripped down to its concrete essentials, and usually playing hardcore techno. It styles itself as an 'experimental space', but largely sticks to raves of the most traditional kind; but recent names have included Asian Dub Foundation, Royksopp and Faithless.

Years of smears and smokescreens have added to the mystery that now surrounds Prague. It is the capital of Bohemia, which has been a byword for outlandishness for centuries. The kingdom began its ascent into the clouds in the mid-1400s: the Pope spread the word that Bohemians made love on the streets, while in France a group of expelled gypsies waved their safe-conducts as they passed through, and the French duly noted that *un bohémien* was a gypsy – as he still is today. By the early 1600s, Shakespeare could get away with describing the landlocked and forested kingdom as 'a desert country near the sea' (*The Winter's Tale*). In 1938, disingenuous ignorance was elevated to foreign policy by British prime minister Neville Chamberlain. Ten years later, Prague – farther west than Vienna, and considerably closer to Dublin than to Moscow – became lost in 'Eastern Europe'. The city of dreams began a 41-year nightmare; but, in the West, Bohemia did little more than hover somewhere between Bloomsbury and Hampstead. And then, in 1989, a few million people pinched themselves, the tinpot emperors of Communism shivered, and the city returned to where it belongs: the heart of Europe.

Prague is now the capital of the Czech Republic – made up of Bohemia, Moravia and a slice of Silesia – comprises some 1,213,800 inhabitants (with an inexplicably decreasing proportion of men); 503 spires, towers and sundry aerial protrusions; 495 square kilometres; 10 districts; eight islands; seven hills (like most legendary cities); and an agglomeration of what were historically five separate towns. Since 1989 it has barely stopped echoing to the rhythm of pile-drivers and, under the glare of oxyacetylene torches, the magical metropolis is being transformed into a city fit for the 21st century. It is still scarred by the barbed-wire wounds of the Cold War but, as it busks, dances, works and kisses its way back to the light, the old divisions are being healed on its streets. Prague doesn't always feel so dreamy – particularly as you chew through its accursed dumplings, wade through hordes of beer-hunting tourists or cross swords with a hobgoblin of the bureaucracy – but, if you pack your senses of humour, adventure and romance, a visit is an unforgettable jaunt into a city where history is in the making, and where a thousand years has already been made.

History

The First Přemysl

The story begins with the establishment of Bohemia's first ruling dynasty, the **Přemysls**, at the end of the 8th century. Myth and history are intertwined but, according to the former, the **Čech** tribe had established itself at Vyšehrad ('higher castle'), a rocky outcrop on the Vltava River that still bears the name. Čech was a mass-murderer on the run, but it was his son, Krok or Crocus, who went down in legend as the putative founding father. Unable to produce a male heir, he was succeeded by his daughter **Libuše**.

When the men of the tribe insisted Libuše needed a husband, she went into a trance. Pointing towards distant hills, she told them to follow her horse, which would take them to a ploughman whose descendants would rule over them for ever. The

Food and Drink

There are several types of eating and drinking establishments in Prague: beer joints (*pivnice, hostinec* or *hospoda*), wine bars (*vinárny*), cafés (*kavárny*) and restaurants (*restaurace*). The most distinctive delicacy of the Czech kitchen is the *knedlík*, or **dumpling**. Praguers treat it as the highest culinary expression of the country: if you say that you recently ate an unexciting one, you are almost certain to be told that you just have to know where to go. The main distinction is between floury *houskový knedlík* and *bramborový knedlík*, made of mushy potato. Both are usually served with a lump of meat in a thick gravy, and are staple fare in beer halls. *Špekové knedlíky* are marginally more interesting, mixed with bacon, while *kynuté knedlíky* are downright wild in comparison, centred on lumps of stewed fruit.

You're on tastier ground when it comes to **cold meats**. Prague ham (*yunka*) is of high quality, but it's generally agreed that the best salamis are the harder Hungarian varieties, particularly the flat *lovecký salám*, and both *Uherský salám* and *salám alékum*. Sausages are much loved, and you can pick up a *párek* (two long porkers) in stands across the city. The frankfurter-like *Liberecký párek* and the paprika-flavoured *čabajka* are the best varieties. If you avoid pork, you can eat *hovězí párky* and *drubeží párky*, made of beef and chicken respectively.

Freshwater **fish** are a healthy alternative: carp and trout are bred in the lakes of southern Bohemia and, along with the pike and eel that are occasionally found with them, are widely available in Prague. **Soups** (*polévky*) are often delicious, and in cheaper beer halls and cafés they are often the most likely winners on the menu. *Dršt'ková* is one of the most popular soups and comprises floating pieces of a cow's stomach, while *zabijačková polévka* is a pungent concoction made largely of pigs' blood. The name, roughly translated, means 'slaughter soup'.

There are a few other **snacks** that you'll probably encounter. *Vafle* (waffles) are everywhere, and to find one you generally need do no more than follow your nose. There are also stalls across the city selling *bramborák*, a garlicky potato pancake that is delicious if not too greasy. *Dábelský toust* is a fiercely tasty mixture of meat (usually beef) on toast. *Smažený sýr* is fried cheese, which is more appetizing but no less unhealthy than it sounds.

Czech **beer** needs little introduction: Plzěn is the home of Pilsner Urquell, the first lager and the father of a thousand German imitators, while the brewing town of Budweis (České Budějovice) has become part of the American dream. In fact, US company Busch borrowed little more than the name, and the potent concoction produced in the Czech Republic puts the US slop to shame. (Perhaps realizing that, Busch has kept Czech Budweis off the US market for decades.) Both Czech beers are chock-full of alcohol and sugar, all created naturally during the brewing process, unlike that in additive-laden Western rivals. You may already like sweet beers, and if not you should acquire the taste: look out for beer halls and bottles marked Plzěnský prazdroj and Budvar. Prague also produces beers of its own – Staropramen, Braník and Smíchov – which are slightly more bitter. Czech **wine** might yet become a force to be reckoned with, but at present is more suitable mulled; ask for *svařené víno*.

horse trotted off, and a sturdy farmer named Přemysl was brought back to wed Libuše. A dynasty had begun. The city of Prague owes its legendary origins to one of Libuše's prophecies too. According to Bohemia's venerable chronicler, Cosmas of Prague (c. 1045–1125), she was overcome by a vision involving 'a town, the glory of which will reach the stars'. Again the loyal subjects trooped off to a spot described by Libuše, where they found a man building a door-sill (in Czech, *práh* – hence the name Praha or Prague) for his cottage. This spot was said to be in Hradčany. Building started in earnest and the rest, as they say, is history.

Scanty archaeological evidence suggests, in fact, that the first people in the area were a Celtic tribe known as the **Boii**, who lived here long enough to leave the name Bohemia. In the 5th century, the Čechs, a Slavonic tribe from Croatia, did establish a strong presence in the area, but there is no record of Crocus, and it is only in the later 9th century that the first historically attested Přemysl, **Bořivoj**, appears on the scene as ruler of Bohemia. The princedom was still an insignificant cog in the Greater Moravian Empire, which included most of the Slavs of central Europe, and was engaged in endless bloody tussles with the Holy Roman Empire to the west.

The **Great Schism** between the Roman and Byzantine Churches had by now begun to open up, and German monks scurried across the Moravian Empire with their version of the Good Book. In about 863, the Empire's ruler, **Rostislav**, turned to the Eastern Church for help. Byzantine Emperor Michael sent along Brothers **Methodius and Cyril**, who arrived with a Bible and a liturgy written in a new Greek alphabet (Glagolitic, or Cyrillic script) that could deal with the grunts peculiar to the Slavs. Jealous Germans levelled charges of heresy, but the two men remained on good terms with Rome until their death. Bořivoj was dunked into the new religion by Methodius in about 874. Mass abandonment of storm and fertility gods followed.

Bohemia Takes Off

Although the Slavs had little sympathy for the Holy Roman Empire, its power could not be ignored. As the Přemysls struggled to control Bohemia, they began to turn away from the East. The influence of Germans in Bohemian affairs, which was to become a tragic motif over the next millennium, began to grow. In 885, **Pope Stephen V** declared the Slavonic liturgy to be heretical. The Přemysls took his word for it and began the switch away from Cyrillic, for which Western tourists can be eternally grateful. Bohemia remained subservient to the Moravian Empire until the beginning of the 10th century, when that empire suddenly disappeared from the map, seized by rampant Magyars, who chose to spare little of Bohemia.

In about 921, **Prince Wenceslas** (Václav) became Bohemia's ruler. A gentle Christian, he may have been a suitable subject for a 19th-century carol but he was not up to the rough-and-tumble of Dark Age intrigue. In 935, he was murdered on the way to Mass by his brother, **Boleslav the Cruel**. What Boleslav lacked in kindness, he made up for with political skill: he exterminated his rivals, extended his dominions, married his daughter into the Polish ruling family, and resisted political pressures from Rome.

In 973, under the rule of **Boleslav the Pious**, Bohemia's strength was acknowledged by the pope, who consented to the founding of a bishopric in Prague. Two more

Boleslavs followed: **Boleslav the Third**, who reverted to type and murdered several unruly nobles at a banquet, and his brother, **Boleslav the Brave**.

Over the next two centuries, Bohemia was pulled deeper into the tangled web of the Holy Roman Empire. In the early 13th century, both pope and emperor allowed Bohemia's princes to call themselves kings and wear a crown – which laid the ground for future emperors to appoint Bohemia's king. An explosive brew was also building up at lower levels of society. Under the reign of **King Wenceslas I** (1230–53) German merchants were invited to Prague and other parts of Bohemia, where they were allowed to govern themselves according to their own laws.

Wenceslas' successor, **Přemysl Otakar II**, gave further ground to the colonists, literally, by founding Malá Strana on the left bank of the Vltava in 1257. During his reign (1253–78), the city developed into three autonomous units – the Old Town, the Castle District and Malá Strana. A Jewish community was expelled from Malá Strana to make way for the Germans. The Jews joined another Jewish community to the north of the Old Town, which had already been walled into a ghetto. Romanies ('gypsies') first came to Bohemia about this time in the wake of the short but savage incursions of the Tartars. Trade and finds of silver deposits around Kutná Hora helped to fund Prague's first building boom, and its Romanesque basilicas and houses gave way to Gothic grandeur. However, the city's expansion was soon halted – a victim of Přemysl Otakar's own success. By the early 1270s, he had created a Bohemian kingdom that stretched from the Baltic to the Adriatic, and shook Germany's princes out of their internecine struggles. Otakar made a lunge for the emperor's throne in 1273. He missed, and **Rudolf, Count of Habsburg**, stepped into the imperial driving seat.

Anarchy and Chivalry

In 1306, the Přemysl dynasty sputtered to a halt with the murder of the 17-year-old **Wenceslas III**. Finding a successor was not easy: anarchic Bohemia needed a monarch, and by 1310 everyone was longing for a strong hand. They finally settled on 14-year-old **John of Luxembourg**, the son of the new German emperor, Henry VII. The king spent most of his reign on a warring spree across Europe. He cared little what Prague got up to as long as it kept the royal coffers full, so burghers and nobles made the most of the new opportunities: the Old Town got a town hall, a legal code and formal supremacy over every other town in the kingdom.

The Golden Age

John's son could hardly have been less like his father. The German princes elected him **Emperor Charles IV** and offered him the Bohemian crown. In 1356, he regularized the imperial electoral system, putting power in the hands of the princes, undercutting those who had voted against him and dealing a body blow to the temporal ambitions of the papacy, which had had a veto for centuries. He took advantage of France's battering at the hands of the English (the Hundred Years' War had only just begun) to reduce it almost to vassal status. He spoke fluent Czech and encouraged the country's language and traditions. The emperor wrapped his reign in a series of legends, going back to Libuše and St Wenceslas. With the help of his friend and former tutor, Pope Clement VI, Prague had already been elevated to an archbishopric in 1344; Charles invited monastic orders from the far-flung reaches of the Eastern Church. While the Black Death devastated the rest of Europe in 1348, Bohemia lay protected by a screen of mountains and emerged as the Continent's most vital centre of Gothic art and architecture. As befitted a medieval town with pretensions of grandeur, it got a new bridge, cathedral and the first university in central Europe. For decades this was an academic vortex, sucking in scholars from as far away as Oxford. In the same year Charles founded the New Town, incorporating the straggling settlements outside the city walls into broad streets and marketplaces – the most successful and lasting piece of urban planning in Europe since the Romans.

Nationalism and Hussitism

The peace and prosperity enjoyed by Bohemia during Charles' reign were not to last. Tensions had long been building between German and Czech populations. The native nobility, although far from homogenous, resented the political influence of the Germans, and workers were jealous of their economic influence. Popular anger found potent expression in a religious reform movement, a century before the birth of Luther – one of the first signs of the conflict that was to tear Europe apart. Charles' policy of inviting scores of religious orders to Prague aroused hostility as Praguers realized that medieval monks and nuns were prone to fool around, and were being subsidized for it. The Church was brought further into disrepute by Charles' mania for collecting relics. In reaction to the corrupt Church, anticlericals, reformists and chiliastic lunatics flooded into Prague. The next decades saw the fissures in Western Christianity grow ever wider. Charles IV's eldest son, **Wenceslas IV**, took over as king of Bohemia and emperor. He spent most of his reign in an alcoholic stupor, and was replaced as emperor by his wily half-brother **Sigismund** in 1400.

In 1402 a young priest, **Jan Hus** (John Huss), influenced by the teachings of Oxfordshire parish priest John Wycliffe, was appointed rector of Charles University. Hus would never have regarded himself as anything but a Catholic, but his fiery sermons moved a long way from the party line. His assertion that clerical and papal decrees had to be tested against Scripture amounted to a direct political attack on the power of the Church. The Hussites preached in the vernacular, and in about 1414 began the practice that came to characterize the movement: allowing the congregation the wine of the Eucharist as well as the bread. They became known as the **Utraquists** (from the Latin for 'in both kinds'). Hus was excommunicated in 1411 and burned at the stake on 6 July 1415. Wenceslas sympathized with the nationalists, but was under constant pressure from his brother to control the heretics. In 1419 things went from bad to worse when councillors at the New Town Hall were **defenestrated**, a novel form of political violence that was to become a regular feature in Bohemia's history. Wenceslas finally succumbed to one of his repeated apoplectic fits.

In 1420, sneaky **Sigismund** tried to succeed his brother as King of Bohemia. It soon became clear, however, that he intended to restore Church privileges and suppress the Utraquists. The last straw came in 1420 when **Pope Martin V** declared a crusade against Bohemia, the first of four in a decade, leaving the Turks to hammer into

Christendom. Bohemia found itself at war with Europe – even Joan of Arc took an interest in 1429. As early as 1421, a division developed among the Utraquists, between moderates, who sought compromise with Rome, and a radical group which now thought in terms of rupture with the Church. The conflict came to a head in 1434 when **Pope Eugenius IV** granted rights to administer and receive communion in both kinds (the Compacts of Basle). The radical Táborites rejected the rights as insufficient, so the moderate aristocrats wiped them out at the **Battle of Lipany** in 1434.

Sigismund, finally recognized as King of Bohemia, died a few months later. His successor, **Albert of Habsburg**, followed suit in 1439, remaining alive just long enough to impregnate his wife, who produced **Ladislav the Posthumous**. He reigned briefly from 1453 to 1457, but the real ruler of Bohemia from 1440 to 1471 was an Utraquist nobleman, **George of Poděbrady** (Jiří z Poděbrad), who ruled as king from 1458. He hoped to establish a native dynasty, but was forced to sign a deal with the pro-Catholic Polish **Vladislav II of Jagellon**, in order to fight off the equally pro-Catholic **Matthias Corvinus** of Hungary.

Vladislav was elected king in 1471, and it was under his reign that the last flickers of popular Hussitism were extinguished. Anti-Catholic feelings still ran high among the population – a riot against Vladislav's officials in 1483 brought Prague's **second defenestration**, this time from the Old Town Hall, but the nobility increasingly looked after their own interests. Taking advantage of the king's absences (he preferred Buda Castle), nobles introduced serfdom in 1487, and began to brew beer (a long-standing privilege of the towns) on their feudal estates. Many kept to the Utraquist faith, but it came to signify little more than a tipple at communion. But even if the first flush of Czech nationalism was over, Bohemia was established as a centre of anti-Catholicism – and paid heavily over the next centuries.

The Habsburgs Arrive

Another would-be dynasty bit the dust when Vladislav's heir drowned; princelings from across Europe headed for Prague to vie for the throne. The divided electors' fateful choice was **Ferdinand I of Habsburg**. He seemed tolerant for a Catholic and, after years of fratricide, many hoped that a strong monarch might repel the voracious Turks.

In the 1520s, many of Bohemia's Germans fell under the Lutheran spell, while the Bohemian Brethren found affinities with Calvinism. Ferdinand was Catholic, but his opposition to Protestantism was strengthened by mundane concerns: Catholicism was a universal ideology to establish centralized rule; and, in Bohemia, Protestantism still had a dangerously nationalistic tinge. In 1547, Ferdinand sweet-talked Prague's Protestants into financing an anti-Turkish army, which then marched west to attack Protestants in Saxony. Incensed nobles met in Prague to bemoan the ruse, but Ferdinand's troops massacred the Saxons in weeks, and were back in Prague before the Estates had found an army. The ringleaders were decapitated and Prague's privileges drastically curtailed.

Ferdinand ensured his eldest son, **Maximilian**, was crowned king and introduced the fiercely proselytizing Jesuit Order into Prague in 1556 to counteract the spread of

Lutheranism. In 1563, **Pope Pius IV** launched the militant programme of the **Counter-Reformation** at the Council of Trent.

Ferdinand died in 1564, to be succeeded as Emperor by Maximilian (already king of Bohemia). In return for continued funding for his anti-Turkish forays, Maximilian granted Bohemia's Lutherans the right to organize independently of the old Utraquist church. The concessions enabled him to have his son elected king of Bohemia with little difficulty in 1576 and, when Maximilian died later that year, he was succeeded by **Emperor Rudolf II**.

Rudolfine Prague

The Turks were within 100 miles of Vienna, the traditional seat of the Habsburgs. The Czech Estates offered to pay off a chunk of the empire's debts, and rebuild the castle, if Rudolf moved to Prague. By 1583, the emperor had decamped to his new capital. Prague became the centre of an empire for the first time in two centuries.

Rudolf was the most singular monarch Prague had seen since Charles IV. The papacy had high hopes for the young emperor but Rudolf turned out to be a strange fish, imbued with a mystical spirituality that was far from the new orthodoxy the Church was trying to promote. Fanaticism was alien to him, but his education left him torn between the ideal of a universal truth and the reality of a Christianity that was being reduced into two armed camps. The sensitive emperor was never able to resolve the dilemma, and teetered between profound pessimism and mild insanity for most of his reign. Legend and history remember Rudolfine Prague as a fantastic city of alchemy and astrology, suspended in time, but its atmosphere was very much a product of the moment: the Counter-Reformation was gathering force in Austria and Styria; a part-time lunatic and full-time melancholic was on the throne; and mystics and zealots were massing in the city. Prague had become the embodiment of Europe's schizophrenia. It would have taken a genius to steer the empire through its crisis, and Rudolf's temperament was ill-suited to the job. His younger brother **Matthias** had intrigued against him since his first major bout of insanity in 1600. By 1606, Matthias had launched an open mutiny and two years later he forced his brother to hand over all his realms save Bohemia, a posthumous gift.

From Defenestration to Massacre

In 1617, **Emperor Matthias** proposed his fiercely anti-Protestant cousin **Ferdinand** as his successor to the crown of Bohemia. The policies of Matthias and the new monarch turned more militant. The Bohemians finally took a stand against Catholic rule on 23 May 1618 when they hurled two of Ferdinand's most hated councillors and a secretary, out of a window. All three survived the 15-metre drop: the Catholic Church claimed a miracle; others claimed that a dung heap had saved them. Prague's **third defenestration** threw Europe into the religious fratricide of the Thirty Years' War. Prague's nobles looked for a royal champion to oppose Ferdinand, and found **Frederick of the Palatinate**. The Bohemians could not have made a worse choice. His allies flaked away and it became clear that the 'Winter King' had never fought before in his life. The two armies finally met at the **Battle of the White Mountain** (Bílá Hora), just outside

Prague, on 8 November 1620. The Czech and Hungarian allied armies scattered into ignominious retreat, a sorry end to two centuries of anti-Catholicism.

The Bohemian Counter-Reformation

The **Thirty Years' War** ravaged Europe until 1648. It had begun as a struggle to assert Habsburg power, but by the 1630s the entire Continent was sorting out its political differences by fire and sword. In Prague, Bohemian Protestantism and nationalism were inseparable. Ferdinand, who had become emperor after Matthias' death, soon hitched the imperial cause firmly to that of the Church. He and his monkish allies extinguished the city's ancient powers: Protestantism was made a capital offence, and the independence of the Czech Estates was destroyed. When the dust settled, Bohemia was left with its population reduced by over a third; the country plunged into a decline that lasted two centuries.

Frederick the Great invaded Prague twice in the mid-18th century, but otherwise the city became a backwater, where you went when the bright lights of Vienna became too much. The Jesuits led the consolidation of the new faith with a Baroque building programme that transformed the face of the city, but were placed under a worldwide ban by a jealous pope in 1773. In 1781, the enlightened despot **Emperor Josef II** abolished most of the empire's other monasteries and convents. The corollary was the restoration of individual religious freedom for all save the weirdest sects, and Prague's Jewish population was finally allowed out of its ghetto.

The Nationalist Revival

During the early 19th century, Bohemia began to breathe again. Europe's tide of nationalisms swept across the country and, after centuries of German meddling and oppression, Czechs began to hanker for a purely Slavic alternative. The Czech language, which had all but died out, was resuscitated by a handful of writers and researchers – František Palacký and Josef Jungmann the most notable. In **1848** the citizens of Prague were up in arms again, joined by the rest of the empire in a revolt against Metternich's iron rule from Vienna. The Habsburg empire was slowly dying. It was to prove incapable of accommodating the new power of nationalist sentiment. As the empire sickened, the Czech nation quickened.

From Independence to Dependency

As the pattern of European alliances emerged in the years before 1914, many Czechs and Slovaks felt with apprehension that their interests lay firmly in the enemy camp. Lingering pan-Slavism encouraged sympathy even for the corrupt Russia of Nicholas II, while democratic ideals and anti-German sentiment made others look towards France and Britain. When war broke out, two men – **T.G. Masaryk** and **Edvard Beneš** – began a four-year tour to persuade the world that the time was ripe for Czechoslovakia. In 1918, Masaryk signed a deal with Slovak émigrés in Pittsburgh, which persuaded President Woodrow Wilson to give 'Czecho-Slovakia' the green light.

Independence was declared on 28 October 1918 and, within two weeks, Masaryk had been elected president of the new Czechoslovakian Republic. With Beneš, now foreign minister, he staked out the borders of the new state. These encompassed the largely German-populated Sudetenland to the west, as well as areas claimed by the Hungarians and the Poles, but in the peace treaties the victors ratified the *fait accompli* with little discussion and no plebiscite.

Although the country's political structures rode the **Depression** with an astonishing stability, the ancient problem of the German minority was soon to explode with unparalleled ferocity. The Sudetenland separatist movement found a champion in Hitler, and Czechoslovakia became the eye of a building European storm. In the infamous 1938 **Munich Agreement**, Britain, France and Italy gave Hitler *carte blanche* to seize the Sudetenland. Within six months, the German army had invaded Czechoslovakia as Britain and France remained silent. Only after the invasion of Poland six months later did they declare war on Germany. The war left Prague's buildings almost unscathed, but its population was less fortunate. Thousands of intellectuals, politicians and Romanies were killed or imprisoned. Of the 90,000 Jews who remained in the Protectorate in 1939, only 10,000 survived the war.

When war broke out, Beneš, who had taken over as president in 1935, went to London to establish a government-in-exile. Within the Protectorate itself, armed underground movements began to operate, directed largely by the London government. On 5 May 1945, the capital's Resistance groups broadcast a call to arms and thousands rose up against the occupying Nazi forces in the city. The **Prague Uprising** lasted only four days, but street fighting and last-minute executions left up to 5,000 Czechs dead. On 9 May 1945 the Soviet Red Army entered Prague to a rapturous reception. A provisional national assembly, with Beneš again as president, was set up in October. Mobs lynched collaborators, and the country's three million Sudeten Germans were expelled, resulting in the deaths of thousands.

Communist Consolidation

The Czechoslovakian Communist Party led by **Klement Gottwald** swept the board in the 1946 elections, with 38 per cent of the votes. Beneš appointed Gottwald prime minister of a coalition government, but Uncle Joe Stalin had no intention of letting his protégé go to bed with a bourgeois. Gottwald's rabble-rousing skills and the weakness of Beneš led to the former's assumption of the presidency in February 1948. Within a month the popular foreign minister, **Jan Masaryk** – son of T. G. – who was less accommodating to the Communists, had died in a mysterious fall from his office window late one night. A **fourth defenestration** began 40 years of Communist rule; the Party was pleased to report 89 per cent support in new elections in May. Within a year the Terror had begun.

From Socialism to Normalization

During the mid-1960s, reformers at the lower levels of the Party began to work on revitalizing its links with the rest of society. In January 1968, Alexander Dubček was elected to the post of First Secretary. Dubček was no closet liberal: his politics were formed in the crucible of the 1930s Soviet Union but, in the heady days of 1968, he finally began to listen, and learn. During the so-called **Prague Spring**, he proposed a radical reform of the country's political and economic institutions, partly out of his changing convictions but largely at the urging of more committed forces and individuals both within and outside the Party.

The Soviet Union, which had actually backed pliant Dubček for the leadership the year before, began to stir. General Secretary Brezhnev was soon considering how to help the Czechoslovak proletariat stave off 'a return to the bourgeois-capitalist system'. He took soundings of the other Warsaw Pact leaders and, on 21 August 1968, Czechoslovakia was invaded by five armies: the Prague Spring suddenly turned very cold. The cultural and political renaissance of the mid-1960s had been strangled in its cradle. The times were desperate. Fourteen philosophy students at the Charles University drew lots, and agreed to burn themselves alive one by one until press freedom was restored. 'Torch No.1' was **Jan Palach**. On 16 January 1969, the 20-year-old emptied a can of petrol over himself in Wenceslas Square, and flicked a lighter. Over the next month, so too did many others. In April 1969, Dubček was replaced by Gustáv Husák – Resistance hero, victim of the Terror and supporter of the Prague Spring. Brezhnev is said to have murmured, 'If we can't use the puppets, we'll tie the strings to the leaders.' Within a year, Husák began to dance. Some 500,000 people were deprived of Communist Party membership, in a process that was called 'normalization' (*normalisace*). When all was normal, the government declared that Czechoslovakia had achieved a state of *reálný socialismus*, an eerie phrase that is usually translated as 'real existing socialism'. A new generation grew up without even the memory of hope.

The Velvet Revolution

Even as late as mid-1989, with Hungary and Poland well on the path to reform, few observers saw Czechoslovakia as likely to follow in the near future. But as the East German regime tottered, refugees began to flood into the West German embassy in Prague. The revolutions of 1989 had begun. On 10 November the West woke to the news that bulldozers were demolishing the Berlin Wall, and on 17 November Prague's students confronted a baton-wielding police force. The filmed scenes of police brutality against students armed with candles and flowers aroused the population from two decades of torpor. For the next six weeks, Prague was enfolded by its **Velvet Revolution**, an anarchic hubbub of strikes, pickets and celebrations, which culminated in the election of playwright and recently released political prisoner **Václav Havel** to the presidency on 29 December 1989.

Truth Will Out

The most dramatic of the messy truths to emerge since 1989 was the realization that Czechoslovakia itself was based on a fiction. The rhetoric of internationalism spouted by Communist leaders had both fuelled and concealed domestic rivalries and, within three years of the Velvet Revolution, Slovakian nationalism grew into a full-blown independence movement. On New Year's Eve 1992, each more or less amicably waved goodbye to the other, and the **Czech and Slovak Republics** were born.

The new nation's social conflicts do not have a solution as simple as Velvet Divorce. The country's Romanies have suffered from official neglect and public ignorance for decades, and the replacement of totalitarianism by majority rule has in many cases done nothing but add a veneer of legitimacy to their stigmatization. The psychological legacy of Communism also fractures the country. As late as May 1988, the Party had more than 1.7 million members – that is, one in 10 of Czechoslovakia's total population – and humdrum compromises with the regime were struck by millions more. As a result, measures taken since 1989 to break the institutionalized power of the Party have often had an irrational quality, scapegoating individuals for a system in which almost every adult was implicated to some extent. So far the Czech Republic has steered a precarious course between demands for revenge and the temptation of forgetfulness, but it is only when today's twenty-somethings reach middle age that it will be possible to say if normality has replaced the 'normalization' which plagued Czechoslovakia for 30 years.

But whatever else may happen, it is unlikely that the country will stumble back into Communist dictatorship. Under the leadership of its first prime minister, **Václav Klaus**, it anchored itself steadily into the mainstream of Europe, joining NATO in 1999 and placing itself on the fast track to **European Union membership**, which was formalised in May 2004. The Social Democratic party won the 1998 and 2002 elections and, in July 2004, 34-year-old Stanislav Gross rose from the ranks to become the youngest leader in Europe. A former train technician, he has been touted by some as a working-class hero, though he is yet to articulate his vision for the Czech Republic – a cause for concern among many commentators. Meanwhile, the nation's moral figurehead Václav Havel quietly stepped down as president of the republic, to be replaced in late February 2003 by former prime minister Václav Klaus.

With all the political to-ing and fro-ing of recent years, many difficult questions for the future remain unanswered. The Czech economy remains the sore thumb of the new regime, long skewed by hidden subsidies and sclerotic industries. In the light of new EU membership, these are set to be tackled with radical reforms. But tourism continues to thrive and the country is gaining an ever-stronger foothold in the international community. Whatever hurdles may lie round the corner, it is certain that Prague has faced them all before.

Art and Architecture

Romanesque

In 965, when most urban centres in northern Europe comprised a few wooden hovels, Prague was a thriving town of stone and mortar. The earliest architecture was Romanesque and the first churches, after the 9th-century arrival of Christianity, had a basilican ground plan. Buildings supported by pillars were topped with wood or simple tunnel vaults and tiny rotundas were built. Prague's best surviving Romanesque church is **St George's Basilica**.

Gothic

Architecture inspired by late 12th-century French cathedral design was called 'Gothic' by Renaissance Italians, who were sure it was produced by Vandals. The first glimmers of this style arrived in mid-13th century Prague with **St Agnes' Convent**, and Gothic features crept into the **Old-New Synagogue**. In church and synagogue, arches and steeples soared heavenwards; rich sculptural decoration crowded walls; and glass framed by fine tracery flooded interiors with light. In the late 1200s, the Vltava submerged the town once too often and the burghers retaliated by burying their town. A new one was built in Gothic style, taking the use of arches, decoration and glass to new pinnacles.

Under Emperor Charles IV (1346–78) Prague stormed on to the European stage. **Matthew of Arras** came from France to begin a new cathedral, but by the mid-14th century, Germany led the field in church design. In 1353 Matthew's timely death brought 23-year-old **Peter Parléř** to Prague, where he built **St Vitus' Cathedral**, one of the grandest late Gothic churches of Europe. Artists began to produce unique Bohemian work too. Paintings dating from the early 13th century show artists breaking free of rigid Byzantine rules. The Bohemian trend manifested itself in heavy modelling, which peaked in the work of **Master Theodoric**. His portraits of saints rank among the most distinctive work of the era in Europe.

The Renaissance

Bohemia's first Habsburg king, Ferdinand I, crowned in 1526, encouraged the flow of Italian ideas to Prague. He built his sublime **Royal Summer Palace** (1538–63) and, after a fire on the left bank in 1541, nobles built a series of imposing **Renaissance palaces**.

Mannerism

Under Emperor Rudolf II (1576–1611), Prague became a centre of Mannerist culture in Europe. Mannerism, originally a term of abuse, was a retreat from the notion that art could capture the essence of the world by reproducing it in its most noble form. In a century of religious uncertainty, attempts to penetrate beyond the visible were part of a quest to find a more solid basis for universal truth. Rudolf summoned artists to Prague from across Europe, notably the Milanese painter **Giuseppe Arcimboldo** (1527–93), best known for his surreal allegorical portraits. Other favoured painters came from the Low Countries, among them **Bartholomeus Spranger** (1546–1611). The apotheosis of Rudolf – Christian hero and art patron against dark ignorance – was a theme to which most of his artists turned. **Hans von Aachen** (1552–1615), from Köln, created elegant portraits and religious scenes, but, like Spranger, also painted nudes tinged with an unusual eroticism. Rudolf's curiosity extended to the natural world; and among his still-life artists was the Flemish **Roelandt Savery**, who arrived in 1604 and painted exotic animals. The next emperor, Matthias, spirited parts of Rudolf's collection to Vienna. Prague's visual arts went into crisis in an atmosphere of quasi-Calvinism, and the Estates sold off more paintings in 1619; most of the rest was stolen in 1648 by Swedish troops.

Baroque

The Baroque style arrived from Rome in the late 16th century, as the Council of Trent laid down its demand that art was to glorify the Church. Within a century it had utterly transformed the face of the city. The Baroque used movement, unnatural light and disproportion with a consistency that overwhelmed rather than intrigued. The new architecture elbowed its way into the **Waldstein Palace**, representing a transitional period. When the Thirty Years' War ended in 1648, building began in earnest. Most of Prague's Baroque architects came via Vienna; the most prolific were **Francesco Caratti** and **Giovanni Alliprandi** (1665–1720).

By the early 18th century, Prague and Vienna had grasped the baton of Baroque. Two of the city's greatest architects were the Bavarian **Kristof Dienzenhofer** (1655–1722), and his son **Kilian Dienzenhofer** (1689–1751); their joint masterpiece, the Jesuit **Church of St Nicholas**, is one of 18th-century Europe's finest.

The Baroque reintegrated architecture and sculpture, after the Renaissance insistence that they were independent elements, establishing a tradition that influenced design into the 20th century. Baroque sculpture began with the relative restraint of **Jan Bendl** (1620–80) and **Matthias Jäckel** (1655–1738) and culminated in the epic works of **Matthias Braun** (1684–1738) and **Ferdinand Maximilian Brokof** (1688–1731).

Baroque painting in Bohemia is not up to sculpture. **Karel Škréta** (1610–74) followed Italian art of the cinquecento, and **Michael Willmann** (1630–1706) painted religious anguish and passion. The most accomplished works of Prague Baroque were experiments with light and colour by **Petr Brandl** (1668–1735) and the frescoes of **Franz Anton Maulpertsch** at the **Strahov Monastery**.

Neoclassicism to Neo-Gothic

Under Emperor Josef II, the city's culture suffered a series of rapid blows. Fripperies had no place in the monarch's coolly rational world. What remained of Rudolf II's collection was auctioned off, and monks were turfed out of their monasteries, which were turned into barracks. Architecture was typified by a dry French classicism; the change was most notable in Baroque Prague, but neither classicism nor Empire style had much impact.

Nation-building

In the mid-19th century, Prague's architecture was engulfed by the national revival movement, and a vogue for rehashing older architectural styles. The Renaissance was the favoured choice. Huge pediments triumphed, and stacks of disordered columns were considered noble. The result appears most clearly in the bombastic **National Museum**. The late 19th century also saw a wave of restoration of Bohemia's Gothic architecture. Artists also played a heroic role in the national revival, adorning buildings with mythological and allegorical works to express patriotic aspirations.

Art Nouveau

Prague's architecture at the turn of the 20th century was dominated by Art Nouveau and a Europe-wide attempt to escape the tyranny of historicism. The

Bohemian *secese* was actually a confluence of two currents. The first came from France, and aimed to create a unified style from natural forms, using sculptural decoration in building, as with the **Hotel Evropa** and **Municipal House**. The second form of Art Nouveau originated in Glasgow and used rectilinear structures, abstract and stripped of ornamentation. Its leading light was **Jan Kotěra** (1871–1923).

Art Nouveau found decorative expression in the work of sculptors like **Ladislav Šaloun** (1870–1946), **Stanislav Sucharda** (1866–1916) and, notably, **Alfons Mucha** (1860–1939). Two of the most original artists to emerge in the 1890s were mystical types unconcerned with new forms. The first was sculptor **František Bílek** (1872–1941), who linked ideas spanning music, literature and religion to produce a fascinating body of work. **František Kupka** (1871–1957) settled in Paris after 1896; his earliest paintings concentrated on ideas of rebirth and renewal, but, after several years as a medium, he moved on to produce some of Europe's first deliberately abstract art.

Cubism

Prague's first modernist painting came out of **Osma** (The Eight), a group of artists founded in 1907. Its initial inspiration was the raw force of Munch but, as early as 1910, Czech artists such as **Emil Filla** (1882–1953), **Bohumil Kubišta** (1884–1918) and **Antonín Procházka** (1882–1945) had picked up on Parisian Cubism. For the next decade, Prague was the most important centre of the new art outside its birthplace. **Josef Čapek** (1897–1945) and **Jan Zrzavý** (1890–1977) also dabbled with Cubism, but were more interested in the primitivism that had inspired it.

Prague's painters largely followed the lead set by Picasso and Braque, but the sculptors and architects in the Cubist **Skupina** group produced maverick works. The leading sculptor was **Otto Gutfreund** (1889–1927), whose early work reflects the ideas of **Cubo-expressionism**. The most extraordinary Czech Cubism was in architecture. Three members of the Skupina, **Pavel Janák** (1882–1956), **Joseph Gočár** (1880–1945) and **Josef Chochol** (1880–1956) tried to restore depth and flexibility to buildings by using 3D geometrical forms on the façades.

Devětsil and Surrealism

The interwar years were among the most exciting in Prague's cultural life. The old world did not look good after the carnage of war, but Czechoslovakian independence had been won and, in the East, a rosy Bolshevik dawn was beginning. In 1920, a group of young artists led by **Karel Teige** (1900–51) founded **Devětsil** ('Nine Forces'). The political philosophy of the group was Soviet-style Marxism but, after a brief tinker with 'proletarian art', Devětsil spent the 1920s in a maze of artistic experimentation. In 1924 Teige hurled the group into the mêlée of the European avant-garde with a *First Manifesto of Poetism*. Like the Soviet constructivists, he embraced the abstract beauty of the machine age, but also laid down his theory of 'Poetism', 'the art of pleasure', which was to condition the art produced.

Though Teige spent most of the early 1920s calling for 'the liquidation of art' (and the artist), early Poetism joyfully celebrated the imagination. The lyrical poets **Jaroslav**

Seifert (1901–86) and **Vítězslav Nezval** (1900–58) worked on 'film poems'; the sculptor **Zdeněk Pěsánek** (1896–1965) created visual pianos and perhaps the world's first neon fountain; one of the group's most common forms of art was the collage, or 'pictorial poem'. The group took the view that photography would replace the bourgeois art of painting, though its only full-time photographer was **Jaroslav Rössler** (b. 1902). Two other photographers emerged during the 1920s, **Jaromír Funke** (1896–1945) and **Josef Sudek** (1896–1976). The group approved of cinema's popular non-élitism, and Devětsil also set up the **Liberated Theatre** in 1926. Devětsil had interests in common with French Surrealism, and the darker questions raised by Surrealism began to make inroads into the happy-go-lucky early Poetism of painters like **Toyen** (Marie Čermínová) (1902–80) and **Jindřich Štyrský** (1899–1942). Another Devětsil member, **Josef Šíma** (1891–1971), settled in Paris in 1921, and became a contact between the two movements. In 1932, one of the first international exhibitions of Surrealist art was held in Prague and in 1934 the **Prague Surrealist Group** was established.

Between the wars, internationalism and ideology led Prague's architects towards **constructivism** and **functionalism**. The first claimed that mass production and modern materials were beautiful; the second theoretically did not care, so long as a building served its purpose. By the 1930s the aesthetic differences, although still loudly argued over, were little more than nuances. Already primed by Art Nouveau, Prague hurled itself into a brave new world of glass and concrete. In 1924, Teige organized Czech participation in the first international **Bauhaus** exhibition and Adolf Loos built his **Villa Müller** on the outskirts of the capital. Standing outside any movement was radical Slovenian architect, **Jože Plečnik** (1872–1957), who modernized the castle and designed the Church of the Sacred Heart, one of the most extraordinary religious buildings of the 20th century.

From Nazism to Normalization

The Nazis rolled into town in March 1939 and Prague's cultural life was crushed. Then, three years after liberation, another tyranny moved in. With the accession of the Communists in 1948, creativity was sacrificed on the altar of **Socialist Realism**. A monolithic, officially controlled programme, extolling class struggle and socialist progress, it produced monumental buildings, and Stakhanovite murals and sculptures.

After Stalin's death, cultural constraints were slowly eased. The **Surrealist movement** whooped into life again in the late 1950s. Important artists were **Mikuláš Medek** (1926–74), **Václav Tikal** and, most impressive of all, **Jiří Kolář**, who experimented with collage assemblages of image and word. In 1965, Prague's students elected Beat poet **Allen Ginsberg** as their king and carried him shoulder-high up Wenceslas Square. By 1968, the mildly insane **Milan Knížák** was slaughtering chickens to loud rock music.

The party ended on the night of 21 August 1968 as 200,000 Warsaw Pact troops turned the Prague Spring into winter. Potential centres of ideological resistance, such as theatre companies and the Writers' Union, were dissolved, and artists who had supported the uprising were anathematized. Intellectuals and artists found work as taxi-drivers, or found fame abroad. The most courageous signed the **Charter 77** manifesto.

Resurrection

Since 1989, some of the artists who left after 1968 have returned. Foreign influences pour in, and the city is engulfed by aesthetic debates that began in the West years ago, such as where to draw the line between erotica and porn – Czech art often has an unselfconscious lasciviousness that offends Western eyes. The work of photographer **Jan Saudek**, known in the West for his portraiture, ranges from tender kisses to spanking scenarios with uniformed girls.

Note also **David Černý**, who has painted a tank pink, sprayed a Trabant gold, and put up anonymous posters in London to advertise a day of random killing. His latest unsettling gag is to send a fleet of creepy giant babies crawling up the TV tower in **Žižkov**.

The architecture of Prague also endures. The most striking contemporary building is the **Tančící Dům** (Dancing House), by the Canadian-born American **Frank O. Gehry** and Czech **Vlado Milunič** (*see* p.160). Over the last few years, there has also been a flurry of renovation, and some of the city's loveliest monuments have been restored to their former opulence. The developers are moving in, but the ancient stone jigsaw of the centre will survive. Even the Communists did not dare to tamper with that.

Around the City

Old Town (Staré Město)

Founded and fortified in the 13th century, the Old Town is the central European fantasy in microcosm, a topsy-turvy world of Baroque colour and Gothic gloom, public executions, legends and wonder-working rabbis. A stroll along alleys near the stone Charles Bridge will lead you though centuries of legend and history. You'll sometimes feel you have stepped back amid the pied pipers and magical playgrounds of a half-forgotten childhood dream. The eastern part of Staré Město takes you into the very heart of medieval Prague – Staroměstské náměstí (the Old Town Square), with the town hall granted to Prague's burghers in the 13th century and the clockwork marionettes of its astronomical clock that have relentlessly counted out Prague's time for five centuries. The modernized façades of the squares now pay lip-service to the 21st century, but the streets around remain a labyrinth; though they are swamped by tourists, negotiating the maze will at the very least be enjoyable.

Charles Bridge (Karlův Most)

For centuries the city's energy has squeezed through the narrow channel of Charles Bridge and, although the coronation processions and fairs of yesteryear have given way to endless troupes of guided tourists, it remains Prague's jugular vein.

There was a wooden way across the river more than 1,000 years ago, if Cosmas the chronicler is to be believed: an incidental detail of his account of the murder of St Wenceslas is that the bridge was damaged in 932, requiring a spot of Divine

Intervention to fly the pallbearers across. Nothing is left of that structure, but remnants of the Judith Bridge, built in 1158, survive in the piers of the present work. The Judith Bridge was destroyed by floods in 1342, but the civic pride of Charles IV, who ascended the throne four years later, ensured that Prague didn't remain bridge-less for long. Astrologers were asked to find a suitably auspicious celestial configuration, and in 1357 Charles' architect, 27-year-old Peter Parléř, got to work. Construction was completed in the early 1400s and, for more than 400 years, the bridge was Prague's only river crossing. This feat of medieval engineering has survived centuries of deluges and, until 1950, the trundle of motor traffic.

Old Town Bridge Tower (Staroměstská Mostecká Věž)

Open April–May daily 10–7; June–Sept daily 10–10; Nov–Feb daily 10–5; Mar daily 10–6; adm

Designed by Peter Parléř and completed during the reign of Wenceslas IV, the titanic Old Town Bridge Tower is part of the city's fortification walls, and has had both symbolic and practical functions. After the execution of Bohemian nationalists in 1620, 10 heads hung putrefying from its first floor for a decade. In 1648 the final hours of the Thirty Years' War raged around the tower, when Sweden's army went on a last-minute looting spree and the Old Town was saved by a motley alliance of bearded students and Prague Jews. A Europe-wide peace had been negotiated, but another truce was clearly necessary. It was signed on the middle of the bridge, in a wooden cabin partitioned to keep the factions from each others' throats. That battle destroyed most of the decoration on the western façade of the tower. The east still has its orig-inal 14th-century decoration, with sculptures of SS Adalbert and Procopius at the top, Wenceslas IV and Charles IV enthroned below, and St Vitus in the centre.

Admission includes entrance to a small exhibition of old musical instruments, on two floors. The view along the bridge from the first floor is impressive: so much so that the Communist secret police used to sit here and point eavesdropping equip-ment and lenses at suspicious conversationalists down below.

Sculptures on the Bridge

The stark structure of the bridge is perfectly complemented by the 30 sculptures that now line it. The 14th century saw a simple wooden crucifix placed on the bridge; the Counter-Reformation knew a propaganda opportunity when it saw one and, during the late 1600s and early 1700s, an entire avenue of Baroque saints was added, inspired by Bernini's 1688 work on the Ponte Sant'Angelo in Rome. The hapless commuters of Prague were a captive audience to what would then have been an awesome array of gesticulating saints. Many of the works have now been replaced by copies to protect the originals from pollution, and there is some lifeless neo-Gothic statuary from the 19th century, but the overall effect of the sculpture is still superb.

The oldest work is the bronze *Crucifixion* (1657), third on your right going east to west, flanked by 19th-century works. The Hebrew inscription on the statue was the contribution of an outspoken Jew, who wandered past in 1695 muttering blas-phemies. The fifth statue on your left shows **St Francis Xavier** being borne aloft by grateful bearers. It's a copy of a 1711 work by F. M. Brokof which was swept away by a flood in 1890. Ignatius used to stand on the opposite side of the bridge; after sinking in 1890, he was replaced by the youngest statue here, Karel Dvořák's 1938 sculpture of **SS Cyril and Methodius**.

About halfway across on the right there is said to be a small bronze **Lorraine Cross** embedded in the wall. According to rumour, the Dalai Lama recognized this point as the centre of the universe during his visit to Prague in 1990. It also marks the spot where **St John Nepomuk** was hurled into the river. If you can find it, put your hand on it, make a wish and then go to his statue, the eighth on the right. John was a vicar-general of Prague who was put in a sack and dropped into the Vltava in 1383 by Wenceslas IV. He will get you across any bridge safely, despite his own misfortune, and he's the saint to turn to if you're wrongly accused.

Further along, **SS Vincent Ferrer and Procopius** deserve a mention: among the feats noted on their statue are the salvation of 100,000 souls, the conversion of 2,500 Jews, 70 exorcisms and 40 resurrections. A downcast devil, Turk and Jew support the saints. If you look across the bridge here, you'll see the statue of **Bruncvík**, a chivalrous character linked to the legend of Roland – a sanguinary epic of crusading Christianity.

Of the petrified melodramas that remain, take a look at Matthias Braun's **St Luitgard**. Generally agreed to be the best-crafted sculpture on the bridge, it shows Christ letting the blind saint nuzzle His wounds, a vision she enjoyed late one night. Two statues along is F. M. Brokof's pantomime-like tribute to the **Trinitarian Order**, established for the age-old purpose of ransoming Christian hostages from infidel clutches. The founders of the Order stand above a little grotto full of captives, guarded by a pot-bellied pasha and a mad dog.

The western end of the bridge is punctuated by the **Malá Strana Bridge Tower**, which was built in the early 1400s, and the stumpy **Judith Tower**, which despite its Renaissance decoration belonged to the 12th-century predecessor of the Charles Bridge (*open April–Oct daily 10–6; adm*). The inseparable duo, wearing tiled top hats and forming the parapet and arch into Malá Strana, frame St Nicholas' Church, forming one of the most tempting photo-opportunities in Prague.

Mariánské Square (Mariánské Náměstí)

Despite the magnificence of the buildings which border it, Mariánské Square, just north of Karlova up Seminářská, is now sadly little more than an overgrown passage with a car park in the middle. On the eastern side is Prague's modern **Town Hall**. The façade and roof are decorated with relaxed nudes peering down at the street, and reliefs representing various virtues.

The **Clementinum** (*Mariánské náměstí 5, Seminářská 1, t 221 663 111; Baroque Library and Astronomical Tower open Tues–Sun 10–7, Mon 2–7*) dominates the western side of the square. During the uneasy peace that preceded the Thirty Years' War (1618–48), the Clementinum became the nerve-centre of the Czech Counter-Reformation, relighting the Catholic flame in a city that had become 90 per cent Protestant. The Jesuit Order made up the Counter-Reformation's advance platoons. One of its most successful weapons was education. The Clementinum's success was such that, by the

17th century, non-Catholic families were queuing up to enrol their little ones. The college swallowed up its arch-rival, the Protestant Carolinum in 1622, and only in 1773 did it lose its religious nature. It now lives on as the **Czech State Library**.

The Jesuits took their architecture seriously too. They moved into this site in 1556, but the present complex was built in protracted stages between 1653 and 1723, on the site of 30-odd houses, three churches, 10 courtyards and several gardens. Just two sections are open to the public – the Baroque Great Library and the Astronomical Tower, both handsomely restored in 2000. On display for visitors are some of the oldest illuminated manuscripts in the library's collection, a selection of Baroque astronomical instruments, and a pair of intriguing clocks made by Jan Klein, a maths teacher at the Clementinum. His clocks illustrate the contemporary dithering over the positioning of the earth in the heavens: on the left, the earth sits firmly at the centre of the universe, while, on the right, it circles the sun as Copernicus insisted.

A step away is the **Great Library**, the grandest of all the Halls on the upper floor and the only one open to the public. It was designed by Kaňker in 1727, and its cherub-topped rococo bookshelves are overlooked by an enormous fresco in three parts. In the centre is a spectacular collection of Baroque globes. The **Astronomical Tower** at the very centre of the complex was the last part to be built (1721–3, remodelled in 1749). It was the college **Observatory** right up until 1928. Creak up the original wooden staircase to see the measuring device for establishing noon; light pierces through a tiny hole in the wall, and the narrow beam strikes a paved section in the wooden flooring. Kilian Dienzenhofer designed the **Chapel of Mirrors** in 1724, fusing glass and stucco decoration in a shimmering display.

The **Clam-Gallas Palace** (Clam-Gallasův Palác) at Husova 20 contains the city archives and is only open to visitors for concerts. Its colossal atlantes, built in 1713–19, were designed by one of the masters of Austrian Baroque, J. B. Fischer von Erlach.

The ground floor of Franz Kafka's birthplace in U Radnice was converted into the **Expozice Franze Kafky** in 1991, with a few photos and a large selection of souvenir booklets.

South of Mariánské Square

Řetězová, a narrow cobbled alley of 18th-century cottages, is home to the Renaissance building of the **House of the Lords of Kunštát and Poděbrady** (Dům pánů z Kunštátu a Poděbrad; *Řetězová 3, t 224 212 299, ext. 22; open May–Sept Tues–Sun 10–6, closed Mon; adm*), which stands over part of an even older Prague. The ground floor (the first floor of a buried Romanesque building) has a permanent display devoted to George of Poděbrady, who lived here until promoted to king in 1458. At the end of the main room, a staircase descends to the damp odours and street level of 13th-century Prague.

With panache, the Bohemians centred the **Bethlehem Chapel** (Betlémská Kaple; *Betlémské náměstí, t 224 248 595; open April–Oct daily 9–6, Nov–Mar daily 9–5; adm*) to the south around the pulpit rather than the altar; and with the Protestant preference for scripture to saints, they, like Milíč, thumbed the Bible for a name. Jan Hus began preaching in the chapel in 1402, the same year that he became rector of the

Jan Hus

Heretical Hus was burned alive in 1415. His death marked the beginning of decades of war in Bohemia. Two centuries later, his Protestant heirs were eradicated at the Battle of the White Mountain (*see* pp.110–11) but, although the population reverted in droves, Hus never lost his position as the pre-eminent symbol of Czech nationalism. In 1900, as the Austro-Hungarian empire doddered towards extinction, Prague's authorities commissioned a monument to their man, in preparation for the 500th anniversary of his martyrdom. The artist chosen was Ladislav Šaloun, whose lifelong attachment to Art Nouveau techniques (until 1946) placed him outside both the mainstream and the avant-garde of Czech sculpture. When this sculpture was unveiled in 1915, it was predictably showered with abuse. It shows Hus flowing from the bronze base, standing tall between two groups representing the crushed and the defiant. Some complained that Šaloun had created a sprawling mess, by letting his fascination with light-effects run away with him; others found the very idea of allegory too disrespectful, although it's doubtful that they would have preferred Hus to be portrayed as the bald midget that he is thought to have been.

Carolinum. His sermons filled the 3,000-capacity chapel, which set alarm bells ringing in the Church. Prague's archbishop warned him to pipe down; Hus was excommunicated and an exasperated pope finally roasted him in 1415. The second Vatican Council voided the sentence in 1965. The building is a modern copy of the original, which was all but demolished in 1786, and there's now little to see inside other than daubed sermons preserved on three walls.

Old Town Square (Staroměstské Náměstí)

The Old Town Square is the Brothers Grimm in stone: Gothic towers, a sparkling white church and a pastel wave of pink and blue Baroque rooftops. It is the strolling intersection of Staré Město, and the perfect spot to soak up rays, history and a beer on a summer's day. The best place for an overview is from the steps of the **Monument to Jan Hus**. A bronze line in front of the sculpture marks Prague's former meridian: a Marian column, erected in 1649 to celebrate the Bohemian Counter-Reformation, sent its midday shadow along here until it was toppled by a patriotic mob in 1918. With independence, Prague gave up the inconvenient tradition of calculating its own time.

The triangular junction known as the **Small Square** (**Malé Náměstí**), which leads into Staroměstské Náměstí, threw up some historical riddles in 1994, when workers stumbled on an 800-year-old cemetery. Archaeologists were drafted in to ponder the bones, and unearthed a village beneath the graveyard, only 15 years older. Nowadays, the square is dominated by more Aleš-inspired paintings on the 1890 neo-Renaissance **Rott Haus**, house of connoisseur, patriot and ironmonger Mr Rott (it is now a huge shop devoted to Bohemian glass). Legend has it that the three Rott sisters were, unbeknown to each other, simultaneously courted by the same man. He married them, murdered them and stole their fortunes – without anyone being any the wiser.

Old Town Hall (Staroměstská Radnice)

*Staroměstské náměstí 1, t 224 482 909; open April–Oct Tues–Sun 9–6,
Mon 11–6; Nov–Mar Tues–Sun 9–5, Mon 11–5; adm; guided tours available.*

The Staré Město had fortifications built and a royal charter in the mid-13th century, and Wenceslas II grudgingly let Praguers have a clerk in 1296; but when they asked for a town hall to put the clerk in, he put his foot down. The townspeople had to wait until 1338, when they were able to take advantage of blind King John of Luxembourg. The burghers bought a house and turned it into the tower – the beginning of the Town Hall. As the receipts poured in, they were slowly able to add all the buildings to the left. It was a piecemeal process, involving the destruction of spinners' sheds and the roofing-over of the lane to the goose market, but the maroon and white 18th-century façades – encrusted with Gothic and Renaissance survivals from earlier days – now house a single interior, stretching from the tower to the end of the block.

The town hall's pride and joy is its **astronomical clock** (Orloj; *the clock chimes daily on the hour between 9am and 9pm for a couple of minutes*). Prague woke up late to the idea of clocks – by the time this one was installed in 1410, every other major city in Europe had one – but they were still exotic devices, and the city's burghers were concerned that things should stay that way. Legend has it that when it was remodelled by a certain Master Hanuš in 1490, the Municipal Council took the precaution of blinding him to protect its copyright. A peeved Master Hanuš scaled the building, tossed a medieval spanner in the works, and promptly died. Prague's timepiece was out of joint for almost a century; but since 1572 it has ticked away without interruption, the occasional fire and artillery blitz notwithstanding.

Even into the 17th century, the connected notions of clocks, clockwork and perpetual motion were imbued with a mystery that is hard to imagine today. This one purports to tell the time, but that's only the beginning. Its astronomical symbols, pointers and interlocking circles also register the phases of the moon, the length of the day, the equinoxes, Babylonian time and the dates of innumerable mobile feasts. Every hour two cuckoo-clock windows open and statues of the 12 Apostles mince past while bony Death tinkles his bell. The great leveller is pooh-poohed by preening Vanity, and those bugbears of 15th-century Europe, the Turk and the Jew. The latter now lacks his beard and horns, and is politely referred to as Greed, having been sanitized following the Town Hall's bombardment in 1945. The post-Holocaust decision was understandable, but the paradoxical effect was to whitewash the bloody feature of central Europe's history that had just reached its culmination. A cock, and delighted children, screech when the ceremony is all over. The temporal theme is taken up by the painted calendar below the clock showing the monthly labours of rural folk.

The town hall's modern entrance is situated under the **Renaissance window** (1520). The Latin phrase means 'Prague, head of the kingdom', and was a motto extracted by the burghers from devil-may-care John of Luxembourg.

The small **Gothic chapel** on the first floor dates from 1381. A Nazi tank shelled it to smithereens at the height of the Prague Uprising, but it has been restored well. The chapel's main attraction is up on your right as you face the oriel: through a glass door, the figures of the 12 Apostles wait on the spokes of two wheels for their moment of glory. If your timing is right, you can be here to see the windows open and the figures twirl into life when the hour strikes.

From the chapel, begin the trek to the top of the **tower**, now made much easier by the construction of a glass lift – though the queues can be long enough for you to consider slogging up on foot. After gasping – and gasping – at the view, descend again for the guided tour of the **town hall's rooms**. The tour passes a **memorial cross** made from two charred wooden beams. At least 14 men died in the building during the Nazi assault; it was the headquarters of the committee that led the Prague Uprising. The resistance fighters holed themselves up in the network of late 12th-century **cellars**. The clammy warren comprises a number of halls, a well, and a dungeon for those women who were thought to talk too much.

The rest of the tour takes you under painted Renaissance joists on the first floor; on the second, faded Gothic murals and a turn-of-the-century drawing of Prague from Petřín Hill, minus the housing estates on today's horizon. The next two rooms contain four works by Václav Brožík (1851–1901), whose speciality was portraying turning-points of Bohemian history with a turgid solemnity. Until 1526, the country's king was chosen in the town hall, and *The Election of King George of Poděbrady* in the Assembly Room shows Hussite George being given the nod by the country's nobles in 1458. The equally monumental *Jan Hus's Trial at Constance* is one of several churned out by Brožík for the nationalist movement.

The **Old Council Chamber**, dating from about 1470, does most to conjure up the years when municipal powers were at their height. The haunting figure of Christ (c.1410) implores them in Latin to 'Judge Justly, Sons of Man'. The councillors found themselves at the receiving end of some rough justice in 1483, when a Hussite mob threw the Catholic mayor and several cronies out of the window, in the second of Prague's four defenestrations (*see* 'History'). The reformers then continued the 'good work' with a pogrom in the Jewish Quarter; eradicating Judaism was widely held to be a precondition of the Messiah's expected return in 1500. The scene of the defenestration is no longer known; the Renaissance window through which light now trickles into the chamber was installed 40 years later.

Other Buildings in the Square

The striking cream and brown façade of the **House at the Minute** (Dům u Minuty), adjacent to the Old Town Hall, fronts one of Franz Kafka's many childhood homes in Prague (1889–96). The only explanation that has been offered for its name is that 'minute' does not refer to time, but to the very small bric-a-brac that was once sold here. The *sgraffito* scenes that cover the building date from around 1610.

The dainty **Goltz-Kinský Palace** (Palác Goltz-Kinschych; *t 224 810 758, www.ngprague. cz; open Tues–Sun 10–6; adm*) dates from 1755–65, by which time Prague's Baroque frenzy had begun to exhaust itself. This is one of the best examples of Rococo archi-tecture in the city, with its frilly stucco garlands and pink and white façade. Kafka studied here from 1893 to 1901, and the family connection was resumed some years later when his father, no-nonsense Hermann, moved his haberdashery store into the ground floor. But its moment came in February 1948, when a vast crowd gathered in the square to hear Czechoslovakia's first Communist president, Klement Gottwald, roar from the balcony that the dictatorship of the proletariat had arrived. The gracious palace now hosts exhibitions of graphic art for the National Gallery.

The creamy façade of the **Stone Bell House** (Dům u Kamenného Zvonu; *t 224 827 526; open Tues–Sun 10–6; adm*), named after the stone bell set into the corner, belongs to the oldest intact Gothic house in Prague, built in the mid-13th century. Thorough remodellings after the late 1600s left it concealed until restorers in the 1960s realized what lay behind its unremarkable neo-Baroque façade. The onion-skins were peeled away, thousands of fragments pieced together or reconstructed and the house was opened to the public in 1986. It's now used for concerts and some of the city's best exhibitions of modern art, but may be closed if there's nothing on. The Gothic tower, fronting a Renaissance courtyard, is the richest part of the building, but you'll find fragments of murals, pointed doorways and ribbed vaults throughout. The most complete decoration is in the chapel to your right as you walk towards the courtyard, once entirely covered with murals of the *Passion* (*c*. 1310).

The 16th-century façade of the Týn School falls and rises in bulbous imitation of the **Týn church** (Kostel Panny Marie před Týnem) that fronts it. The church (*access in Celetná; open for Mass only, Mon–Fri 5.30pm, Sat 1pm, Sun 11.30am and 9pm*), with its multi-steepled towers bristling like Gothic missile batteries and dominating the square, was founded in 1385; it was a hub of Hussitism right up to the 1620 rout, when it was commandeered by the Jesuits.

Enter the church through the passage running from the vaulted arcade. After a fire in 1679 the central vault was rebuilt in Baroque style. The altars and decorations are also largely Baroque, but even more than in St James's (*see* p.128), they are swamped by the cavernous Gothic structure of the triple-naved church. At the end of the northern nave, past the 1493 stone baldachin (which now canopies a 19th-century altar) and the tombstone of the dwarf to your left, is a powerful Gothic *Calvary* of around 1410. From here, cross the central nave. Walk across the high altar and, on the pillar to your left, you'll find the **tomb of Tycho Brahe** (1546–1601), Emperor Rudolf II's imperial mathematician for two eventful years. The red marble relief is quite flattering, hardly hinting at the gold and silver nosepiece worn by the moustachioed Dane after he lost the original organ in a duel.

Near Brahe's tombstone, at the end of the southern nave, is the oldest font in Prague, a tin pot dating from 1414. The Gothic pulpit on the next pillar to the west dates from the 15th century, although the painting and canopy are 19th-century additions. It was from here that rabble-rousing preachers incited generations of congregations to sprees of destruction. Near the pulpit is the rich foliage and drapery of an early-16th century carving of Christ's baptism by Master I. P., an artist influenced by Dürer, with work in St Agnes' Convent (*see* p.136). The convent also holds the original Gothic **tympanum** from the arched portal on the flank of the church, by members of Peter Parléř's workshop. The one in place today, visible from around the corner on Týnská, is a copy.

The buildings lining the south side of the square are constructed over older subterranean houses. Almost all of them bear a painted or carved house sign: the **Štorch
House**, at No.16, has a swirling depiction of a prissy St Wenceslas on horseback,
painted at the end of the 19th century. The **House at the Stone Ram**, at No.17, is older,
more discreet but no less whimsical with a delicate carving of a miniature shep-
herdess dwarfed by an enormous ram.

Estates Theatre (Stavovské Divadlo)

Ovocný trh 1, t 224 215 001; open for performances only.

The pediment and pillars of the theatre flow from the body of the building in
concave curves, with all the elegance of neoclassical architecture at its best. It was a
bastion of German opera for 150 years until 1945, and its early history has made it a
minor place of pilgrimage among Mozart groupies for two centuries. In 1786, it saw a
performance of Mozart's *The Marriage of Figaro*, which had been panned by the
snooty Viennese, but Prague's critics could not praise too highly. Wolfgang came to
town and was fêted by the city's bourgeoisie and nobility. The management knew a
box-office success when it heard one and collared the composer. Commissioned to
write another opera, he returned with the score of *Don Giovanni*, which he conducted
here for the first time in October 1787, and the theatre's place in musical history
was assured.

Also on this square is the **Carolinum** (Karolinum), the core of the Charles University,
founded by Emperor Charles IV in 1348. It was central Europe's first university, as
Prague's tourist brochures proudly state, and the 35th in the rest of the Continent, as
they generally forget to say.

Further East: Celetná

Celetná is one of the oldest streets in Prague. Behind the Baroque and rococo
façades are remnants of earlier Gothic buildings and, below them, cellars that were
once ground floors, buried along with the rest of the capital during the drastic flood-
prevention programme of the late 13th century. Nowadays, it is a busy shopping
street, packed with smart boutiques and Bohemian crystal outlets.

Where Celetná meets Ovocný trh is the **House of the Black Madonna** (U černé
Matky boží; *Celetná 3; open Tues–Sun 10–6; adm*), a 20th-century Cubist curiosity
housing temporary exhibitions and a permanent collection of Czech Cubist art (sadly
one of the least exciting collections in Prague). It's worth trying to sneak past the
ticket office, however, for a quick glimpse of its keyhole staircase. Designed by Josef
Gočár, and built in 1911–12, the building is recognizable by the caged Virgin suspended
above the portals, a 16th-century remnant of an earlier house on the site. Black
Madonnas have long been a popular sideline of the Marian cult in Catholic Europe.

Just north of Celetná, off Štupartská, is **Týn Court**, a handsome, arcaded courtyard.
The name 'Týn' comes from the same Germanic root as the English 'town'; this courtyard, dating from the 11th century, was the enclave of the eastern traders and formed
one of the first settlements on the right bank of the Vltava. It had everything: church,

inn, and even a hospice in which moribund merchants could expire in comfort. The traders abandoned it in the late 1500s and now the courtyard has emerged from an expensive renovation with a stack of chichi shops, terrace cafés and restaurants. It is surrounded by buildings from several centuries, but the loveliest is undoubtedly the graceful **Granovský House**, built by the customs officer of Týn in 1560.

St James's Church (Kostel sv. Jakub)

Malá štupartská, t 224 828 816; open Mon–Sat 9.30–12.15 and 2–4, Sun 9.30–12 and 2–6.

The nearby St James's Church), founded in 1374, escaped the overkill that turned some of Prague's churches into grotesqueries during the Counter-Reformation. Its interior is now one of the most elegant in the city. Although the Gothic proportions of the hall-church keep the 21 Baroque altars firmly under control, the splendid tableau of the **Tomb of Count Jan Václav Vratislav of Mitrovice** (1714–16) tries its hardest to break free, at the far end of the northern aisle. Mitrovice was imperial chancellor of Bohemia at a time of strict control from Vienna, when the most important qualifications for the job were dull ambition and knee-jerk reflexes. He may have slipped out of the history books, but when the daunting late Baroque duo of Vienna's J. B. Fischer von Erlach and Prague's F. M. Brokof set to work on this monument, his posthumous fate was clearly seen in more elevated terms.

Municipal House (Obecní Dům)

Náměstí Republiky 5, t 222 002 100, www.obecni-dum.cz; open daily 10–6; guided tours in English of the Smetana Hall and main rooms daily every 2hrs in summer, weekends only in winter; adm.

The Municipal House, with exhibition halls and auditorium, is an Art Nouveau masterpiece. The ornate façade, built between 1906 and 1911, is a successful contribution to Czech national revival. Scores of Prague artists and architects contributed, notably Mucha, and the effect is a cacophonous *charivari* rather than a tight symphony in the new style. It is a forest of crystal and mirrors, whiplash curves, organic excrescences and sensual homages to Czechdom and civic virtue. It now hosts exhibitions of all things Art Nouveau, from poster art to photography.

A wander around the staircase between the ground-floor restaurant, the elegant *kavárna* (café) and the basement bars is free and gives a heady sense of the opulence of the age. But to see most of the interior, finally restored to its original lustre in 1997, you'll have to join a tour, starting with the massive cloakroom (*šatna*). Rising through two storeys at the core of the building is the **Smetana Hall**. Just off the Hall is the glittering **Confectioner's Room** (*cukrárna*), complete with gilded display cases and an original samovar (1912), still gracefully dispensing coffee. The **Slovatsky Room** has an Art Nouveau aquarium encrusted with brass snails, and the Turkish delights of the **Oriental Hall** are among the best-preserved in the building. The sumptuous Art Deco **Gregr Hall** is still used for chamber concerts and dances. In the circular **Mayoral Hall** (Sál Primátorský) are violet windows, and paintings by Mucha – sombre late works.

Powder Gate (Prašná Brána)

Originally one of the gates into the Staré Město, this Gothic hulk (*Na příkopě; open April–Oct daily 10–6; adm*) is now marooned in a 20th-century sea. Tethered by a small bridge to the neighbouring Municipal House and hemmed in by grim banks and a shiny shoe shop, it's a stately but forlorn reminder of a glory that never was. As long ago as the 11th century, traders with turbans, pelts, spices and slaves would roll into Prague from the east through a gateway here. Although this tower was begun in 1475 amid general festivities and merriment, it was rapidly abandoned by the mercurial Hussites. Later, it was given a temporary roof, a use (gunpowder storage) and an unimaginative name. It was bombarded by Frederick the Great, and emerged in an even sorrier state than before. It was finally put out of its misery by the zealous neo-Gothic touch of the Czech Josef Mocker; the ornate decoration of the façade, and much of the interior, is his work (1875–86).

Josefov

With its central location and august feel, post-Communist Josefov has at last become the bourgeois district of boulevards and avenues that its Paris-inspired designers always wanted it to be. But as you walk through the quiet streets, under the façades of fantastic neo-Gothic strongholds and Art Nouveau citadels, you can't help but hear whispers from the past. You'll shadow the life of the last Jewish storyteller of Prague, Franz Kafka, and then wander among the synagogues and ancient cemetery of Prague's former Jewish ghetto. Alongside those parts of it that still stand, there are hundreds of passageways and rooms, silent oubliettes and medieval refuges. Now, however, they form the cellars of the airline offices, French *parfumiers* and antique stores that have taken over the area. Elsewhere in Prague, history reeks from every stone, but in the Jewish Quarter, it's the transformation that speaks.

Jewish Museum (Židovské Muzeum)

The Jewish Museum comprises six major sights in the former Jewish Ghetto: the Maisel Synagogue, the Spanish Synagogue, the Pinkas Synagogue, the old Jewish Cemetery, the Klausen Synagogue, and the Ceremonial Hall, t 224 819 456, f 223 819 458, www.jewishmuseum.cz. Open Sun–Fri except Jewish holidays, April–Oct 9–6; Nov–Mar 9–4.30; adm, tickets sold at the Pinkas Synagogue and next to the Klausen Synagogue. Reserve in advance in summer.

Pinkas Synagogue (Pinkasova Synagóga)

The present building of the Pinkas Synagogue stands over the 11th-century foundations of what may have been the first synagogue in Prague, at the southern edge of the cemetery. Rabbi Pinkas began the present building on this site in 1479, and the first Jews of Prague may have worshipped on this spot. After the Second World War the synagogue was chosen to house the Czech monument to the victims of the

The Jewish Ghetto

No one knows when the first Jews came to Prague. Historical sources suggest that it was probably in the 10th century, and that Jews first lived in two separate communities on either side of the river. By the mid-13th century, however, an unhappy set of events had combined to create a single community here: Přemysl Otakar II wanted the left bank for his new town of Malá Strana; Staré Město was fortified; and, most crucially, in 1179 the Church had announced that Christians should avoid touching Jews, ideally by building a moat or a wall around them. Another set of walls was built within the Staré Město and, three centuries before the word was coined in Venice, Prague Jews began life in the ghetto.

The daily routine was much the same as that of Jews elsewhere in central Europe: pogroms, ritual murder allegations, and occasional banishments from the land. By day movement was free, but as the sun set, the portcullis was lowered. The gates would be locked throughout the Easter/Passover flashpoint. Jews didn't mind, as it kept out the crowds eager to avenge Jesus on Good Friday, but the authorities' concerns were no different from those of the mob. Medieval Christendom assumed that the Passover lamb was a cunning codeword for Christ and that, unless the gates were locked, Christian babies and virgins would end up on a Passover plate.

During the 16th century, the ghetto became a vortex of mysticism as interest in the kabbalah grew among both Jews and Christians throughout Europe. The mysterious cabalistic tradition – handed down orally from Adam – was reflected in the intellectual questing of Rudolf II's court; the exchange of cryptic data between rabbis and castle scholars was legendary. The period was to inspire a powerful image of the ghetto as a dank universe of miracles and poverty, its 7,000 inhabitants living cheek-by-jowl in a labyrinth of cramped lanes, subterranean passages and hypertrophied buildings. There's more than a little truth to the picture, but although the ghetto was sealed, it wasn't all poor. The richest man in Rudolfine Prague was Jewish.

In 1784, under Emperor Josef II, the gates were thrown open. Josef, enlightened despot that he was, was being liberal only in an academic sense. The idea was to wipe the Jews out as an independent community: the use of Hebrew or Yiddish in business was prohibited, and separate schools were banned. That didn't stop him being honoured after 1848, when Jews were finally granted civil rights. The ghetto was formally incorporated into Prague in 1850 and renamed Josefov. Integration proceeded apace: rich Jews moved out, poor Christians moved in. By the end of the 19th century, the district was a set of 288 stinking slums, brothels and bars, a breeding ground for typhoid and tuberculosis. The authorities chose to destroy the buildings, along with an irreplaceable part of Europe's history. Broad streets, crowded with turn-of-the-century mansions, now stand over winding medieval alleys. Of the old ghetto, only six synagogues, the town hall and the cemetery were spared, and survive thanks to Hitler's macabre decision that they would house a postwar 'Exotic Museum of an Extinct Race'. Of the Jews themselves, some 80,000 of the 90,000 who remained in Bohemia and Moravia in March 1939 were killed.

In 1994 the State, which had taken over the Nazi collection after the war, finally relinquished control and the new Jewish Museum was opened by President Havel.

Holocaust: under the gilded ribs of the brick-red vault were listed the names of each of the 77,297 Czech Jews who died at Nazi hands. The synagogue was reopened in 1991, after being closed for over 20 years of so-called restoration, during which the Communist authorities allowed the memorial to crumble into indecipherability. They excused themselves by blaming rising damp. As you gaze at the thousands of names, now repainted, only their tragedy can dwarf the scale of that insult.

Upstairs is a heart-rending permanent exhibition of children's drawings from the camp at Terezín. Of the 8,000 children who were sent to the concentration camps further east, only 242 survived the war.

Old Jewish Cemetery (Starý Židovský Hřbitov)

Entrance through Pinkas Synagogue.

Known in Hebrew as **Beth-Chajim**, or the House of Life, this Jewish graveyard is the second oldest in Europe and is an astonishing sight: the flash of a lost world that imprints itself on your memory. For more than three centuries until 1787 it was the only burial ground the Jews were permitted, its elder trees the only patch of green behind the ghetto walls. As space ran out, it was covered with earth, older gravestones were raised, and a new layer of burials was begun. Subsidence has turned the graveyard into a forest of some 12,000 madly teetering tombstones. Many are half-interred themselves; many have migrated far from the person they commemorate; and as you walk through, there are thought to be some 20,000 people under your feet, buried in up to 12 subterranean storeys. Tens of thousands of people now visit annually, and for many reasons – including religious sensibilities and the fact that the cemetery was being padded down by a millimetre each year – walking routes have now been marked out.

The oldest known plot is that of poet **Avigdor Kara**, dating from 1439. In 1389, Kara lived through and lamented the most vicious pogrom in Prague's history, in which 3,000 were massacred: more than half the ghetto's inhabitants. His original gravestone, now in the Maisel Synagogue, has been replaced by a copy which you'll find on the path running along the eastern wall of the cemetery.

Along the western wall of the cemetery, near the Pinkas Synagogue, is the grave of **Rabbi David Oppenheim** (1664–1736), whose 5,000-volume library went on a tour across Europe, making it to Oxford's Bodleian in 1829 as the Oppenheimer Collection.

Just as you emerge from the Pinkas Synagogue courtyard into the cemetery, you can find the grand tomb of **Mordechai Maisel** (1528–1601), the mayor of the ghetto during the reign of Rudolf II. Maisel had to wear a yellow wheel and high hat like any Jew in Rudolfine Prague (badge and hat were an intermittent requirement throughout the ghetto's history) but he died one of the wealthiest men in Europe.

The best-known of all the cemetery's occupants, the subject of tales that are still told to awestruck New York children, is **Rabbi Loew ben Bezalel** (1512–1609). His tomb, covered in pebbles, is along the western wall, opposite the entrance gate. Loew, born in either Poznan or Worms, was one of the leading scholars of 16th-century Jewry. Most of his life was spent in Prague and, in 1597, he took over as chief rabbi of the ghetto; by the time of his death, he was already a legend (*see* box overleaf). His powers apparently extended even beyond the grave: he is surrounded by 30 faithful disciples, among whom is his grandson Samuel. Solemn Samuel set his heart on being buried next to his grandfather; Loew vowed that he wouldn't be disappointed. Bungling ghetto authorities filled the precious plot with another lucky corpse but, dead though he was, Loew had not forgotten. When Samuel expired, the rabbi and his sepulchre budged a couple of feet. Samuel's grave is the thin one on the left.

Ceremonial Hall (Obřadní Síň)

Entrance at exit of Old Jewish Cemetery, on U Starého Hřbitova.

The crooked little neo-Romanesque building squatting by the cemetery was built in the early 1900s for the Prague Burial Society Hevrah Kaddishah (founded in 1564). The Jewish Museum uses each of its exhibition spaces to explain a different area of Jewish life and customs. Here, the rites and rituals of Jewish burials are expounded with slightly disconcerting matter-of-factness. Plain white kittels (shrouds), tools for cleaning the nails and hair of the newly dead are laid out, along with explanations of various Jewish customs.

Klausen Synagogue (Klausová Synagoga)

Entrance by the exit gates for the Old Jewish Cemetery, on U Starého Hřbitova.

The late 17th-century synagogue, remodelled in 1884, was built on the site of a mess of schools and prayer halls. Rabbi Loew taught in an older building. The synagogue now houses exhibits devoted to Jewish customs and traditions in daily life.

Maisel Synagogue (Maiselova Synagoga)

The Maisel Synagogue was another of the mayor's gifts to the ghetto, but it was dully remodelled in neo-Gothic style at the end of the last century. The hall contains an exhibition devoted to the history of Jews in Bohemia from the 10th to the 18th century, including a spectacular silver collection.

Spanish Synagogue (Španělská Synagoga)

The Spanish Synagogue, on the corner of Široká and Dušni, is the last of the synagogues to survive the great tidying-up of 1897–1917; three were destroyed, along with some 30 smaller prayer halls. Its arabesques and keyhole-shaped windows are the last reminder of the Sephardic Jews who settled in this part of the Staré Město after their mass expulsion from Spain at the end of the 15th century. They commandeered an ancient synagogue on the site, but this neo-Moorish structure dates from the end of the last century. It has been magnificently restored, and the extravagant gilding which covers every inch now glimmers once again. It contains a permanent exhibition devoted to the history of Czech Jews from the late 18th century to 1945, including a small exhibit devoted to Kafka and the Prague Circle – pictures, journals and mementos of the famous story-teller and his friends.

The Legendary Rabbi Loew

Every community mythologizes its history, but with the legendary Rabbi Loew, Prague's Jews personified it. The legends begin on a touching note. When young Loew arrived in the capital, he was smitten by Pearl, daughter of one Reb Schmelke, who promptly went bankrupt. Loew was so in love that he agreed to wait until the dowry could be raised. Impetuous it may have been, but it was only 10 years before Reb Schmelke was back on his feet, thanks to a bag of gold that a contemptuous cavalier tossed at Pearl as he stole a loaf of bread. Loew, by now steeped in the Talmud, declared that that had been no ordinary horseman, but Elijah. The stage was set for an exceptional life.

Certain themes run through all the tales. The ghetto is under constant threat from Christians, the wickedest of whom is Brother Thaddeus, whose very mention brings a hiss to the throat. There is also the occasional good goy, most notably the weak but fundamentally sympathetic Emperor Rudolf. Pulling the strings together is mild-mannered Rabbi Loew, who checks Brother Thaddeus at every turn, dares to reveal to the emperor that his real mother was Jewish, and exchanges tips with other super-rabbis across Europe in his dreams. On the innumerable occasions that Rudolf begs him for help, the rabbi rescues him from jail, dethrones an impostor and overturns expulsion edicts. When a jealous flunky persuades the vacillating emperor to order Loew to hold a banquet, the scholar transports a shimmering palace from a distant land into his humble ghetto abode; and to the now jovial Rudolf II's uproarious laughter, the luckless lackey pockets a goblet and is rooted to his seat.

The legend now inextricably linked to Loew is that of the *golem*, or artificial man. The word, meaning 'unformed substance' (or 'unmarried woman') in Hebrew, is first found in Psalms 139:16. The idea that humanity could create life comes from the mystical cabalistic tradition that each mortal contains a spark of the divine. Jewish history is littered with pre-Loewian *golems*, but Rabbi Loew's has become the most famous, turned into a German silent film (1920), a French talkie (1937) and a tale to alarm good Jewish boys and girls. It all began while Loew communed with the cosmos one night. He was warned that danger loomed and told to make a *golem*, pronto. With his two youthful rabbi sidekicks, he hurried to the banks of the Vltava and built a man out of mud, walked around it several times and then placed the unknown name of God (the *shem*) in its mouth. 'Joseph Golem' was born. His adventures are laced with slapstick ghetto humour, but most are of a grimly heroic nature. Joseph once rescues a girl from being forcibly baptized and, when the community is on trial for ritual murder, he arrives with the exonerating evidence just as the verdict is to be announced.

Joseph was eventually laid to rest in the roof of Prague's Old-New Synagogue. The annihilation of the capital's Jews gave rise to the last *golem* legend. It had been said that he would return if needed, but as the Nazi cattle trains filled and emptied, those Jews who remained declared that he had died forever. It sounds likely, but Praguers still claim that on stormy nights, Joseph's footsteps can be heard on those streets of the ancient ghetto that survive.

Old-New Synagogue (Staronová Synagoga)

On the corner of Pařížská and Červená; open Sun–Thurs 9.30–5, Fri 9.30–2; adm; tickets (Jewish Museum sites not included) can be bought at the Jewish Museum gift and bookshop in the Jewish Town Hall, opposite its entrance. Men are required to cover their heads – a yarmulke will be provided.

One of the oldest functioning synagogues to survive in Europe, the Old-New Synagogue is still used today by Prague's Orthodox community. There are two explanations for the synagogue's name. The more prosaic offering is that it was coined when the building was newly constructed on an older synagogue, but Jewish legend springs to the rescue with the claim that *alt-neu* ('old-new' in German) is actually a corruption of *al-tenai*, or 'with reservation' in Hebrew. Angels and/or outriders of the Diaspora are said to have built the synagogue from the rubble of the last Temple in Jerusalem, which they carried over in about AD 135. The name stands as a reminder that when the Messiah finally arrives, Prague's Jews have to take it back.

Unless the legend is true, the synagogue appeared around 1270. The date was about 10 years before the level of the Staré Město began to be raised and, as you enter, you sink several feet to the level of (not quite) antediluvian Prague. The first chamber is the vestibule, and through the door on your left is the section where women are segregated during services. The gorgeous Gothic **tympanum** over the portal, a stylized vine, is divided into sections that represent the 12 tribes of Israel and the three continents of the world then known to Europe. The splayed chinks of light, and the pillar supports, show how much the synagogue owed to Romanesque building techniques; but the vaulted naves, and the slenderness of the octagonal pillars themselves, represent the beginnings of Gothic architecture in Prague.

In the centre is the *almemar* (pulpit), surrounded by a 15th-century wrought-iron grille. Rabbi Loew apparently fought his final and most heroic battle here when, alerted by a dream, he hurried to the darkened synagogue and found an apparition waving swords, dripping with gore and ticking off a list of all Prague's Jews. Ninety-six-year-old Loew realized that this was Pogrom personified, and lunged for the beast. He ripped the scroll from Death's bloody grip, saved the ghetto from extinction, and missed only a scrap containing his name.

On the eastern wall is a screen covering the Torah (the scrolls containing the Pentateuch – the first five books of the Old Testament), in front of which are four messy cushions, where the rabbi used to circumcise wailing infants. The Hebrew psalms on the walls date from 1618 and were recovered in the 1960s, after the neo-Gothic restorer Josef Mocker (whose aesthetic sensitivities often recall those of the Communists) had obliterated them during restoration in 1883. Among the other features that ham-fisted Mocker restored to oblivion were the bloodstains of those who barricaded themselves in the synagogue during the 1389 pogrom. For 500 years the unwashed walls had been a memorial to those elegized by Avigdor Kara, 'destroyed in the House of God by the bloody sword of the enemy'.

Rabbi Loew's *golem* (whose full name was Joseph Golem according to Jewish legend) eventually ran amok, as man-made creatures do, and went on a rampage through the synagogue. Loew was holding a service when he heard the news and, after consulting the scriptures to work out whether *golems* could be deactivated on the Sabbath, he stalked Joseph and eventually turned him back to clay. Suitably chastened by his dabblings with the laws of creation, he announced that he would never make another *golem*; lifeless Joseph was taken up to the steep brick roof, and has apparently been there ever since.

Jewish Town Hall (Židovská Radnice)

The wooden clocktower of the Jewish Town Hall (*closed to visitors*) was donated to the ghetto by Mayor Maisel in 1586. Originally Renaissance in style, it was given a rococo revamp in 1765, when the tower and the clock below it were also added. The lower clock has Hebrew figures and, as the Jewish alphabet is read from right to left, its hands turn backwards. The town hall is still the administrative centre of Prague's Jewish community. For years it was a symbol of the moribund state of Jewish culture in the capital, but like so much else in the city it has fizzed back into unexpected life since 1989. There are still only about 1,500 registered Jews, but the number is growing and their average age (which used to be about 65) has begun to sink.

West of the Ghetto

Dominating **Náměstí Jana Palacha**, a square named after the student who burned himself to death in 1969 in protest at the Red Army invasion of Prague, is the **Rudolfinum** (Dům umelcu; *Alšovo nábřeži, t 224 893 111; Galerie Rudolfinum, t 227 059 205, www.galerierudolfinum.cz; open Tues–Sun 10–6; adm*). The neo-Renaissance building's walnut-panelled and cut-glass rooms, ranging around a vast glass-roofed atrium, host temporary exhibitions (which usually showcase cutting-edge contemporary art), but the Rudolfinum is best known as the home of the Czech Philharmonic Orchestra. Its history is not purely cultural: the musicians perform under the globe-clustered chandeliers of the glorious **Dvořákovy Sál** (Dvořák Hall), which used to host the legislative sessions of the Czechoslovak parliament until that was prorogued by the Nazis in 1938.

Opposite the Rudolfinum is the **Museum of Decorative Arts** (Uměleckoprůmyslové Muzeum; *17 Listopadu 2, t 251 093 111; open Tues–Sun 10–6; adm*), founded in 1885, and inspired by the English Arts and Crafts Movement's dream of elevating public taste in the industrial age. Many of its holdings are in storage, or have been moved to the National Gallery of Modern Art, but the collection displayed is sumptuous: four rooms of household and palace furnishings from the Renaissance through to the mid-19th century. The work includes *escritoires* and cabinets inlaid with gemstones, timepieces, Baroque bureaux and chests, porcelain (including works from Meissen, the first European factory to unlock the thousand-year-old Chinese mystery), Gobelins tapestries and furniture.

Up Dušni and Eastern Josefov

The area south of the river and east of Kozí is one of the loveliest parts of Staré Město. The small houses and cobbled lanes, bathed in a sleepy hush, are a tantalizing glimpse of what a restored Josefov might have become. Off Dušni at Elišky Krásnohorské 10–14 stand some **Cubist Houses**, built by Otakar Novotný. With their jutting geometrical balconies, they were constructed between 1919 and 1921 when the old ghetto slums were still being cleared. They originally housed a teacher's collective, but are now plush private residences.

On the corner of Dušní and U Milosrdných, the now deconsecrated church of **SS Simon and Jude** (Kostel sv. Šimona a Judy) has a net-vault that's an example of Prague's tenacious use of Gothic motifs into the early 17th century. Mozart and Haydn played on the organ in its heyday and nowadays it occasionally hosts chamber concerts featuring the Prague Symphony Orchestra. The Baroque front, along with that of the one-time hospital next door, dates from the 1750s.

St Agnes' Convent (Klášter sv. Anežky)

The oldest remaining Gothic building in Prague, the former convent now houses the National Gallery's collection of **Bohemian and Central European Gothic Art** (*U Milosrdných 17, t 224 810 628, www.ngprague.cz; open Tues–Sun 10–6; adm*). The convent was founded by King Wenceslas in 1233, at the urging of his sister Agnes (Anežka) who had just signed up with the Order of the Poor Clares. Agnes was canonized as recently as 12 November 1989; the 750-year delay was because her body was never found. The long wait meant that by the time she got the papal thumbs-up, the inevitable legend had arisen that her canonization would be accompanied by great marvels. The prophecy was duly fulfilled five days later, with the advent of the Velvet Revolution. In 2000, the convent was dramatically refurbished to house the National Gallery's newly expanded Gothic art collection. The earliest Gothic art in Bohemia dates from the beginning of the 14th century. The slender and elegant *Madonnas* in the **opening gallery**, their faces half turned away, show how Bohemian art was beginning to escape the rigid formality of its Byzantine progenitors, with ever more robust representations of the human form.

In the next room is the *Vyšší Brod (Hohenfurth) Altarpiece*. The most notable feature of the nine paintings is their use of contrasting colours to create an illusion of depth, a hundred years before the laws of perspective twinkled in the eyes of the clever Florentines. It is most remarkable in *The Descent of the Holy Ghost*: huddled Apostles swirl in a sea of reds and greens and indigos, yet the space around them appears almost three-dimensional.

The loud-mouthed creature with the droopy ears is called *Gargoyle-ibex*, though less goat-like a beast you never did see. Beyond its howling canine companion is the room containing the work of **Master Theodoric**, the first of Bohemia's painters to emerge from misty anonymity; as you gaze at the six paintings on display here, you'll understand the reasons for his fame. Bohemian artists' experiments with colour values and facial modelling reach their culmination in these panels, which have a vitality that survives six centuries. The panels are from the Chapel of the Holy Cross at Charles IV's castle at Karlštejn, where there are over 100 more (*see p.168*).

With Charles' death and the coronation of his wastrel son Wenceslas IV in 1378, Bohemian art became increasingly refined. Sophistication replaced spiritual mystery, and the paintings of women take on a doll-like charm. Look, for example, at the languid rosy-cheeked depictions of SS Catherine, Mary Magdalene and Margaret in the *Třebon (Wittingau) Altarpiece* of c.1380. The line of Madonnas become romanticized images of motherhood: the *St Vitus' Madonna* shows the phenomenon in all its treacle; it's also apparent in the sculptures. The humanization trend takes a different form in most of the depictions of men of late Gothic art; the galleries are filled with hirsute and/or bald saints, while Christ suffers and is tortured with a greater intensity than ever before. The work in the following galleries represents the final period of Bohemian Gothic art. By the time you get to the *Lamentation* of c.1510–20, the regular cast of characters mourning the dead Christ show a restraint that's still utterly Gothic, but have begun to sprout the extra inches and shrunken pin-heads so characteristic of Mannerist art. The tour of the ground floor ends with the carvings of Monogrammist I. P., a shadowy character who lived in Prague from 1520 to 1550, and left behind a series of masterful woodcuts, showing a devotion to north European foliage characteristic of the Danube School.

Prague Castle (Pražská Hrad)

Metro Malastranská, then follow the signs uphill. **Castle grounds** *open summer 5am–midnight, winter 6am–11pm;* **castle monuments** *open summer daily 9–5, winter daily 9–4; adm for St Vitus' Cathedral except nave, the Old Royal Palace, the Basilica of St George and the Powder Tower; other museums within the castle grounds charge separately. Guided tours in English (one hour) available Tues–Sun 9–3.* **Changing of the Guard,** *summer, hourly on the hour 5am–11pm; winter, 6am–11pm. Fanfare and ceremonial changing of the guard daily at noon.*

From its beginnings as a pagan mound to the day when Václav Havel was sworn in as president, Prague Castle has been the backdrop for Prague's history. Its neoclassical veneer now stretches half a lazy mile over the capital, but it is the cathedral's onion domes and demented prongs, rising from its core, that hint at the true nature of what lies within. It is almost certainly the oldest continuously inhabited part of the city and, until the end of Bohemian independence in the 17th century, it was home to most of the oddballs to rule the country. It is still the seat of the president. Every building has its secrets, from the laboratory of Emperor Rudolf II's alchemists to the minuscule pastel cottages of the 400-year-old Golden Lane.

The **façade** of Prague Castle dates from 1753–75, when neoclassical façades were added with dull abandon although, behind it all, huge chunks of the medieval castle survive.

First Courtyard (První Nádvoří)

Enter the castle from Hradčanské Náměstí through the main gateway under the Art Nouveau **Battling Giants**. Between the pine flagpoles of the First Courtyard is the **Matthias Gate** (1614), thought to have been designed by Vincenzo Scamozzi, a close follower of Andrea Palladio. The **Roman triumphal arch** is now unhappily immured in a building dividing the first two courtyards, but it originally stood proud and alone between two bridges crossing the outer moats of the castle.

The north wing is approached by way of the **Hall of Columns** (Sloupová sín), built between 1924 and 1926 and the work of Jože Plečnik (*see* p.118). Three rows of Ionic columns line the walls around the stone staircase, which marches up to double iron doors under a copper-panelled roof. Plečnik was appointed castle architect in 1920, with an unenviable brief: to modernize the castle in a way unimposing enough to suit the democratic ideals of the new Czechoslovakian state, dignified enough to honour that democracy's president, and tactful enough to complement the existing architectural scheme of the castle. In the context of the monumentalism that surrounded him, he carried off the balancing act with aplomb. The staircase leads up to the **Spanish Hall** (Španělský Sál), which is used for concerts but otherwise accessible to the public only occasionally. On those occasions, queues of Praguers snake through, all curious to see the stucco-encrusted room that used to host the regular meetings of the Communist Party Central Committee. Opposite the Hall of Columns another glass doorway leads to the **presidential rooms**.

Second Courtyard (Druhé Nádvoří)

The most notable feature of the Second Courtyard is the **Chapel of the Holy Cross** (Sv. Kříz), which is now used for exhibitions. At the north end of the courtyard, beyond a Baroque fountain (1686) and a disused well, a gateway leads to the **Powder Bridge** where it crosses the Stag Moat. To the right of the gateway are the **Castle Stables**, once the home of 300 thoroughbred horses and now a sanitized exhibition space. To the left, another part of the former stables houses the Castle Picture Gallery.

Castle Picture Gallery (Obrazárna)

t 224 375 531; open Tues–Sun 10–5; adm.

The holdings of the gallery, including works of art kept in the castle since the reign of Emperor Rudolf II, are worth a brief visit to get a feel of the emperor's eclectic tastes and the decline of his Habsburg successors. No inventory survives, but as well as rhino horns, nails from the Ark and the like, Rudolf is thought to have installed some 3,000 pictures and 2,500 sculptures. The gallery was pillaged by occupying Protestant forces in the Thirty Years' War: a mild pruning by the Saxons in 1631–2 was followed by a systematic ransack by Swedes in 1648. What's left includes works by Massari, Guido Reni, Gentileschi, Tintoretto, Titian and Rubens.

Third Courtyard (Třetí Nádvoří)

Castle Information Centre, Third Courtyard, Prague Castle, t 224 373 368, www.hrad.cz; open Tues–Sun 9–4. You can buy tickets and audioguides, book guided tours and pick up maps and leaflets here.

An arched tunnel leads from the Second Courtyard into the Third Courtyard, bringing you up short before the looming St Vitus' Cathedral (Katedrála sv. Víta).

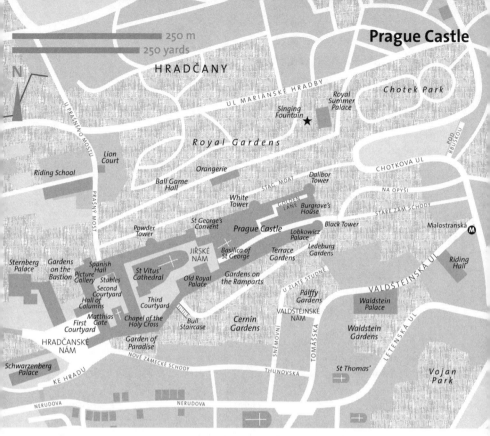

On the southern façade of the church is the **central tower**, which dominated the front of the cathedral until its modern completion.

The tower is almost 100 metres high, although a fair chunk of that (38 metres) is made up of the multi-storey Baroque dome. Four bells hang in the tower, of which the largest is **Sigismund**, an 18-ton monster on the first floor, dating from 1549. Bells caused no end of trouble in the 16th century. They couldn't be touched by anyone impure (a category that included all women), and pubescent boys dressed in white had to be engaged to transport them from foundry to belfry. The ornate golden grille in the arched window dates from Rudolf II's reign (hence the 'R' just above), as do the two clocks, the higher of which shows the hour, the lower the minute.

To the right of the tower is the **Golden Portal**, once the cathedral's main entrance. Above the gate is a **mosaic** of *The Last Judgment* dating from 1370–71, featuring Charles and his fourth wife, Elizabeth of Pomerania. Restoration funded by the Getty Foundation was carried out in 1998 and 2000, and the epic theme now shines out in glorious Technicolor.

Directly opposite the mosaic façade is the **Bull Staircase**, another ingenious Plečnik construction, which runs down to the **Garden on the Ramparts**. The garden contains pavilions and two obelisks that commemorate the miracle that followed Prague's third defenestration, in 1618 (*see p.110*).

St Vitus' Cathedral (Katedrála sv. Víta)

Open April–Oct daily 9–5; Nov–Mar daily 9–4; adm to the nave free, to the
crypt and chapels with Prague Castle ticket.

It was under Charles IV that the cathedral, one of the finest 14th-century churches
in Europe, began to take shape; building commenced in 1344. Charles hoped to make
Prague into a great imperial metropolis and the cathedral its centrepiece. Brought up
in Paris, he turned first to a French architect, summoning Matthew of Arras from the
papal court at Avignon. Matthew built the east end of the chancel on standard French
lines but, luckily for Prague's Gothic architecture, he died in 1352. His replacement,
called to the court from Swabia, was Peter Parléř, the scion of a distinguished family
of German masons. His new plan for the nave inaugurated a half-century during
which Prague became the most significant centre of Gothic architecture in Europe.
However, the entire western part of the church, including its grand façade, was only
completed between 1871 and 1929, the neo-Gothic architects giving Prague's skyline a
focus it had lacked for 500 years. The cathedral was dedicated to St Vitus because in
pagan times a four-headed war and fertility god of that name was worshipped here.

The Nave

Mammoth pillars line the noble arch of the nave. The stained glass is a modern
addition dating from the 1930s. The original Gothic church is thought to have had
only one coloured window, and its bold use of clear light was one way in which architect Parléř broke from the church's French origins. The windows have a garish
splendour, but here it's hard not to wonder how different a completed 14th-century
church might have been. The window in the third chapel was paid for by an insurance
company, and celebrates prudent risk-assessment with the psalm, 'Those Who Sow in
Tears Shall Reap in Joy'.

The original part of the building contains the **tower** of the old cathedral, which
offers the highest vantage point in Prague; the view is as breathtaking as you would
expect from a climb of 287 steps (*open as cathedral; adm*).

On the left of the building is the **choir** (1557–61), designed by Ferdinand I's court
architect, Bonifaz Wohlmut, and surmounted by a tremendous organ dating from the
later 18th century. Originally, it closed the western end of the church, but the whole
shebang was moved in the 1920s.

St Wenceslas' Chapel, St Andrew's Chapel and the Crypt

To the right of the choir is Peter Parléř's shining goldmine of a chapel, built between
1362 and 1367. Gentle Wenceslas died at the hands of his brother Boleslav in 935, and
has wielded more influence from his grave than he ever did during his life.

There are two doorways. The northern portal in the nave contains the ring to which
the saint allegedly clung as he was hacked to death, although the church where the
deed occurred, outside Prague, has always indignantly claimed to have the knocker
concerned. The arch is flanked by sculptural warnings: on the left, a crumbling figure
of Peter denying Christ and, on the right, a vicious demon yanking Judas' tongue from

his mouth; but the interior is an inviting mosaic of gilt plaster and semi-precious stones, unevenly framing and crowding over the painted Passion scenes below.

The chapel is a Gothic painting in three glittering dimensions, suffused with the shot of mysticism that ran through the otherwise eminent worldliness of Charles. The number of stones (about 1,370) corresponds to the date of its construction (and, if Prague's clerics were to be believed, the rough date of the Second Coming).

The emperor also gave the chapel tremendous secular significance by establishing a new coronation ceremony linked closely to the cult of Wenceslas. Much of it took place here, and the forged door in the southwest corner leads to a small room containing the **old crown jewels of Bohemia**. You'll have a job getting to see them, though: the door is closed with seven different locks. In any case, any pleb who puts them on signs his own death warrant. The legend was last fulfilled (or just possibly created) in 1942, when Reichsprotektor Reinhard Heydrich is said to have sneered with Teutonic arrogance when the grizzled guardian of the jewels warned him of the curse; shortly after trying on the crown, he was cut down by assassins. St Vitus' in its heyday, like any cathedral worth its salt, served as a necropolis for the corpses of the high and mighty. In the central aisle is the white marble **Habsburg Mausoleum** (1566–89), containing the remains of the first two generations to rule Bohemia.

Prague did not yield second place to Rome for want of trying. **St Andrew's Chapel** used to contain a picture known as the *vera icon* (true image). The Vatican also has one; a messy state of affairs, given that the *vera icon* is the miraculously imprinted hanky used by the (anagrammatical) St Veronica to wipe the sweat off Jesus on the road to Calvary.

The tour is a confusing journey through the convoluted architectural history of the cathedral, leading you to the 11th-century **crypt** of the basilica (*open same hours as cathedral; adm with Prague Castle ticket*), the cathedral's foundations and those of its original choir, 20th-century masonry and the northern apse of Wenceslas' rotunda. The wooden steps take you back into the nave, but first take a look at the **royal crypt** in the room to the right, next to more foundations, containing the bodies of Charles IV and Rudolf.

Back in the Nave

From the crypt, you emerge back into the centre of the nave. The line of chapels on the right continues with the **Royal Oratory**. Opposite the **Waldstein Chapel**, with the Gothic tombstones of the cathedral's two architects, is a relief showing what looks a very orderly iconoclastic rampage through the cathedral, which occurred in 1619. You're now entering the oldest part of the church, but to go any further you have to get round the incandescent Baroque **Tomb of St John Nepomuk**. St John's not-so-humble abode was fashioned from 3,700 pounds of solid silver, after a design by Fischer von Erlach the Younger. Larger-than-life angels support the coffin, the swooning saint clutches a crucifix above the lid and four heavenly bodies float over it all. As you pass the centre of the cathedral, pay your respects to the altar to **St Vitus** on your left. Vitus has not done well over the years, outshone first by Wenceslas and then by John Nepomuk; his tomb is an insignificant 19th-century affair.

On the right just past the choir is an amazing **wooden altar** (1896–9) by the Czech sculptor František Bílek. Its simplicity, and the pain that it exudes, owe much to the humanistic traditions of late Gothic art in Bohemia. Bílek's sculpture is a modern addition that works; the Art Nouveau **stained glass** by Alfons Mucha (a 1931 comic-strip celebrating SS Cyril and Methodius) is one that doesn't.

Old Royal Palace (Starý Královský Palác)

Open April–Oct daily 9–5; Nov–Mar daily 9–4; adm with Prague Castle ticket.

Since the castle was first fortified, the Old Royal Palace has been the site of the royal residence, and inside are three layers of palace, spanning the Romanesque and the Renaissance. The older halls are now below ground level – a feature you come to expect in Prague – as a result of the original unevenness of the Third Courtyard, which sloped steeply towards the east until paved during Rudolf II's reign.

The topmost palace, and the one you'll see first, is the **Vladislav Hall** (Vladislavský sál). The hall was built between 1486 and 1502 by Benedict Ried, Vladislav II of Jagellon's court architect. The structure represents the culmination of the Bohemian late Gothic style named after the Polish king. In its magnificent vault, ribs shoot up like monstrous tendrils from its wall shafts, intertwining across five gently articulated bays and somehow meandering into star-like flower petals in the centre. Ried used anything that seemed to fit the opulence required: the broad rectangular windows are pure Renaissance, sneaking into Bohemia years before the Italian influence began to be felt in western Europe; spiralling pillars and classical entablatures frame the doors of the hall. Horses fitted in here comfortably; mounted stewards and cupbearers lined the sides during banquets, and tournaments were a regular feature. Since 1918, the president of the Republic has been sworn in here.

To the right of the entrance is a door leading to the **Ludvík Wing**, and it was here that Prague's most significant **defenestration** took place on 23 May 1618. Count Thurn and a few other Bohemian Protestant noblemen confronted the two hated Catholic governors appointed by Ferdinand I and, after explaining their grievances, tossed both out of the window to your left; they survived after landing on a dung heap. The Church declared it a miracle, and two obelisks were set up in what is now the Garden on the Ramparts to commemorate the glorious event.

At the foot of the staircase, more steps lead down to the predecessors of the Vladislav Hall. At the lowest level is the Romanesque gloom of the 12th-century **Soběslav Palace**.

Basilica of St George (Bazilika sv. Jiří)

Open April–Oct daily 9–5; Nov–Mar daily 9–4; adm with Prague Castle ticket.

The majestic chancel of St Vitus' looks across Jiřské náměstí (St George's Square) to the charming early Baroque façade of the Basilica of St George, with its asymmetrical towers (medieval rules said that a fat male tower had to protect a slim female tower from the midday sun). The perky orange-on-brown pilasters and dunce's cap of a dome cover an incongruously sombre Romanesque interior. The church was the second to be founded in the castle (921) and pre-dates St Vitus' Cathedral. Strictly speaking, its interior dates back to 1142, when it was rebuilt after a fire, but zealous restoration at the end of the last century has robbed it of gloom and turned it into a spanking-clean model of neatly hewn pillars and masonry.

Between the Baroque steps winding up to the chancel is the 12th-century **crypt**, containing the Romanesque **tympanum** that used to crown the southern portal of the church. At the top of the steps is the **chancel**, decorated with fading Romanesque frescoes of the Heavenly Jerusalem, and to the right is the **Chapel of St Ludmilla**. The saint was Prince Wenceslas' grandmother and spiritual adviser, strangled at prayer with her veil by his pagan mother Drahomirá, who hoped to coax her son back into the cock-worshipping fold. It was an optimistic scheme, and it soon collapsed: Wenceslas took Ludmilla's side and had her remains transferred here in 925. Sadly, the chapel is inaccessible, having been firmly closed off since a 17th-century German workman temporarily absconded with some of the saint's bones.

St George's Convent (Jiřský Klášter)

Open Tues–Sun 10–5; adm.

This Benedictine convent, neighbouring the Basilica, was the first in Bohemia, founded in 973. Since the Gothic art collection once held here was moved to St Agnes' Convent, the convent has been left with the **National Gallery of Czech Baroque Art**. One of the most striking works of the collection is the *Epitaph of the Goldsmith Müller* by Bartholomeus Spranger, exuding a rather incredible eroticism. The collection also contains a rippling *Hercules with the Apples of the Hesperides* by Rudolf II's sculptor, Adriaen de Vries, and landscapes by the Flemish Roelandt Savery. Then come the statues of Maximilian Brokof and Matthias Braun, the two greatest sculptors of Baroque Prague, of which Braun's *St Jude* is the most spectacular example – a whirlwind of frenzied rags and varicose veins. Past the paintings by the Czech Petr Brandl, you'll find the remarkable work of Jan Kupecký (1667–1740), a melancholy Czech exile who spent most of his life shuttling between Vienna and Nuremberg.

Golden Lane (Zlatá Ulička)

The huddled cottages along Golden Lane date from the later 16th century and look like a Matisse painting come alive: tiny blocks of colour stretching higgledy-piggledy down the street. There's barely enough room inside to fit a cat, let alone swing one. The cottages, built into the castle fortifications, originally housed 24 of Rudolf II's marksmen. Take a look at the powder-blue hovel at **No.22**, now a shop swallowing coachloads of avid tourists. Between December 1916 and March 1917, Franz Kafka lived here and wrote most of the short stories that were published during his lifetime.

The White Tower, Dalibor Tower and Lobkowicz Palace

The **White Tower** (Bílá Věž; *open April–Oct daily 9–5, Nov–Mar daily 9–4*) was built in the 15th century as part of Vladislav II's fortifications of the castle, but for about 200 years after 1584 it also served as Prague's central prison. The tower's torture chamber (*mučírna*) still contains a rack, stocks, branding irons and so on.

The **Dalibor Tower** (Daliborka; *open April–Sept 9–5*), built in 1496 as another part of Vladislav's fortifications, was the work of Benedict Ried, but his flamboyant tendencies are firmly under control. The tower served as a prison for the nobility, and is named after its first inmate, a knight named Dalibor of Kozojed, who landed up here in 1498 in connection with a revolt of serfs. At the top level, a corridor, filled with suits of armour, lances, maces and muskets, runs the length of Golden Lane.

The **Lobkovický Palác Museum** (*open summer Tues–Sun 9–5, winter Tues–Sun 9–4; adm*) in the Lobowicz Palace contains copies of the elusive **coronation jewels**. The crown was designed on the instructions of Charles IV for his new coronation ceremony. The original contains the largest sapphires then known to Europe, as well as a hole to accommodate the Crucifixion thorns that Charles had just acquired.

The Royal Gardens (Královské Zahrady)

Open April–Oct daily 10–6.

The Royal Gardens stretch to the northeast of the castle; a gate links them with the **Chotkev Park** (Chotkovy Sady) which in turn links up with **Letná Park** for a wonderful walk.

The Royal Gardens are best reached across the **Powder Bridge** (Prašný Most), in the Second Courtyard. Ferdinand I built it and, in his weird Habsburg way, included a not-very-secret tunnel underneath, so that he could sneak off to his newly built Royal Summer Palace. His weirder grandson Rudolf II built a warren under the castle. The Communists constructed even more escape routes and hideaways, but suddenly got cold feet and filled the castle tunnels with concrete blocks in case anyone tried to invade through them.

Far below is the **Stag Moat** (Jelení příkop). At first, it was a useful natural ditch, but with the invention of artillery, Vladislav II sensibly decided to rely instead on the powerful fortifications that you can see on the right. The Habsburgs filled the fissure with stags, who multiplied and gambolled here until 1743.

Over the bridge to the left is the **Riding School of Prague Castle** (Jízdárna Pražského hradu; *now home to temporary exhibitions of the National Gallery*). Animals were an important part of the life of a self-respecting 16th-century monarch, and just opposite the school, you'll see the **Lion Court** (Lví dvůr), once the Habsburg zoo.

Beyond the house is the *sgraffito*-covered **Ball Game Hall** (Míčovna), dating from 1567–9. The sculpture in front is *Allegory of Night* by Antonín Braun. Examine the monochrome façade closely. When restoring it after the war, the authorities, in a fit of Communist whimsy, added a few new details to the Renaissance decoration, such as the hammer and sickle discreetly tucked away next to the figure of Justice.

The one-time **Orangerie** stretches along the slope below the garden.

Royal Summer Palace (Královský Letohrádek)

Also known as the **Belvedere**, the palace (*no public access*) was built between 1538 and 1564 for Ferdinand I. More particularly, it was built as a token of love for his wife – although he loved her to death: she died while giving birth to their 15th child, before the palace was completed. It's the purest example of Italian Renaissance architecture in Prague.

There are several pretty gardens on the hillside south of the palace, known collectively as the **South Gardens** (Jižni Zahrady), with picturesque views of the red rooftops of Malá Strana. They can be reached via the Bull Staircase south of St Vitus' Cathedral.

Hradčany

The shadow of the castle has always fallen between Hradčany and the city below. The district was founded in 1320 as a set of hovels in which the royal serfs could sleep and breed – and although it slipped out of the castellan's personal control in 1598, it never grew into a normal town. Locked into a slowly turning backwater, monks and nobles indulged their peccadilloes here for centuries; today, its cobbles and courtyards are a silent suburb of the castle which many visitors never see.

Hradčany Square (Hradčanské Náměstí)

The **Martinic Palace** (Martinický Palác), plastered with cream-on-brown scratchings, was built by the count of the same name in 1620, two years after his defenestrated descent into a dung heap had plunged him into the footnotes of history as one of the minor causes of the Thirty Years' War. The *sgraffito* decoration was uncovered during restoration in 1971. It's a merry Renaissance retelling of Old Testament stories. On the front is Joseph (of dream-coat fame). The wife of his master Potiphar is eagerly trying to lie with him, but he does not want to know her. On the other angle of this corner of the square is a house that film buffs might recognize: Milos Forman chose it as Mozart's house for *Amadeus*, which was largely filmed in Prague.

A row of butcher's shops was demolished to make way for the haughty, early Baroque building of the **Tuscany Palace** (Toskánsky Palác; *closed to visitors*), which was handsomely restored in the late 1990s. It now belongs to the Czech Foreign Ministry. Upstaging the Martinic Palace opposite is the **Schwarzenberg Palace** (Schwarzenberský Palác; *closed to visitors*), with its eye-catching façade: endless *sgraffito* triangles crawling in diagonal formations across its Renaissance splendour. The **Archbishop's Palace** (Arcibiskupský Palác; *closed to visitors*) was built in Renaissance style, but given the present rococo façade in 1763–4.

Sternberg Palace (Šternberský Palác)

Hradčanské Náměstí 15, t 233 090 570, www.ngprague.cz; open Tues–Sun 10–6; adm.

The **National Gallery of Pre-modern European Art** in the Sternberg Palace, which used to be the finest in Prague, was decimated by a double-whammy in 2000: its superb modern collection was hived off to the new Trade Fair Palace (*see p.163*), while many of its older works were returned to the monasteries and nobles from whom they were confiscated by the Communists. However, it still contains a few excellent pieces, and is worth a visit if you're in the mood for another gallery.

On the **first floor** you'll find 14th- and 15th-century Italian art, ancient and classical art and icons, and 15th- and 16th-century Flemish art. The triptychs and diptychs that make up the bulk of the work on this floor are no great shakes, but there are a few notable paintings in the Flemish section. One that you can't avoid is *St Luke Drawing the Virgin* (1513–16) by Mabuse (Jan Gossaert), which once adorned the altar of St Vitus' Cathedral. This floor also contains Pieter Brueghel the Elder's *Haymaking* (1565), a happy landscape of rural harmony which originally formed part of a cycle; only four other *Months* survive, in Vienna and New York. Finally, have a look at the exquisite *Bouquet* (1607–8), by Jan Brueghel, flower-painter *extraordinaire*.

The first rooms on the **second floor** contain work by **German artists** of the 14th–16th centuries, including a much-reduced selection of works by Lucas Cranach the Elder. The highlight is Albrecht Dürer's *Feast of the Rose Garlands* (1506), regarded as one of the most important paintings of the northern Renaissance. It represents Dürer's deliberate attempt to marry his country's late Gothic art with the technical tricks and new visions of the south, and this work – with its shimmering colour, noble proportions and beauty, and its use of perspective – was an attempt to beat the Venetians at their own game (Dürer painted it on a visit to the city). France and Spain are represented by a few minor works, least unremarkably Goya's *Portrait of Don Miguel de Lardizábal* (1815). The next wing continues with Prague's collection of **Italian Renaissance art**. The big names disappeared when the Swedes pilfered Rudolf II's massive collection in 1648. Of those that remain, look out for the two works by Agnolo Bronzino, *Cosimo de Medici* (1560) and *Eleanor of Toledo* (1540–43), both examples of the portraits produced by the artist for his Florentine patron.

Prague's **Mannerist** collection was unmatched in northern Europe until the Swedish heist. Although El Greco probably did not feature strongly, the gallery now holds one work by him, *Head of Christ* (1595–7), one of the most unforgettable in the gallery.

Baroque light effects fill the next few rooms. The works include Guido Reni's idealized *Salome with the Head of John the Baptist*; and Domenico Fetti's masterful *Christ on the Mount of Olives* (1615), convulsed by rippling movement and illumination. The gallery's Italian collection ends with Canaletto's *View of London from the Thames* (1746), painted from the balcony of Lambeth Palace.

The next wing of the gallery contains its collection of **Flemish and Dutch art** from the 17th and 18th centuries. The first room has two works by the Flemish Roelandt Savery: *Paradise* (1618) and *Landscape with Birds* (1622). Each is an excellent showcase for Savery's claim to art history fame as Europe's first painter of exotic animals. He developed his skills during the decade he spent at Emperor Rudolf II's court, and more particularly, during the time he spent in the imperial menagerie. The room also contains several works by Rubens, including the superb *Expulsion from Paradise* (1620), a preliminary sketch for one of 39 depictions commissioned by the Jesuits for their church in Antwerp. In the next room are landscapes by Salomon van Ruysdael, still lifes by Jan Jansz den Uyl, and a number of notable minor works.

The oval heart of the palace that you enter next contains the grandest Dutch and Flemish painting in the gallery. Rubens holds centre stage with his *Martyrdom of St Thomas* (1637–8), showing the dramatic skills of the artist at their larger-than-life best. Frans Hals, who like Rubens didn't waste a brushstroke, is represented by a masterful *Portrait of Jasper Schade van Westrum* (1645). The very different portraiture of Rembrandt, kneaded from the palate and laboriously formed on the canvas, is reflected in his *Scholar in his Study* (1634); an unknown character painted early in the artist's career, but showing the quizzical mystery of facial expression that was to obsess him in later life. The art of the Low Countries ends with some minor gems in the next room, including the eerie monochrome of *Ships in the Estuary* (1646) by Jan van Goyen, whose lifelong fascination with moody clouds placed him at the forefront of Dutch landscape painting of the 17th century. There are three notable still-lifes: *Still Life with Lemon* by Willem Kalf, which depicts sparkling glasses and glistening fruit set off against a dark rug; Jan van de Velde's *Still Life with Smokers' Requisites* (1647), a strikingly simple example of Dutch still life; and Jan Davidsz de Heem's *Still Life with Fruit* (1652), which exemplifies the more opulent Flemish still-life tradition.

Nový Svět

The name Nový Svět means 'New World', and refers to both a street and a hamlet. Dvořák's symphony is appropriate, although it is Hovis commercials rather than the Land of the Free that come to mind. The quarter grew up during the 1500s as ramshackle hovels for workers to trudge back to after a hard day's work at the castle. The last house at the eastern end of the street was the **home of Tycho Brahe** during his stay in Prague as imperial mathematician to Rudolf II (1599–1601; *see* box, over).

Around the corner on U Brusnice is the **Church of St John Nepomuk** (Kostel sv. Jana Nepomuckého), the first work of Dienzenhofer junior built independently of his father in Prague. It dates from 1720–8, roughly the same time that he was finishing the elegant façade of the Loreta. Continue into **Černínská**, with its little mess of cottages sinking into a dell of grassy cobbles.

Loreta Square (Loretánské Náměstí)

Loreta

t 220 516 740; open Tues–Sun 9–12.15 and 1–4.30; adm.

The original Loreto in Italy was one of the most visited shrines in Europe: it was the house where Archangel Gabriel told Mary the good news, rescued from pagan hands and flown over from Nazareth by a flock of angels in 1291. The cult was wildly popular, and hundreds of imitations appeared in the following centuries. After the Battle of the White Mountain (*see* pp.110–11), 50 were built in Bohemia as part of the re-Catholicizing miracle-culture. The Prague Loreta was the grandest. The shrine was begun in 1626, and three generations of architects perfected it.

The **façade** (1716–23) was the work of both Kristof Dienzenhofer and his son Kilian and it's a charmer: a boisterous mob of cherubs, green onion-domes and dinky towers cheerfully taunt the armed might of the Černín Palace opposite. Inside, the atmosphere is less sunny. The Loreta was established by Benigna Kateřina of Lobkowicz, one of the minor relatives of the Spanish Habsburgs. It was owned and run by an order founded by a Spanish warrior-saint, and it speaks the unearthly language of Spain's

Seers, Stargazers and Mathematicians

The ear of Rudolfine Prague was attuned to speculations on all the highest planes, and soothsayers, croakers, necromancers and prophets of every description found the court of Emperor Rudolf II a congenial staging-post. In Rome, the shadow of the stake was a powerful disincentive to weirdness; in Prague, the character of an emperor whose horoscope had been cast by Nostradamus demanded it. His vast curiosity cabinet included mandrake root fetishes; he apparently carried moss from the bones of a hanged man in his back pocket; and wherever there was a mystery to be pondered, Prague thinkers could be guaranteed to deepen it.

The scope for quackery was immense. Notwithstanding, alchemists would soon become chemists, and the stargazers of Rudolfine Prague stood at a turning point in the history of science. In a few decades, the universe had been shaken to its core. For some 1500 years, the moon, planets, sun and stars had orbited the earth attached to Ptolemy's harmonious crystal spheres, but in 1543 the Pole Nicolaus Copernicus had revived the ancient heresy of heliocentricity. No one knew how to look at the universe any more. Successive imperial mathematicians at Rudolf II's court personified the critical juncture to which the heavens had come. The work of the first, the little-remembered Nicholas Ursus, was inextricably linked to that of the second, the Danish Tycho Brahe, who served at the court between 1599 and 1601. While still in Denmark, Brahe accused Ursus of plagiarism, setting off an arcane intra-Continental row that became vitriolic even for an age when scientists didn't mince their words. Brahe never quite matched his opponent's invective, but he was no more stable; and although his stellar observations did their bit for rationalism by putting the boot into Ptolemy's crystal spheres, in Prague he subjected poor Rudolf to endless astrological prophecies of doom. The emperor was told variously that he would die before 50, that he would be killed by a monk, and that he would follow his pet raven to Hell.

Counter-Reformation, the mixture of fanatical cruelty and sensual mysticism that spawned the Inquisition and the art of El Greco. Pleasure and pain are part and parcel of any shrine, but in Prague the new cult was being thrust on a people who had fought Catholicism for two centuries: it tapped into a morbid superstition and voyeurism that permeate it still.

The **cloisters**, built in 1661 to protect the hundreds of homeless pilgrims from heavenly deluges, are lined with rows of painted saints in pine cabinets. Halfway round the cloister, you're led into the **Santa Casa**, a replica of the Nazarene hovel itself, complete with rich Baroque stucco reliefs. You may feel that it is all slightly at odds with your understanding of the Gospels, but have faith: the exterior may be the work of mid-17th-century Italians, but inside is what it really looked like. The brick room is something of an anti-climax: a sombre box, with a cedar Virgin on the altar, surrounded by smiling silver cherubs who look as though they were put together with tin foil. Set into the bricks on the left are two beams from the original Loreto. The relief on the back shows the story of the angelic transportation.

Behind the Santa Casa is the **Church of the Nativity** (Kostel Narození Páně), which is well suited to the cruel and surreal spirit of the shrine. On the far right is a painting of the tortured martyr St Agatha – the patron saint of women with breast complaints – handing her own severed breasts like poached eggs on a dish to a welcoming angel. Even more macabre are the dummies in the glass cases on either side of the altar. The wax masks and dusty costumes shroud the skeletons of SS Felicissimus and Marcia, another Spanish addition to Loreta's box of tricks.

The most preposterous Iberian addition to the shrine is in the chapel on the corner. The figure with the Castro beard, on the cross to your left, is not Christ (as you may realize from the sky-blue dress with silver brocade) but the Portuguese **St Wilgefortis**. She prayed on the eve of her wedding to be saved from her heathen suitor, and God in His mysterious way decided that the best remedy was facial hair, which she sprouted overnight. The prospective groom was suitably awed, and hastily withdrew from the wedding. Her father was less impressed; he crucified her.

Up the stairs just before the entrance is the **Loreta Treasury**, a priceless collection of glittering monstrances and reliquaries. The most impressive bauble is a diamond monstrance, more than 6,200 of the stones sprayed out like the quills of a horror-struck hedgehog. It was designed by Fischer von Erlach in 1699, and formed part of the gift of Ludmilla Eva Franziska of Kolovrat, who left her entire estate to the Madonna of the Santa Casa.

Walking around the shrine, you may have heard the appealing but cacophonous chimes of Loreta's **carillon**, 27 mechanical bells that have been urgently trying to learn a recognizable tune every hour for three centuries. They were among the few to survive a central European bell holocaust in the First World War, when the Austro-Hungarians turned most of the metal they could find into cannons (Prague's 267 bells were rung for the last time on St Wenceslas' Eve in 1916). They're synchronized, for want of a better term, by grooved cylinders.

Černín Palace (Černínský Palác)

The Černín Palace (*closed to visitors*) is the largest palace in Prague, and it is a beast, with 30 Doric half-columns ranged along a length of 150 metres. In form, its façade is still Renaissance; in its scale and deliberate repetition it belongs to the Baroque; and its awesome pomp is redolent of past power. Humprecht Černín was one of the wealthiest of the *arrivistes* who moved in after the Catholic victory at the Battle of the White Mountain in 1620. When he died in 1682 the palace remained unfinished. It became a barracks in 1851, and then a ministry. Reichsprotektor Reinhard Heydrich decided that it should house his operations, and from 1941 to 1945 swastikas framed its façade. In 1948, Prague's fourth (and so far last) defenestration occurred here, when Foreign Minister Jan Masaryk 'fell' from his office window.

Strahov Monastery (Strahovský Klášter)

*Strahovská, **t** 220 516 671, www.strahovmonastery.cz; open daily 9–noon and 1–5; adm.*

Strahov Monastery gets its name from Strahov, derived from *stráž* ('guard'). It dates from the 14th century, when the western gateway of Charles IV's new fortifications around the left bank of Prague was built here. The Premonstratensian canons were an austere order – their insistence on celibacy did not make them popular among the licentious monks of the day – but they were also an honest and hardworking crew. On their hilltop retreat, they assembled a library that, despite sacks at the hands of Hussite swarms in 1420 and oafish Swedes in 1648, became the finest in Bohemia. The books came in useful in 1782, when Josef II announced the dissolution of almost all the monasteries and convents of the empire. While nuns and monks everywhere were being clapped in jail or told to find honest work, the wily abbot of Strahov, Václav Mayer, saved the day by turning it into a research institute for scholars. Strahov was one of very few monasteries to survive in Bohemia.

The Communists were tough cookies – in 1950 they mounted a night-time raid, sent the canons to gulags, and turned the cloisters into the national literary museum – but the Premonstratensians proved tougher still. Eight hardy survivors shuffled back after the 1989 revolution, and Strahov is once again a functioning monastery.

The canons have been multiplying steadily, and by early 1996 there were 32 living in Strahov, cohabiting with several parish priests. But although you might glimpse the flash of a white robe, they live in segregated quarters and tend to avoid visitors; the flipside is that to pay the bills, they exploit tourism like never before. To that end, they have leased the 12th-century beer cellars to a well-known Italian family, opened an art gallery, and established a brewery opposite the copper-lidded towers of their church.

Church of St Roch (Kostel sv. Rocha) and Galerie Miró

Strahovské nádvoří 1, t 233 354 066; open daily 10–5; adm.

Just as you enter, you'll spot the crooked little church of St Roch, now the Galerie Miró, on your left. The church was built after Rudolf II promised the plague-resistant saint a church if he protected Prague from the approaching pestilence. It dates from 1603–12. St Roch did not share the luck of the monastery: it was closed down by Josef II in 1784. It is now an impressive gallery featuring work by contemporary Czech artists and paintings by Picasso, Miró and Braque.

Philosophical Hall (Filosofický Sál)

The Philosophical Hall library (*access with Strahov Monastery ticket*) was built in a frenzy between 1780 and 1782, after Abbot Mayer got wind of the new Emperor Josef's monastery-razing plans. After climbing the staircase, you'll find yourself in the **ante-room**. It contains a few illuminated manuscripts and monkish doodles, but it's hard to resist being dragged into the opulence of the hall beyond. Walnut bookcases, strung with overripe gilt rococo decoration, rise two levels. Any sensible library would stop at the gallery, but here the tomes march on, climbing 15 metres in all to the ceiling. There are more than 40,000 books, comprising works that Strahov had picked up from benefactors and monasteries less fortunate than itself, all lined up to prove to Josef that it was providing a useful social service.

The ceiling **fresco**, rising from the sombre stacks into a celestial blue, was the last work of the Viennese artist Franz Maulpertsch, and dates from 1794; it's called *The Struggle of Mankind to Know Real Wisdom*.

Strahov's Premonstratensians did not just bury their heads in books. They also stared at their collection of curiosities, displayed in the cabinets outside the hall: monstrous creatures of the deep, a sad crocodile and cases of shining beetles and butterflies. The musty, dusty leather-bound books that line the corridor lead up to a display case containing a replica of the oldest manuscript in the library: a 10th-century New Testament bound in fussy 17th-century encrustations.

Theological Hall (Teologický Sál)

The Theological Hall library was built in 1671, during the restoration of the monastery after the Thirty Years' War. It does not have the solemn majesty of the Philosophical Hall, but its stucco-laden barrel vault is even more sumptuous. Its ceiling frescoes extol the virtues of True Wisdom, painted by a member of the Order in 1723–7. The clerics were liberal, but only up to a point. They observed the prohibitions of the Vatican *Index*, but kept choice selections to tantalize the canons in the cabinet above the far door. If a prurient preacher wanted to flick through one of Galileo's potboilers or a diabolical Hussite tract, he had to explain his reasons in detail to the abbot, a cumbersome process that was swept away during the *glasnost* of the 1780s, when the books were removed to the profane Philosophical Hall.

Strahov Art Gallery

Open Tues–Sun 9–noon and 12.30–5; adm.

Most of the works in the gallery, acquired over the centuries by the monastery, were confiscated by the Communists after 1950. Those that remain are unified by a humanistic and sometimes downright secular quality that is rare for monastic collections. The most notable early work is the *Strahov Madonna* (1340–50), whose matronly bulk and squirming infant clearly show Bohemian art's departure from the orthodoxies of Byzantium, while Lucas Cranach the Elder's *Judith* (*c.* 1530) turns the Old Testament head-hunter into a coquettish girl-about-town. There are several works from the Mannerist court of Rudolf II, including a portrait of the avuncular emperor by Hans von Aachen (1604–12) and an *Allegory of the Reign of Rudolf II* (1603) by Dirck de Quade van Ravesteyn. The latter is typical of many apotheoses that were produced to celebrate a pipe-dream vision of the emperor's crisis-ridden reign: Peace, Justice and Plenty fondle each other's breasts, while an iron-clad imperial bouncer keeps a curious Turk at bay. Most impressive of all the Rudolfine works is Bartholomeus Spranger's shimmering *Resurrection of Christ* (*c.* 1576), in which the superhuman saviour shoots skyward from his tomb and the phrase 'faster than a speeding bullet' comes inexorably to mind.

Malá Strana

The name Malá Strana translates roughly as 'Lesser Quarter' or 'Little Side'. Sloping from the castle to the left bank of the Vltava, its swirling canopy of orange tiles and chalky-green domes covers one of the finest Baroque preserves in Europe. The quarter was founded way back in the 13th century, but a fortuitous fire and the Thirty Years' War cleared out the rotundas and Gothic clutter in time for the carpetbaggers of the Counter-Reformation. Formerly a hive of opposition activists and artists, it has now become one of the most desirable residential districts in Prague.

Church of St Nicholas (Kostel sv. Mikuláš)

Open daily 9–4.

The Baroque mass of St Nicholas' Church and adjoining one-time Jesuit College towers over **Malá Strana Square** (Malostranské náměstí). The church exudes the confidence and ideology of Prague Jesuitry at its height.

The **façade** was the work of Munich-born Kristof Dienzenhofer. It is a development of the undulating rhythm used by Borromini in 1667 for his church of San Carlo alle Quattro Fontane in Rome, but this one was not completed until around 1710. It is only when you enter the church that the mobility of Prague's late Baroque architecture finally overwhelms you. All of the city's churches built during this period sought to capture hearts and minds for the Church Militant, but none other has the potency of this Jesuit cocktail of illusion, threat and promise.

The nave's piers jut out at a diagonal, dragging your attention upwards, while the balconies sway forwards from pier to pier, over vast saints urging you onwards to the high altar. The vault adds to the intoxicating confusion, flowing almost imperceptibly from the pillars into three central bays, while the *trompe l'œil* extravaganza of the 1,500-square-metre **fresco** (1760) makes it almost impossible to say where construction ends and illusion begins. The fresco was the work of Johann Lukas Kracker, and opens the vault into the dark drama of the life of St Nicholas (better known to pagans as Father Christmas). The east of the church, from the third vault on, is the work of Kristof's son, Kilian Ignaz Dienzenhofer, home-grown and educated by the Jesuits themselves in the Clementinum.

From the nave, the **choir** and **altar** seem almost irrelevant, a result not of an unsuccessful union between the work of father and son, but of the overpowering effect of the church as a whole. But by the time you're standing under the diffuse light of the painted **dome**, it is the nave that has become an appendage. The size of the dome caused terror; no one would enter the church until a commission of experts certified in 1750 that it would not collapse. The painting, by Franz Xavier Palko, is the *Celebration of the Holiest Trinity* (1752–3).

God moves in mysterious ways while you keep your eyes heavenward, but there's little room for doubt when you notice the colossal statues (1755–7) stationed above and around you. The venerable **Doctors of the Church** standing at each corner of the stunted transepts have physiques more often associated with steroid abuse than religious devotion. Their brutality was no accident. SS Basil, John Chrysostom, Gregory of Nazianzus and Cyril of Alexandria are all associated with the early Christian struggle against heterodoxy in the East, and the Jesuits were drawing a parallel with their own cause in Bohemia. There are equally gargantuan statues of the Order's heroes, SS Ignatius and Francis Xavier, flanking the copper St Nicholas on the high altar.

Waldstein Palace and Around

The majestic maze of beech hedges, gravel paths and gurgling fountains lazing under the silhouetted spires and halls of Prague Castle make the **Waldstein Gardens** (Valdštejnská Zahrada; *Valdštejnské nám. 4 (entrance from Letenská Street), t 257 07 11 11; gardens open May–Sept daily 9–7, April and Oct daily 10–6; the palace is now home to the Ministry of Culture and closed to visitors*) an idyllic summer retreat from the overheating city, as well as a monument to General Albrecht Waldstein (1581–1634), Prague's most epic megalomaniac.

Waldstein's character oozes out of both his garden and his palace, built between 1623 and 1629. The magnificent terrace, or *sala terrena*, is approached through an

Waldstein

Waldstein belongs to the dubious band of men whose influence on Europe is difficult to exaggerate. Friedrich Schiller turned his life into *Wallenstein*, a three-act tragedy, and the general himself was one of the first to recognize his own genius.

In 1618, while his countrymen were lobbing Emperor Ferdinand's men out of Prague's windows, Waldstein threw in his lot with the Imperial cause. The defenestrators were executed; Waldstein snapped up confiscated lands for a song, and was put in charge of the imperial army, which he led through a decade of almost continuous victories over motley Protestant forces. But he was no employee. He provided the army to Ferdinand under a series of lucrative contracts and, with the help of an inflated currency scheme and manic organizational skills, Waldstein soon became the largest creditor of the Habsburg empire. Without the money to pay his general, Ferdinand had to reward him with other assets. Lands and honours poured through his hands, culminating with a princedom in 1627.

Ferdinand's Jesuit advisers already loathed Waldstein for his pragmatic attitude to a war that they saw as a crusade and, to many, the fact that he could now keep his hat on while chatting to the emperor was the last straw. The intrigues intensified until 1630, when Waldstein was relieved of his command. It was too late – his superbly run army had become indispensable. When Saxon Protestants retook Prague the following year, Ferdinand hastily recalled his champion, and appointed him *generalissimo* of the imperial forces. An almost omnipotent Waldstein finally decided to slip the leash. He began to negotiate with the enemies of the empire and, in January 1434, launched open mutiny against Ferdinand. Historians have spent three centuries discussing his reasons. Few doubt that he wanted to be king of Bohemia, but the riddle is whether he had been a Bohemian nationalist all along, whether he grew into one, or whether he was a power-mad traitor. The nuances did not really matter to Ferdinand, and the *dénouement* unfurled. As Waldstein crossed northern Bohemia in a crimson litter, looking for the allies who were suddenly and mysteriously fading away, Vienna's churches were put on alert and ordered to pray, for 'a matter of the first importance'. Four days later, placards appeared across the city blaring that the legendary Waldstein was to be taken dead or alive. The noble renegade's game was up, and he and the commanders who remained loyal to him were finally done to death by Scottish and Irish officers in the town of Cheb.

avenue of sculpture by Adriaen de Vries (1545–1626). These green-streaked deities were among the last works to be produced by Netherlands-born de Vries, who died before completing his master's commission. The path of sculptures ends with a fountain of Venus, beyond which is Waldstein's terrace, designed by Milanese architect, Giovanni Pieroni, following the 16th-century rules of proportion to the letter. Waldstein clearly appreciated the triumphal possibilities of Baroque architecture, but his greatest tribute to his own genius lies under the stucco vault, in the **frescoes of the Trojan Wars** (1629–30) by Baccio Bianco.

In a small *salon* on the left as you face the *sala terrena*, the general would dine in the summer, under more heroic frescoes of the Argonauts' quest for the Golden Fleece. A **grotto** on the opposite side contains a door leading to what was once Waldstein's **observatory**. The general would stare at the grotto wall and listen to the warblings of his pride of peacocks when the pressures of devastating Europe became too much. Grottoes had become popular across the Continent during the later 1500s, and this pendulous foliage, growing tumour-like into a mass of hidden faces and shapes, reflects Waldstein's mystical pursuits. He had spent some years studying in Padua, a hotbed of the quasi-sciences of the day, and his astrological mania was public knowledge.

South of the Waldstein Gardens, **St Thomas' Church** (Kostel sv. Tomáše; *Josefská 8, t 257 530 556; open 10.35–1 and 2.30–6*) was originally built for the friary of Prague's Augustinian beer-drinking hermits by Kilian Dienzenhofer. The late Baroque façade looms over the tiny cul-de-sac, demanding a level of respect that the humble alley cannot muster. The powerful nave of the church is decorated with **frescoes** (1728–30) by Václav Reiner, as is the light-filled **dome**.

Locked behind a wall and watched by the castle high above, the almost hidden **Vojan Park** (Vojanovy Sady; *U lužického semináře; open April–Sept 8–7; Oct–Mar 8–5*) is the oldest in Prague, laid out in 1248 by the Carmelites, taken over by English Virgins and now an integral part of the Finance Ministry.

The former 18th-century Hergetova Cihelna complex (Herget Brickyard), down on the river near Vojan Park, was renovated to house the new **Prague Jewellery Collection** (*Hergetova Cihelna, Cihelna 2, t 257 535 738; open daily 11–6; adm*), which features jewellery and decorative items from the 17th to 20th centuries. The collection, which was put together by the Museum of Decorative Art, traces the evolution of the art, with original Czech pieces alongside Fabergé eggs and items by Tiffany.

Nerudova

This street is named after Jan Neruda (1834–91), a 19th-century Czech poet and journalist who lived here. His name was later filched by the Chilean writer, 1971 Nobel Laureate and inspiration for *Il Postino*, Pablo Neruda, who apparently chose it at random, although he deposited flowers outside Jan's birthplace after finding out who he was. More a chasm than a street, its Baroque and Renaissance façades cling on to the incline. The street has more **painted house signs** than any other in Prague: multicoloured beasts, birds and apparently random objects which sometimes date back 600 years. Walking west from Malostranské náměstí, at No.6 on the right is the narrow 18th-century façade of the **Red Eagle** (U červeného orla), one of the innumerable variations of the 26 avian species that adorned Prague's houses. There is another sign at the **Three Little Fiddles** (U tří housliček), a small restaurant at No.12. Three generations of violin-makers lived in the house, but legend insists that the sign has more to do with satanic fiddlers who gather here when the moon is full. Other signs to decipher as you walk up the street include a **Golden Goblet**, at No.16 and a **Golden Key** at No.27, both from the 17th century, when castle goldsmiths used to heat and beat their metals along Nerudova.

The **Morzin Palace** (Morzinský Palác; *Nerudova 5*), from 1713–1714 and now the Romanian Embassy, shows the inventiveness of Giovanni Santini, one of Prague's late Baroque greats. Santini adapted three older houses into a palace, placed a balcony in the middle and curved both sides of the façade out towards it, making the asymmetry almost unnoticeable at first glance. The tension is thrown into even higher gear by the two atlantes, sombre Moors (the Morzin family emblem) who carry the balcony with ease and make a good job of supporting the rest of the façade.

Atlantes became fashionable during the 18th century, but if you look at the portal of **Thun-Hohenstein Palace** (Thun-Hohenštejnský Palác; *Nerudova 20*), now the Italian Embassy building, you'll see that they did not always work. It was built in 1721–6 for the Kolovrats, very soon after the Morzins had moved in at No.5. The newcomers liked the idea of the family emblem supporting the portal. Unfortunately, the Kolovrats' was an eagle, and Matthias Braun duly sculpted these two preposterous creatures. Next to the embassy a stairway leads up the hill to the **New Castle Steps**, which in turn lead up to Prague Castle.

At No.32 is the former **Dittrich Pharmacy**, established in 1821 and now restored to house a small exhibition of antique pharmacies. The ghoulish will like the descriptions of leeches and blood-letting and everyone else can admire the handsome old fittings.

Lobkowicz Palace (Lobkovický Palác)

This Lobkowicz Palace on Vlašská Ulice (confusingly, there are four Lobkowicz Palaces in Prague), now home to the German Embassy, dates from the early 18th century. The top floors of the side wings were added in the later 18th century, and have disrupted the scale originally intended for the building. The elliptical plan, inspired by the work of Fischer von Erlach, originally bore a close resemblance to a 1665 project by Borromini for the rebuilding of the Louvre in Paris.

The English layout of the **gardens** dates from the late 1700s, but they are still recuperating from the most momentous event in their sheltered history: in September 1989, thousands of East Germans arrived in Prague, dumped their Trabants, and clambered over these railings in the hope of being allowed to go west; they lived on the flower beds for a fortnight until permission was granted for them to emigrate. A whimsical tribute to the fleeing Ossies now stands in the garden, called *Quo Vadis*. It's a gold Trabant on four long legs. Sadly, someone has seen fit to sanitize it by knocking off the scrotum with which it was originally endowed. The gardens are closed to the public, but you can glimpse the statue through the railings.

Ledeburg, Cernin and Pálffy Gardens

*Entrances at Valdštejnské náměstí 3, or through the Garden on the
Ramparts. Open 28 Mar–31 Oct 10–6; adm.*

The Baroque Terrace Gardens of Malá Strana ascend the castle hill in terraces. After
decades of neglect, they were handsomely restored and reopened in the late 1990s.

Originally laid out in the 18th century as three separate gardens adjoining aristocratic residences, they have now been merged. They are beautifully manicured formal
gardens with immaculate walkways, balustraded staircases, and observation terraces.
Many of the former pavilions are no longer standing, but the Ledeburg garden
contains a delightful pavilion onstructed by Santini and Allipandi. In the Pálffy garden,
you'll find a whimsical sun clock painted above the entrance to the covered staircase.

Southern Malá Strana

Church of Our Lady of Victory (Kostel Panny Marie Vítězně)

Karmelitská 9, t 257 533 646; open April–Oct daily 8–6.

This sits on the site of Prague's first Baroque church (1611), given by Ferdinand II to
the Order of Barefooted Carmelites. The structure is unimpressive, but the church has
a famous exhibit: the **Bambino di Praga**, venerated throughout the Hispanic world.
The Bambino's rise to stardom began when Polyxena of Lobkowicz, one of many
Spanish brides taken by Czech Catholics during this period, gave the figure to the
friars in 1628. Numerous miracles followed, and in 1741 enough money had been made
to buy the doll its silver altar. It has been given scores of costumes: after the
Carmelites were expelled in 1784, an Order of English Virgins was allowed to continue
dressing it, and even through the Communist era a prelate of St Vitus' Cathedral
changed the Bambino regularly. Look out for outfit No.5, an apple-green number with
gold embroidery, which was handed over personally by Queen Maria Theresa in 1754.

The John Lennon Wall

Opposite the very proper charm of the apricot and white French Embassy in the
Buquoy Palace in Grand Prior's Square (Velkopřevorské náměstí) is the polyglot scrawl
of the John Lennon Wall, a colourful tribute to the Beatle-saint. The singer became a
non-conformist symbol in Communist-ruled Europe after his murder in 1980, and this
wall became the site of a surreal struggle between Prague's youth and the police. The
wall is now encrusted with several years worth of obscene non sequiturs and the
scrawled greetings of hooligans from across the Continent. If you're around on the
anniversary of Lennon's death on 8 November come and join the dreamy types who
spend much of the night imagining no possessions, greed or hunger.

Kampa Island

Kampa Island (from the Latin *campus* for field) is one of the gentlest spots in
Prague. A mere sliver of the Vltava, known as the Čertovka (Devil's Stream), separates
it from the mainland. Kampa's grassy enclaves, water-wheel and quiet, cobbled

streets are a step away but a world apart from the hubbub of nearby Charles Bridge. The island spreads around a tree-filled square, crossed at one end by the rough Gothic arches of the bridge and lined with quietly decaying Baroque houses.

New Town (Nové Město)

The New Town is actually not very new, having got its name way back in 1348, when Emperor Charles IV established it to cater for the monks and merchants flooding into his new capital. Over the last century, Nové Město has become the commercial and administrative centre of the capital. Apart from Václavské náměstí (Wenceslas Square), these districts are overlooked by most visitors, but if you want to see what Praguers get up to while the tourists are not watching, take a walk.

Wenceslas Square (Václavské Náměstí)

Wenceslas Square and the Charles Bridge were founded almost simultaneously in the mid-14th century by Emperor Charles IV. The square, in fact a half-mile boulevard, was the horse market that Charles needed for his new town; now it is the commercial centre of the city and significant for its recent history.

St Wenceslas

The equestrian figure silhouetted against the National Museum is one of the motifs of Bohemian nationalism. Although a familiar name to English carol singers since the 1850s, Good King Wenceslas ruled as a prince rather than a king, until murdered by his notoriously cruel brother, Boleslav the Cruel, in 935. The saint's reputation arose from his Christianity, but over the years Wenceslas has metamorphosed from religious to national hero.

The symbolic importance of the statue came to obsess its designer, J. V. Myslbek, the grand old man of 19th-century Czech sculpture. He began work in 1887 on Wenceslas with the idea of a shaggy Slav, but, as the reality of a nation state grew closer, he transformed the Dark Age prince into the serene and noble leader you see today. Ever since its unveiling, it has been a public rallying point. In 1918, Czechoslovakian independence was announced at Wenceslas' feet. After 1948, Communist May Day parades marched along the square. And following the Soviet-led invasion of August 1968 the monument became the focus of Prague's desperation. The happiest moment of the monument's recent history came in November 1989, when Wenceslas and his stallion Ardo made it on to millions of television sets across the world, at the head of the demonstrations that finally saw off the shoddy dictatorship.

National Museum (Národní Muzeum)

Václavské náměstí 68, t 224 49 71 11, www.nm.cz; open May–Sept daily 10–6, Oct–April daily 9–5; closed first Tues of each month; adm.

A museum of Bohemian history was a dream of early 19th-century patriots. They launched an appeal for objects, but as the domestic appliances and folk art poured in, it became apparent that Bohemia's traditions needed a home more glorious than what was so far available. In the 1870s Prague's council stepped in with this rent-free site. The grandeur of the neo-Renaissance building (1885–90) was meant to express the confidence of the Czech national revival movement; the effect was to shatter the balance of old Václavské náměstí. It encouraged the almost complete renewal of the street's architecture in the 20th century. Paradoxically, the symmetry of the museum, its bulk set off by a central golden dome, now makes it an almost elegant point on the 20th-century exclamation mark that Václavské náměstí has become.

The museum is worth a visit just for the open staircase that greets you beyond the entrance: three floors of veined marble pillars and banisters, globular lamps and swaying palm fronds. Wait for a very, very rainy day before exploring the rest of the building, which houses a stupefying collection of stuffed animals and anthropological knick-knacks.

Around the Square

The global fast-food chains flashing neon signs from every corner of Václavské náměstí are a reminder of how things have changed in Prague during the last decade. Bobbing serenely above the strident call to spend is an undulating skyline of Art Nouveau mansions, offices and hotels, of which the most famous is undoubtedly the **Grand Hotel Evropa**. Revolving doors spin you from the glorious Art Nouveau façade into a shabby and beautiful room of mirrors, mahogany, crystal chandeliers and carriage lamps. It all conforms to a clichéd theme of faded *Mitteleuropäische* elegance, but the sterility makes it little more than an overpriced tourist-trap.

Across Jindřišská is the **Polish Cultural Centre**, which once housed the insurance company where Franz Kafka began his first job in 1907. Moving north, the rest of Václavské náměstí is a hotchpotch of 20th-century Prague architecture, but wedged between the functionalist Alfa and Tatra buildings on the left is the **Hotel Adria**, one of the last Baroque façades on the square. Further down on the same side of the street, at No.8, is the **Peterkův Dům**, perhaps the most elegant Art Nouveau façade in the capital; it was designed by a 28-year-old Jan Kotěra and shows the precision that would later inspire some of the finest Czech constructivist architecture; one example is the **Bat'a shoe shop**.

The north end of the square opens into the so-called **Golden Cross**, a junction of shoppers and idle youth which – along with Ardo's tail – is Prague's most widely-used meeting point, and roughly marks the northern extent of Nové Město.

Northwest Nové Město

Off **Jungmannovo Náměstí** is the **Church of Our Lady of the Snows** (Kostel Panny Marie Sněžné; *open daily 6am–7.30pm*), one of the last remnants of Charles IV's New Town; he founded it in 1347, five years before the 1,000th anniversary of its Roman namesake, Santa Maria Maggiore. The interior is dominated by a splendid early Baroque altar.

Bristling with bizarre crenellations and turrets, the **Adria Palace** is a striking example of the 'rondo-Cubist' architecture that Pavel Janák tried to develop into a

Czechoslovakian national style fit for the 20th century. Modern Prague would have been a curiosity of titanic proportions had he succeeded, but this urban citadel (1923–5) is one of only a few examples that got off the ground.

Národní Třída (National Street) was built in the early 20th century when the New Town's defensive moat was filled in. At the end of it stands the **National Theatre** (Národní Divadlo), erected at the height of the 19th-century Czech national revival. As the inscription at the entrance states, it was the 'nation's gift to itself', paid for entirely by a subscription to which almost every Czech contributed. It opened on 11 June 1881 with a performance of Smetana's opera *Libuše*: less than a fortnight later, it was a smoking shell after workmen accidentally set fire to the building. Once again, the Czech people dug deep and the National Theatre opened again just nine months later. Special trains were laid on to bring the Czechs to see their new theatre, decorated by the most famous artists of the day, and bursting with statues and paintings trumpeting the glories of the Czech nation and its people. It is still a potent symbol of Czech nationalism, and one of the first places that local Czechs recommend visiting.

Charles Square (Karlovo Náměstí)

The hub of southwest Nové Město is Charles Square, which marks the boundary between commercial city and residential neighbourhoods. The broad streets may be medieval in origin, but they are 19th century in feel; wide, confident and lined with handsome mansions. Charles Square was laid out as a park in the 19th century. Until then, cattle changed hands here, and Charles IV used it for gruesome relic displays.

Today's **New Town Hall** (Novoměstská Radnice; *tower open May–Sept Tues–Sun 10–6; adm; exhibition hall open May–Sept Tues–Sun 10–5.30*) is descended from the 14th-century original. Only the tower (1425–6) looks its age, however, since the rest was completely rebuilt during the 19th and early 20th centuries. In 1419 its former windows were the venue for Prague's **first defenestration**. Jan Želivský, a Hussite firebrand of a priest, led a rabble to the building to demand the release of some heretics, and the Catholic councillors lobbed stones at his monstrance – a misjudgement: the crowd stormed the building, hurled the councillors from the windows, and bludgeoned to death anyone who survived the fall.

The **Church of St Ignatius** (Kostel sv. Ignác; *Ječná 2; open daily 6am–6.30pm*) once formed the Jesuit base in the New Town, along with the neighbouring college (now a hospital). The powerful arches of the chapels and broad nave are laden with half-immured cherubs and angels, and the gold and creamy-pink interior has the usual ostentatiousness of Jesuit architecture. It was built in 1665–70.

Just off Charles Square, a two-minute walk down Resslova St, the Orthodox **Church of SS Cyril and Methodius** (Kostel sv. Cyril a Metoděj; *church and crypt open Tues–Sun 10–4; adm to crypt*) is recognizable by a pock-marked section of wall that commemorates one of the most dramatic events to occur in Prague during the Second World War. After the killing of loathed Nazi Reichsprotektor Reinhard Heydrich, seven members of the group responsible holed themselves up here. They were betrayed and during the early hours of 18 June 1942 over 300 SS and Gestapo soldiers took up positions around the building. Through the night, wave upon wave of machine-gun fire slammed into the church, but only as dawn broke did the shooting from within stop. The Nazis entered to find that they had spent the night battling three men: four remained in the crypt. Gunfire resumed, and for another two hours the fighters held out in the catacombs against bullets, tear gas and hand grenades, until they finally took their lives after reaching the end of their ammunition. German troops had pushed a high-pressure hose through a vent, and with water flooding into the pitch-black crypt, and the Nazis on the point of blowing open the long-disused staircase, both men blasted themselves with their final bullets. The gashes of the shots still mark the walls. At the far end of the crypt is a metre-long hollow, smashed away with a pipe while the Nazis pumped gunfire and water through the ventilation hole over-head. Although hundreds of troops had been stationed at sewage outlets along the Vltava to forestall any escape, the crypt is next to a Grand Central of Prague sewers. Had they hit the drain, the men would have been home and dry. They were 30 centimetres away from doing so. A small exhibition includes photographs of the Nazi assault, taken by a Czech police officer with a camera in his lighter.

Along the Vltava

Resslova Street emerges by the riverside at Jiraskovo Náměstí, an innocuous little square which is overlooked by the swaying, glassy **Dancing House** (Tančící Dům). Designed by Frank Gehry and Vlado Milunič, it was completed in 1996 and got its name because it reminded its creators of the dance duo Fred Astaire and Ginger Rogers. The top floor contains a swish French restaurant, La Perle de Prague (see p.101), and there's a café-bar on the ground floor too.

Art Nouveau mansions line the embankment in a more or less unbroken string from the Charles Bridge as far as Vyšrehad (see p.161). Havel famously lived in the top-floor flat of the house adjoining the Dancing House, and chose to stay here after the Velvet Revolution rather than move to the plusher surroundings at Prague Castle. After he had made his point, he found discreetly luxurious lodgings in a smart neighbourhood behind the castle.

South of Charles Square

Effortlessly perched on a craggy curve, the **Church of St John Nepomuk on the Rock** (Kostel sv. Jana Nepomuckého Na skalce; Vyšehradská 49) is one of the most elegant of all Kilian Dienzenhofer's churches in Prague. A double staircase swoops serenely up the west front, and inside is a wooden version of the statue of St John of Nepomuk on the Charles Bridge. The twin towers of the narrow façade are echoed by the bizarre peaks of the **Slavonic Monastery** (Klášter na Slovanech) across the street. This Gothic monastery had its roof obliterated during an Allied bombing run in February 1945; the 1960s replacement, flowing into two spires, is one of the most distinctive pieces of postwar architecture in the capital.

Further east, the small **Dvořák Museum** (Muzeum Antonína Dvořáka; Ke Karlovu 20, t 224 91 80 13; open Tues–Sun 10–5; adm) is housed in a gorgeous Baroque summer-house designed by Kilian Dienzenhofer and set among sculptures by Antonín Braun. It contains photos, notebooks and other memorabilia.

A few hundred metres further down Ke Karlovu is the strange **Police Museum** (Muzeum Policie; *open Sept–June Tues–Sun 10–5; adm*), housed in a former convent. Once devoted to the activities of the National Security Corps, it has been cleaned up since the revolution and is now intended to laud the acceptable face of authoritarianism. Children will enjoy the outdoor playground with helicopter.

The crimson dome of the **Church of Our Lady and Charlemagne** (Kostel Panny Marie a Karla Velikého; *open Sun and hols 2–5.15*), also known as Na Karlově, glows at the end of the road. It was founded by Charles IV in 1358, for French Augustinians. Its unusual octagonal plan was loosely modelled on the Aachen burial church of Charlemagne. The most awe-inspiring feature of the church is its remodelled interior, shaped like a single star, 24 metres in diameter. Legend has it that the architect was a novice who built it with the devil's help; others claim that it was designed in about 1575 by Bonifaz Wohlmut, court architect to Ferdinand I. Either way, it is one of the grandest flourishes of (extremely) late Gothic architecture in Prague.

Outside the Centre

Vyšehrad

www.praha-vysehrad.cz; metro Vyšehrad; tram 3, 17 or 21.

This ancient crag over the Vltava has spun a web of nationalistic lore. Praguers still reel off the myths, but its romantic heyday was a century ago, when it was infested with poets and painters in search of patriotic inspiration. It is now a pleasant retreat on a lazy afternoon, with grassy parks covering the remnants of ancient walls.

According to the city's oldest legend, soothsaying Princess Libuše was standing here when she prophesied Prague. In the later 11th century, Vratislav II moved to the rock, prompted by dislike of his brother, who lived in the castle. The change of royal address lasted a century, but the only evidence is the heavily restored Romanesque **Rotunda of St Martin** (Rotunda sv. Martina). Near it are remnants of the fortification walls built by Charles IV in the mid-14th century.

Before leaving the area, be sure to see the **Cubist houses** designed by Josef Chochol between 1911 and 1913. There is a trio on the embankment below Vyšehrad, at Podolské nábř. 6–10, one at Libůina 3, and, most impressively, the prismatic apartment block jutting outwards and upwards from the corner of Přemyslova and Neklanova.

Smíchov

Metro Anděl; tram 4, 6, 7, 9, 10, 12.

This is one of Prague's most intriguing suburbs, minutes from the centre but a world apart from the golden city. Smíchov was Prague's 19th-century industrial powerhouse and brewery. Today the Staropramen brewery still belches out greenhouse gases, but the unique atmosphere now owes more to the concentration of Romanies living here. On warm evenings the streets have the liveliness of a central European New York City. Gangs loaf around the back streets, and no-good kids yell obscenities or invitations (or both) from tenement windows, but things are changing; the construction of a massive new shopping centre and cinema complex has enticed fleets of developers and yuppies. Catch old Smíchov while you can.

The charming Villa Bertramka is one of the few houses of the suburban gentry to survive the dark advance of industry into Smíchov in the 19th century. It now houses the **Mozart Museum** (*Mozartova 169, t 257 318 461, www.bertramka.cz; open daily April–Oct 9.30–6; Nov–Mar 9.30–5; adm*); Mozart stayed here on three of his visits to Prague.

Petřín Hill

The funicular railway can take you up and down the hill between 5am and midnight.

Petřín Hill is the green and wooded hump on the left as you cross the Charles Bridge from Staré Město. The forest that used to stretch for miles to the south has disappeared, and vineyards no longer clamber up the hill, but its patchwork of gardens still makes for a perfect retreat. You can stroll as far as the gardens of the Strahov Monastery. One of the loveliest walks in Prague is down from Nebozízek on the path which turns from asphalt to forest as it sinks into Malá Strana's sea of olive domes and orange tiles.

Nebozízek, the first stop on the funicular, is marked by an eponymous terrace restaurant, on the site of a vintner's cottage. In the woods is a monument to the Romantic poet Karel Mácha, where generations of Praguers necked for the first time.

At the **summit** is a rose garden. On the left is the **Štefaník Observatory** (*open Tues–Sun, hours vary*) and the Baroque Church of St Lawrence. To the right is a **model of the Eiffel Tower** (*open April–Oct daily 9.30am–7pm; Nov–Mar Sat and Sun only 10am–5pm; adm*), built in 1891 (two years after the original) by the Club of Czech Tourists. The club was proud of its tower, but at 60 metres it falls well short of the Gallic symbol. The Tourists also contributed the nearby **Magic Maze** (Bludiště; *adm*), with a diorama depicting the Swedish attack on the Charles Bridge in 1648.

As you wend your way over the hill, look for remnants of the **Hunger Wall** (Hladová zed'), the crenellations and battlements of which form a scar across Petřín as far as the Strahov Monastery. Charles IV constructed the wall in 1360 to enclose the inhabited left bank of Prague. The name is born of a legend that Charles did not really need a wall and built it solely to create jobs for peckish Praguers after a failed harvest (although it seems no less functional than all the other walls, churches, castles and bridges Charles built).

Letná Park

Metro Staroměstská, then tram 17 (or walk) across the Čechův Most; tram 12, 17.

This expanse of greenery offers a stroll with views of the city. You can walk to the gates of the Royal Gardens in one direction and Stromovka Park in the other. Steps from the **Čechův Most** (Czech Bridge) lead up to the graffiti-scrawled plinth of the former Stalin statue. (A giant metronome sits there now.) Uncle Joe was blown up in

1962, but his rocky remains are in chambers below. The nearby **Hanavský Pavilion** is an Art Nouveau exhibition piece that was moved here in 1898. To the north is the barren expanse of **Letná Plain**, devoid of interest save that it used to host Communist speech days (1 May) and, on 25 November 1989, it was the site of the demonstration that marked the death of the old regime, when a million people saw Václav Havel shake hands with Alexander Dubček. You could stop for coffee on the terrace of the **Letenský Zámeček**, a 19th-century château with great views.

Trade Fair Palace (Veletržní Palác)

Dukelských hrdinů 47, Holešovice, t 224 301 122, www.ngprague.cz; metro Holešovice Nádraží, then tram 5, 12, 17. Open Tues–Wed and Fri–Sun 10–6, Thurs 10–9; adm, audiotours included in ticket.

The **National Gallery of Modern Art** is housed in the spectacular functionalist interior of the Trade Fair Palace, built between 1925 and 1928. In 2000 the collection was completely reorganized by its new director, Milan Knižák, a one-time member of the Fluxus movement. Many of the city's other museums have contributed pieces to enable the Trade Fair Palace to display its art works in context, and wallpaper, furniture and fittings have been brought in as theatrical backdrops (explaining the paucity of the displays at the Museum of Decorative Arts).

Fourth Floor (1800–1900)

The 19th-century collection opens with the work of **J. V. Myslbek**, the country's most influential 19th-century sculptor. The following galleries are devoted to the great names of the Nationalist Revival movement of the 19th century, which produced terrible art; the **Manés family** dominates. Pay your respects to the out-of-place talents of **Josef Navratil** (1798–1865), represented by a number of accomplished still lifes and luminous lakeside scenes.

The next few galleries are piled high with the work of the 'National Theatre generation'. These heroes were firm believers in the unity of art and architecture, and many worked on the Municipal House. There are a couple of smouldering paintings by Sarah Bernhardt's favourite poster artist, **Alfons Mucha**, and a few feisty, bitter-sweet portraits by **Karen Spiller**, who created the mosaic above the entrance to the Municipal House. The prolific **Mikoláš Aleš** (1852–1913) defaced almost every public edifice of the era in Prague. Mainstream Czech **Art Nouveau** sculpture is represented by **Ladislav Šaloun** and a series of gentle copper and bronze reliefs by **Stanislav Sucharda**. The belated influence of Rodin, who exhibited in Prague in 1902, is reflected in the early works of **Josef Mařatka** and **Bohumil Kafka**, both of whom spent a couple of years working in the great man's studio.

There are several notable works by Germanic artists, including **Gustav Klimt**'s luscious *Virgin* (1913). It hangs opposite **Egon Schiele**'s contrasting vision of feminine fecundity, *Pregnant Woman and Death* (1911), in which a cadaverous couple dolefully contemplate life's bloody terror. Another tortured spirit, **Edvard Munch**, is represented by three paintings.

Each floor has been allocated a series of galleries devoted to the **architecture** and **decorative arts** of each period. On this floor, there are models and architectural plans of the National Theatre, the pinnacle of the Nationalist Revival movement, and several of the city's finest Art Nouveau buildings including the Municipal House and Hlavní nádraží train station.

Third Floor (1900–1930)

Prague's artists discovered Impressionism, post-Impressionism and Cubism within a few years of each other in the first decade of the 20th century, and the collection shows the profound effect of this ferment. **František Kupka**'s mystical and ever more abstract art is well represented, and **Emil Filla**'s unique work is worthy of note, permeated with the moody tension of Expressionism but given form in a fluent style.

The most Czech work of this period is the **social realist** work of the 1920s and '30s, which was inspired by a genuine regard for the real lives of 'ordinary' people. **Otto Gutfreund** was one of the earliest practitioners, but his work went on to influence a whole generation of Czechoslovakian sculptors, including **Karel Pokorný**, **Jan Lauda**, **Karel Dvořák** and **Karel Kotrba**. Their works are complemented by the gentle naive painting of **Jan Zrzavý**, and a collection of Czech **Surrealist** dreamscapes. **Toyen**, **Štyrský** and **Šíma** are the most eminent painters.

There is a distinctive collection of non-Czech art, including several works by **Rodin**, among which are the seminal *Age of Bronze* and the dominating *Balzac* (1898). When the latter was unveiled, others called it 'a toad in a sack'. It has to be said that, on the purely visual level, this is an accurate description, but the psychological mystery and Expressionistic power of the sculpture make it perhaps the most original ever produced by the artist.

The gallery's collection of early **Cubist** works is the best in central Europe. The director of the National Gallery in the 1920s, Vincenc Kramář, had lived in Paris during the early years of the century and unerringly appreciated the emerging style. Works by **Pablo Picasso** form the core of the collection. The plum is the artist's *Self Portrait* (1907), painted while he was still thinking his way out of the world of appearances. Other works include his *Woman* (1907) and *Nude Woman* (1908), and his first truly Cubist piece, *Woman in an Armchair* (1910). The style develops through *Mandolin and Glass of Pernod* (1911) and *Woman with a Guitar at the Piano* (1911), and explodes into obscurity with *Clarinet* (1911) and the murky mystery of *Toreador Playing the Guitar* (1911). The co-creator of Cubism, **Georges Braque**, is less well represented, but his *Violin and Glass* (1910–11) is an interesting still life.

As well as pieces of hazy Impressionism, there are a handful of works by the romantic heroes of **post-Impressionism**. **Gauguin**'s lifetime preoccupation with colour is reflected in his *Bonjour, Monsieur Gauguin* (1889), and his erstwhile friend **Van Gogh** is represented by the swirling undercurrents of *Green Rye* (1889). Considerably less anxious is **Le Douanier Rousseau**'s *Moi-même, Portrait paysage* (1890), the artist's only known self-portrait; look out too for the no less joyful *Circus* (1927) by Marc Chagall, and some sensuous nudes by Matisse.

Keep your eyes open for two unnerving **Expressionist** portrayals of powers-that-be by **Wilhelm Thony** and **Max Oppenheimer**. *Thony's Verdict* (pre-1929) is Kafka in monochrome, while Oppenheimer's excellent *Operation* (1912) indicts the medical profession: a turbulent sea of white coats surround the patient, fingers grasping for the jagged wound while Mephistophelian doctors fascinate themselves with everything other than their charge's well-being.

Racked up in the Decorative Arts and Architecture galleries are dozens of stage sets for shows from the 1920s and '30s. There is also an assortment of wind-up gramophones, early telephones, vacuum-cleaners, irons and kettles, beautifully beaded flapper dresses and sketches for stage costumes.

Second Floor (1930–Present)

This floor opens with a bang: the gruesome **Surrealist** visions of **František Janonšek**, all swirling entrails and eyeballs. Behind them flicker **Zdeněk Pešánek**'s light-kinetic sculptures, created in 1936 and given a garish neon splash in the 1980s. There is Surrealism of a more contemplative bent too in **Josef Šima**'s dreamy landscapes. A small gallery is devoted to **Josef Sudek**'s early photography, exquisite experiments with light and shadow. Look out, too, for exceptional paintings by **Oskar Kokoschka**, most painted during his stay in the capital between 1934 and 1938.

After decades of restrictions, Czech artists were liberated to some degree by the death of Stalin. There are powerful **Abstract Expressionist** paintings by **Mikuláš Medek**, and some quirky pieces by **Petr Štembera**, who 'grafted' a twig to his body and recorded the process. The director of the Trade Fair Palace, former Fluxus artist **Milan Knižák**, was an outspoken critic of the Communist regime; there is a photographic record of his *Demonstration of One* (1964), in which he asked spectators to crow as they passed.

Little art could flourish in the two decades which followed the horrors of the Prague Spring. The work which has appeared post-1989 is a mixed bag: **Ivan Kafka**'s *Potent Impotency* is an installation of furiously ticking clock mechanisms which do not tell the time, and **Kurt Gebaner**'s *Swimmers*, floating across the ceiling, are poignantly nostalgic. In the 'laboratory of contemporary trends', the city's youngest and most talked-about artists are featured; **Filip Turek**'s *From the History of Art* is a witty, irreverent piece which uses found images to recreate famous works of art – Botticelli's *The Birth of Venus* is illustrated by three 1960s waterskiiers in flowery bathing caps.

The **First Floor** is devoted to temporary exhibitions.

Troja Château (Trojský Zámek)

*U trojského zámku 1, **t** 283 851 625, www.citygalleryprague.cz; metro Holešovice Nádraží, then bus 112. Open April–Oct Tues–Sun 10–6; Nov–Mar Sat–Sun 10–5; adm.*

The château houses an extensive collection of 19th-century Czech art. But unless you're a fanatic of Symbolism or patriotic Czech history paintings, it is the gaudy, illusionistic decoration of Baroque Troja itself that is worth the trip. The castle was built in the 1600s by an ambitious Czech nobleman so anxious to please Bohemia's masters that he covered his main hall with an apotheosis of the Habsburgs. Painted by the Flemish-born and Roman-trained Abraham Godyn between 1691 and 1697, it is the capital's richest *trompe l'œil*. Austrian triumphalism is the order of the day. The gaudy masterpiece heaps scorn on the Turks, who had been defeated at Vienna in 1683.

Day Trips from Prague

Karlovy Vary

Carlsbad, as the Germans called it, was long one of central Europe's most elegant watering holes. Goethe and Schiller drank deep of its draughts; its casino and promenades were the playground of Russian aristocrats and European monarchs; every Romantic composer took the cure. The frolics ended in the 20th century. As part of the Sudetenland it was stolen by the Nazis in 1938, and after the war the toffs were dispossessed by the Communists. A dreary parade of postwar potentates, from Haile Selassie to Kurt Waldheim, came to dip their toes in the waters. But although the beau monde has been replaced by German tourists, lovers of bygone charm will find few better spots in Bohemia. Le Corbusier called Karlovy Vary a 'cream cake' – an insult from a modernist – but less doctrinaire types will revel in the confectionery. Built along the bubbling Teplá river, the town climbs wooded hillsides in pastel blocks.

The town's famous springs are forced up from subterranean hot rocks two kilometres down, and reach the surface at temperatures of 30 to 72°C, but until Emperor Charles IV stumbled upon it in 1358, little Wary was just a village of clean and healthy folk. It received its royal charter in 1370, and now 12 of the 60 springs have established medicinal benefits. Beware the hypochondriacal regulations that apply along the promenades – no dogs, smoking or loud noises – and in the colonnades, where 'long objects' are forbidden too.

Up the Teplá from the landmark **Thermal Hotel**, you pass **Dvořák Park** (Dvořákovy sady), featuring a lily pond and the wrought-iron colonnades that survived a Habsburg cannon-metal hunt during the 1914–18 war. Further upriver is the neoclassical splendour of the **Mill Colonnade** (Mlýnská kolonáda), where five springs hiss and gurgle to the surface. It is the favourite ambulatory of the town's hydrophiles, who drink waters through the spouts of teapot-like *pohárky*.

In the centre of town is the wooden **Market Colonnade**. Here you will find the **Vřídlo** ('Spring'), the fountain responsible for Karlovy Vary's rise to glory, housed in a glass Communist-era temple. When Charles IV chanced upon a spring while deer-hunting he was advised by his physician that it was suitable only for bathing; but in 1522, its oral advantages were publicized by early spa maniac Václav Payer, who recommended a daily dosage of 60 cups and 12-hour baths.

The street that runs up the hill from the plague column takes you past the circular colonnade of the **Castle Spring**, under a tower built by Charles, to **Stag Leap** (Jelení skok), the tall rock where Charles' quarry was sighted – leading him to the spring.

Getting There and Around

Karlovy Vary is 132km west of Prague. By **car** join the E48 on Milady Horákové running north by Letná Park. **Coaches** leave Florenc bus station more or less hourly and take 1½–2 hours; a one-way ticket costs around 100kčs. **Trains** leave from Masarykovo nádraží train station three times a day and take 3 hours; tickets cost around 140kčs one way.

There are two **funiculars** in the town.

Tourist Information

Karlovy Vary: Infocentrum, Lázenská 1, **t** 353 236 377, **f** 353 232 858, *www.karlovyvary.cz*.

Spa Treatments, Specialities and Souvenirs

The town's clinics handle conditions from indigestion to quadriplegia. Treatments can be booked at Čedok offices abroad. In the town, Infocentrum (next to the Vřídlo; *see* opposite) can tell you if Karlovy Vary can treat your ailment. It can also book hotels and guides.

Of the municipal baths, Baths III and V, luxurious Bath I and the new Bath VI are open to foreigners. They offer watery services from massage to low-voltage electric shock. If you just want a dip, there's an outdoor pool on the hill behind the Thermal Hotel, filled with water from a cool spring. Sparkling clean and with a breathtaking view over the town, there are few more satisfying swims in Bohemia (*open Mon–Sat 8–8, Sun 9–8*).

The town also has a few dietary specialities. Look out for *oplatky*, sweet wafers designed to mitigate the foul taste of the waters, and the ubiquitous Becherovka, a herbal tipple developed by town chemist Dr Becher in the 19th century. Porcelain from its factories and Moser snifters are the town's most popular souvenirs – the latter balloon-sized glasses that have the sole purpose of making superior cognac taste even more superior.

Eating Out

Embassy, Nova louka 21, **t** 353 22 11 61 (*expensive*). To dine in the style that Karlovy Vary deserves, make a reservation at the dark and discreet Embassy, and gorge yourself on smoked eels and asparagus tips. The cure wouldn't be worth it without the indulgence.

Promenáda, Tržiště 31, **t** 353 22 56 48 (*moderate*). Huge, Baroque vinotheque for fine dining or sampling the regional wines.

Zámecký Vrch, Zámecký Vrch 14, **t** 353 22 13 21 (*cheap*). Sprawling old mansion with a garden near the river; wooden beams, vaults and classic Czech dishes like stuffed pork and cottage cheese dumplings.

Salvation of the soul always took second place to sins of the flesh in Karlovy Vary. The town was blessed with just one Counter-Reformation masterpiece, the oval **Church of St Mary Magdalene** (Kostel sv. Marie Magdalena), built by Kilian Dienzenhofer in 1732–6, on the hill across the river. An enjoyable approach is by **funicular** (*lanovka*), walking down again past bulbous spires. In the same square is the **Vítězslav Nezval Theatre** (Divadlo V. Nezvala), financed by toilet admission fees. Its stage curtain was painted by three Viennese painters in 1885, one of whom was a young Gustav Klimt. The embankment beyond the theatre is called **Old Meadow** (Stará louka), and is lined with the oldest houses in town. On the right at the end is another **funicular**. It takes you to a view so good that it is disillusioning, revealing the spa as a tiny oasis in the greyness of a 20th-century town.

The 500-bed **Grand Hotel Pupp**, the core of which is 300 years old, marks the end of the town. The twilight splendour of the neo-Renaissance **Bath 1** (Lázně 1), opposite the hotel, offers the chance to munch water biscuits in Emperor Franz Josef's imperial bathtub, before heading upstairs for the roulette tables. A few hundred metres down **Goetheova stezka** is a bust of Goethe, who paid Carlsbad thirteen visits.

Karlštejn

*Statni hrad Karlštejn, **t** 311 681 617, **f** 311 681 211, www.hradkarlstejn.cz.*
Ppen 1 Mar–24 Nov, and two weeks at Christmas, at the following times:
Christmas weeks Tues–Sun 9–3; April and Oct Tues–Sun 9–4; May, June and
Sept, Tues–Sun 9–5; July–Aug Tues–Sun 9–6; closed noon–12.30 in high
season, noon–1pm in low season; adm by guided tour only. The chapel tour
is for groups of 12 or fewer and must be booked in advance.

Bohemia is full of Gothic castles. Karlštejn is one of the closest to Prague; its slate roofs and towers perched on their limestone peak are almost too perfect to believe. Karlštejn was begun in 1348 by Charles IV, and by 1367 it had been turned into a vast symbol of the strange universe that the emperor inhabited. Its three components were designed to mark a mystical ascent from the mundane level of temporal power (the emperor's quarters), up 260m to the pinnacle of the castle, the Chapel of the Holy Rood. In the late 19th century it was restored according to the neo-Gothic theories of Josef Mocker. Much of its interior suffered, but it is still well worth a visit.

The tour of the lowest level takes you into a richly panelled **Audience Hall**, past an altarpiece by Tomaso da Modena (1325–79), and into the **Luxembourg Hall**. A minuscule model shows how the original room looked.

Spiritual concerns begin to take over in the **Church of the Virgin**, where Charles is still honoured with a requiem on 29 November. Its lively *Relic Scenes* (c.1357) are among the earliest European portraits. They show the emperor receiving oddments of the Passion from Charles V of France (left), and placing them in his Reliquary Cross. *Scenes of the Apocalypse* cover the other walls; you can just make out hallucinations suffered by John on Patmos, including a city collapsing into topsy-turvy destruction, and the fiery seven-headed and ten-horned Beast itself.

Next to the church is **St Catherine's Chapel**, consecrated to one of Charles' patron saints, adopted by the emperor after she saved his life on an Italian battlefield. The oratory is studded with chalcedonies, amethysts and jaspers set in gilt stucco. Paintings of the seven Bohemian patron saints line the side of the chapel. On the altar is a votive scene of the emperor kneeling under the Virgin.

In the third and last stage of Karlštejn the fervent chiliasm of the emperor and his age reaches an unparalleled climax in the **Chapel of the Holy Rood** (Cross). Accessible

Getting There and Around

Karlštejn is 28km southwest of Prague. To get there by **car** follow signs on Strakonická (south), the western embankment of the Vltava. **Trains** to Karlštejn leave Smíchovské nádraží hourly, taking 35 mins, for 55kčs.

The castle is a stiffish (2km) **walk** from the railway station. Walking routes through the hills and forests are marked on tree trunks and cairns. If you don't fancy the walk from the station, there are hundreds of Prague-based tour operators who'll deposit you at the door in a coach.

Eating Out

The road up the hill to Karlštejn is lined with cafés eager to sap the pockets of day-trippers. Eat in Prague before leaving, take pot luck wherever there's a table, or picnic in the woods.

only via a corkscrew staircase and fortified with walls that are up to 5½ metres thick, the chapel was designed by Charles to house his crown jewels and Reliquary Cross. It also represented the promised Heavenly City, where he could contemplate the bliss of salvation after the tribulation of revelation in the church below. Under its gilt vaults, studded with hundreds of glass stars, a moon and a sun, he would pray in the light of 1,300 candles. The emperor's painter, Master Theodoric painted over 120 saints, prophets and angels to guard Charles and his jewels – Gothic gems.

Kutná Hora

Kutná Hora means 'mining mountain'. The town grew out of nothing in the late 13th century, when silver and copper were discovered in the hill. The Přemysl kings muscled in on the operation, and the city boomed as it began to yield up thousands of tons of precious ores annually. It was granted a royal charter (1308), grew into one of the largest towns in Europe, and became the second home of King Wenceslas IV in 1400 – and then, in the mid-16th century, its silvery life-blood was finally exhausted. But its crumbling Baroque and rococo townhouses are peppered with some of the finest Gothic architecture in Bohemia.

The highlights of the town are packed south of the main square, including the 82m tower of the **Church of St James** (Kostel sv. Jakub), which rises incongruously from a curving lane of pastel cottages. The citizens started to build it in 1330, but splendid as it is, it was just a trial run for their later effort.

The **Church of St Barbara** (Kostel sv. Barbora; *open April and Oct Tues–Sun 9–11.30 and 1–4; May–Sept 9–5.30; Nov–Mar Tues–Sun 9–11.30 and 2–3.30; adm*) was built between 1388 and 1558 and ranks among the most splendid Gothic churches in Europe. Its three steeples and web of gargoyle-bedecked flying buttresses can be seen from across the town. The church is even more fantastic when you consider that it was miners who financed it, in honour of their patron saint (shared by anyone who faces sudden death). Bohemia's finest architects worked on the church for over 150 years. Peter Parléř began the eight eastern chapels. The most striking feature of the church, the wondrous flowers and stars of the nave's vaulting, was the work of Benedict Ried. The Jesuits moved in their Baroque baggage – the chapels at the west end have altars dedicated to SS Ignatius and Francis Xavier – but the original Gothic decoration is superb. Three of the chapels are covered with late 15th-century frescoes: the Crucifixion; the Queen of Sheba; a colossal St Christopher fording a fishy stream (he is another protector against sudden death); and miners at work. Local traditions have influenced the art of the period with striking effect in the church's architectural grandeur. At the southwest end an entire wall is covered with images of coiners and angels, neither group more glorified than the other.

As you walk through the streets of the town, look out for the late 15th-century **stone fountain** in Rejskovo náměstí, the **plague column** of 1715 at the junction of Husova and Šultysova, and the Gothic façade of the **Stone House** (Kammený dům) on Radnická.

Getting There and Around

The scenic route by **car** is the 333 (from Vinohradská); the fast route the D11 motorway to Poděbrady, then the 38 via Kolín.

There are regular **buses** from Florenc station. It takes 1hr 20mins, 60kčs one way.

Regular **trains** from Hlavní nádraží take 50mins and cost 60 60kčs; add 20–30mins if you have to change at Kolín.

You can **walk** everywhere, and the town is well signposted.

Tourist Information

Kutná Hora: Infocentrum, Palackého nám. 377, **t** 327 515 556, *www.kutnahora.cz*.

Eating Out

U **havířů**, Šultysova 164 (near the plague column) (*cheap*). Pub serving beer and tasty daily specials. *Closed Mon.*

U **Mikulase Dačického**, Rakova 8, **t** 327 51 22 48 (*cheap*). Big wooden beer hall serving beer and Czech pub grub. Breezy summer house.

The **Italian Court** (Vlašský dvůr; Havličkovo náměstí *552*, *t 327 51 28 73; open Mar and Oct Tues–Sun 10–5; April–Sept Tues–Sun 9–6; Nov–Mar Tues–Sun 10–4; adm by guided tour only*) was set up as a mint in 1300 by Wenceslas II after Florentine financial experts suggested he make money by producing coins. The *groschen* became the euro of its time, used by merchants across Europe. You can see it in the museum, alongside the *taler*, precursor of the dollar. Wenceslas IV moved his royal residence here in 1400, with a **Session Chamber**, used when troublesome nobles wanted a word. Diets (parliaments) assembled here into the 16th century. The same king built the chapel, smothered by garish neo-Gothic painting from 1904.

The **Hrádek Mining Museum** (*Barborská 28, t 327 51 21 59; open April and Oct Tues–Sun 9–noon and 1–5; May–Sept Tues–Sun 9–noon and 1–6; adm by guided tour only*) is built over a mine shaft, and is the perfect spot to contemplate the drowning, burning and asphyxiation that were the causes of premature death in medieval Kutná Hora.

Beyond the museum on Barborská is the former **Jesuit College**, built in the mid-17th century and the largest outside Prague; to your left is an avenue of the Baroque sculpture so loved by the Society of Jesus.

Hungary: Practical A–Z

07

Average temperatures °C											
Jan	Feb	Mar	April	May	June	July	Aug	Sept	Oct	Nov	Dec
−1.2	0.8	5.6	11.4	16.3	19.8	21.7	20.9	16.8	11.1	5.2	0.8

Climate and When to Go

In summer Budapest can be uncomfortably hot. Many establishments close in July and August. Winter can be bitterly cold, the average temperature around the freezing mark, troughing in January. So the best time to visit is late April–June or September and October.

Crime and the Police

Police: t 107 or t 112
Tourist police (Budapest): V. Vigadó u. 6,
  t 4388080
Ambulance: t 104
Fire: t 105

Most of the crime in Budapest is organized crime. It is generally safe to walk at night, but use common sense in outlying districts, especially District VIII. Beware pickpockets in the tourist areas, especially around crowds and on public transport.

Beware tricksters. Never change money on the streets. A common ploy is for a girl to pick up a foreign male and take him to buy her drinks. The bill is extortionate, and the man pressurized to pay. The same tactic is used in red-light venues. If anyone claiming to be the police asks to see money or a credit card, it is a scam. Demand to be taken to the police station and watch them run.

Call the police or contact the **Complaints Office**, Budapest Municipal Police HQ BRFK: XIII, Teve u. 6.

Disabled Travellers

Budapest is not geared up for disabled travellers. Wheelchair access is limited. Most sights and museums are housed in 19th-century buildings with copious steps, and most major roads can only be crossed by subway. Apart from the M1 metro line and the Airport Minibus, transport is also equally unadapted for wheelchairs.

For more information contact the **Hungarian Disabled Association**, San Marco utca 76, **t/f** 3882388.

Electricity

The Hungarian electricity supply is 220 volts and the plugs are of the standard Continental type with two round pins. Bring an adaptor.

Embassies and Consulates

In Budapest
Australia: XII. Királyhágó tér 8–9, t 457 9777, *www.australia.hu. Open Mon–Fri 9–12.*
Canada: XII. Budakeszi út 32, t 392 3360, f 392 3390. *Open Mon–Thurs 8.30–10.30 and 2–3.30.*
Ireland: V. Szabadság tér 7/9, t 302 9600. *Open Mon–Fri 9.30–12.30 and 2.30–4.*
New Zealand: VI. Teréz krt. 38, gr. floor 16, t 4282208. *Open Mon–Fri 11–4.*
UK: V. Harmincad utca 6, t 266 2888, f 266 0907. *Open Mon–Fri 9.30–12.30 and 2.30–4.30.*
USA: V. Szabadság tér 12, t 475 4400, f 475 4764. *Open Mon–Fri 8.15–5.*

Hungarian Embassies and Consulates Abroad
UK, 35 Eaton Pl, London SW1X 8BY, t (020) 7235 2664, *www.huemblon.org.uk.*
USA, 3910 Shoemaker St, NW, Washington DC 20008, t (202) 362 6730, *www. huembwas.org.*
Canada: 299 Waverley Street, Ottawa, Ontario, K2P 0V9, t (613) 230 2717, f (613) 230 7560, *www.docuweb.ca/Hungary.*

Health and Insurance

No vaccinations are required to enter Hungary. Medicines can be obtained with prescriptions written abroad, and most common over-the-counter drugs are available.

Foreign citizens are entitled to first-aid and emergency ambulance treatment free of charge if injured. EU citizens are now entitled to free treatment with a stamped E111 (available from post offices), but travel insurance is still recommended.

See **Budapest**, p.180, for English-speaking doctors, dentists and pharmacies.

Money

Hungarian currency is the **forint** (Ft in this book, sometimes HUF elsewhere). Coins come in 1, 2, 5, 10, 20, 50 and 100Ft; notes in 200, 500, 1,000, 2,000, 5,000, 10,000 and 20,000Ft. The rate of exchange at the time of writing was approximately £1 = 357Ft, €1 = 247Ft, $1 = 190Ft. Hungary is set to switch to the euro in 2009.

The best way to travel is using a bank card and **ATMs**, which are very numerous. Major **credit cards** are also accepted just about everywhere. Rates for exchanging cash vary wildly, the worst from hotels and tourist spots, the best from banks and certain exchange offices. In the latter, always double-check the rate and commission that apply to you.

Traveller's cheques are hard to change, and the commission/rates are unfavourable. The AEB Bank is best (there's one at Astoria). The Magyar Külkereskedelmi Bank, V. Szent István tér 11, transfers money from abroad.

There's a **24-hour exchange service** at V. Apáczai Csere János u. 1. Leftover forints can be exchanged up to 20,000Ft, more with an exchange receipt.

National Holidays

1 Jan New Year's Day
15 Mar Revolution Day.
Mar/April Easter Monday
Mar/April Whitsun
1 May Labour Day.
20 Aug St Stephen's Day.
23 Oct Remembrance Day.
24–5 Dec Christmas (*Karácsony*).

On these dates, public buildings will all be closed. See p.181 for an explanation of what goes on during these and other festivals.

Price Categories

Hotel Price Categories

Prices for hotels are almost always quoted in euros (€), even when payment is expected in forints. The approximate price you should expect to pay, for a double room with bath in high season, is as follows:
luxury over €200
expensive €140–200
moderate €80–140
inexpensive less than €80

Restaurant Price Categories

The approximate price for a three-course meal with wine is as follows:
luxury over €25
expensive €18–25
moderate €10–18
inexpensive less than €10

Telephones

The **international code** for Hungary is **t** (00) 36. The **code for Budapest** is **t** 01, which is not necessary to dial not necessary if you're there. To dial Budapest from abroad, dial **t** 00 36 1 (i.e. drop the 0 from the code).

The code for **long-distance calls within Hungary** is **t** 06. You also have to dial **t** 06 before calling mobile phones.

For **international calls from Hungary**, dial **t** 00, wait for the dialling tone, then dial the country code, area code and number.
Operator: **t** 191
Domestic directory enquiries: **t** 198
International enquiries: **t** 199
Sending a telegram in Hungary: **t** 192

Public phones are common. Some take 20, 50 or 100Ft coins, but most take cards, available from post offices, hotels, supermarkets and newsagents, costing 800Ft or 1,800Ft. International calls are very expensive, much cheaper if using an international card (from tourist offices, Vista (*see* p.179), or news stands).

Time

Summer time, from early March to late October, is GMT +2hrs, Eastern Standard Time

+7hrs, Pacific Standard Time +10hrs. In winter clocks go back an hour to GMT + 1hr.

Note that Hungarians represent times in a way which can be confusing to Westerners: ½8 means 7.30.

Tipping

Service in restaurants is usually 10%. Tell the waiter how much change you expect. If you say 'thank you' (*köszönöm*) when handing over the bill, it means you expect them to keep all the change. Give a small tip to cloakroom attendants, taxi drivers or changing room attendants at the baths. Most people leave 10% where appropriate or 50Ft.

Toilets

Public toilets (*WC* or *toalett*; *női* or *nők* is women and *férfi* or *férfiak* is men) usually charge a small fee and have a concierge.

Tourist Information

Tourist information abroad is available from embassies (*see* above). The following websites are useful:

www.budapestinfo.hu: Budapest's official home page.

www.budapest.hu: A site maintained by the mayor's office.

www.livebudapest.com: Articles and listings.

www.timeout.com/budapest: Background information and listings.

www.budapestweek.hu: Listings.

Hungary: Budapest

08

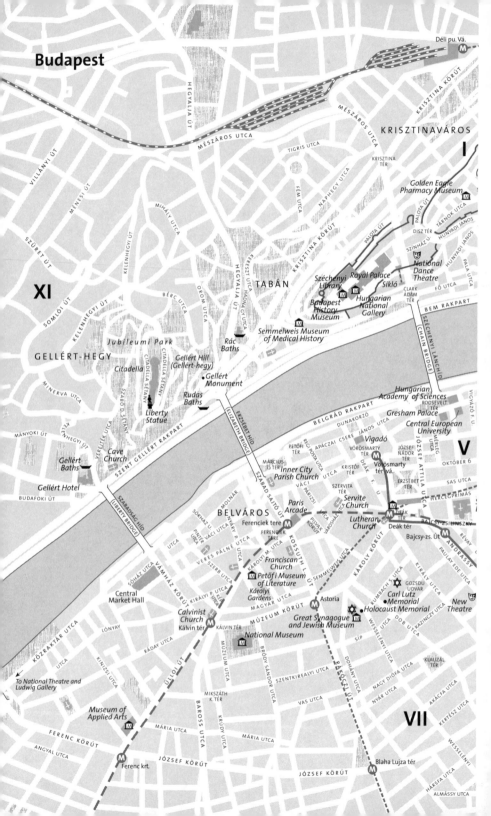

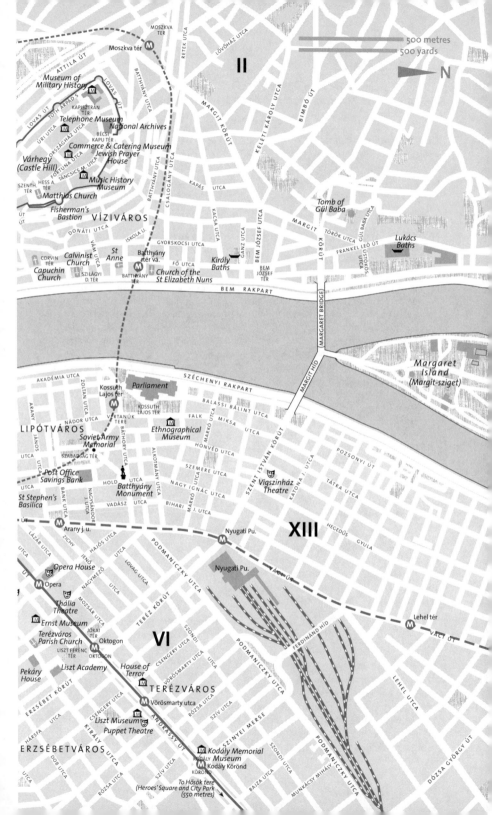

Getting There

See **Travel**, pp.4–5, for details of airlines flying to Budapest. You can also travel by train or coach, see pp.5–7.

Getting from the Airport

Budapest's Ferihegy Airport is 15 miles (20km) southeast of the city. Ferihegy 1 (**t** (01) 269 9696) has just been reconstructed for use by budget airlines. Malév (the ex-state airline) uses Terminal 2A (**t** (01) 296 7000 Departures; **t** (01) 296 8000 Arrivals); all other airlines use 2B (**t** (01) 296 5052 Arrivals; **t** (01) 296 5883 Departures).

LRI, the airport administration, runs a **minibus service**, bookable at its counter in Arrivals, that will take you anywhere in Budapest (2,100Ft single, 3,600Ft return). To arrange pick-up for the return, call **t** (01) 296 8555 one day in advance.

The **93 bus** runs from just outside the terminals (buy a ticket from the machine, and validate it on the bus) to its terminus at the M3 metro station in Kőbanya-Kispest. The total journey to the centre is about an hour. The last bus leaves the airport at 11.45pm. The last **metro** leaves at 11.10pm, the there's the **50É night bus** from the metro station.

To get from the airport to the centre by **taxi**, look for the board indicating fixed prices in the Arrivals area. The fare should be c. 5,000Ft.

Getting Around

The Budapest transport company **BKV**, www.BKV.hu, runs a fast, efficient and cheap network consisting of three metro lines (a fourth is planned), buses, trams, trolley-buses and local trains (HÉV). All run between about 4.30am–11.30pm. A few night buses ply the busier routes.

www.utak.hu has route planners, maps, ticket prices, traffic news and other info.

Tickets and Passes

The same tickets are used for all modes of transport, one ticket good for one ride on one vehicle only: if you change metro lines, you need to have another validated ticket. Tickets can be bought at any metro station, from some news stands, and from vending machines at busier bus/tram stops, which only accept change and often don't work. To minimize frustrating moments when a ticket just isn't available, buy a **book of tickets** or a **pass**. Don't be tempted to travel without one: plain-clothes inspectors will fine you 2,000Ft. Pleading ignorance does not work.

Tickets must be validated (punched) for each journey. In the metro, this is fairly obvious, but on some buses and trams you might have to watch someone else first. Tickets cost 145Ft, 1,250Ft for 10, 2,450Ft for 20; a day pass is 1,150Ft, a 3-day pass 2,300Ft, a weekly pass 2,700Ft, a 2-week pass 3,500Ft, a 30-day pass 5,400Ft (requires an ID card: bring a photo). Children up to 6 travel free.

By Metro

Trains are identified by destination rather than direction or name, Paris-style. There are three lines: yellow (M1), red (M2) and blue (M3), all connecting at Deák tér. A Metro Section ticket for 3 stops on one line costs 105Ft. A Metro Transfer ticket, allowing you to travel on two lines consecutively, costs 240Ft. See p.283 for a metro map.

By Tram

At rush hour, though packed, these are a godsend. The most useful routes are 4 and 6, which follow the Nagykörút (see p.208) all round Pest, terminating at Moszkva tér in Buda. Line 2 hugs the Danube on the Pest side, affording great views, and line 19 follows the Buda embankment from Batthyány tér to beyond the Gellért hotel.

By Bus

Most buses are very modern, with displays showing the next stop. When you want to get off, press the button on the rail next to the doors. Especially out of the centre, the distance between stops can be very large. Buses with a red square around their number are express and make fewer stops. Those with red numbers follow different routes. A useful route is the 86, following the Buda embankment from Óbuda past the Gellért hotel.

The 6É night bus follows the 4/6 tram route round the Nagykörút; 50É follows the M3 line, 78É follows the M2 line. They run every 15mins or so, and begin as normal transport ends.

By Local Train

There are four suburban train (HÉV) lines; you are most likely to use the one from Batthyány tér (M2) to Óbuda and Szentendre. A normal ticket is valid as far as Óbuda, since it is officially within city limits.

By Boat

Ferries (t 369 1359, *www.ship-bp.hu*) run every couple of hours from May to early September between Boráros tér, at the Pest end of Petőfi Bridge, and Római part, just north of Aquincum. The last ferry stops at the Pest end of Margaret Bridge.

By Taxi

Taxis that hang around outside major hotels, tourist spots, stations and the airport often overcharge; phoning a taxi is always a safer bet. Ask roughly how much the journey will cost before getting in, and check the meter is working. Taxis are prohibited from charging more than the following rates anywhere in Budapest, and should issue a receipt on request. **6am–10pm**: 300Ft basic fee, 240Ft/km, and 60Ft/min waiting fee; **10pm–6am**: 420Ft basic, 340Ft/km and 85Ft/min waiting. The following have good reputations, and dispatchers speak English: **Fő Taxi**, t (01) 222 2222.
City Taxi, t (01) 211 1111.

Car Hire

Driving in the city itself is a bad idea. If you do drive, be aware that the use of dimmed headlights is obligatory even during daylight out of city limits. The speed limit is 80km/h unless stated. In city limits it is 50km/h.

All the major companies are at the airport.
Avis, V. Szervita tér 8, t (01) 318 4859, airport t (01) 296 6421, *www.avis.hu*.
Budget, I. Krisztina krt 41–3, t (01) 214 0420, airport t (01) 296 8197, *rentacar@budget.hu*.
Hertz, V. Apáczai Csere János u. 4 (Hotel Marriott), t (01) 266 4361, airport t (01) 296 0988, *www.hertz.hu*.
Dollar Thrifty, XIII. Váci út 175, t (01) 237 7300, *www.thrifty.hu*.

Bike Hire

Riding a bike around town is no more recommended than driving. However, it can be a very good idea in the Buda Hills, or on Margaret Island.
Nella Bikes, V. Kalmán Imre u. 23, t (01) 331 3184, *www.nella.hu*.
Yellow Zebra, V. Sütő u. 2, t (01) 266 8777, *www.yellowzebrabikes.com*.
Bringó Hintó, XIII. Hajós Alfréd sétány 1, Margaret Island, t (01) 329 2073.
Charles Rent a Bike and Accommodation, II. Hegyalja út 23, t (01) 212 9196, *www.charleshotel.hu*.

Tourist Information

TOURINFORM, *www.hungarytourism.hu*, is the very helpful state-run tourist office. It can be found at:
V. Vigadó u.6 (Vörösmarty tér). *Open 24hrs.*
V. Sütő u. 2 (Deák tér), t (01) 317 9800, f 317 9656; 24hr infoline t (01) 438 8080. *Open 8–8.*
I. Szentháromság tér (Castle Hill), t (01) 488 0475, f 488 0474, *var@budapestinfo.hu*. *Open June–Sept 9–9; Oct–May 9–7.*
VI. Nyugati Station, t (01) 302 8580, f 473 1436, *nyugati@budapestinfo.hu. Open 9–7.*
VI. Liszt Ferenc tér 9–11, t (01) 322 4098, f 342 9390, *liszt@budapestinfo.hu. Open April–Oct 9–7.*
Tourism Office of Budapest: V. Március 15 tér 7, t (01) 266 0479, f 266 7477, *www.budapest info.hu*, *info@budapestinfo.hu*.
Hungarian National Tourist Office: II. Margit körút 85, t (01) 355 1133, f 375 3819, *htbuda pest@hungarytourism.hu*.

Infotouch electronic information terminals are scattered around town at: Astoria passenger underpass; Blaha Lujza tér; upper station of Castle Sikló; Deák tér; Déli, Nyugati and Keleti railway stations; airport terminal 2; Grand Market Hall; Moszkva tér; Tourinform.

For less official but equally helpful advice, go to **Vista Café and Visitor Centre**, where they cater very intelligently to all a traveller's needs: VI. Paulay Ede u. 2, t (01) 267 8603, f 268 1059, *www.vista.hu. Open Mon–Fri 8–8, Sat and Sun 10–6*.

Budapest Card

The Budapest Card currently costs 4,350Ft (2 days) or 5,450Ft (3 days). It covers unlimited use of public transport, free entry to most sights, and discounts in many shops, spas, etc. Children under 14 accompanied by the card-holder receive the same benefits. Available at big metro stations, TOURINFORM offices, travel agencies and hotels. There is also a **Hungary Card**, www.hungarycard.hu, 7,935Ft.

Guided Tours

Boat tours: **Mahart, t** (01) 384 1765, www.mahartpassnave.hu, run up to 9 sightseeing tours daily from the dock at Vigadó tér. The *Duna Bella* combines a 1hr tour with an hour on Margaret Island. The *Danube Legend* does 1hr night cruises with sound and vision shows. They also run a 2hr folklore tour with a three-course dinner and gypsy music and dancing, and a similar trip with operetta. Tickets and information from the dock.

Bus tours: **Budatours, t** (01) 374 7070, reservations **t** (01) 353 0558, run a recommended 2hr tour with tape-recorded guiding, departing from the corner of Andrássy út and Bajcsy-Zsilinszky. **Cityrama** offer a whole host of different tours; pick up their booklet from Vista, ticket offices or V. Báthory utca 22 for details, or call **t** (01) 302 4382. **IBUSZ, t** (01) 485 2700, organize 'live' English tours from Erzsébet tér at 10.30 year-round and 3pm May–Sept, as well as lots of other tours. **Queenybus, t** (01) 247 7159, run 3hr tours from the Basilica, some in an open-top bus.

Walking tours: **Budapest Walk** run tours from Hősök tere (M1) stop. Informative commentaries. **Budapest Walks, t** (01) 340 4232, the original walks company, host tours in English daily 15 April–30 Sept. The Pest tour leaves from Gerbeaud in Vörösmarty tér and lasts 2hrs. The Buda Castle tour leaves from the Matthias Church. **I.A. Tours** offer 3hr tours including all the major sights, leaving from the steps of the Palace of Arts in Heroes' Square daily. **Jewish Heritage walking tours** start at the Great Synagogue every day but Sat. At the end there is a chance to taste traditional non-kosher Central European Jewish food (except Sun).

In the air: **Indicator, t** (01) 249 9824, organize 20min pleasure flights on request, *Mar–Nov only*. **Sup-Air Balloon Club, t** (01) 322 0015, can arrange balloon flights for at least two people (depending on the weather).

Internet Cafés

AMI, V. Váci u. 40, **t** (01) 267 1644. *Open 9am–midnight.*
BudapestNET, V. Kecskeméti u. 5, **t** (01) 328 0292. *Open 10–10.*
CEU Net Pont, V. Október 6. u. 14, **t** (01) 328 3506. *Open Mon–Fri 8am–10pm, Sat–Sun 9am–10pm.*
Matáv Pont, V. Petőfi S. u. 17–19, **t** (01) 485 6612. *Open Mon–Fri 9–8, Sat 10–3.* Also in all major malls, such as Westend City Centre by Nyugati Station.
Westel-Enternet, V. Váci u. 1. *Open daily 10–9.*

Post Offices

The main post office is at Petőfi Sándor u. 13, *open Mon–Fri 8–8.* The *poste restante* address is Magyar Posta, 1364, Budapest; the office is at the back of the building on Városház u., *open Mon–Fri 8–8, Sat 8–2.* Post offices at Keleti and Nyugati stations *open Mon–Sat 7–7.*

Emergencies and Medical

Police: **t** 107 or **t** 112.
Tourist police: V. Vigadó u. 6, **t** (01) 438 8080.
Ambulance: **t** 104; fire: **t** 105.
Complaints Office, Budapest Municipal Police HQ BRFK: XIII, Teve u. 6.

24hr emergency departments are at V. Hold u. 19, **t** (01) 311 6816, and II. Ganz u. 13–15, **t** (01) 202 1370. **Országos Baleseti Intézet** at VIII. Fiumei u. 17, **t** (01) 333 7599, specialize in broken limbs and accidents.

24hr medical care is offered by **Falck SOS Hungary**, II. Kapy u. 49b, **t** (01) 200 0100, which has an ambulance service. **IMS** at XIII. Váci u. 202, **t** (01) 329 8423, has English-speaking staff.

24hr dental services: **Profident**, VII. Károly krt. 1, **t** (01) 267 9602; **SOS Dental Service**, VI. Király u. 14, **t** (01) 267 9602.

A notice on the door of **pharmacies** indicates the address of the closest 24hr pharmacy. Those with a night service include: II. Frankel Leó út 22, **t** (01) 212 4311; IV. Pozsonyi u. 19; VI. Teréz krt 41, **t** (01) 311 4439; VIII. Rákóczi u. 39; IX. Boráros tér 3, **t** (01) 217 5997; XII. Alkotás u. 1b, **t** (01) 355 4691; XIV. Bosnyák u. 1a.

Festivals

An asterisk denotes a public holiday when shops and businesses are closed.

1 Jan: *New Year's Day

6 Jan–Ash Wed: *Farsang*. Celebrates the end of winter and fattening up before the fasting of Lent. Open-air music, carnivals and balls, culminating in a fancy-dress parade.

Early Feb: Hungarian Film Festival. Weekend event highlighting the best Hungarian films. Main venue is the Corvin cinema. Some films are subtitled in English.

15 Mar: *Revolution Day. Commemorates Petőfi's recital of his National Song outside the National Museum. Events there and around his statue in Március 15 tér.

Late Mar/early April: Budapest Spring Festival. The major annual arts event. Classical music, opera, jazz and folk; dance, including folk dance; painting and sculpture; theatre and cinema, often subtitled in English.

Easter: Mainly passes off quietly with church processions and egg painting. Arts and crafts fairs, e.g. in the Ethnography Museum; free performances of Bach's *St John Passion* in the Lutheran Church. *Easter Monday is a rowdy drunken occasion, when men douse women in cheap perfume in exchange for shots of *pálinka*. It can start as early as 6am, gets ugly by about 10am, and by the afternoon it is better to be off the streets.

Mar/April: *Whitsun

1 May: *Labour Day. No longer involving compulsory homage to Communist bigwigs, this is still a big event organized by trade unions in the parks, especially City Park.

Nearest weekend to 21 June: World Music Day. Most venues participate in this French innovation, and stages are set up in open places.

30 June: *Budapesti Bucsú*. A celebration of the withdrawal of Soviet troops in 1991. Music, theatre and dance in squares and parks.

Early–mid-July: World Music Festival (WOMUFE). A 2–3-day event as good as the performers at the time, becoming more established every year. In the Budai Parkszínpad by XI. Kosztolányi Dezső tér.

Second weekend in Aug: Hungarian Grand Prix (at Hungaroring). A major event; all the hotels are full and jack up their prices, restaurants are often fully booked, and every bar and café sets up its TV or screen.

Mid-Aug: Sziget Festival. Possibly Europe's biggest rock and pop festival, transforming Óbuda Island into a giant open-air party

with big-name international acts, beer tents, rave-marquees and every type of music, plus dance, theatre, films, etc. Budafest. Opera and ballet festival in the State Opera House.

20 Aug: *St Stephen's Day. Rites at the Basilica, craft fair and folk dancing in Castle Hill, and the procession through the streets with the Holy Right Hand leads up to a firework display from the Citadella.

Early Sept: Budapest Wine Festival.

Mid–late Sept: Budapest International Music Competition.

Late Sept: European Heritage Days. Public buildings open up for a weekend.

Late Sept–mid-Oct: Budapest Autumn Festival. Like the Spring Festival but more contemporary arts.

Late Sept–Oct: Budapest Music Weeks. The classical music season kicks off as close to the anniversary of Bartók's death as possible (25 Sept). City-wide events follow, focusing on the Vigadó and the Academy of Music on Liszt Ferenc tér. Music of our Time: two weeks of contemporary classical music.

Around 1 Oct: Budapest Marathon and Running Festival.

23 Oct: *Remembrance Day. Commemorates the 1956 Uprising. Wreath-laying at Imre Nagy's statue, at his grave in the New Cemetery, and in Kossuth tér.

1 Nov: All Souls' Day. Make an evening trip to the cemeteries, which stay open late for people to light candles to their departed.

6 Dec: Mikulmás. The night before, children put cleaned shoes out on the windowsill, expecting the national Santa Claus to fill them. If they've been bad, Krampusz the bogeyman might turn up instead.

24–5 Dec: *Christmas (*Karácsony*).

31 Dec: New Year's Eve (*Szilveszter*).

Shopping

Like most formerly Communist cities, Budapest has gone consumer-mad, opening its doors to all the major brand names from the West, and embarking on a passionate love affair with shopping malls, the bigger the better. The best is the **West End Mall** behind Nyugati station. High-street fashions are still a few steps behind but a number of talented young native designers are producing original, quality garments. Getting clothes made is an affordable option, and trawling the second-hand shops and flea markets for a quirky retro bargain can be fun. The specialist local products most suitable as gifts include folk art (although much of it is mass-produced), handmade porcelain and ceramics from the world-famous factories of Herend and Zsolnay.

Budapest excels in the range and quality of art and artefacts. A staggering quantity of galleries carry works from Hungary's past, as well as showcasing the talents of today's artistic community. The many antique shops around **V. Falk Miksa utca** and the southern end of **Váci utca** will let you know what you are legally entitled to take from the country. For real bargains, junk and kitsch head to a flea market and haggle. The best window-shopping is on Váci utca and its many side streets and courtyards, the north end overflowing with souvenirs, folk art and Western clothes shops, the south lined with antiques, jewellers, boutiques and cafés.

Department Stores and Malls

Duna Plaza, VIII. Váci u. 178. Mall.

Luxus, V. Vörösmarty tér 3, **t** (01) 318 2277. One of Budapest's last remaining ancient stores, with suitably old-fashioned staff.

Mammut, II. Széna tér, **t** (01) 345 8020. Mammoth indeed, with two giant wings, one packed with designer label outlets, the other still holding onto some smaller, older names. Huge food store in the basement.

West End City Center, VI. Váci út 1–3. A giant Postmodern mall next to Nyugati station, with a large food court, all the major designer stores, bars, and rides in a hot air balloon from the roof.

Flea Markets

These can be great fun, though you'll have to turn up early to get the bargains among the junk: things that haven't yet come back into fashion in Budapest or kitsch memorabilia. Even the inflated tourist prices can be extremely low, though haggling is essential. Decide on your maximum, start haggling at a third or half of what you're willing to pay, and don't ask the price unless you're willing to buy.

Ecseri Piac, XIX. Nagykőrösi út 156 (bus 52 from Boráros tér). In a vast lot in an industrial area: follow the crowds, or get off the bus at the used-car yard and walk through it the way you came. *Mon–Sat 8–4.*

Józsefvárosi piac, VII. Kőbányai út 21–3 (tram 28 or 37). There are no used goods or antiques here, just regular goods, such as clothes, of dubious provenance. It's known locally as the Chinese market: most of the phoney brand-name goods were probably made there. There are bargains to be found, but be careful, of pick-pockets and of being cheated. *Daily 6–6.*

Városligeti Bolhapiac, in the Petőfi Csarnok in City Park (Széchenyi fürdő, M1). A Hungarian garage sale full of old books, records, toys and Communist relics. *Sat and Sun 7–2.*

Folklore and Souvenirs

Anna Antikvitás, V. Falk Miksa u. 18–20. Good selection of beautiful embroidered linens.

Folkart Centrum, V. Váci u. 14. The first stop for all kinds of authentic Hungarian souvenirs.

The **Great Market Hall**, near Kálvin tér. Authentic costumes and linens: first floor.

Herend Porcelain, V. József Attila u. 7, **t** (01) 317 8133. Hungary's finest porcelain since 1826.

Majolika, V. Váci u. 46, **t** (01) 266 3165. Colourful folk pottery.

Tangó Romantic, V. Váci u. 8. Clothes made from Hungarian linens; the shop opposite sells the fabrics.

Zsolnay Porcelain, V. Kigyó u. 4, **t** (01) 318 3712. Bolder, more modern styles than Herend, but equally respected.

Where to Stay

Budapest t (01) –

Breakfast-lovers will be horrified to learn that the morning meal doesn't really fit into the Hungarian scheme of things. Few places bother with it at all.

Buda

★★★★art'otel, I. Bem rakpart 16–19, **t** 487 9487, **f** 487 9488, *www.artotel.hu* (*luxury*). This well-located boutique hotel is refreshingly innovative. The stylish, modern interior was designed down to the smallest detail by US artist D. Sultan, while the west wing consists of four renovated Baroque houses on Fő utca, whose high vaulted ceilings and old doors retain a genuine sense of history. The rooms are a good size and very attractive, with nice bathrooms. Those on the west side have views of the Matthias Church. Parking and sauna. *Batthyány tér (M2).*

★★★★★**Budapest Hilton**, I. Hess András tér 1–3, **t** 488 6600, **f** 488 6644, *www.hilton.com* (*luxury*). Luxury in the heart of the Castle district. Described by the Hilton president as the most beautiful pearl in the whole string, the building incorporates medieval remains, its wings linked by corridors running through a Gothic church tower. Rooms have been extensively refurbished recently. *Várbusz from Moszkva tér (M2).*

★★★★★**Danubius Grand Hotel**, XIII. Margit-sziget, **t** 329 2300, **f** 329 3923, *www.danubiusgroup.com* (*expensive*). Situated at the northern end of Margaret Island, this mansion-like building and its 19th-century period furnishings offer the comfort and grandeur of a bygone age. Rooms are decorated in fine taste, and those on the park side have balconies. You can take the waters for free in the attractive bathing complex of the Thermal Hotel, reached by an underground tunnel. *Bus 26 from Nyugati station.*

★★★★**Danubius Hotel Gellért**, XI. Gellért tér 1, **t** 385 2200, **f** 466 6631, *www.danubiusgroup.com* (*moderate*). A sumptuous and historic Art Nouveau building, as much tourist attraction and thermal bath as hotel; old-fashioned rooms of a good size, with decent bathrooms and large windows, though renovation is long overdue. First-floor rooms have balconies. Baths are free to guests, a major bonus. *Trams 47 and 49 from Deák tér.*

★★★**Astra Vendégház**, I. Vám u. 6, **t** 214 1906, **f** 214 1907 (*moderate*). Beautiful 300-year-old building whose spacious rooms are luxuriously decorated with furniture from Italy or Transylvania, original paintings and big beds. Cellar bar with pool table. The manager goes out of his way to be helpful and there is a 24hr reception. Highly recommended. *Batthyány tér (M2).*

★★★**Victoria**, I. Bem Rakpart 11, **t** 457 8080, **f** 457 8088, *www.victoria.hu* (*moderate*). Simple, tastefully decorated rooms with big beds but rather small bathrooms. Front rooms offer river views, while garden rooms have nice patios. Buffet breakfast. Polite and friendly English-speaking staff. *Bus 86 from Batthyány tér (M2), or walk.*

Uhu Panzió, II. Keselyű u. 1a, **t** 394 3876 (*moderate*). Hard work to get to, but this lovely turn-of-the-century villa is situated in a quiet forested valley in the Buda Hills. Nine simple but tasteful rooms, and a lovely flower garden with views. 10pm curfew. *Tram 56 from Moszkva tér (M2) and a 1km walk, mostly uphill.*

Ábel Panzió, XI. Ábel Jenő u. 9, **t/f** 209 2537 (*inexpensive*). A beautiful ivy-covered villa set on a quiet street away from the centre. Common areas are exquisitely decorated with antique furniture and the owner's fabulous paintings; the veranda overlooks a tree-filled garden. Highly recommended. Breakfast included. *Tram 61 from Moszkva tér (M2) or Móricz Zsigmond Körtér.*

Beatrix Panzió, II. Széher u. 3, **t/f** 394 3730, *www.beatrixhotel.hu* (*inexpensive*). This friendly, well-placed B&B has won awards. Good-sized rooms with decent bathrooms. Lovely front garden with terraces and a pond. Sauna, safes, and a helpful owner with good English. *Bus or tram 56 from Moszkva tér (M2), then a 200m walk.*

Helios Panzió, XII. Lidérc u. 5a, **t** 246 4658, *roomheli@matavnet.hu* (*inexpensive*). Classily decorated rooms, some with balconies. Excellent views. Big, beautiful garden at back, and a terrace at the front. Parking, and helpful staff. Recommended. *Bus 8 from Ferenciek tere (M3).*

Kulturinnov, I. Szentháromság tér 6, **t** 355 0122, **f** 375 1886 (*inexpensive*). Sixteen big, simple and clean rooms with high ceilings, housed in the neo-Gothic Hungarian Cultural Foundation building right opposite Matthias Church. Those on the road side can be noisy, but the staff are friendly, the price is right, and the location amazing. Buffet breakfast included. *Várbusz from Moszkva tér (M2).*

Central Pest

★★★★★**Four Seasons Hotel Gresham Palace**, V. Roosevelt tér 5–6, **t** 268 6000, **f** 268 5000, *www.fourseasons.com* (*luxury*). Spacious and stylish, decked out in marble, granite and polished wood, the rooms in this newly restored historic gem adhere to its exquisite

Art Nouveau mood (*see* p.226) and breathtaking grandeur.

★★★★★**Sofitel Atrium**, V. Roosevelt tér 2, **t** 266 1234, **f** 266 9101, *www.sofitel.com* (*luxury*). The exterior may be ugly, but the Sofitel's inside really is an atrium: a glass-roofed courtyard with palm trees, plants hanging from the balconies, and a glider plane suspended in mid-air. Even the lift is beautiful. Rooms are decent enough, but you'll be drawn back to the lobby.

★★★★★**Kempinski Hotel Corvinus**, V. Erzsébet tér 7–8, **t** 429 3777, **f** 429 4777, *www. kempinski-budapest.com* (*expensive*). A Postmodern extravaganza: glass, granite and steel put together with taste and imagination. The interior is equally well executed. Rooms are nicer and larger than most, with many distinctive touches, and the best bathrooms in town. Facilities include parking, pool, sauna, and fitness rooms. Its Corvinus restaurant is one of Budapest's finest.

★★★**City Panzió Mátyás**, V. Március 15 tér 8, **t** 338 4711, **f** 317 9086; **City Panzió Pilvax**, V. Pilvax köz 1–3, **t** 266 7660, **f** 317 6396; **City Panzió Ring**, V. Szent István körút 22, **t** 340 5450, **f** 340 4884. All *www.taverna.hu* and (*moderate*). This small chain of hotels offers modern, clean no-nonsense rooms with no real personality but handy locations. The Mátyás is best for both location and exterior.

Kálvin Ház, IX. Gönczy Pál u. 6, **t** 216 4365, *www.kalvinhouse.hu* (*moderate*). Simple, white, huge rooms with high ceilings and wooden floors in a handsome building nicely located near the National Museum and Market Hall. TVs and tubs. Great value.

Peregrinus Elte Hotel, V. Szerb u. 3, **t** 266 4911, **f** 266 4913 (*moderate*). Small gem of a hotel in a quiet but central location. Good-sized airy rooms with high ceilings. Good value.

Mellow Mood Central Hostel, Bécsi u.2, **t** 411 1310, **f** 411 1494, *www.mellowmoodhostel. com* (*inexpensive*). A superior hostel, with small and simple but decent rooms, lockers, shared kitchens, and a common room/bar. Great central location, surprisingly quiet.

Around Andrássy Út

★★★★★**Andrássy Hotel**, VI. Andrássy Út. 111, **t** 462 2100, **f** 322 9445, *www.andrassyhotel. com* (*luxury*). Attractive building with a

striking, chic interior, but certainly overpriced. Deluxe rooms (€30 extra) are much bigger, with tubs and balconies.

★★★★★**K & K Hotel Opera**, VI. Révay u. 24, **t** 269 0222, **f** 269 0230, *www.kkhotels.com* (*luxury*). This large chain-hotel feels smaller and more friendly than most, thanks to its bright, upbeat décor. Rooms are modern and tastefully furnished with big windows. Health club, sauna and buffet breakfast.

★★★★**Hotel Liget**, VI. Dózsa György u. 106, **t** 269 5300, **f** 269 5329, *www.liget.hu* (*moderate*). Situated near Heroes' Square (M1), this building is a mish-mash of shapes, colours and textures. The lobby is bright and shiny, centred on a long, curving bar. Rooms are small but agreeable. Well run with professional staff. Breakfast included.

★★★**Hotel Pest**, VI. Paulay Ede u. 3, **t** 343 1198, **f** 351 9164, *hotelpest@hotelpest.hu* (*moderate*). Plain outside, but a wonderful classical building inside, with a pleasant courtyard. Rooms are simple with big windows. Buffet breakfast included.

★★**Medosz**, VI. Jókai tér 9, **t** 374 3000, **f** 332 4316 (*inexpensive*). The only advantages here are its location, close to the most happening area in town, and price, one of Budapest's cheapest. The exterior is ugly, the lobby poor and the rooms small and rather tawdry.

★★★**Radio Inn**, VI. Benczúr u. 19, **t** 342 8347, **f** 322 8284 (*inexpensive*). Close to Kodály körönd (M1), the institutional and dated feel of this large hotel is made up for by the huge apartments with big windows, separate toilets and bathrooms, and small kitchens. In the back are two nice gardens surrounded by trees. A good option at this price.

Elsewhere in Pest

★★★★★**Corinthia Grand Hotel Royal**, VII. Erzsébet krt 43–9, **t** 479 4000, **f** 479 4333, *www.corinthiahotels.com* (*luxury*). The views as you enter this magnificent, newly restored 1896 palace are breathtaking: an atrium courtyard crossed by a glass bridge with perspective-hugging staircases and gorgeous chandeliers. A vast labyrinth, the building features five restaurants and 414 rooms, which are plush and comfortable.

★★★★★**Sydney Apartment**, XIII. Hegedűs Gyula u. 52–4, **t** 236 8888, **f** 236 8899, *www.*

sydneyaparthotel.hu (luxury–moderate). These spacious flats come with a bedroom, lounge, kitchen and bathroom, with all the accessories you could want. Indoor pool, Jacuzzi, sauna, steam room, gym, in-house masseur, laundry facilities, car park, and terrace. *A 5min walk from Lehel tér (M3).*

★★★★**Ambra Apartment Hotel**, VII. Kisdiófa u. 13, **t/f** 321 1533, *www.ambrahotel.kozep.com (moderate).* Fully equipped, decent-sized apartments, with modern décor in pastel shades. Sauna, Jacuzzi and buffet breakfast. A great deal, just *5min walk from Opera (M1).*

★★★**Corvin Hotel**, IX. Angyal u. 31, **t** 218 6566, **f** 218 6562, *corvin@mail.datanet.hu (moderate).* Close to Ferenc körút (M3), in a building with lots of character, this modern little hotel has small but clean and pleasant rooms, a car park, a good restaurant and a big, attractive garden at the back.

★★★**Ibis Centrum**, IX. Ráday u. 6, **t** 215 8585, **f** 215 8787 *(moderate).* This pleasant, professional hotel gives value for money. Rooms are modern, clean, simple and quiet. Windows are a bit small, and bathrooms are small with showers but no tub. Three no-smoking floors. There's an open-air 'garden' on the first floor. Parking and a safe.

★★★**Sissi Hotel**, IX. Angyal u. 33, **t** 215 0082, **f** 216 6063, *www.hotelsissi.hu (moderate).* Smart, modern and a bit more stylish than most, with tasteful if simple rooms in an eclectic building with a terraced facade. There's a garden, and breakfast.

★★★**Unio Hotel**, VII. Dob u. 73, **t** 479 0400, **f** 479 0401, *www.uniohotel.hu (moderate).* Very spacious rooms with high ceilings, big windows, and wood furnishings. Good value. *Walk from Oktogon (M1), or tram 4 or 6.*

★★★**Hotel Queen Mary**, VII. Kertész u. 34, **t** 413 3510, **f** 413 3511, *www.hotelqueenmary.hu (inexpensive).* Smart, well-located building with simple, quiet rooms. Buffet breakfast included. Good value. *Walk from Oktogon (M1), or tram 4 or 6.*

Marco Polo Hostel, VII. Nyár u. 6, **t** 344 5367, **f** 344 5368, *www.marcopolohostel.com (inexpensive).* An attractive building, with a courtyard and cavernous cellar bar-restaurant that has TV, pool tables, computers, and live music. Rooms are small and clean, but childishly decorated. Shared bath and kitchenette. *Free bus service from Keleti station. Astoria is the nearest metro (M2).*

Private Rooms

Private rooms and apartments represent a growing business in Budapest, and offer better value than hotels. Rooms often have bath and kitchen shared with other guests or the owner. Apartments are self-contained and can be very nice, if small.

IBUSZ, V. Ferenciek tere 10, **t** 485 2767, **f** 337 1205, *accommodation@ibusz.hu*, organize rooms for €21, apartments for €40–50, will show you pictures, and can be very helpful.

Vista, VI. Paulay Ede u. 2, **t** 26 78603, **f** 268 1059, *www.vista.hu*, offer a similar service. Otherwise, try **t** 922 5680, *www.nott-ltd. com/pgr.* for decent rooms at Astoria; or **t/f** 250 4918, *www.kurreisen.hu*, who have a number of rooms/apartments downtown.

Eating Out

Budapest **t** (01) –

In Budapest, there is often a fine line between a restaurant, café and bar, so see these categories for more options. Restaurants in expensive hotels are almost always excellent, and only mentioned here if exceptional.

Traditionally, culinary class barriers have not existed, so menus in the cheapest and most expensive restaurants can be virtually identical. The food in the expensive place will normally be superior, as will the surroundings, but the greatest difference will be in the service. You can generally expect even the cheapest place to have a menu in English and a waiter who knows enough English to take your order. Check to see if service is included: that the menu says it won't be doesn't mean a thing. And check the price of drinks.

In bars and some restaurants, wine, juices and soft drinks are often sold by the *deci*, which is a tenth of a litre (100ml). A glass of wine usually costs twice the number on the menu, which is the cost per deci.

Buda: Castle Hill

Alabárdos, I. Országház u. 2, **t** 356 0851 *(luxury).* In a 15th-century Gothic building, this feels like a banquet hall, with paintings of knights, swords and shields. Specialities of ancient Hungarian cuisine are put together with an expertise that explains the prices. The service is impeccable, the selection of drinks vast. *Closed Sun.*

Arany Kaviar, I. Ostrom u. 19, t 201 6737, *www. aranykaviar.hu* (*expensive*). Good portions of authentic Russian dishes, including some reasonably priced caviar, smoked salmon, and beef. A good range of vodkas and wines.

Pest Buda Vendéglö, I. Fortuna u. 3, t 212 5880 (*expensive*). Intimate and old-fashioned with a pianist playing schmoozy favourites. Gourmet meat-based food, excellent wine list. Lunch is more affordable.

Rivalda, I. Színház u. 5–9, t/f 489 0236, *www. rivalda.net* (*expensive*). By the Castle Theatre, decorated with classy but over-the-top theatre regalia. There's also an expansive cobbled courtyard and live music every night. Co-owned by an ex-Gundel chef, with a European-Hungarian menu that aims at quality rather than range of choice

Víziváros

Belgian Brasserie (Belga Söröző), I. Bem Rakpart 12, t 201 5082 (*moderate*). Popular Belgian-style bar-restaurant, stylishly fitted out, with a pleasant Hungarian crowd. A staggering range of beers, including Belle Vue Kriek and Leffe (light and dark) on tap. Starters include brioche, snails and frogs' legs, followed by mussels or meat dishes with a French slant. Tasty, plentiful food, good service, and a riverside terrace. *Batthyány tér (M2), then tram 19 or walk.*

Horgásztanya Vendéglő, I. Fő u. 27, t 212 3780 (*moderate*). Famous for their spicy fish soup, with décor to match, including an upside-down boat complete with plastic fisherman stuck to the ceiling. They also rustle up marjoram veal steak with brains, mushroom and bacon, or dishes fried on lava stone.

San Remo, II. Török u. 6–8, t 212 1991 (*moderate*). Simple, clean Italian-style cellar close to Margit Bridge. Lots of pizzas and seafood, a good range for vegetarians. *Closed Mon. Batthyány tér (M2), tram 4 or 6.*

Elsewhere in Buda

Remíz, II. Budakeszi u. 5, t 275 1396 (*expensive*). In the Buda Hills next to a tram depot.

Highly recommended for the best of traditional Hungarian cuisine. Barbecues in the wonderful garden are particularly popular in summer. *Bus 22 from Moszkva tér (M2).*

Náncsi Néni, II. Ördögárok u. 80, t 397 2742 (*moderate*). The most famous place in town for home-cooked Hungarian cuisine. Top marks for quality and quantity, and a thoroughly authentic experience. Try the braised wild boar cutlets, or seafood Thunderbolt. Booking is essential. *Bus 56 from Moszkva tér (M2), or Children's Railway (p.254) then walk.*

Marcello, XI. Bartók Béla u. 40, t 466 6231 (*inexpensive*). Popular and intimate Italian: an incredible range of pizzas, a good salad bar and a no-smoking policy. One of the few options in Gellért. *Closed Sun.*

Pest: City (Lipótváros)

Lou Lou, V. Vigyázó Ferenc u. 4, t 312 4505 (*luxury*). Two beautiful little rooms covered with small pictures. Perfectly prepared, sophisticated French-Hungarian *haute cuisine*, well presented, and an impressive wine list. Attracts a well-to-do crowd. *Closed Sat lunch and Sun.*

Café Kör, V. Sas u. 17, t 311 0053 (*moderate*). Small, popular bistro near the Basilica, with a simple, tastefully trendy interior. The menu is small yet more diverse and exciting than most places in town, and the food is excellent. *Breakfast until 11.30am. Closed Sun.*

La Fontaine, V. Mérleg u. 10, t 317 3715 (*moderate*). French specialities in well-furnished, spacious surroundings. The menu focuses on seafood and salads. Good wine selection, friendly service and reasonable prices, especially if you have the 3-course lunch special.

Majd Léonard, V. Balassi Balint u. 7, t 301 3891 *www.majdleonard.hu* (*moderate*). Decked out in a classic, old-fashioned coffee-house style, popular with a well-heeled local crowd. The menu is *nouvelle* Hungarian, with lots of European influences.

Szeraj, V. Szent Istvan krt 13 (*moderate*). Self-service Turkish restaurant near Margit Bridge, whose food is fast but far from junk. Great if you're in a rush, hungry, or have kids. *Open 9am–4am* and always packed.

Via Luna, V. Nagysándor József u. 1, t 312 8058 (*inexpensive*). The dining room resembles an Italian country villa. Various pastas and sauces, including some for veggies. Risottos, lots of fish and pizzas, salads and steaks.

Kisharang Étkesde, Október 6. u. 17, **t** 269 3861 (*inexpensive*). Typical small Hungarian diner. Chequered tablecloths, the whole bit. One of the survivors round here, which says a lot. Daily specials, tasty food, very cheap.

Govinda, V. Vigyázó Ferenc u. 4, **t** 269 1625 (*inexpensive*). Vegetarian set meal changing daily but basically an Indian thali: dal, two vegetable dishes, puri, rice, chutney. Healthy, filling and tasty, not necessarily spicy. Drinks are good, especially the lassis. The small cellar is calm and relaxing.

Lugas Étterem, V. Bajcsy-Zsilinszky 15, **t** 302 5393 (*inexpensive*). Best views of the back of the Basilica from this terrace across the main road. Laid-back and friendly, offering good portions of well-cooked Hungarian fare. There are a few veggie choices, like grilled courgette (zucchini) with dill and cheese sauce, plus salads.

Pest: Belváros

Corvinus (Keminski Hotel), V. Erzsébet tér 7–8, **t** 429 3777 (*luxury*). Considered one of the city's best restaurants. Setting, presentation and service are impeccable. The menu is small, international and clever.

Fausto's, VII. Dohány u. 5, **t** 2696806 (*luxury*). High-quality, genuine Italian food. The pasta is home-made, the sauces exquisite. A gastronomic delight with service to match. *Closed Sun. Not really Belváros, but a few minutes' walk from Astoria (M2).*

Iréne Légrádi Antique, V. Bárczy István u. 3–5, **t** 266 4993 (*luxury*). Close to Deák tér. Considered one of the best restaurants in Hungary for traditional Hungarian food. If it feels like dining in an antique shop...well, it is. Gypsy music in the evening. *Closed Sun.*

Képíró, V. Képíró u. 3, **t** 266 0430 (*luxury*). Bright artistic interior of an eclectic nature: Art Nouveau stained glass, Japanese windows, Greek columns, with gentle jazz. Shame about those very big, ugly paintings. The frequently changing menu is eclectic *haute cuisine*, like beef tenderloin *torte* baked with sweetbreads and goat cheese. Highly recommended, though portions tend to be small. Good selection of wines and whiskies. More affordable lunch specials.

Oroszlános Kút, Vörösmarty tér 7, **t** 429 9023 (*luxury*). The hallowed Gerbeaud institution is behind this fairly recent fine-dining venture, so it's understandably classy, and the Hungarian cuisine, with a few innovative touches, is about as good as it gets. Great outdoor seating also.

Cyrano, V. Kristóf tér 7–8, **t** 266 4747 (*expensive*). The menu, essentially French-international fusion, is one of the most daring and imaginative in town. Try the goose liver urban-style or the fresh butter-fish. Also gourmet salads and sandwiches. Just off Váci utca, the terrace is wonderful for people-watching, while the interior is dark and cavernous.

Kárpátia, V. Ferenciek tere 7–8, **t** 317 3596 (*expensive*). An extraordinary interior, bold, busy and very medieval, the walls covered in heavy patterns, much like the Matthias Church. There is a pleasant covered area outside. The food is traditional Hungarian cuisine cooked to perfection.

Múzeum Kávéház Étterem, VIII. Múzeum körút 12, **t** 267 0375 (*expensive*). Established in 1885, still with much of the original décor, including Károly Lotz frescoes. Good food in sumptuous surroundings. The menu is enormous. Very good wine list. *Booking essential. Closed Sun.*

Pest: Around Andrássy Út

Articsóka, VI. Zichy Jenö u. 17, **t** 302 7757 (*expensive*). Light and airy, popular and lively. The menu is sophisticated Mediterranean, with some nice innovations. Vegetarian dishes include baked artichoke hearts with gorgonzola. Lots of wines and cocktails. Reservations recommended.

Chez Daniel, VI. Szív u. 32, **t** 302 4039 (*expensive*). Real French food cooked by a real French chef using the freshest ingredients. The menu is small and select, with an ever-changing specials board. The bright little courtyard is delightful. *Booking essential.*

Cotton Club, VI. Jókai u. 26, **t** 354 0886 (*expensive*). Comfortable and classy lounge with dim lighting and a 1920's theme. Exceptional *haute cuisine* menu full of items like deer steak rosé with truffles. Quartets are set 4-course meals for €20–30. Live song and dance show nightly.

Cactus Juice, VI. Jókai tér 5, **t** 302 2116 (*moderate*). Basement pub with an unfortunate Wild West theme and speakeasy feel but excellent food. Well-prepared Hungarian fare with imaginative twists, and portions so big, some dishes require two plates. Try the Giant Pork BBQ with pickles. Some choices for veggies, and a good selection of beers.

Fészek Művész Klub Étterem, VII. Kertész u. 36, **t** 322 6043 (*moderate*). The best of meaty Hungarian cuisine served in a leafy interior courtyard surrounded by arcades and old street-lamps, or in the expansive, sophisticated interior, with live music. Large portions at surprisingly reasonable prices, popular with locals and tourists alike. *Recommended. Tram 4 or 6 or walk from Oktogon (M1).*

Karma Café, VI. Liszt Ferenc tér 11, **t** 413 6764 (*moderate*). A stunning interior that doesn't overplay the Eastern angle, with subdued lighting, plenty of brick and wood, and multiple layers. The very eclectic international menu features tandoori oven specialities. Equally suitable for drinks.

Marquis de Salade, VI. Hajós u. 43, **t** 302 4086 (*moderate*). Owned by an Azerbaijani lady, and featuring chefs from many different countries, the menu here is vast, international and very mixed, with plenty of meat, seafood and vegetarian choices. Reserve a table in the small, intimate cellar scattered with Eastern rugs.

Premier Étterem, VI. Andrássy út 101, **t** 342 1768 (*moderate*). The menu and terrace here are decent enough, but the real draw is the stunning Art Nouveau decor, focusing on a long vaulted ceiling with swirling patterns.

Két Szercsen Kávézó, VI. Negymező u. 14, **t** 343 1984 (*moderate*). Terracotta-coloured Mediterranean-style bistro and *tapas* bar with a changing blackboard menu. Decent wine selection and summer terrace. Always packed. *Open from 8am for breakfast.*

Elsewhere in Pest

Gundel, XIV. Állatkerti u. 2, **t** 321 3550 (*luxury*). Founded in 1894, Gundel is a legend: the most famous restaurant in Hungary, the highest-praised in Central Europe, and among the best in the world. The interior is exquisite, the garden a delight and the menu adds refinement to traditional Hungarian dishes. Of course it is expensive, and a little stiff and formal. The Sunday lunch buffet, served 11.30–3, is a bit less so. *Hőrök tere (M1).*

Robinson, XIV. Városligeti tó 5, **t** 422 0222 (*expensive*). An island restaurant (about 12ft from the shore) in City Park, bravely placed opposite Gundel. A friendly, laid-back atmosphere in beautiful surroundings. The French-inspired, cleverly planned menu changes regularly. Excellent, well-presented food. *Hőrök tere (M1).*

Bagolyvár (The Owl's Castle), XIV. Állatkerti u. 2, **t** 343 0217 (*moderate*). Gundel's sister restaurant is in a rustic Transylvanian building with wooden beams. The emphasis is on traditional cooking, prepared and served only by women. *Hőrök tere (M1).*

Costes Restaurant, IX. Ráday u. 4, **t** 219 0696 (*expensive*). International fusion food involving some imaginative combinations, served in a plush, intimate environment. Lots of salads and seafood. One of several good options on this happening street.

Soul Café and Restaurant, IX. Ráday u. 11–13, **t** 217 6986 (*moderate*). Large, trendy but comfortable interior with high vaulted ceilings, leather armchairs and soft lighting. Small but intelligent international menu. *Open daily till 1am.*

Kádár Étkezde, VII. Klauzal tér 9, **t** 3213622 (*inexpensive*). Small, very authentic Hungarian eatery with a nice atmosphere and a great menu of well-balanced meat dishes. *Open Tues–Sat 11.30–3.30.*

Cafés

Buda

Angelika, I. Batthyány tér 7, **t** 212 3784. On the river side of St Anne's Church, this is a bastion of old-fashioned style, complete with vaulted ceilings, gilt mirrors, lamps, chandeliers, marble tables and terrace views of parliament. Impressive selection of coffees, cakes, juices, teas, wines, spirits, cocktails, ice creams, beers and breakfast.

Café Miró, I. Úri u. 30, **t** 375 5458. The most successfully stylish modern spot in Castle Hill, decked out to resemble a large-scale piece of art by Miró, and with a terrace offering views of Matthias Church. Mixed clientele in the day, buzzing with locals in the evening. Good drinks, but if you're hungry, eat elsewhere.

Pierrot Café, I. Fortuna u. 14, t 375 6971. At the Béksi Kapu tér end of the street, this comfortable little café is bursting with eclectic charm. It is halfway to being a restaurant, with crêpes, seasonal specials like asparagus, vegetarian dishes and lunch deals (*expensive*). The bar has a good range of beer and wine as well as speciality coffees and cocktails. Live piano after 7pm.

Ruszwurm Cukrászda, I. Szentháromság tér 7. Budapest's oldest *pâtisserie*, open since 1827, its interior featuring some fine chaises-longues and an old stove. Views of Matthias Church. Staggeringly busy. *Closed eves.*

Pest

Auguszt Cukrászda, V. Kossuth Lajos u. 14–16, t 337 6379. Delightful little old-style coffee shop hidden away in the corner of a court-yard near Astoria. Good coffee and cakes, and an oasis of sophistication away from the downtown bustle.

Café Cinema, V. Semmelweis u. 2. Big café near Astoria with a low funky ceiling and subdued lighting. Very atmospheric, alive with the chatter of a young, cheerful crowd. Good prices for coffee, cakes, juices and a fair selection of wines, liquors and cocktails.

Café Eckermann, VI. Andrássy út 24, t 374 4076. A calm, modern place with great art, a nice terrace and a decent selection of coffees, teas, snacks, juices, wine and beer.

Café Mediterrán, VI. Liszt Ferenc tér 10, t 344 4615. The selection of drinks here is inexplicably poor, but the atmosphere is great and the clientele cheerful. Its summer terrace is one of the town's busiest. The action goes on till late then moves downstairs.

Café Miró Grande, VI. Liszt Ferenc tér 9. The comfy armchairs, funky furnishings, aquarium and stylish long bar make this yet another satisfying spot on the square for any kind of drink. Live Latin music nightly.

Café Mirákulum, V. Hercegprímás u. 19, t 269 3207. Tasteful, bright café-bar with Art Nouveau prints and a laid-back atmosphere. Fair selection of beers and wines, coffee, teas, juices and shakes. Some food.

Café Picard, V. Falk Miksa u. 10, t 311 8273. Tiny, stylish continental café near Parliament. Excellent strong coffee, tasty *tapas*, plus beer, wines and juices.

Café Vian, VI. Liszt Ferenc tér 9, t 342 8991. With its big, bright, comfortable interior decorated with wonderful art, and a small, elegant terrace, this still stands out despite the stiff competition. Excellent selection of bottled beer and wines, plus coffees, juices and cocktails. Food includes omelettes, salads, croissants and desserts. Clientele sophisticated and not necessarily young.

Central Kávéház, V. Károlyi Mihály u. 9. Vast old-style coffee house on Ferenciek tere with extremely high ceilings. Leather upholstery, marble tables and the gold, green and orange colour scheme add to the grandeur. Reasonable prices; intimate seating upstairs. The food is surprisingly good.

Gerbeaud, V. Vörösmarty tér 7, t 429 9000. The place to sit and enjoy coffee and cake at the social heart of Belváros. Sit out on the terrace to watch the crowds. Inside is replete with turn-of-the-century antique furniture and fittings. They also do breakfast, cold food and beer, but at a price. Round the corner is a slightly cheaper stand-up version and an expensive restaurant. The whole affair is quite touristy, and service is rushed.

Komédiás Kávéház, VI. Nagymező u. 26, t 302 0901. Small, old-style theatrical café, all wood, mirrors, brass and plush seating.

New York Kávéház, VII. Erzsébet körút 9–11, t 322 3849. Budapest's last remaining genuine coffee house from the pre-war era was still closed for renovation at time of writing. A glorious neo-Renaissance/Art Nouveau building overflowing with sumptuous details, if it's reopened.

River Café, V. Párizsi u. 6. On a quiet side street, with an atmosphere like a small French café, the perfect place to escape the bustle of nearby Váci utca. Meals also (*moderate*).

Zsolnay Kávéház, V. Váci u. 20. The nicest spot for a coffee on this busy stretch. Outside is a slightly raised terrace, inside is an old-style lounge, all wood and windows with a piano-player and fountain. Another contender for the best cakes in town. Also upstairs in the Béke Radisson Hotel at Teréz körút 43, near Nyugati Stn.

Entertainment

The monthly *Where Budapest* magazine has excellent listings for music and English-language shows. *Budapest Program* is also very useful. *Pesti Est* and its sister *Pesti Súgó* are more comprehensive but published in Hungarian. Or look in one of the ticket agencies on Váci u. **Ticket Express, t** 303 0999, *www.tex.hu*, have 6 counters around the city, including Deák tér 19 and the Ferenciek tere IBUSZ. Note that nearly all the theatres close for the summer (*June–Sept*).

Theatre

International Buda Stage, II. Tárogató u. 2–4, **t** 391 2500. English and Hungarian theatre, music, dance and concerts. Simultaneous translation into English during Hungarian shows. *Box office open daily 10–6. Tram 56 from Moszkva tér (M2).*

Katona József, V. Petőfi Sándor u. 6, **t** 318 6599. The best-reputed mainstream theatre company. *Box office open daily 2–7. Ferenciek tere (M3).*

Kolibri, VI. Jókai tér 10, **t** 312 0622. Small theatre showing some productions in English, usually by amateur companies. *Box office open Mon–Fri 9–5. Oktogon (M1).*

Merlin International Theatre, V. Gerlóczy u. 4, **t** 317 9338. The most professional venue offering English-language performances. *Box office open daily 2–7. Deák tér metro.*

Thália Szinház, VI. Nagymező u. 22–4, **t** 312 1280. Very attractive venue hosting theatre (often in English), dance, musicals and foreign troupes. *Box office open daily 10–6. Oktogon (M1).*

Trafó, IX. Liliom u. 41, **t** 215 1600. Very lively venue, with all sorts of events, often crossing over between art forms: art, poetry, music, theatre, exhibitions, dance, comedy, etc. *Box office open daily 5–8pm. Ferenc krt. (M3).*

Vígszínház (Comedy Theatre), XIII. Szent István krt. 14, **t** 329 2340. Wonderful Baroque theatre focusing on comedy; some big musicals. *Box office open Mon–Fri 1–7, Sat and Sun 1hr before curtain. Nyugati pu. (M3).*

Classical Music and Opera

The classical scene in Budapest is booming, and audiences are well known for their enthusiasm. Yehudi Menuhin called this 'the town of Bartók, Kodály, Doráti and the very responsive concert public'. It is thanks to these first two, who scoured the country for folk melodies which they incorporated into their own works, that Hungary found its own true classical voice. The best orchestras are the **Budapesti Fesztivál Zenekar,** the **Nemzeti Filharmonakusok,** the **MRT Szimfonikus Zenekara,** and the **Liszt Ferenc Chamber Orchestra.** Choirs are generally even better, the **Nemzeti Énekkar, MRT Énekkar** and **MRT Gyermek Kórusa** (a children's choir), all rated very highly. The **Bartók String Quartet (Bartók Vonósnégyes)** are also always worth seeing. The **Hungarian State Opera** company puts on a wonderful show, and a night spent at the magnificent Opera House is one of the most truly memorable experiences Budapest has to offer. They publish their own monthly schedule, available at the Opera House or at ticket agencies.

As well as the venues listed below, look out for events at **St Stephen's Basilica,** the **Lutheran Church,** the **Great Synagogue, Kiscelli Museum** and the **Old Music Academy** in the Liszt Museum. Note that most venues close for summer, when open-air venues are set up for music of all kinds, the main ones being **Budai Park Stage,** XI. Kosztolányi Dezső tér, **t** 466 9849 (*tram 49 from Deák tér/Kiskörút*); **Vajdahunyad Castle** in City Park, **t** 342 3198 (*Hősök tere, M1*); **Városmajor, t** 356 1565, just east of *Moszkva tér (M2).*

Bartók Béla Memorial House, II. Csalán u. 29, **t** 394 2100. Chamber concerts, usually on Fridays. *Bus 5 from Moszkva tér (M2).*

Hungarian State Opera House (Magyar Állami Operaház), VI. Andrássy út. 22, **t** 353 0170. Everything you could want from an opera house. Productions are lavish and dramatic. *Box office open Tues–Sat 10–7, Sun 10–1 and 4–7 (show days only). Opera (M1).*

Erkel Színház, VIII. Köztársaság tér 30, **t** 333 0540. The number two opera house, with a totally different feel. A vast, socialist building, usually hosting less high-profile productions, ballets and musicals. *Box office open Tues–Sat 10–7, Sun 10–1 and 4–7 (show days only). Blaha Lujza tér (M2).*

MATÁV Zenehá z, IX. Páva u. 10–12, **t** 215 7901. Home of the MATÁV orchestra, recently renovated, with great acoustics and an intimate capacity of 200. *Box office open Mon–Fri 9–6, in June 9–2. Closed July and Aug. Tram 4 or 6 to Boráros tér.*

Mátyás Templom, I. Szentháromság tér 2, **t** 355 5657. A striking venue, usually used for organ recitals. The audience cannot see the player. The poor acoustics are unsuitable for the choir and orchestra works also performed here. *Tickets from the door of the church. Várbusz from Moszkva tér (M2).*

MTA Music Hall, Roosevelt tér 9, **t** 332 7176. Housed in the Hungarian Academy of Sciences, this is one of the busier classical venues in town, with excellent acoustics. Seating is on a first-come, first-served basis.

Óbuda Társaskör (Óbuda Society Circle), III. Kiskorona u. 7, **t** 250 0288. Small venue surrounded by high-rise blocks, but hosting very good chamber concerts, recitals and an eclectic range including some jazz. *Box office open daily 10–6. HÉV to Árpád híd, or tram 1 from Árpád híd (M3).*

Vigadó, V. Vigadó u. 5, **t** 338 4721. A beautiful building and location, but terrible acoustics. *Box office Mon–Fri 10–6, Sat 10–2, Sun 5–7. Closed July and Aug. Vörösmarty tér (M1).*

Zeneakadémia (Franz Liszt Music Academy), VI. Liszt Ferenc tér 8, **t** 342 0179. The Nagyterem (Large Concert Hall) is the best and busiest venue in town, with excellent acoustics and a gorgeous interior. *Box office open Mon–Fri 10–8, Sat and Sun 2–8. Closed late July–Aug. Oktogon (M1).*

Jazz and Blues

Birdland, VI. Liszt Ferenc tér 7, **t** 413 7983. Classic interior with plain walls and B&W jazz prints. Live jazz Thurs–Sat. Small meat-based menu (*expensive*).

Fat Mo's, V. Nyári Pál u. 11, **t** 267 3199. Open till 2 or 4am nightly. Done up as a speakeasy, with one very long bar and B&W gangster prints, always staggeringly full. The restaurant is Tex-Mex (*expensive*), with either live or DJ music every night.

Jazz Garden, V. Veres Pálné u. 44a, **t** 266 7364. With plastic trees and a black ceiling dotted with stars, the sensation of being in a garden is a little eerie. Jazz nightly. The pastel-coloured restaurant offers the regular fare plus some veggie choices (*expensive*).

Reasonably priced drinks. Cover charge. *Open daily 6pm–1am. Kálvin tér (M3).*

New Orleans, VI. Lovag u. 5, **t** 268 0802, *www.neworleans.hu.* A spacious, comfortable venue that has hosted some pretty big names in the jazz and blues world.

Vera Jazz Café, VII. Osvát u. 11, **t** 322 3611. Klezmer, jazz, Latin, etc.

Folk Music and Dance

Dance houses (*táncház*) were formed during the Transylvania-inspired folk-tradition revival in the 1970s. A few places around town have weekly gatherings, at which outsiders are welcome, usually with the chance to learn the steps beforehand. More polished, less authentic folk dancing or gypsy concert shows aimed at tourists take place more or less nightly at the **Budai Vigadó** (I. Corvin tér 8), the **Duna Palota** (V. Zrínyi u. 5) or the **Bábszinház** (VI. Andrássy u. 69). Phone **t** 317 2754 or pick up one of their leaflets.

Belváros Cultural Centre (Belvárosi Művelődési Ház), V. Molnár u. 9, **t** 317 5928. Very popular for dance Sat night. Children learn from 5pm, adults from 7pm. *Ferenciek tere (M3).*

City Cultural Centre (Fővárosi Művelődési Ház), XI. Fehérvári u. 47, **t** 203 3868. Dance house Tues/Fri 5.30–6.30 for kids; Fri 6.30–12 for adults. *Tram 18 from Moszkva tér or 47 from Deák tér.*

Csángó Dance House, XII. Marczibányi tér 5a, **t** 212 5660. Loud energetic, *Csángó* music and dancing (Wed from 8pm). On Thurs the popular group Muzsikás play from 8pm in a relaxed atmosphere with little dancing. *Moszkva tér (M2).*

Fonó Budai Zeneház, XI. Sztregova u. 3, **t** 206 5300, *www.fono.hu.* Alight at Fehérvári u. 108. In a former aluminium factory, one of the best music venues. Acoustic music: folk, jazz, etc. Transylvanian groups every Wed. Outdoor stage in summer. *Tram 18 from Moszkva tér (M2) or 47 from Deák tér.*

Gyökér Club, VI. Eötvös u. 46. Transylvanian dance house (Thurs from 8pm), and straight Hungarian (Fri from 9pm). *Nyugati pu (M3).*

Cinema

There are plenty of English-language cinemas. *Pesti Est* often has an English-language film listing. Many old movie houses survive, a few showing art-house films. The best multiplex, in a graceful old building, is **Corvin**, VIII. Corvin köz 1, **t** 459 5050, *www. corvin.hu*. *Ferenc krt. (M3)*. Arthouse venues include: **Cirko-gejzír**, VIII. Balassi Bálint u. 15–17, **t** 269 0904, *tram 2*; **Hunnia**, VII. Erzsébet krt. 26, **t** 322 3471, *Blaha Lujza tér (M2)*; **Metro**, VI. Teréz krt. 62, *Nyugati pu (M3)*; **Művész**, VI. Teréz krt 30, **t** 332 6726, *Oktogon (M1)*; **Odeon-Lloyd**, XIII. Hollán Ernő u. 7, **t** 329 2065, *tram 2,4 or 6*; **Örökmozgó Filmmúzeum**, VII. Erzsébet krt., **t** 342 2167, *tram 4/6 to Wesselényi u.*; **Tabán**, I. Krisztina krt. 87–9, **t** 356 8162, *tram 18 from Moszkva tér*; **Toldi Stúdió**, V. Bajcsy-Zsilinszky u. 36–8, **t** 472 0397, *Arany János (M3)*.

Dance

There are a host of modern Hungarian dance groups, most of whom are represented by the **Contemporary Dance Theatre Society**, XI. Kőrösy József u. 17, **t** 366 4776 *(trams 4/6 on the Nagykörút, 47/49 on the Kiskörút; open Oct–May Tues–Thurs 4–7)*. The **Hungarian National Ballet Company (Magyar Nemzeti Balett)** performs at the State Opera House and the Erkel Theatre. See the Opera House's publication for details. The organizers of the dance shows at seasonal festivals provide information on these and most of the main dance companies: **Táncfórum**, I. Corvin tér 8, **t** 201 8779 *(Batthyány tér, M2; open Mon–Fri 9–3)*. Check what's going on at **Trafó** *(see p.190)*. This is where the highly acclaimed company **Moving House** (Mozgó ház) usually perform when they're not touring.

Nightlife

It is hard to identify a typically Hungarian bar culture, unless you mean the many dark, rather desperate-looking places filled almost exclusively with unsteady men: the *borozó*, a cheap wine cellar, usually full of early drinkers; the *söröző*, a beer-cellar, but not like those found in Prague; the *presszó*, a dingy style of café-bar. You won't find many of these listed below, though they're certainly of cultural interest. Budapest's bar scene is vivacious, and too eclectic to classify. Many of the best bars are also cafés, venues or even restaurants, so see above. For the best taste of what's on offer, head to Liszt Ferenc tér or Raday utca.

A38 Ship, moored at Petőfi Bridge, Buda side, **t** 464 3940, *www.a38.hu*. One of Budapest's busiest venues, for all genres of music, is also a dance hall, restaurant and bar, whose door prices deter the younger partiers. *Open daily 11–4*.

Crazy Café, VI. Jókai u. 30, **t** 302 4003. This long cellar bar has an astounding selection of draught and bottled beers. Live music and karaoke. The restaurant is done out like a jungle, with plastic vegetation and stuffed animals. Imaginative menu *(moderate)*. *Open daily noon–1am*.

Fregatt Pub, V. Molnár u. 26, **t** 318 9997. English-style laid-back cellar pub, with live jazz most evenings. *Open Mon–Fri noon– 1am, Sat and Sun 5pm–1am. Ferenciek tere (M3)*.

Gödör Klub, V. beneath Erzsébet tér, **t** 943 5464, *www.godorklub.hu*. A stunning venue for a mixed bag of live or DJ-led sessions, from jazz to techno. *Open 4pm–2am daily*.

Leroy Café, VI. Liszt Ferenc tér 10. An extraordinary interior that has to be seen, featuring high arched stone ceilings, massive chandeliers and a spectacular bar. Menu is new angles on meaty fare with lots of steaks *(expensive)*, but better used for drinks.

Old Amsterdam, V. Királyi Pál u. 14, **t** 266 3648, open till 2am nightly. Stylish little pub with a genuinely European feel. Some great food specials *(inexpensive)*.

Old Man's Music Pub, VII. Akácfa u. 13, **t** 322 7645. Probably the most fun, popular and crowded nightspot in town. Mainly disco, with live blues, jazz or funk earlier in the evening. Book a table if you want to see the stage. The menu is surprisingly good *(moderate)*. *Open daily 3–3. Blaha Lujza tér (M2)*.

Talk Talk, V. Magyar u. 12–14, **t** 267 5758. A modern minimalist interior with tasteful iron chairs and a cosy mezzanine. The clientele is young and trendy, the waitresses aloof. As much a café-restaurant as bar. *Open till 2am Fri and Sat*.

Undergrass, VI. Liszt Ferenc tér 10, **t** 322 0830. Beneath Café Mediterrán. A long, metallic cellar bar with a small dance-floor. Not unbearably crowded: you can hear each other talk in the bar, then nip next door for a boogie. *Open 8pm–4am, closed Sun*.

Wherever you are in Budapest, a point comes in the late afternoon when a magical quality of refracted light calls you to the Danube. The other cities that straddle this most celebrated of Europe's waterways have largely resisted her charms, but here she is queen, and the atmosphere she commands is one of romance. Destroyed and rebuilt many times, Budapest seems to have learned something from other famous riverside cities. It has its bridges and promenades for pedestrians, Paris-like; a castle and a cathedral on the hill, Prague-like; and a London-inspired Parliament building adorning one bank. The key sights here are the two panoramas, so perfect on the Buda side that the whole stretch has been assigned UNESCO World Heritage status.

Budapest is of course two cities, which grew as separate entities until their union less than 130 years ago, and which have maintained their own distinct characters. Buda is hilly and green, lorded over by the elevated Castle Hill area, whose cobbled traffic-free streets and grand old buildings huddle around the vast Baroque Royal Palace and the picturesque Matthias Church, just about maintaining the atmosphere of a medieval village, despite the tour buses. Just two centuries ago, most of its inhabitants still spoke German and kept themselves apart from the expanding metropolis across the water. That flat expanse on the east bank is Pest, a vibrant, thoroughly modern city in all respects but for the complete lack of skyscrapers. There is so much to see here, so spread out, that the onslaught of tourism is easily absorbed.

Almost the entire town was built at the end of the 19th century in an unparalleled period of expansion. After centuries of having to defend itself from invaders and neighbouring empires, Hungary became part of the Austro-Hungarian Dual Monarchy, and set about transforming its newly united capital into a city that would compete with and even surpass Vienna in its grandeur. This rapid development was catalysed by the 1896 Hungarian Millennium, the 1,000th anniversary of the arrival in the Carpathian Basin of the city's Magyar founding fathers. In the four years leading up to this date, at least 3,700 buildings were completed. At 80 square miles Budapest had become the biggest city on the continent, with the mainland's first metro system, electric street-cars running since 1880, three bridges spanning the Danube and a fourth well under way, and, also nearing completion, two of Pest's most important constructions: its cathedral, St Stephen's Basilica, and its Parliament. No wonder Mark Twain had this reaction in 1899: 'Budapest was a surprise for me, really. Civilised, cosmopolitan, spacious. Young and ambitious. Can this Chicago-paced development go on forever, one wonders.' It did so long enough to benefit fully from the exciting Art Nouveau era, of which it ranks alongside Barcelona as the world's premier exponent. The progress was halted, however: by two World Wars, then 40 years of Communism.

Budapest is not what the visitor expects. The predominant characteristic of Hungarian architecture is an almost obsessive love of the eclectic, a mix-and-match combination of Gothic, Baroque, Renaissance, Romanesque and Art Nouveau. Lawns, parks, gardens and great playgrounds abound, making this as child-friendly as cities get. Giant plane-trees line the roads. The city's inhabitants are as varied as its buildings: from the start, Hungary has been a melting pot of Slavs, Serbs, Croats, Romanies, Germans, Austrians, Italians, Turks, and of course Magyars. The visitor expecting the cliché-ridden Russian-style temperament will be surprised at how Mediterranean the Hungarians seem. People here are passionate and fun-loving, needing little excuse to get dressed up.

In fact, on a superficial level, it already feels as if 40 years of enforced Communism, with the implied atmosphere of bleak, apathetic fatalism and crippling inefficiency, never happened. The service in shops and restaurants is not always great, but it has improved even in the last five years. People still have not learned to clear a fast-lane on metro escalators, but maybe this is a symbol for what the Communism-imposed deceleration of Budapest has preserved. Whereas the modern age of advancing technology, multinational corporations and information superhighways has led to cities looking increasingly similar, in Budapest the effect has been dampened. As the generation educated in post-Communist years assumes greater control, however, things are changing fast – for the better and worse. Budapest's tacky and commercial districts are losing their character, but other areas are just finding theirs, with more colours on their palette to choose from. Some believe that the city will be ruined, but Budapest's progressive-minded mayor has other ideas.

History

Migration, Migration

The history of Budapest cannot, technically, be spoken of until the year 1873, when the two municipalities of Buda on the right bank and Pest on the left bank were united. But the human history of the region is older even than St Stephen and his sometimes problematic crown.

The earliest settlements in the area we now know as Budapest can be traced to the 2nd millennium BC. Subsequent waves of migrations left their mark, with the **Scythians** arriving from modern-day Russia in the 6th century BC and the **Celts** from what is now France around the 4th century BC. In the 2nd century AD, the **Romans** built a city called **Aquincum** on the western bank of the Danube, designating it the capital of their easternmost province of Lower Pannonia. Aquincum's population had grown to more than 40,000 by the 3rd century but, as the empire declined, the Romans could not hold off attacks from successive waves of eastern nomadic peoples. When the **Huns**, led by their king Attila, attacked in the 5th century, the Romans abandoned the site. The excavated ruins, now a low-key tourist attraction with its small museum in Óbuda, make a pleasant outing, easily reached by public transport (*see* p.259). The fortifications the Romans built on the eastern side of the river to protect them from the barbarians became the beginnings of the town of Pest.

After Attila's death in 453, the **Avars** took over and ruled for several centuries. Finally the conquering **Magyars** or Hungarians got to Hungary in 896, led by their chieftain Árpád. The nomadic Magyars were similar in habits to other central Asian tribes, except for their everlastingly unassimilable language, which was of Finno-Ugric origin. The Europeans confused them with the dreaded Huns, which may account for the eventual name of Hungarians. In their last attempt at European conquest, the

Magyars were defeated at Augsburg in 955, after which they retreated to the Carpathian Basin to consolidate and establish a kingdom. A descendant of Árpád, King Géza, was the first to be baptized by missionaries from Charlemagne; they also baptized his son Vajk. This son was to be renamed István or **Stephen**.

Stephen was a strong king, who helped organize a feudal state out of the formerly tribal territories. After his death in 1038, the country continued to develop, despite squabbling among former chieftains and 'pagan' revolts, and despite pressure from the Byzantine and Holy Roman Empires. Then in 1241 the **Mongols** arrived, sacking the city and burning Pest to the ground. But the Mongols quickly retreated with the death of their leader, and the Hungarian king **Béla IV** ordered castles – including one at Buda – built to fortify the country.

Matthias and the Hungarian Renaissance

When the House of Árpád died out with the death of King Andrew III in 1301, the throne was taken over by the Neapolitan Angevin kings, who established the royal seat at Buda, encouraged trade and built a university. In 1456, under the leadership of **János Hunyadi**, the Turks – the next set of invaders – were temporarily staved off at Belgrade. This breathing space before the eventual arrival of the Turks (the newly established Habsburgs, too, were eyeing Hungary) was to provide the country with a fertile era during which Buda became one of the most cultivated courts in Europe. Mátyás, Hunyadi's son, reigned from 1458 to 1490, romanizing his name to **Matthias Corvinus** (his emblem was the crow). He was by all accounts a gifted ruler and a cultural visionary, bringing Italian artists and literary figures to the court and amassing a huge and valuable library, the Bibliotheca Corviniana; Matthias' reign became known as the **Hungarian Renaissance**. After his marriage to an Italian, Beatrice of Aragon, Matthias' table evidently became as sophisticated as his library.

First Turks, then Habsburgs

In 1526 the Hungarians were defeated by the Turks at Mohács, and in 1541 Buda Castle fell. For nearly 150 years Hungary became part of the **Ottoman Empire**, with a slice of the country to the west ruled by the Habsburgs, and Transylvania as a separate principality. Buda and Pest were depopulated, and churches were converted to mosques. Little other building occurred except for defensive fortifications. In 1686 a pan-European Christian army led by the **Habsburgs** and partly financed by the Pope mounted a six-week siege to recapture Buda and release the Hungarians from their bondage. At the end, Buda and its castle were in ruins, as was Pest, a result both of the siege and of the post-victory depredations of the 'liberators'.

The Turks left behind little in the way of cultural artefacts except for several fine baths, still functioning, and the tomb of Gül Baba. They had made no effort to convert the Hungarians, and in fact a strong wave of Protestantism had converted many from the Roman Church to a Calvinist faith. But the Turks' real legacies were twofold: the habit of drinking coffee, a custom that became crucial to the social, literary and political life of Budapest; and the use of that quintessentially Hungarian seasoning, paprika.

The Habsburgs are Coming – and Staying

After the defeat of the Turks, Hungary was ruled from Vienna, in a connection that ended only with defeat at the end of the First World War in 1918. The new rulers brought in settlers from Austria and Germany to replace the depleted population, and instituted strong Counter-Reformation measures against the growing power of Hungarian Protestantism. A failed **War of Independence**, led by **Ferenc Rákoczi** between 1703 and 1711, which united nobles and peasantry, is still seen as one of the great moments in Hungarian history. When it was over, the Austrians destroyed fortifications and castles throughout the entire country to make sure no such rebellion would happen again. Reforms that defined the rights of the peasants and initiated public education were introduced under Maria Theresia and Josef II, but they made small inroads on the essentially imperial-colonial relationship between ruler and ruled.

Although Latin was the official **language** of government, German and French were the main languages of the privileged; Hungarian was spoken by peasants and now also by an enlightened intelligentsia looking towards revolutionary nationalist ideas. In 1795, seven of these revolutionaries, the 'Hungarian Jacobins', were executed. As in other countries struggling toward nationhood, language became a powerful issue at the end of the 18th century, along with the attempt to define a specifically Hungarian artistic and architectural style. It was important and threatening enough that Ferenc Kazinczy, a leader in the reform of the language, was thrown in jail. Anyone who has tried to learn Hungarian as a second language will understand how special this linguistic experience is; some might argue that this linguistic uniqueness makes it possible for the best Hungarian minds to think 'outside the box'. A surprising number of Hungarians have won Nobel Prizes in the sciences, including the quantum mechanics physicist Paul Dirac and the father of vitamin C, Albert Szent-Györgyi. Think, too, of Rubik's Cube, an invention almost as baffling as Hungarian grammar.

Independence Gets on the Agenda

The so-called **Reform Period** of the second quarter of the 19th century is notable for the presence of a star, the liberal politician **Count István Széchenyi** (1791–1860). A sophisticated, multi-talented figure, he was an anglophile who admired England's modern inventions, from steam shipping to flush toilets. He founded the Hungarian Academy of Sciences, introduced horse racing, and had the Chain Bridge built. But liberal reforms within the framework of Habsburg rule were not enough for revolutionaries such as **Lajos Kossuth**, who called for immediate and total separation from Austria. With the help of the nationalist poet **Sándor Petőfi**, Kossuth called for the abolition of the feudal system along with a new constitution that would grant Hungary far greater autonomy. The **Revolution of 1848–9** began, in what was to become a typical Hungarian fashion, with a meeting in a literary and political café, the Café Pilvax in Pest. Frightened by the show of support for Kossuth, the Austrians acceded to the initial demands, which included making Hungarian the official language, and instituting a ministry headed by, among others, Széchenyi. But Kossuth, now finance minister, upped his demands for even greater separation from Austria. The rebellious Hungarians were easily defeated in 1849 when the new emperor, Franz Josef, called for help from the Tsar of Russia. In the wake of the uprising, the government outlawed public gatherings, theatre performances, displays of the national colours and Kossuth-style beards. Kossuth himself went into exile. Széchenyi suffered a nervous breakdown, and eventually committed suicide.

But Hungarian independence was permanently on the agenda, and the idea soon fell on more fertile ground. When the Austrians were defeated in 1866 during the Austro-Prussian War, the weakened empire looked for an agreement with the Hungarians. The **1867 Compromise** created the **Dual Monarchy**, with separate governments and parliaments. Under the new arrangement, the Habsburg emperor was King of Hungary, and the two countries shared finance ministries; but the Hungarian government, with a prime minister, cabinet and parliament, took control of its own domestic affairs. The arrangement did not satisfy the most radical reformers, nor did it please members of various ethnic minorities living in Hungary. Still, it marked the beginning of an unprecedented period of peace and prosperity. That period ended with another nationalist eruption and the outbreak of the First World War.

Building a Modern City

One outward sign of the newfound solidity was a population explosion. The 1870s also saw the creation of a public works council, based on the London model. Then, when the two main cities were combined into **unified Budapest** in 1873, an immense architectural plan was implemented, featuring the creation of that still magnificent boulevard, Andrássy út, as well as the rebuilding of Pest's inner city. By 1900, shortly after the millennium celebrations, Budapest had a population of 773,000 and enjoyed modern utilities and transport. Commerce and industry blossomed during this period of relative stability, Hungary's **Golden Age**, and Budapest became the centre of a rich intellectual and social life, with poets and literary figures haunting the coffee houses.

The architecture of today's Budapest reflects the prosperity and style of the turn of the 20th century. The buildings that largely characterize the city's current skyline were built during this period: the faux-Baroque palace, the faux-Gothic Matthias Church, the fantastic Fisherman's Bastion, the Parisian-style Opera House and the London-style Parliament.

The First and Second World Wars

In June 1914, Hungary entered the First World War along with the rest of Austria-Hungary as an ally of the Germans. Luckily for the Hungarians, the war was not fought on their soil, but they suffered heavy losses on the Russian and Italian fronts. The war and the defeat that followed underscored the social weaknesses that lay just beneath the heady pre-war prosperity. Ethnic divisions and economic inequality led to political instability. For a brief moment, an independent republic was established under the leadership of **Count Mihály Károlyi**, and universal suffrage and freedom of the press were proclaimed in 1918. Then in March 1919 a short-lived (4½-month) Communist regime was installed under **Béla Kún**, who dealt brutally with all opposition. On 16 November 1919, **Admiral Miklós Horthy** rode into Budapest on a white horse at the head of a Hungarian army, beginning a right-wing regime that lasted until the regent, as he was called, was kidnapped by the Germans in 1944. Under Horthy's 'White Terror', the Communist Party was banned and a *numerus clausus* restricting the enrolment of Jews in universities was instituted.

Hungary's most devastating wounds from the First World War, politically and psychologically, came from the amputation of its territory by the **Treaty of Trianon**. Romania gained Transylvania and a number of primarily Hungarian towns; and, using the Danube as a convenient border, southern Slovakia got an area packed with Hungarians. But during the Horthy regime prosperity, albeit an uneasy one, settled back on Hungary. Despite the backbeat of hunger and social unrest, tourism rose as celebrities and ordinary people from all over Europe and America came to enjoy Budapest's hospitality, its spas, music and good food. The period came to be designated as the **Silver Age**.

Perhaps the most dangerous result of dismantling Hungary's former territories after the First World War was to send the country into the arms of Nazi Germany at the start of the Second. Hungary was a reluctant and recalcitrant ally of the Germans, although it became a source of natural resources, food and forced labour for the Axis powers. When huge numbers of Hungarians were lost on the Eastern Front in 1943 the government withdrew its troops and began secret negotiations with the Allies. In addition, the Horthy regime, despite its history of home-grown anti-Semitism, refused to go along with the murderous German demands for the ghettoization and deportation of Jews. As the Russians moved in from the east, the British and Americans began bombing the country. Up until now, Budapest had been spared air raids.

In March 1944, the Germans occupied their ally, Hungary, and the round-up of anti-Nazi citizens began. Jews were forced into ghettoes and deported to the death camps. A few thousand of Budapest's Jews survived because of the heroic efforts of Swedish diplomat Raoul Wallenberg. When the Germans kidnapped Horthy in October, Hungary's murderous **Arrow Cross** Fascist party took over. The Nazis occupied Buda Castle, preparing for a siege during the winter. They held out for several months, but the city was finally 'liberated' in February by Soviet forces fighting street by street. The Germans surrendered in April 1945. Seventy-four per cent of the buildings in the city had been damaged and more than a third destroyed. Along with Berlin and Warsaw, Budapest was one of the three European capital cities to suffer the greatest damage in the war.

Communism, Real and Goulash

The Hungarians welcomed their Soviet liberators uneasily; the advance guard of Russian troops were known to be a particularly brutal lot. A kind of local government was established, with elections that gave the Communists only 17 per cent of the vote. A new currency, the forint, was created, helping to stave off disastrous inflation, and a land reform act distributed agricultural land to peasant families. But by 1948 a Soviet-style government was put in place, a Stalinist, one-party system, with typically inefficient five-year plans that succeeded in destroying the Hungarian economy, collectivizing farms and emphasizing heavy industry at the expense of agriculture and commerce. A Communist secret police force, the AVO, took over the building on

Andrássy út formerly occupied by the fascist Arrow Cross party. In 1949, the Moscow-appointed hard-liner **Mátyás Rákosi** became prime minister. In 1951, as part of the effort to extinguish the bourgeoisie, more than 13,000 citizens were deported into the countryside for hard manual labour. Hungary became a failed Soviet-style economy, driven by a deadly combination of shortage and waste. On the death of Stalin in 1953, Rákosi was replaced by a less extreme Communist, **Imre Nagy**. His more relaxed form of government, the so-called **New Course**, permitted economic and social reforms. But the struggle between hard-liners and moderates tipped again toward Moscow, and Rákosi was returned to power in 1955.

The 1956 Revolution

In late October 1956, in the midst of a particularly warm and pleasant autumn, the world watched with horror as Russian tanks rolled into Budapest to crush what Hungarians and others had believed would be a well-supported revolt against Communist rule. The USA and other Western powers, who the revolutionaries had understood were prepared to back their cause with force of arms, were unfortunately distracted by the simultaneous events of the Suez Crisis and did nothing. The revolution was a failure; exhausted and disillusioned, 200,000 Hungarians left the country to start new lives elsewhere. But in the long run, the 1956 revolution meant that Hungarians began once more to see themselves as agents, rather than simply as observers or victims of their own history. Totalitarianism in Hungary was broken; **János Kádár**, Hungary's new leader, was a relatively moderate figure in the Communist spectrum. His oft-quoted formulation, 'Those who are not against us are with us,' suggests an edge of renascent humour, along with the possibility of a new political and cultural freedom. During the 1960s Budapest began once again to rebuild, and a reinvigorated, sophisticated culture was on the rise.

The End of Communism

Budapest, which had come to be known as 'the jolliest barracks' in the Eastern bloc, in a country that practised 'goulash Communism', began to live up to its reputation. During the late 1970s, major **construction** of hotels began, to accommodate foreigners coming to conferences and sporting events. Enormous, faceless housing blocks had been built during the 1950s and 60s but, as prosperity grew, so did the attempt to protect the historic face of the city. In 1983, the City Embellishment Association of Budapest was founded to encourage preservation and restoration.

In June 1989, Imre Nagy was reburied in an emotional ceremony. That summer and autumn, all over the Eastern bloc, walls and barbed wire came down. The Hungarians allowed thousands of East Germans to go west through its territory. In Budapest, streets and squares shed their Communist designations and recovered their old names. With enormous enthusiasm, Hungarians generated over 100 political parties, of which about six survived. That authentic emblem of capitalism, a tiny stock exchange, reopened. After a series of elections and run-offs, the **Hungarian Democratic Forum party (MDF)** eventually took power, with a conservative coalition led by Prime Minister **József Antall**. His government was replaced in the 1994 election by the **Socialist Party (MSZP)** and their coalition partners, the **Free Democrats (SZDSZ)**, with **Gyula Horn** as prime minister. The 1998 elections returned another conservative coalition, **FIDESZ**, with **Viktor Orbán** as prime minister and **Árpád Gönz** as president. The concerns of this government included efforts to preserve the environment, reflected in a struggle over a Danube dam on the Hungarian–Slovak border, and an increasingly comfortable relationship with Western Europe and its capitalist-demo-cratic ideology. In the end, the swing to the right proved too much for the ever-divided Hungarian psyche, especially when Orbán started promoting a return to pre-war Christian and Nationalist values. In 2002, FIDESZ unexpectedly lost the election – albeit narrowly – to the Socialists under **Péter Medgyessy**, a finance minister with the old régime. For Budapest and liberal-progressive mayor **Gábor Demszky**, whose more cosmopolitan values were increasingly at odds with the conservatives, it's great news.

Having joined NATO in 1999, Hungarians voted overwhelmingly in a referendum to join the **EU**, and did so on May 1 2004. They are committed to crossing over to the euro in 2009.

Art and Architecture

The city's greatest period of prosperity came after unification in the 1870s, and the magnificent boulevards of Pest are the manifestation of a dramatic era when Budapest and Chicago were the fastest-growing cities on earth. The building of Pest coincided with Hungary's greatest artistic flowering; its streets are crowded with exquisite architectural decoration and powerful buildings. The wealthy, however, often moved out to the leafy hills of Buda, so the city's finest architecture is widely spread; to see it all is a mammoth undertaking. Whether you have a weekend, a week or a year, the key to the city's architecture is to stroll and look around. Look at the details, the doorways and their wonderful ironwork, wander into the courtyards, sit in the cafés and observe one of Europe's most coherent capitals.

Roman to Ottoman

The history of Hungarian architecture is of dramatic leaps forward and devastating setbacks, a stop-start affair which makes it hard to trace any single line of develop-ment. The earliest surviving works were left by the **Romans**: a few morsels, including the military amphitheatre (1st century AD), are in Aquincum, in modern Óbuda. The art and architecture of Hungary's early years (*c.* 1000–1200) was **Romanesque**; there is little of it in Budapest. The work of art embodying the early Hungarian nation is the **crown of St Stephen**; its blend of Byzantine and Romanesque reflects Hungary's posi-tion between East and West. Mongol invasions from 1241 destroyed much, and, once the barbarians retreated, the focus of Hungarian building efforts was fortification.

The ruke of King Matthias Corvinus (1458–90), who brought the Renaissance to Hungary, was the pivotal period between the **Gothic** and the **Renaissance**; the buildings from his reign blend Gothic and Classical motifs. A few fragments from this period survive throughout the Castle district, a window here, a door there. The brilliant polychromatic **Matthias Church** is a true mish-mash, this incarnation dating from the 13th century. It has been remodelled almost every century since. The **Royal Palace** also dates from the 14th century but only a few Gothic foundations survive. Some of the finest Hungarian art of the period can be seen inside.

The Turkish invasions of the 16th century swept away Hungary's burgeoning Renaissance and artistically the country stagnated for 150 years. The Turks left few monuments, but they are worth seeing. The **Király Baths** in Buda date from the 1560s and survive in almost unaltered form. The dome in the **tomb of Gül Baba** is original; the rest has been rebuilt several times.

Baroque

Turkish occupation was followed by Habsburg domination from the end of the 17th century. For the next 150 years **Baroque**, which crept in during the last years of Turkish occupation, defined the city. Baroque was the architectural language of the Counter-Reformation, its curvaceous forms a riposte to the puritanism of Calvinist and Protestant architecture, and, although it appeared in secular buildings, its greatest expression was in **ecclesiastical architecture**.

Although the great Baroque monuments are churches, most 18th-century buildings were affected by the style. The Castle district presents endless examples of Baroque embellishment. During this period, a lot of foreign artists, mostly Italian, Austrian and German, were at work in Budapest; there was a snob value in employing them, although many were second-rate. Ironically, with so many foreign artists in Hungary, many Hungarian artists were forced abroad.

Neoclassicism and Romanticism

The Baroque remained a powerful force in Hungarian art and architecture through the 19th century, when it was dominant in the historicist rebuilding of Pest. But gradually, under the influence of changes in Germany, Britain and France, the **neoclassical** emerged as the style that would most stamp its mark on the city during the first half of the 19th century. The key building of this era was the **National Museum** (1837–44), the last major neoclassical museum in Europe. Neoclassicism, the style based on the Greek model, seemed everything Baroque was not: cool, urbane and intellectual. Associated with the French revolution and the American republic, it represented democracy, rationalism and science. With Hungary under the yoke of Habsburg oppression, it was inevitable that Mihály Pollack's museum of national history, culture and aspirations, the distillation of the nation's image of itself, should be executed in a grand neoclassicism. In art, neoclassicism was represented by sculptor **István Ferenczy**.

Historically and artistically the turning point of Hungarian art and architecture was the failure of the 1848 Revolution. On one hand the defeat led to a self-pity which penetrated the arts to their core. On the other, Hungary's economic success and growth after the Revolution led to the Dual Monarchy. **Romanticism**'s inherent sense of longing and loss struck a deep chord with Hungarian artists. In France, Germany or Britain, Romantic artists celebrated lost worlds of chivalry, the passion of revolution or an emotional desire for ancient pastoral landscapes; Hungarian artists celebrated death and heroic failure. If you walk through a Hungarian art gallery you will be astounded at the misery, poverty and intense mourning on display. Hungarian art of this period was Europe's most miserable art by far: **Viktor Madarász**, **Mihály Munkácsy**, **Gyula Benczúr** and **Bertalan Székely**. The stronghold of Romanticism and historical genre painting was only challenged at the end of the 19th century, when Hungarian artists brought their Impressionist influences home from Paris.

Eclecticism: Building the Capital

Industrialization, the population boom and the uniting of the city necessitated a huge building programme. Town planning, based around two new concentric ring roads, was based on the Viennese model. The infrastructure and council of public works were based on London. The aesthetic came from the broad, tree-lined boulevards and grand buildings of Paris. The first step was the building of the earliest permanent bridge between Buda and Pest, the **Chain Bridge** (1839–49). It was followed by the layout of key parts of Pest as aristocratic Buda waned and Pest became the engine of Hungarian recovery. The style of the new city was **Eclecticism**, a pompous but urbane blend of neo-Renaissance, neo-Baroque and Parisian grandeur. Eclecticism allowed unprecedented freedom of expression with a pick 'n' mix range of architectural elements. **Imre Steindl**'s fairy-tale **Parliament** (1884–1902) is an ambitious example of extremist Eclecticism, blending Gothic verticality, a Florentine dome, Baroque planning and Ruskinian dreaming spires with great success.

National Expression, National Romanticism and Folk Art

After the failed 1848 revolution there was a great desire to rebuild a Hungarian architecture independent of foreign sources, leading to a surge of interest in Hungarian folk art and the origins of the Magyars. Ethnographers traced the nation's roots to Central Asia and India by similarities between Hungarian folk art's motifs and those of other nations. These researches were often spurious but they prompted some remarkable architectural approaches.

The architect who succeeded (briefly) in reviving the ideal of a truly Hungarian architecture was **Ödön Lechner**, and his masterpiece is the **Museum of Applied Arts** on Üllői út. Lechner's building was created to house the best international applied arts as a resource for Hungarian designers. His fascination with Eastern forms explains the domes and ogee arches, the dragons' heads and Middle Eastern courtyards which so influenced this building. The decorative elements are almost all executed in brightly coloured Zsolnay tiles. **Vilmos Zsolnay** was a ceramicist of world renown who had travelled with Lechner to study design in London. His ceramic factory was pivotal in the spectacular success of Hungarian decorative art. The company's products, in particular its glazed tiles, grace the roofs of a number of buildings that define Budapest's skyline, including the Matthias Church and the **Post Office Savings Bank** (1899–1901), Lechner's other great masterpiece. Lechner was a contemporary of Gaudi, with whom comparisons are instructive.

Influenced by William Morris and the British Arts and Crafts movement, and Finnish National Romanticism, and, inspired by Lechner's attempts, the next generation set about creating a new œuvre. Its rural roots gave this style more success in the country than the city, but Budapest has some examples, the most concentrated area being the **Wekerle Estate** around Kós Károly tér (well off the tourist map), a version of the Arts and Crafts garden suburb. The bastion-like gates around the main square are particularly impressive. Nos.2–3 were designed by **Károly Kós**, the influential leader of this group. Kós continues to exert great influence on Hungarian architects, and the modern architects working in an organic vein are inspired by his use of folk art and architecture. Hungary's most internationally renowned architect, **Imre Makovecz**, who was taught by Kós, owes a deep debt to his mentor's vision.

Art at the End of the 19th Century

If Hungarian art had been morose in the mid-19th century, it underwent a stunning volte face towards the end of the century. **Pál Szinyei Merse**, who spent much of his career in Munich, was a contemporary of the French Impressionists and his work paralleled theirs. Sunny, colourful and *plein air*, Szinyei Merse brought sunshine to the gloom of Hungarian art. He was followed by **József Rippl-Rónai**, who lived in France and represented the post-Impressionist phase of Hungarian art; his works echoed the bold outlines and powerful forms of Toulouse-Lautrec, with graphically simplified figures, but he blended these with the expressive colour of Van Gogh and Gauguin. Rippl-Rónai also designed fine tapestries and ceramics and painted frescoes, and was instrumental in fusing arts and architecture, an ideal of Hungarian Art Nouveau. The artist who stands out from this period as unique and unclassifiable is Tivadar Csontváry Kosztka. Known as **Csontváry**, he was a true eccentric who began painting at 30. His deeply odd paintings blend biblical symbolism, Expressionist emotion and complex symbolism and iconography rooted in Hungarian history.

Art Nouveau and Secession

The *fin de siècle* in Budapest was dominated by the **1896 millennium** of Magyar settlement. A huge programme of rebuilding celebrated both this and the phenomenal progress that Hungary had made in the years since 1867. The legacy of the celebrations is staggering. The **metro**, the first in continental Europe, still runs to Hősök tere, focus of the celebrations. Beyond is the **Városliget park**, built for the Millennium, within which is **Vajdahunyad**, an impressive theme-park re-creation of a 15th-century Transylvanian castle.

In the first few years of the 20th century, artists and architects reacted against the established appearance of the city in Hungary's **Art Nouveau**, known as **Szecesszió** after the breakaway from the academic system of Vienna. By Western European standards, Budapest arrived at Art Nouveau late. The highlights occurred in 1905–15, by when this approach was distinctly *art vieux* in France, Belgium and elsewhere. Nevertheless the Secessionist architecture and decoration in Budapest is fantastically varied, of very high quality and worth examining in detail. Among the larger works of Art Nouveau, the **Ferenc Liszt Music Academy** (1904–7) is the supreme *Gesamt-kunstwerk*. Another towering work of this era is the **Gresham Palace**, designed by **Zsigmond Quittner** and **László and József Vágó** in 1905–7, a similarly mountainous structure adorned with jewel-like inlays of gold and swirling Art Nouveau tendrils.

At this time Budapest was the fastest-growing city in Europe. Pest's phenomenal growth was fuelled by rapid economic and industrial expansion: it was the engine of the Austro-Hungarian Empire, a city of factories, banks and pan-European trade. This industry also gave rise to a new field in Hungarian arts: graphic design. The **poster** became the driving medium in the popularization of Art Nouveau, and **graphic design** as well as illustration became an important part of the new art. Posters for Tungsram light bulbs, Unicum liquor and Törley champagne are among the most distinctive, each developing a specific brand image and style.

Modernism

The First World War, the loss of two-thirds of Hungary's territory and its reactionary post-war regime crippled its art and architecture while Modernism was fermenting throughout Europe. **György Lukács**, the cultural commissioner under Kún in 1919, encouraged radical art and design but the government was not able to put its ideas into practice, and artists who had been associated with it had to flee the country after it failed. Other radical architects left the capital for more promising environments and Hungary lost a generation of brilliant young artists. The **Bauhaus**, the German home of radical Modernism, was full of Hungarians. **Marcel Breuer**, best known for his invention of tubular furniture, designed the UNESCO building in Paris (1953–8). **Vilmos Huszár** was a key figure of the De Stijl movement in Holland. **Ernő Goldfinger** was pivotal in the development of Modern architecture in England. **André Kertész**, perhaps the finest Modern photographer, worked in Paris. **Sándor Bortnyik**, **Andor Weininger** and **Lajos Kassák** all proselytized for European Modernist and Constructivist art in Hungary but were also at the apex of the development of these art forms.

A few artists scraped a living in Hungary during these lean years. By the early 1930s, architects like **Kozma** were beginning to get work once more as the country slowly liberalized and began to prosper. A few Modernist villas appeared in the Buda hills as business began to boom and entrepreneurs and industrialists looked for the latest fashions. By the mid-1930s, the political climate was more receptive, and **Functionalist** buildings were beginning to appear in the city centre.

Towards the end of the decade a more streamlined version of Modernism blended the aerodynamic curves of classic ocean liners and cars with the clean, simple lines of Functionalism. This resulted in a number of wonderful apartment blocks, the best of them the building at **Margit körút 15**, a sleek, travertine-clad apartment block with lifts encased in glass cylinders. Good modern buildings went up in the early years of the Second World War and resumed quickly in the socialist regime of the immediate post-war years. The finest example of architecture from this early, idealistic period of socialism is the **Erzsébet tér bus station** (István Nyíri, 1949). By the early 1950s, however, Stalinism had taken grip and Modernism was out.

Food and Drink

The image conjured up by the words 'Hungarian food' is of stodgy dumplings, thick stews, lots of meat and lard, and paprika in everything. For the most part this is still true, but as Hungary embraces the possibilities of a more global perspective, more and more Budapest chefs are breaking away from the undeniably tasty but heavy traditional meat-based fodder, stretching their range of ingredients and techniques, taking chances, and embracing a lighter, pan-European fusion cuisine.

Often this is coupled with a rediscovery of pre-Communist Hungarian cooking. From the Mongols, the Magyars learnt the secrets of stewing meats in their own juices, the basis of *tokány* stews. The great Renaissance king Matthias is said to have imported the likes of dill, capers, figs, turkey and garlic from Italy. From Austria came *schnitzel*, meats fried in breadcrumbs (*rántott*), and the cooking of vegetables in a roux of lard and flour and/or sour cream (*fő zelék*). In the 19th century, the Francophile tastes of aristocrats encouraged chefs to lighten the traditional fare, substituting butter for lard, and introducing such subtleties as herbs and truffles. The most famous Hungarian flavour, **paprika**, came with the Turks, and is usually surprisingly subtle: sweet and fragrant. Along with onions, fat, and smoked bacon, paprika forms the basis of the classic stews called *pörkölt*, which usually include cubed meat. *Paprikás* is the same thing with sour cream. These are what we know as goulash, while *gulyás* is actually a thick meat soup cooked slowly with onions, vegetables, paprika and potatoes or small noodles. In their milder, unground form, paprika peppers are the basis, with tomato, of the classic summer dish *lecsó*, a kind of ratatouille often served with meat. In winter an old favourite is stuffed cabbage, *töltött káposzta*, made of *sauerkraut*, minced pork and smoked sausage dumplings.

As well as these dishes, a typical menu will offer a range of **meats**, often including pheasant, wild boar, hare, venison, goose, goose liver and duck, cooked in a variety of ways, usually with sauces containing fruit, wine or cheese. They are generally delicious. **Fish** from Hungary's many rivers and lakes is also abundant: the delicious pike-perch and trout, abundant carp and rather bony catfish. Particularly worth trying is the hot and sour fish soup called *halászlé*. **Vegetarians** have always been ill-served here: theirs is a credo alien to the Magyars, for whom healthy eating for centuries meant shovelling down enough fat to make it through the next winter. Breaded and fried mushrooms (*gombafejek rántva*) and cheese (*rántott sajt*) feature heavily. Salad (*saláta*) has no fixed meaning and could amount to a pile of pickled

Socialist Realism to Post-Modernism

Stalin decreed that modern art was decadent, the preserve of an urban bourgeois élite and could only have value if it realistically represented the life and work of the people. This art came to be known as Socialist Realism, or **Soc-Real**. The architecture of the period was derivative, a classicism that appeared bolder and stronger than it was. This heroic period of Socialist Realism lasted only a few years, and the late 1950s and early 1960s were dominated by rebuilding the city after the brutal suppression of the 1956 revolution. By the time Hungarian art and architecture recovered from that cabbage, gherkin or pepper. Among **desserts**, look out for the strudels (*rétes*), apple, cherry or curd-cheese. Curd-cheese balls (*túrógombóc*) are also recommended, as are the pancakes stuffed with walnuts and topped with chocolate sauce named after the famous chef (*Gundel palacsinta*). It's fun to stretch the culinary experience to a second venue and have coffee and a delicious cake or pastry in a *cukrászda*.

Hungary's 20 **wine**-producing areas have a tradition as long and accomplished as those of France, Italy or Spain, broken by 40 years of Communism, from which the industry is still recovering. Grape varieties include cabernet sauvignon, merlot, and pinot noir for reds, chardonnay, sauvignon and riesling for whites, and local central Eastern European varieties. There are also some rosés and natural sweet whites. The Hungarian wine with the greatest reputation is of the latter kind: Tokaji Aszú, which Louis XIV called 'the wine of Kings, the King of wines'. It is made using grapes desiccated by long hours of sunshine and *Botrytis cinerea*, or 'noble rot'. The number of hods of these raisin-like grapes added to each batch of base-wine made from non-botrytized grapes is expressed by a number from three to seven *puttonyos*, the higher the number the greater the quality, the finest known as Tokaji Eszencia. The mixture of grapes is then refermented, without all of the sugar turning to alcohol.

Of the reds, the most famous, not necessarily the best, is known internationally as 'Bull's Blood' and locally as (Egri) Bikavér, Eger being the best-known but not the only region to produce it. Indeed, some of the finest hail from the Szekszárd area, which generally makes some of the best red wine to be found. The other key region for reds is Villány, whose wines are the most full-bodied, with high tannin and alcohol content. Eger reds tend to be more delicate and complex. For whites the North Balaton area is recommended. The small Somló region produces very acidic whites, said to be utterly unmistakable. Otherwise, chardonnays are generally a good bet, as is the Tokaji Furmint or Hárslevelű. Note that Hungarian sparkling wine can be every bit as good as champagne and considerably cheaper.

Hungary is not historically a **beer**-drinking nation and, while the younger generation are moving in this direction, Hungarian brewers are yet to catch up. Dreher, the most common brew, is acceptable ice-cold on a sweltering day. Borsodi is only slightly better. The best bet is to look for Czech beers such as Budweiser Budvar (not to be confused with the inferior American product) and Pilsner Urquell, or Belgian brews like Leffe and Belle Vue. Normally two sizes are offered: a *korsó* is almost a pint, a *pohár* almost a half. Some places sell glasses by the decilitre (*deci*).

---

shock it had fallen into line with Western trends. Architecture from the late 1950s to the 1980s has little to recommend it. The lasting architectural legacy of the Kádár era is the dreadful concrete tower blocks which surround the city.

Art of this era was dominated by a few figures, whose state-sponsored status has inevitably tainted them. **Margit Kovács** was probably the best known. Her naïve, folk-influenced ceramics remain popular. **Imre Varga** was one of the regime's most favoured sculptors. The best-known Hungarian artist of the era was **Victor Vasarely**, creator of Op Art, who studied under Constructivist Sándor Bortnyik in the 1920s but left Hungary to live in France.

The most famous national **spirit** is *pálinka*, a strong fruit brandy or eau-de-vie. The best is apricot (*barack*), but also worth trying are plum (*szilva*), pear (*körte*) and cherry (*cseresznye*). A national institution is Unicum, a dark brown liqueur containing 23 different herbs, with a horribly bitter taste and a kick like a mule.

Coffee was introduced here by the Turks a century before it was heard of in Paris or Vienna. The burgeoning coffee culture reached its apotheosis at the turn of the 20th century, when there were between 400 and 600 cafés in Budapest. At a time when most people lived in cramped, dark surroundings with few amenities, coffeeshops were a convivial place to relax and socialize. These were forums for views to be aired and disseminated. The 1848 Revolution even began in the Café Pilvax, Petőfi's regular haunt, where he spent so much of his time that he advised his friend János Arany to address any letters there. Cafés would list on the wall like a menu those publications to which they subscribed, and provide paper and ink for the journalists and writers, who spent much of their time gaining inspiration from the free flow of ideas and opinions. Naturally, they were favoured by the whole intellectual and artistic community. Different groups or professions, artists, writers or businessmen, would have their own coffee shop. Thus the Japán on Andrássy út was the regular den of artists and architects such as Ödön Lechner, József Rippl-Rónai and Csontváry, whereas the New York was dominated by writers, clustered around dramatist Ferenc Molnár. It says something for the standing of coffee shops that the New York, which opened in 1894, was designed by the architect in charge of the Royal Palace, Alajos Hauszmann.

The New York, now under renovation, is the only survivor of those glory days. Cafés were such renowned bastions of free thought that the Communists closed them down. With those years gone and the the promise of consumerism in the air, even optimists harboured no real hopes that the halcyon coffee house days would return, but somehow, gloriously, it is happening. All over the city, new establishments have opened with a genuine sense of style. The Central Kávéház on Ferenciek tere is a perfect example, and the coffee itself (espresso rather than filter) is probably better than ever. Along with this rebirth, the kind of trendy cafés found in Paris, London or Amsterdam, modern alternatives to pubs and bars, are also represented in abundance, serving alcohol as much as caffeine. Finally, Budapest is famous for its *pâtisseries*, known here as *cukrászda*, selling a variety of creamy *gâteaux*, tortes, tarts, pastries and pies, freshly made on the premises.

By the early 1980s Hungary's more liberal politics and tolerant regime allowed artists a degree of expression unthinkable in neighbouring countries. Conceptual and absurdist art were a vehicle for criticism of the regime. Hungarian **Pop Art** too took on radical overtones, aiming criticism at Soviet political imagery and Western consumer culture. From 1989 the political poster became a powerful and evocative tool, the voice of democracy against the still Communist-controlled mass media. One of the artists loudest against the inhumanity of Communism was **Imre Makovecz**, Makovecz is renowned for his organic approach to building, his revival of forms drawn from folk art and architecture, and his unparalleled use of sculptural timber forms.

Orientation

Finding your way around Budapest is easy. Buda is the hilly part to the west of the Danube, Pest the flat busy area to its east. The river runs near enough north–south, so that when you are in Pest west means towards the Danube, east away from it. Two circular roads service Pest. The inner semi-circle or **Kiskörút** (Little Boulevard) traces the boundaries of the Inner City, called Belváros. It runs from Szabadság (Liberty) Bridge in the south to Széchenyi Lánchíd Bridge at Roosevelt tér, changing names as it goes: Vámház krt., Múzeum krt., Károly krt., and József Attila u. Roughly where the latter two sections meet, Bajcsy-Zsilinszky út strikes north, marking the eastern boundary of Lipótváros (Leopold Town, the City). Together, Belváros and Lipótváros, stretching from Liberty Bridge to Margaret Bridge, constitute district V, and contain the lion's share of Pest's sights. The outer ring-road, or **Nagykörút** (Great Boulevard), running from Petőfi Bridge to Margaret Bridge as Ferenc, József, Erzsébet, Teréz and Szent István krts., possesses its own more gritty appeal and many extraordinary buildings that are being renovated one by one.

Budapest's numbered **districts** fan out from the inner ring, divided by the spokes of major roads. Of these, the most important is Andrássy út, which runs northeast to Heroes' Square and City Park. The Nagykörút continues on the Buda side, almost making a perfect ring, with Moszkva tér as its main transport hub on the west bank.

Around the City

Castle Hill (Várhegy)

The Sikló (funicular), its cars resembling old-fashioned black and yellow trams, glides up to Castle Hill from the Buda side of the Chain Bridge in about a minute (7.30am–10pm daily; closed every other Mon). This model, built in 1986, looks like the original from 1870, which functioned up until 1945 when it was taken out by a Soviet shell. To walk, follow the slope (negotiable by wheelchair to the top) to the left as you face the Sikló, then take the stairs to your right. Or take the M2 metro to Moszkva tér, then pick up the Várbusz from beneath the turret of the castle-like building. However you get up to Castle Hill, it feels like a journey back in time.

Perhaps the best place to start a tour of Buda is at the other end of the **Chain Bridge** on Roosevelt tér. Your first view of Castle Hill will then be in the context of the landscape that it crowns. A mere 60m above the level of the Danube, it's not high enough to be aloof, but demands your attention: the Royal Palace, Matthias Church, the whole centuries-old centre, hanging above the city like a mirage of the past.

First to see the strategic potential of this location was the Hungarian King Béla IV, who, following the Mongol invasion of 1247, had a fortress built here, recognizing it as a more defensible location than Esztergom. A civilian population grew up around it and, when the 'New Palace' was built during the 1387–1437 reign of Sigismund of Luxembourg, it became the new royal seat in an extended period of peace that culminated in Matthias Corvinus' rule (1458–90), a Golden Age when Buda played its part in the European Renaissance.

All that died with the king. A period of decline set in, and this weakness was seized upon in 1541 by the Ottoman Turks, who plundered what they could from the town and left the rest to fall apart around them, a job of destruction finished off in 1686 by the Habsburg-led Christian armies that drove them out. This self-proclaimed royal family built their own palace (though they ruled from Vienna) and restored the town, only to raze it again during the 1848–9 War of Independence. Again the castle was rebuilt and again destroyed, this time in 1945, when German troops, besieged by the conquering Red Army, held out for a month, during which Castle Hill was reduced to rubble. It was the city's 31st siege. Phoenix-like, it rose again.

This persistence is important to remember when roaming these streets, which still follow the course dictated by the shape of castle walls. As the rubble was cleared away after the last destruction, many remains dating back to the Middle Ages were found which would otherwise have been forever hidden. In the rebuilding that followed, these were left visible, and complemented by architectural styles that evoke every period of Buda's eventful history. It would be both easy and unjust to dismiss the whole area as a historical theme park. Instead we should see the preservation of its past as a gesture of pride on the part of a people who have always been a buffer zone between East and West, and have always bounced back.

The Turul Statue

If you ascend by the steps, this great bronze eagle suddenly looms over you, clutching a sword and squawking, wings spread, poised for flight. This is the **turul-bird**, which can also be seen guarding the Szabadság híd and Parliament's main gates. It occupies a curious place in Hungarian myth, beginning its job as national protector by raping the grandmother of Magyar chieftan, Árpád. As the hero led his people to conquer the Carpathian Basin, it flew overhead, bearing the sword of Attila the Hun. Descent from an eagle, symbol of the Creator, implied that holy blood coursed through Magyar veins. It's ironic that this particular turul, created in 1905 by Gyula Donáth, was placed here by Habsburg Emperor Franz Josef to present himself as a second Árpád, founder of a thousand-year Dual Monarchy.

In the palace gardens beside the bird is the **statue of Eugene of Savoy**, considered the finest work of József Róna, a self-made man from a poor background. It pays tribute to the man who liberated Hungary by driving out the Turks, though rumour has it that the Austrian Eugene couldn't stand Hungarians.

The Royal Palace (Budavári Palota)

Plain as it may be, few would be unimpressed by the sheer scale and symmetry of the Royal Palace. Occupying much of the southern portion of Castle Hill and dominating the Buda skyline, its lineage reflects the changing fortunes of the town.

Nothing remains of the castle and fortifications of King Béla IV, and nobody is even sure where it stood. The Angevin Kings, living in less drastic days, built more impressive quarters, bettered in turn by Sigismund of Luxembourg, who commissioned a large Gothic palace, protected by a new set of external walls. Matthias Corvinus went one better, ordering a whole new set of buildings and renovating the old ones to suit the latest Renaissance tastes. As the palace re-invented itself as a melting pot for the new ideas on art, politics and culture, artists and scholars from all over Europe were commissioned to supply paintings, sculptures, fountains and lavish banqueting halls; and stayed on, no doubt, to enjoy the famous hospitality, state-of-the-art hot and cold running water, wine, women and song.

Alas, the Turks were waiting in the wings to trash the place, using the Royal Palace to stable their horses and store their gunpowder. Defeating them entailed reducing Matthias' pleasure-dome to such tatters that the Habsburgs just had to build a new one. It started small under Charles III (early 18th century), grew to 203 rooms under Maria Theresia, and just kept growing through the 19th century, despite the lack of royalty. The Viennese court left it to be enjoyed by their viceroy, which added to the rancour of the Hungarian public and no doubt fuelled their restless desire for independence. After the great Compromise was made in 1867, large-scale extensions were carried out under Miklós Ybl, then Alajos Hauszmann. This neo-Baroque monolith was completed in 1905, and never did house an actual monarch.

After the First World War put an end to the Dual Monarchy (though not to the palace, which came off uncharacteristically unscathed), the locals again had to put up with an impostor walking the corridors, this time in the shape of the Allies' viceroy Admiral Horthy. In 1945, of course, the walls came tumbling down again, more completely than ever. The medieval remains uncovered were incorporated into the new structure, which, alas, was based not on the Matthias model but on the vast Habsburg edifice completed by Hauszmann, though with a simpler roof and the addition of a neoclassical dome, which is probably its finest feature.

The interiors were not designed with royalty in mind but for the benefit of cultural institutions; and today the palace is occupied by the National Gallery (wings B, C and D), the Budapest History Museum (E), and the National Széchenyi Library (F).

Hungarian National Gallery (Magyar Nemzeti Galéria)

Open April–Oct Tues–Sun 10–6; Nov–Mar Tues–Fri 10–4, Sat–Sun 10–6; closed Mon; adm for temporary exhibitions only.

Unlike many National Galleries, this one really is national. Everything is Hungarian, ranging from the Middle Ages to the present. It is a large collection but not intimidating: a couple of hours should be enough. Paintings are labelled in English, but there is no further elaboration and no guidebooks or tapes. It hardly seems to matter, since these are all artists the layman is unlikely to have heard of, with names that are impossible to get a hold on, who often allude to historical events only a Hungarian would know. What does matter is that there is much of quality that will help you understand a little better the national soul of the country.

Ground Floor: First port of call is the Lapidarium, which displays stone objects reclaimed from the past after the 1945 destruction. Note the black marble statue of King Béla III's head, thought to date from around 1200, and the two red marble bas-reliefs of King Matthias and his wife Beatrice. Most people agree that one of the highlights of this museum is the collection of 15th- and 16th-century Gothic altarpieces and panel paintings, found on both the ground and the first floor. Many seem weird and wonderful to the modern eye, but that is part of the fun. Note the *Madonna* from Bártfy, rare among Gothic art in that it is complete, and the *Death of the Virgin from Kassa*. These, like most of this collection, are from Slovakia, once part of Upper Hungary. Those in the Magyar heartland were mostly destroyed by the Turks.

First Floor: Of the late Gothic altarpieces, look out especially for *The Annunciation* by Master GH and *The Visitation* by Master MS. In the Baroque rooms, most notable is the 1712 *Portrait of Ferenc Rákóczi* by Ádám Mányoki, which might prepare you to go back through the middle section and face the vast canvases of battle scenes that you hurried past. The most unavoidable, right at the top of the stairs, is Peter Krafft's *Zrínyi's Sortie*, which captures that suicidal moment when the army defending Szigetvár took on the Turks outnumbered 50 to one. These skilful, but to many unappealing, works form part of a wave of nationalism which shows itself in every aspect of the 19th century, when Hungary was sick of being ruled by the Habsburgs or anyone else. Here the response was a return to the glories, even glorious defeats, of the past. András Török mentions the word *honfibú*, which he translates as 'patriotic sorrow': 'There is the grief of generations behind this word. The grief common to all for their ill-fated country.' The nationalist fervour is only too evident in Bertalan Székely's historical works such as *The Return of Buda in 1686*, but the grief is there also, maybe more profoundly, in his portraits.

It is easy to see the influences from the rest of Europe, particularly France, but for the most part these styles are given a distinctly Hungarian turn, and the artists are at their best when they rise above outside influences and bare their souls, as in László Mednyánsky's dark, brooding, Expressionist oils. A room in wing B is devoted to the works of Mihály Munkácsy and László Paál. The former, who worked largely in Munich and Paris, was one of the few to gain recognition in the rest of Europe. He is well known for paintings with a social conscience such as *The Condemned Cell* and *Tramps at Night*, but also produced landscapes such as the Turneresque *Dusty Road*. Paál mainly painted landscapes of a Realist nature. Also in wing B, look out for works by the 'father of Hungarian Impressionism', Pál Szinyei Merse, such as *Picnic in May*. The varied collection of Károly Lotz – whose frescoes adorn the ceilings of almost every major building in town – includes the beautiful, life-size *Woman Bathing*.

Second and Third Floors: These floors contain the 20th-century and contemporary art collections, plus two major temporary exhibitions. Much of the permanent work is by The Eight, a group from the influential artists' colonies such as Nagybanya, who established Hungary's first avant-garde school. The most notable examples of their work are Róbert Berény's *Woman Playing the Cello*, and Ödön Márffy's *The Old Tollhouse at Vác* and *The Oarsmen*. One of the most immediately likeable artists is Károly Ferenczy. His work seems characterized by a certain serenity, such as in his *Self-portrait: The Painter*, or the informal peasant setting of his *Sermon on the Mount*. Note also the extremely idiosyncratic style of Tihanyi Lajos' portraits.

In the works of the 20th century, general trends are ever more apparent, though the critics are not always sure what to call them. József Rippl-Rónai has been called Art

Nouveau and Impressionist. See his works such as *Woman with a Birdcage* and decide for yourself. Somewhere between Art Nouveau and Symbolism are János Vaszary (*The Golden Age*) and Simon Hollósy (*Dancing Girls at the Outskirts of the Forest*). One artist everyone agrees on, even Picasso, is Tivador Csontváry Kosztka. It seems that this enigmatic, possibly mad visionary discovered that he could draw when he sketched on the back of a prescription form a dozing oxen tied to a cart outside a chemist's shop. He is considered self-taught, though he studied in Rome, Paris and Munich. When Picasso first saw his work he apparently asked to be left alone with the paintings for an hour with the doors locked, and said, 'And I thought I was the only great painter of our century.' Csontváry is represented by a handful of paintings including *Pilgrimage to the Cedars of Lebanon* and *Ruins of the Greek Theatre at Taormina*. Most of his works, apparently saved after his death just as his family were about to sell them off as tarpaulin, are in Pécs, about 125 miles south of Budapest.

Amongst all this, everyone will surely find much that appeals. In spite of, maybe because of, its difficult history, Hungary has quietly amassed a wealth of artistic achievement of which any country would be proud. And this without even mentioning the sculpture. Here you will have to follow the dictates of your own tastes, for if anything this is an even more subjective art form than painting.

At the end, if you still haven't had enough, for a fee you can be taken on a tour of the **Palatine crypt** below, which was built in 1715. Ask at the reception desk for details.

Museum of Contemporary Art

The excessive use of red marble in the atrium used for temporary exhibitions is a hangover from the socialist days when this wing housed the Museum of the Working Class Movement. With the laughably oversized staircase, this makes it difficult to take many of the artworks seriously.

Outside the museum is the **Matthias Fountain** on the south wall. It is based on the legend of Szép Ilonka (Helen the Fair), a peasant girl who fell in love with the king when he was out hunting, accompanied by his head huntsman and Italian chronicler. Upon discovering his identity and understanding the hopelessness of her love, she died of a broken heart. To the left is the chronicler, while to the right is poor Ilonka, cossetting the animal her beloved is intent on killing. To the right, two lions guard the gate which leads into the courtyard named after them, within which are entrances to the National Library and the Budapest History Museum.

Budapest History Museum (Budapesti Történeti Múzeum)

Open Wed–Mon 10–4; closed Tues; adm.

This is definitely worth a visit, since it helps to bring Budapest's tumultuous history to life. It is probably best to start on the top floor, where the history lesson begins with artefacts and accounts of those original Magyars descended from the turul-bird. There is little left to show of the intermediate period of the city's past, when the Mongols and Turks seemed bent on all-out destruction, but this deficiency is made good by the splendid, well-designed permanent collection 'Budapest in Modern Times', from the overthrow of the Turks in 1686 to the present.

Downstairs in the basement are exhibited the remains of the **medieval palace** that in its heyday was praised as one of the grandest in all Christendom. Alas, the rooms that it was possible to restore were only of minor importance. The best are the vaulted royal chapel and a Gothic hall which is home to the collection of Gothic statues unearthed in 1974. Ironically, these only survived the Ottoman ravages because in the 15th century no space could be found for them, so they were dumped out in a yard that was later filled in. In summer, a door leads from here to the bastions and courtyards on the palace's southern side.

National Széchenyi Library (Nemzeti Szécsenyi Könyvtár)

Open Aug–June Mon 1–9pm, Tues–Sat 9am–9pm, closed July and Sun; adm.

This library was founded in 1802 thanks to Count Ferenc Széchenyi, father of the famous reformer and national hero. He scoured the country for books, which he bought out of his own pocket and donated to the nation, a collection of some 17,000 books and manuscripts. Today the library contains five million books, including everything that has ever been published in or about Hungary or written by a Hungarian. There are also newspapers, journals, small prints, and collections of maps, music and theatre history. Chief among its treasures are the earliest surviving records of the Hungarian language, from around the 13th century, and the Corviniani, a collection of ancient books and manuscripts, some beautifully illustrated, which originally belonged to King Matthias. There are usually some items being exhibited.

North to Matthias Church

Castle Hill's biggest asset is its atmosphere. Here the past presents itself through the accumulation of details, so, as you wander these ancient streets, observe how each house distinguishes itself through countless tiny variables, hinting at its own secret story. Look at the huge doors; the windows with their bars and boxes; the roofs dotted with spikes, vents, chimneys or tiny windows; the wrought-iron grilles, torch-carriers, sign-holders; the pastel shades, murals, niches, sculptures, plaques. Take in the street-lamps, the cobbled streets, the tiny alleyways and the listed-building (*műemlék*) signs giving details you won't understand.

As you walk away from the Royal Palace past the Sikló, another giant of a building looms, looking as if it must contain something terribly important. This is the **Sándor Palace**, presently unused. Its only claim to fame occurred on 2 April 1941 when the prime minister, Count Pál Teleki, shot himself as a gesture of disgust when Hungary joined Germany in its invasion of Yugoslavia only months after signing with them a treaty of eternal friendship. Next door is the grand **National Dance Theatre**. Originally built for the Carmelite order in 1736, it housed the first ever play in Hungarian, performed by the first professional acting troupe in 1790.

On the other side of **Dísz tér** (Parade Square) the road splits. Tárnok utca, now sadly all dug up, leads to Matthias Church via the small **Golden Eagle Pharmacy Museum** at No.18 (*open Tues–Sun 10.30–5.30; closed Mon; adm*). This 15th-century house was the second home of Buda's oldest pharmacy, established after the defeat of the Turks and here since the mid-18th century. A reconstruction of an alchemist's laboratory features various dried creatures along with the alembics. Original texts include an early 17th-century Paracelsus, a 13th-century Roger Bacon and a 16th-century Geber. Look out for the 17th-century Italian map showing Buda's fortifications at the time of the Turkish occupation, with Pest nothing but a tiny village. There's no labelling in English but the enthusiastic lady will gladly guide and explain.

Úrí utca (Lord Street), on the left, runs to the northern end of Castle Hill and is probably its finest street. The stand-out house is No.31, its almost entirely Gothic façade thought to look as it did in the late 15th century, though the core dates back to the 14th century. In 1862 it was redesigned in a Romantic style but, after these decorations were destroyed in 1945, great efforts were taken to restore the medieval façade. No.49, the former Poor Clares' cloister, houses the **Telephone Museum** (*open Tues–Sun 10–6, closed Mon; adm*), containing everything from ancient Bakelite contraptions to state-of-the-art technology, presented in a fun, hands-on way.

Buda Castle Labyrinth (Budavári Labirintus)

Úrí u. 9, t 489 3280, www.labirintus.com. Open daily 9.30–7.30; adm.

Castle Hill is topped by an 11m-thick layer of limestone, within which thermal springs have hollowed out a series of natural cavities. The first Magyar inhabitants of the hill developed and connected them. Through centuries of invasions, the cave network repeatedly proved its worth, growing in length and sophistication all the while. Sometimes it was the invaders themselves, such as the Turks, who saw their military potential. In peaceful times, the caves were partitioned and used as cellars. In the Second World War they were used as air-raid shelters for up to 10,000 people and contained a hospital. During the Cold War they held a secret military installation. Nowadays you can visit a small section of the 10km labyrinth of passages. Attractions include copies of the most famous European cave paintings such as Lascaux, reconstructions of historical scenes, images of labyrinths from different ages and cultures, and the chance to test your courage and sense of direction by walking around alone. After 6pm the tour is by oil lamp.

Szentháromság Tér

Dominated by the Matthias Church and Fisherman's Bastion, the broad, cobblestoned Szentháromság tér is the focal point of Castle Hill, thronged by tourists, tricksters, leaflet-distributors and buskers. All the more reason to arrive early or late. At night the church is more beautiful, and the whole area timelessly romantic.

The large bronze equestrian **statue** between church and bastion represents King Stephen, justly, as a grim and powerful figure. At the end of the 10th century he unified the Magyar tribes into one nation, of which he was the first king. Born Vajk, he became Stephen (or István) when he converted to Christianity and forced his nation to do the same, a move that facilitated their integration into Europe. He is depicted here wearing the famous crown sent for his coronation by Pope Sylvester II. The relief at the back shows Frigyes Shulek (*see below*), who designed the neo-Romanesque plinth, kneeling modestly before the king, offering him a model of the Matthias Church. Nearby, a spiral staircase leads down into the **Szent Mihály Kápolna**, an atmospheric, cavernous brick and stone chapel full of modern artworks. The square is named for its central **Holy Trinity Column**, erected in thanksgiving for the end of the plague in 1713, and in the hope of fending off another.

On the square's southwest corner is the former **Buda Town Hall**, bearing a statue of Pallas Athene, protector of cities. Turn west for the famous **Ruszwurm Cukrászda** (*see* p.189), whose lavish antique interior makes it as much a part of the historical tour as a great place for coffee and cake. Opposite is the statue of András Hadik, better known as the **Hussar Statue**. These infantrymen, first organized by King Matthias in 1480, wore no armour because their weapon was speed. Armed with sabres, pikes and pointed daggers, they specialized in fast, unexpected attacks, with such success that soon every army in Europe had a similar regiment. As well as capturing the poise of effortless understanding between horse and rider, this statue has another interesting feature: its gleaming, smooth testicles. Touching them is said to bring luck in exams.

Matthias Church (Mátyás Templom)

Open daily 7am–8pm; adm. Mass 7am, 8.30am and 6pm, also Sun and hols 10am (Latin mass) and noon.

Matthias Church is undoubtedly one of Budapest's finest buildings, though its effect is diminished by the surrounding fence and scaffolding on the spire. Its chequered past began way back in the early 13th century, following the Mongol invasion. It originally resembled the northern French Gothic, before Sigismund of Luxembourg remodelled it into a hall-church in high Gothic style. Matthias made his own improvements and was married here twice. Under the Turks, the furnishings were destroyed, the walls whitewashed and the church restyled as a mosque. Back in Christian hands after the siege, it was given to the Franciscans, then the Jesuits, who decorated it in a Baroque style. Poor as its condition was by 1867, it was still considered worthy to host the coronation of Franz Josef as King of Hungary, for which Liszt's *Coronation Mass* was specially composed.

Like so much of Castle Hill, this building is neither old nor new, but rather a composite of many past ages. When much-needed reconstruction was undertaken between 1873 and 1896, architect Frigyes Schulek was so keen to preserve its multi-layered past that he noted all the original features revealed as the walls were pulled down, and built them into his new structure, including much of the wall decoration. He also added a lot of his own. Thus, he kept the original tower intact up to the third floor, after which he followed his own vision.

It takes a while to realize why the church makes such an impact. Partly it is the proliferation of detail and the colourful tiling of the roof, but mainly it is the sheer height of the tower. At 80m, it could lose a whole section without appearing squat. Before going inside, have a closer look at the front left **Béla Tower**, named after the church's original founder, which has retained many Gothic features; and the stained-glass rose window, which is unfortunately hidden inside by a pipe organ. Above all, have a good look above the door at the **Mary Portal**, Schulek's reconstruction of one of the greatest pieces of Gothic stone carving in Hungary, depicting the *Assumption of the Virgin Mary*.

Inside, every inch of wall space has been painted, not like the Sistine Chapel – there are few biblical scenes or figures – but with repetitive patterns of a floral or geometrical nature, sometimes resembling Polynesian, Aboriginal or Native American art, and adding up almost to an Art Nouveau effect. They were designed by Bertalan Székely. The overall effect is one of infinite warmth, in marked contrast to the starkness of so many churches. Here the worshipper – for this is still above all a place of worship – is not overawed and intimidated, but cheered and welcomed. The God who resides in this house feels much more approachable than most. But he still has a penchant for gold. Much of that present is on the altar, whose design was based on Gothic triptychs, and which repeats the Trinity figures from the column outside.

The three arched stained-glass windows on the south wall were designed by Schulek, Székely and Károly Lotz. The participation of these latter two artists helps to explain the overall quality of the art present. Above the Mary Portal are five circular paintings by Lotz showing the birth and childhood of Christ. To its right is the original coat of arms of King Matthias. Nearby, inside the **Loreto Chapel** below the south tower, is a Baroque *Madonna* in Italian style from the 17th century. Legend has it that the original was set into a wall during the Turkish occupation. When the walls were crumbling during the siege of 1686, she reappeared, scaring the Turks out of their wits and assuring them of their imminent defeat.

On the north side in the **Trinity Chapel** lies the tomb of King Béla III and his wife Anne de Châtillon. Their double sarcophagus lies below a richly carved stone canopy. In the crypt is a red marble sarcophagus housing bones from the royal tombs in Székesfehérvár, and a small collection of ecclesiastical treasures and relics. From here a staircase leads to **St Stephen's Chapel**, containing a bust of the king, and various scenes from his life. More stairs lead to the **Royal Oratory**, exhibiting a replica of the Hungarian crown jewels (the real ones are in the Parliament), and coronation thrones of Emperors Franz Josef and Karl IV.

Try to attend a concert in the church; the acoustics are excellent.

Fishermen's Bastion (Halászbástya) and Hilton Hotel

In the Middle Ages there was a fish market near to this spot, and the Guild of Fishermen were responsible for defending this part of the **wall**. Nowadays, this rampart fulfils a strictly aesthetic function. It was designed by Schulek to complement the Matthias Church. In both, the mood is one of romantic chivalry, playfulness and an almost childlike sense of wonder. With its zigzagging white ramparts, curving stairways and ice-cream-cone turrets (seven, symbolizing the Magyar tribes who founded the nation), it looks as if it leapt from the pages of a fairytale book. It also offers some of the best views of Pest available.

Opposite is the ugly **Hilton Hotel** which, despite the funky reflections of church, statue and bastion thrown off by its dated copper-glass façade, looks all wrong here. It does have some redeeming features, though. Follow the bastion to its northern end and go through the (normally open) gate that leads behind the hotel, and you will find yourself in the remains of a medieval church from 1254. This Dominican courtyard, uncovered during excavations in 1902, was incorporated by architect Béla Pinter into the hotel's design, and now provides a stage for concerts and operettas during the summer season. The hotel's **Faust Wine Cellar** is a reconstruction from remains of the original monastery wine cellar. Round on Hess András tér, the hotel's frontal façade has been built to integrate remains of a late Baroque Jesuit college. To the left of the entrance is **St Nicholas' Tower**, containing a copy of the 1486 *Matthias Relief* from Germany, generally considered to be the only genuine likeness of the great man. The overall achievement is admirable, and from the Pest embankment the hotel's bulk looming behind the church is discreet enough to take little away from the scene.

North of Matthias Church

Three streets run north from Szentháromság tér, roughly parallel to and east of Úri u. Furthest east is Táncsics u., which contains the **Music History Museum** at No.7 (*open April–Oct Tues–Sun 10–6; Nov–Mar Tues–Sun 10–5; closed Mon; adm*), in the grand Erdödy Palace where Beethoven stayed in 1800. In this fascinating selection of 17th–19th-century instruments, the classical exhibits include finely ornamented lyres and a unique tongue-shaped violin, while the folk section has a gardon (a primitive cello), bagpipes, zithers and cowhorns. The emphasis is on the instruments as works of art. As well as temporary exhibits, there is a collection of Bartók's scores and scribblings. Down the street at No.26 is the **Medieval Jewish Prayer House** (*open May–Oct Tues–Fri 10–2, Sat and Sun 10–6; closed Mon*). Foundations of a large synagogue dating back to the 15th century were discovered here. The interest of the museum lies not so much in the small exhibition of tombstones and liturgical objects, but in the space itself, used as a house of prayer during the Turkish occupation.

The **Museum of Hungarian Commerce and Catering** (*Fortuna u. 4; open Wed–Fri 10–5, Sat and Sun 10–6; closed Mon and Tues; adm*) is much more interesting than you'd expect. The commerce section includes early 19th-century advertisements, antique shopfronts, a provincial grocery store, Hungary's first electric billboard (advertising beer) and, the *pièce de résistance*, an HMV dog that taps its paws against the window to catch the attention of passers-by. In the catering section we learn about the men behind the names Gundel and Gerbeaud.

Hess András tér was named after the man who established the nation's first printing-press. His workshop is believed to have occupied the site of the Fortuna Restaurant. At No.6 is the **House of Hungarian Wines** (Magyar Borok Háza; *open June–Sept Mon–Fri 1–9, Sat and Sun 11–9; Oct–May daily 11–7*), whose extensive cellar holds some 550 different wines from Hungary's 20-odd growing regions, making it one of the biggest wine collections in Europe. For a mere £5–6 you can help yourself to a selection of 60 or 70 of these, taking as much time as you like, and learn everything about Hungarian wine. Farther west, Országház u. (Parliament Street) gained its name from a period in the 1790s when the Parliament (Diet) met in the large building at No.28, originally a convent of Poor Clares.

At the northern end of Castle Hill, all streets converge on two conjoined squares. To the east is Bécsi Kapu tér, named after the **Vienna Gate**, built to celebrate the 250th anniversary of the recapture of Buda. Climb on top of the gate for a better view of the Lutheran Church, built at the end of the 19th century, with its unusual spire. Through the gate and to the right is **Europa Grove**, so named because in 1972 city mayors from all over Europe planted 16 types of tree in honour of the centenary of the unification of Buda, Óbuda and Pest. Lovas u., curving left under the castle walls, has a collection of Budapest street-lamps dating from 1844 to 1944.

Back on the square, the hulking neo-Romanesque **National Archives** building is saved from total po-facedness by the multicoloured roof. Next door is the **Military History Museum** (*open Tues–Sun 10–4, closed Mon; adm*) in a former barracks. Permanent displays include 'The History of Hand Weapons from the Stone Axe to the Pistol', exhibits on the 1848 Revolution, and an evocative look at the 'Thirteen Days' of street-fighting during the 1956 Uprising (*newsreel footage at 11am and 2pm*). Outside is a **statue of Friar John Capistranus**, after whom this bigger square, Kapisztrán tér, is named. This zealous Italian Franciscan urged the Crusaders on to victory in the siege of Belgrade in 1456. Here he stands over a dead Turk, exhorting the soldiers to produce more. Over the road is the **Mary Magdalene Tower**, modelled on the original Baroque spire, after the war destroyed the rest of the church. In the Middle Ages, Hungarians worshipped here, while the Germans got Matthias Church. The remains of the foundations stand between this strangely solitary tower (housing a private art gallery) and the even more eerie sight of a single tall window. Adding to the oddness is the tower's peal of ornamental bells, apparently capable of rattling through a melody compiled by a jazz pianist.

A chestnut-tree-lined street, Tóth Árpád sétány, hugs the western ramparts of the hill, offering views of the Buda Hills, Gellért and Tabán. The entrance to the Military History Museum is on this street, announced by a collection of historical cannons. Round the corner is the **Abdurrahman Memorial**, a tomb with an inscription in Hungarian and Turkish that reads: 'It was near this site that the last governor [pasha] of the 143-year-long Turkish rule in Buda fell in battle at the age of 70. A valiant foe, may he rest in peace.'

Gellért Hill and Tabán

These two areas line the Buda embankment from the Liberty Bridge (Szabadság híd) in the south to the Chain Bridge (Széchenyi Lánchíd) in the north.

Gellért Hill (Gellért-Hegy)

As well as providing a backdrop to the Buda skyline, the 460ft dolomite cliff of Gellért Hill offers the best views of Pest and Castle Hill. For centuries its lower slopes were used for cultivating grapevines. The name Gellért derives from an 11th-century Benedictine abbot from Venice, Ghirardus (Gellért in Hungarian, Gerard in English), whom King Stephen asked to help convert the Magyars to Christianity, as well as tutoring his son, Imre.

The Gellért Hotel and Baths

Budapest's most famous hotel sits like a country mansion at the end of the elegant Liberty Bridge, which looks as though, like a driveway, it were constructed for this purpose alone. (In fact it was built for the Millennium celebrations in 1896, when it was opened by Franz Josef, whose name it originally bore.) It is a spectacular, unabashedly Art Nouveau building, with cylindrical towers and turrets and many fine details, such as the lyre and bird motifs on the elaborate balustrades of the balconies. Purpose-built as a spa hotel in an attempt to promote Budapest as a spa town, it occupies a spot whose hot springs have been revered for their healing properties for at least seven centuries. An old legend has it that spring comes to Gellért Hill three weeks earlier than the rest of Budapest thanks to the dynamic power of the thermal waters. In the Middle Ages a hospital stood on the site, and the Turks, who know about such things, constructed their own baths. Sadly, the year after its completion the hotel was taken over by Béla Kún's Communist régime, then by the Romanian army, and finally by Admiral Horthy following his entry on a white horse and declaration of intent to cleanse the 'sinful city'. Despite this interlude, the Gellért lived up to the hopes invested in it, becoming in the 1920s a social high spot for Budapest's upper classes and later enjoying an international reputation that attracted the royal, powerful, rich and famous from all over Europe. After the party-pooper of 1939, it was goodbye to all that: only the outer walls survived the war. Though not original, the interior is as magnificent as the outside, and should not be missed. Step into the busy entrance hall to admire the mosaics and statues. On the right, at the top of a flight of stairs, is a radiant stained-glass window, which recounts the story of the magic stag, an old Hungarian legend famously rendered in the poetry of János Arany.

Entrance to the **baths** is on the hotel's right flank as you face it (*t 466 6166; trams 47 or 49 from the Kiskörút; open May–Sept daily 6am–7pm; Oct–April Mon–Fri 6am–7pm, Sat and Sun 6am–5pm; adm, reduced rate after 5pm*). They offer sheer opulence, decorated throughout in ornate Art Nouveau style replete with statues, columns, mosaics, glazed tiles, ornate ceilings, lion-headed spouts and myriad other details only the wealthy could once afford. Ignore those around you and imagine that you are royalty. Rarely does life offer the opportunity to partake of so much grandeur for so little money. The baths are mixed-sex, with segregated hot-tubs and steam-rooms. They offer all the variety of pools, plus an outdoor swimming pool and sunbathing terrace.

The Cave Church (Sziklatemplom)

Opposite the entrance to the baths, a path leads a short way uphill (to the right) to the Cave Church (*wheelchair accessible*). Established in 1926 and based by designer Kálmán Lux on the shrine at Lourdes, the church was intended for the Pauline order of monks. This is the only order indigenous to Hungary, traditionally confessors to the king, founded in 1256 by Eusebius of Esztergom and dissolved in 1773 by Josef II. It was built and they came – 15 of them, back from a 150-year exile in Poland. Unfortunately, in the 1950s the Communists jailed the monks for 'treasonable acts' and sealed the entrance of the church. It was reopened in 1989.

It may be in a cave, but everywhere the coldness of ceiling and walls is enlivened by potted plants, stained glass and art. At the very back a giant bronze Polish eagle contains a copy of the *Black Madonna* of Czestochowa. In the chapel, look for Béli Ferenc's wooden sculptures, and check out some of the whimsical art in the area behind the altar. All of this is rather let down by the gaudy plastic Christ above the altar. But then this is not a tourist attraction: it is a working church, and a busy one at that. A large congregation attends the hour-long masses at 11am, 5pm and 8pm, during which times tourists are asked to remain outside and silent.

The Citadella and Liberty Statue

On the summit of Gellért Hill squats the low, bulky **Citadella**, not an attraction as much as a pinnacle from which to see everything else. The site was chosen by the Habsburgs with this in mind. After quashing the 1848–9 Revolution, they constructed this grim edifice, a stronghold from which to survey and control, and which was impossible to ignore. After the Compromise of 1867, citizens breached its hated walls and called for its destruction. For all that, only in 1897 did the Austrian soldiers leave. Since then it has housed a prison camp, an SS regiment, the homeless, an anti-aircraft battery and, nowadays, a restaurant, café, hotel, nightclub and a small museum about the Celtic Eravisci, the first inhabitants of this hill, 2,000 years ago.

Mainly, though, people come for the views, among them that of the adjacent **Liberty Statue**, which is far too tall to take in from below. Designed by Hungarian sculptor Zsigmond Kisfaludi Stróbl, Lady Liberty stands 46ft high (100ft if you include her colossal pedestal), and can be seen clearly from anywhere in Pest. The story goes that this statue was originally commissioned by Regent Miklós Horthy to commemorate his son István, killed in a plane crash on the Russian front. But after the German units were finally prised out of Castle Hill, a Russian marshall supposedly saw this figure in a sculptor's workshop and had the propeller she was intended to hold swapped for a palm leaf, thus creating a monument to the Soviet soldiers who died in the 'liberation'. Funnily enough, this really is just a story: it was a Communist monument from the start. When the Communists retreated, many locals wanted the statue destroyed or removed. In the end it was simply recycled: the figure of a Russian soldier (now in the Statue Park, see p.257) and a plaque listing Russian war casualties were removed. For all that, something about the pedestal marks this out as a Soviet creation.

The Gellért Monument

A quarter of the way up Gellért Hill, facing Elisabeth Bridge, stands this statue of the eponymous saint (bear left on your way down from the Citadella). The pagans he was converting put up with Gellért's evangelising while King Stephen was alive, but legend tells that in 1046, eight years after the ruler's death, a rebellion erupted against Christianity during which the saint was put into a barrel and pushed off this hill into the Danube. The barrel could have been nail-studded or merely a wheelbarrow, depending which version you choose to believe.

Now that Christianity again has the upper hand, Gellért has been restored to his full dignity. Built in 1904, this near-40ft statue shows him holding his cross aloft in perpetual reproach to the sinners across the water in Pest, while at his feet kneels one of the newly converted Magyar heathen.

An alternative way down the hill involves following the paved road past the viewing spot until you hit a junction, then bearing right and getting lost amidst the maze of lanes and narrow streets. This would appeal to lovers of grand houses and mansions, with which this green area is overflowing. Most of them are embassies. If you keep going down you will, of course, eventually get back to the river and the jumble of roads that carve up the area of Tabán.

Tabán

This area gets its name from the tanning workshops here during the Turkish occupation. The Turks took advantage of the thermal waters, building two magnificent baths, the only part to survive the siege of 1686. When the Turks retreated from Hungary, they still occupied the Balkans, and many Serbs fleeing from them settled here. Around 1700, 95 per cent of the area's inhabitants were Serbian (Rácok in Hungarian). As Greeks and Romanies followed suit, a dense, cosmopolitan and essentially impoverished population gave the quarter a run-down, bohemian flavour, famous for its bars, brothels and gambling dens, ancient rambling streets, whitewashed houses with red tile roofs, wine gardens and orchards. Unfortunately, this nostalgic simplicity also entailed open sewers, and in 1908 the City Council declared the whole area a health hazard and razed it. Thankfully the baths survived, as did the splendid Tabán Parish Church on Attila út. The arterial roads that now choke it were constructed during the Communist years and mean that the area is only worth visiting for one of its notable sights.

The **Rác Baths** (*I. Hadnagy u. 8–10, t 356 1322; open 6.30am–7pm; women Mon, Wed, Fri; men Tues, Thurs, Sat; adm*), at the foot of Gellért Hill where it meets Tabán, are named after the Hungarian word for Serb. The building contains a Turkish octagonal pool and dome, though its exterior is 19th century. The waters are good for chronic arthritis and muscle and nerve pain, though the baths are now more famous for their gay scene. Currently closed for renovations which are due to add a big spa hotel and a funicular up to the Citadella.

The **Rudas Baths** (*I. Döbrentei tér 9, t 356 1322; open Mon–Fri 6am–6pm, Sat and Sun 6am–1pm; adm*), built in the 16th century on a site occupied by baths since the 14th century, are the most atmospheric of the Turkish baths. The original octagonal pool and cupola combined with the dim, rather dank interior, saturated with steam and echoing sounds, make for a timeless experience. Light slants in at different angles through small octagonal windows in the dome. As well as six pools of differing temperatures, including the hottest in town at 46°C, there are three saunas and two steam rooms. A fountain allows you to drink the warm, sulphurous water, said to be good for gastric complaints. Occasionally, the Rudas pays host to a uniquely Budapestian phenomenon known as *Vizimozi*, basically a rave in the main swimming pool accompanied by silent movies shown on a big screen, or ethno-trance music in the Turkish baths. It also offers bars, a gallery, and a dance floor in the hallway.

The **Semmelweis Museum of Medical History** (Semmelweis Orvostörténeti Muzeum; *I. Apród u. 1–3, t 201 1577; open Tues–Sun 10.30–5.30, closed Mon; adm*), near the Rudas Baths, exhibits items relating to medicine, including a medieval chastity belt and some 18th-century beeswax anatomical models. It's based in the house where Dr Ignác Semmelweis was born.

The striking white **Elisabeth Bridge** which leads from the jumble of roads across to Pest was named after Franz Josef's wife. Nicknamed Sisi, she was a beautiful and tragic figure, unsuited to the straitjacket of royalty. Much loved by the Hungarians, whose language she spoke, she was greatly mourned following her assassination in 1898 (see p.56). This was the only bridge destroyed in the war not rebuilt according to its original form, although it does imitate the old chain bridge's much loved arch. Constructed in 1964, this bridge has almost become a symbol for the city.

The Chain Bridge (Széchenyi Lánchíd)

Before the 1840s, Buda and Pest were by necessity separate towns because they were divided by the Danube. It was impossible to build a bridge of wood and stone over a river this wide. A pontoon bridge operated between autumn and spring, there were occasional ferries, and in winter the water froze so that sometimes even carts could cross, but still people got stuck on the wrong side for weeks when a sudden thaw set in. Like many examples of 19th-century progress, the first permanent bridge across the Danube was István Széchenyi's initiative. In 1820 he had to wait a week for a ferry across to attend his father's funeral, and decided it wasn't good enough. He sent to Britain for an English engineer, William Tierney Clark (who designed London's Hammersmith Bridge), and a Scottish masterbuilder, Adam Clark (no relation), and even had the iron shipped over. In 1849, before it was completed, the Austrians tried to blow it up, but Adam Clark thwarted their plans by flooding the anchorage chambers and destroying the pumps that could have been used to drain them. The colonel who tried to use explosives despite this was blown to pieces. But the Uprising failed, and the bridge was completed under Austrian command. As a further irony, the first person to cross the bridge at its opening was the cruel and much hated General Julius Haynau, at whose behest the equally despised Citadella would be constructed.

A story has it that Adam Clark was so proud of his masterpiece that he swore he would drown himself if the slightest fault was found with it. Eventually it was noted (erroneously) that the splendid lions at either end had no tongues, and Clark duly topped himself. Again, just a story. Actually, Clark liked the city so much that he married a local girl and stayed to construct the **tunnel** that runs under Castle Hill as a direct continuation of the bridge, whose style it complements. Flanked by two pairs of Doric columns, it was clearly built with an eye to the aesthetic. The joke amongst Budapesters at the time was that it would be a good place to put the new bridge when it rained. Today the Chain Bridge is a symbol of the city, for its beauty as much as its technological prowess. When, 95 years after its construction, the Germans blew up all the Danube's bridges, this was the first to be reconstructed, to the same design.

The **Sikló** running up to Castle Hill starts its journey in Clark Ádám tér. At its foot, a small garden contains a curious concrete doughnut. This is the **Kilometer Zero stone**. Sculptor Miklós Borsos intended it to express not just zero but the beginning of everything, the origins of all life. It signifies that this is the centre of Budapest: all distances in the country are measured from here; and justly so, for this is where the three component towns of Pest, Buda and Óbuda were given their first permanent physical link, paving the way for their official union in 1872.

Víziváros

The thin stretch of land north of the Chain Bridge and east of the river has been called Víziváros or 'Water Town' since the Middle Ages. While the royal court and its associated gentry enjoyed the views from the hill, people down here were mainly fishermen, craftsmen and traders. The Turks depopulated the area, turned its churches into mosques and left behind the Király baths. The 18th century witnessed a boom time when some of Buda's more socially elevated citizens built many of the grand houses that can be seen here today, but extensive construction a century later put an end to the small-town atmosphere and the advent of the car killed it off.

Today Víziváros has the feel of a neighbourhood that has known better times and will know them again. In contrast to Castle Hill, many grand old buildings have been let go; the churches are closed, the principal square feels seedy, and the main road heaves with traffic. Yet on a Sunday morning, when the churches are open and the roads less busy, it is still possible to catch a whiff of the history that permeates these buildings. It is not dead, only sleeping.

Fő Utca

Literally meaning 'Main Street', this thoroughfare leading northwards from Clark Ádám tér dates back to the times of the Romans. Looking up at the façades, it is clear that this has the potential to be a beautiful, refined district when future waves of yuppies restore the faded buildings. Check out the three-sided Romantic building at No.2, or the 1811 remodelling of a medieval house at No.20, with its unusual turreted cylindrical window and reliefs. Past the ugly Postmodernist pile of the French Institute with its Constructivist sign, already looking dated in a way these older buildings never will, past the **Capuchin Church**, whose fine statue of St Elizabeth has unfortunately been painted brown, pretty **Corvin tér** stands newly renovated. Across the road are four striking houses, recently renovated and painted in pastel shades to form the western face of the art'otel, demonstrating what could be done with the whole street. A statue of St John of Nepomuk stands in the niche on No.3's Baroque façade, whilst the neoclassical No.5 carries four reliefs, the three above the windows depicting King Matthias as farmer, scholar and commander, the one above the door showing the interior of an alchemist's shop. Fő utca continues in its unrenovated form practically to Margaret Bridge and contains at least two churches that shouldn't be missed. If the traffic gets too much, try the quieter Iskola utca, parallel on the left.

The Calvinist Church (Református Templom)

On Szilágyi tér off Fő u., this neo-Gothic church (finished in 1896) was planned by Sámuel Pecz according to a design traditionally used for medieval Catholic churches. It is one of the most distinctive points of the Buda landscape and an extremely complex, impressive construction. Castle-like and angular, squat and solid rather than elegant, and buttressed on all sides, it still manages to achieve a certain sublime beauty: maybe thanks to the three shades of brick used and the glazed, polychromatic roof-tiles, maybe due to its very complexity. Note the unusual shape of the central 10-sided tower, its roof splaying at the last moment to connect with the walls, or the way the spire is set off to one side. Whatever the appeal, viewed from Pest it stands out as one of a trio with the Matthias Church and Fishermen's Bastion. The inside is similarly unornamented but aesthetic, its most showy feature the intricate upper half of the pulpit. Unfortunately, it's usually closed.

The **statue** on a fountain in this square is of the church's architect Pecz dressed as a medieval master builder, a guise the sculptor claimed to have seen him wearing at a fancy-dress ball. The square itself is remembered for one of the more grim events of 1945. This stretch of water is one of the areas where Jews and anti-Fascists were brought to be shot. Even after the departure of the SS, the Fascist Arrow Cross rounded up and massacred hundreds of Jews here and dumped their bodies in the river. A plaque commemorates the spot.

Church of St Anne (Szent Anna Templom)
Open only for services, Mon–Fri 6.45–9 and 4–7, Sun and hols 9–1.

Located on faded Batthyány tér off Fő u., this twin-towered parish church is one of Budapest's most beautiful Baroque buildings. Commissioned by the Jesuits, work began in 1740 but was interrupted by financial constraints, an earthquake in 1763, and the abolition of the Jesuit order in 1773. It was not consecrated until 1805. It was badly damaged in the Second World War, and almost pulled down during the construction of the metro due to fears that its foundations would be undermined. On the **façade**, note, from bottom to top, the allegorical figures of Faith, Hope and Charity above the entrance, the central niche with a statue of St Anne and the child Mary, the Buda coat of arms in the tympanum, and above it the eye-in-the-triangle symbol representing the Trinity, flanked by two kneeling angels. Farther up loom the distinctive twin towers, crowned by magnificent Baroque spires with funky green square domes.

Much of the **interior** dates from the 18th century. The spectacular **high altar**, representing in typically Baroque fashion the child Mary being presented by her mother Anne at the Temple of Jerusalem, was completed in 1773, the finest work of Károly Bebó, who also created the gilded Baroque pulpit swarming with cherubs. The painted **ceiling** in the cupola of the chancel is a 1771 depiction of the *Holy Trinity* by Gergely Vogl, while the side altars by Antal Eberhardt date from 1768. Note also the delicately carved baptismal font and the figurative scenes carved into the wooden panels of the choir pews. Yet, for all the gold and excess of decoration, the green wallpaper, carved wooden Stations of the Cross, vases of flowers and oval portraits create a homely, small-town atmosphere, such that, as in the Matthias Church, the God who resides within these walls comes across as welcoming rather than intimidating.

Batthyány Tér and on down Fő Utca
Batthyány tér epitomizes the current nature of Víziváros, surrounded as it is by grand edifices gone shabby. Note, for instance, the old market building that resembles the best kind of railway station but now houses a supermarket. Worth seeing, though, are the bas-reliefs on the façade of the 18th-century **Hikisch house** at No.3. Reminiscent of sketches from an alchemical treatise, they are depictions of the four

seasons. The rococo-style house next door is the former **White Cross Inn** where Casanova is reputed to have stayed. The square is good for views of Parliament.

Carrying on down Fő utca, you will pass the **Church of the St Elizabeth Nuns**, looking like a big cake. Inside, the Baroque decoration is absurdly rich, with gold-draped figures everywhere: fixed to the walls, loafing around the edge of the pulpit or flanking the paintings, admiring them or pointing to encourage us. The altarpiece of St Francis receiving the stigmata is worth seeing, as is the fresco of St Florian saving Christians from a fire in 1810. All the more pity that it too is locked outside service times. Farther on are the Turkish **Király Baths** (*II. Fő u. 84*, *t 201 4392; open Tues, Thurs and Sat 9–8 for men; Mon, Wed, Fri 7–6 for women; adm*). One of Budapest's most striking and atmospheric baths, featuring a 16th-century Ottoman pool and several smaller pools beneath the original cupola. They were completed by the third Turkish pasha in 1570 just inside the Víziváros castle gates, so that the garrison could bathe even during a siege. The classical section was added in the early 18th century. All the normal baths are here. The surviving Turkish section faces Ganz utca; the neoclassical wing facing Fő utca dates from 1826.

Bem József tér is named after the Polish general whose statue it contains. He fought in the Polish uprising of 1830–31, the Vienna revolt of 1848 and the War of Independence in 1848–9. Demonstrations often begin here, as did the march on Parliament at the beginning of the 1956 Uprising.

The road changes name but continues, leading (maybe farther than you would want to go) to the peaceful neoclassical complex of the **Lukács Baths** (*II. Frankel Leó u. 25–9*, *t 326 1695; open May–Sept Mon–Sat 6am–7pm, Sun 6am–5pm; Oct–April Sat only 6am–5pm; adm*). These mixed-sex baths are set in attractive grounds containing two outdoor swimming pools and the normal thermal pools. The waters are said to be good for orthopaedic diseases.

A short detour off Frankel Leó u. takes you to the **Tomb of Gül Baba** (*Mecset u. 14; open April–Sept Tues–Sun 10–6; Oct 10–4*). The name of this Turkish Dervish, a member of the Sufi Bektaşi order, means 'Father of the Roses'. Legend has it that he introduced the rose to Hungary and gave Rózsadomb, this area, its name: Hill of Roses. Hungarians revere him for this even though he participated in the hated Turkish capture of Buda (after which he died at the thanksgiving service). His life has inspired works by the Danish writer Hans Christian Anderson and the Hungarian composer J. Huszka. The site has been restored by the Turkish government and surrounded by a colonnaded parapet. The octagonal tomb is a 1962 reconstruction of the one built in the 1540s by the third pasha of Buda, but the dome that covers it is original. The interior is decorated with Arabic calligraphy citing the Koran, pictures and Turkish carpets.

The City (Lipótváros/Leopold Town)

Covering the northern section of inner Pest, this is the financial, banking and business heart of the capital, containing its Parliament and cathedral. Planned in the early 19th century and named Lipótváros after Leopold Habsburg II, it is buzzing on weekdays with people in suits talking on mobile phones, and a ghost town at weekends and in the evenings. Since what is of most interest here is the buildings (of which there are too many striking examples to take in), these quiet times are probably the best ones for a visit. There is a lot to see here, and the selection below is only the cream. But, as is so often the case, it is a good idea just to stroll around, get slightly lost, and see what you see.

Roosevelt Tér

Situated at the Pest end of the Chain Bridge, Roosevelt tér is a big grassy expanse, choked by relentless traffic. Its main draw is the **Gresham Palace**, an Art Nouveau gem designed by Zsigmond Quittner and brothers József and László Vágó in 1906, with details crafted by many of the leading artists of the day. Built for an insurance company, it became an apartment block with exclusive boutiques in the arcade, a famous café, and a cabaret. Badly damaged by the retreating German army in 1944, it was used by Allied military for a while, became a library, then Communist state offices, before slipping into complete neglect. Fortunately, the Four Seasons hotel group have recently completed the painstaking reconstruction that has restored its former glory, sticking as close as possible to the original design. The fresh white façade is very subtle, dotted with fragments of glistening gold mosaic designed by Miksa Róth. The relief of a male head in a ruff at the top portrays Sir Thomas Gresham, who first commissioned the building. Guests pass through exact copies of the original delicate wrought-iron peacock gates into an interior that is far more overtly Art Nouveau. The floor is a swirling mosaic; the lobby, inner courtyards and sweeping staircases overflow with showy details in stained-glass, wrought-iron, and Zsolnay ceramic. Arched glass ceilings focus on the restored original glass cupola. The only blot on the landscape is the building site next door.

At the north end of the square is the neo-Renaissance **Hungarian Academy of Sciences**. The six statues on the main façade represent the Academy's original six departments: law, sciences, mathematics, philosophy, linguistics and history. On the same level are statues of six scientists: from the river, Newton, Lomonosov, Galileo, Miklós Révai (a Hungarian linguist), Descartes and Leibnitz. The building was finished by German Friedrich August Stüler in 1865. The statue in the middle of the square is Széchenyi, surrounded by Minerva (trade), Neptune (navigation), Vulcan (industry) and Ceres (agriculture). Farther south is a **statue of Ferenc Deák**, a moderate, liberal politician known as 'the nation's sage'. It is appropriate that his statue should be close to that of Széchenyi, whose belief in the gentle path of reform he shared throughout the turbulent 1840s. Ever opposed to war, he was largely responsible for the 1867 Compromise with Austria that led to the Dual Monarchy. Here he is shown with figures representing Justice, Patriotism, Popular Education, National Progress and Compromise. In 1858 he wrote, 'Primarily the task is to keep alive in the nation a sense and enthusiasm for constitutional liberty, because in a more favourable moment the Hungarian constitution can be restored by the stroke of a pen, and within 24 hours we can again be a free constitutional state.'

The large bronze relief on the Akadémia u. side of the Academy depicts the moment of its formation. On 3 November 1825, Count István Széchenyi (dressed here in a

Hussar officer's uniform) announced to the Diet (Parliament) that he would donate a year's income towards the establishment of a learned society for the development of Hungarian arts, science, language and literature. When asked what he would live on, he answered, 'My friends will support me.' It was the first major act of a life of extraordinary philanthropy.

Between Roosevelt tér and Parliament, **Akadémia u.** is recommended for its buildings, though Nádor u. has the appealing **Central European University**, whose best feature is its interior. Nip inside for a look: just say you're going to the fine academic bookshop if anyone asks. It was established by George Soros, a billionaire economist born in Budapest in 1930 at the tail end of a period which saw an unfeasible number of geniuses educated in the city.

St Stephen's Basilica (Bazilika)

t 317 2859; basilica open Mon–Fri 9–5, Sat 9–1, Sun 1–5, and daily 7–7.45pm; treasury open daily 10–5; adm.

Sitting on Szent István tér with its back to the main road, and surrounded by buildings almost as high as itself, Budapest's cathedral tends to creep up on you. It's hard to get a good look at it except from the front, which is easily the most attractive part anyway. The back is too overcrowded with competing architectural features for its own good, and has provoked accusations of ugliness. Detractors are silenced now, however. Freshly cleaned and free of scaffolding, the basilica looks fantastic.

History has hitherto been unkind to the building. Over 50 years and three architects were required to complete it, to the point that it became a standing joke: 'I'll pay up when the Basilica is finished.' After decades of talk and three years of a failed Revolution, work finally began in 1851 under József Hild, whose neoclassical design followed a Greek-cross floor plan. When Hild died in 1868, Miklós Ybl took the helm and was shocked to find cracks in the walls. He had the site fenced off, just in time: eight days later during a storm the dome tumbled down, breaking more than 300 local windows. Ybl began afresh with new plans, including the neo-Renaissance dome that is the church's finest feature today. After he died, the church was finished by József Kauser and consecrated in 1905. During his opening speech, the story goes, Franz Josef was seen to throw nervous glances at the dome. Though it is not shaped like a basilica, it received the title Basilica Minor in 1938, the 900th anniversary of the death of St Stephen, to whom it was dedicated.

The city around the Basilica changed long before it was finished. Originally it had backed on to low buildings and narrow streets but, by the time Ybl took over, the major thoroughfare now called Bajcsy-Zsilinszky had been built, necessitating a second façade. He cleverly provided this by adding the Ionic colonnade surmounted by statues of the 12 apostles. The dome is 96m high (315ft), the same as the Parliament's dome, this number alluding to the date of the legendary arrival of the Magyar tribes, AD 896. Its four niches carry statues of the four Evangelists. The tympanum between these contains figures of Mary surrounded by Hungarian saints. The main door features carvings of the 12 apostles. Above it is a bust of King (St) Stephen, and higher still a mosaic of the Resurrection.

The **interior**, which can hold 8,500 people, is spacious, impressive but not oppressive. The marble walls and pillars carry mosaics, paintings and sculptures of a very high standard, mostly produced by Hungary's finest 19th-century artists. The mosaics were designed in Hungary (the dome's by Károly Lotz) and made in Venice. Highlights of the statues are the mournful St Rita, and the subtle Joseph, which has Jesus looking like a normal little boy yet with something intangible extra. Of the paintings, Gyula Stettka's *Golgotha* on the left middle deftly portrays Christ's passion as realistic yet larger than life. Opposite, also excellent, is Gyula Benczur's treatment of a famous scene from Hungarian legend. King Stephen, left heirless after Imre's premature death, is portrayed shrewdly offering his crown, and therefore his country's future, not to the Pope or the Holy Roman Emperor but to the Virgin. Since then she has been considered the Patroness of Hungary. Stephen is featured on the main altar, wearing a halo and a sword, a combination that raised no eyebrows in the past. (Note, for instance, the statue of St Ladislaus, the hilt and blade of his sword held up as a cross, a tell-tale crescent symbol protruding from beneath his foot.) The reliefs behind Stephen depict scenes from his life.

Strangely, it was in death that the great king provided the church with its most famous attraction. His mummified **Holy Right Hand** (and forearm), Hungary's most important relic, is daily taken from its chapel and displayed in front of the painting of Stephen offering his crown. It lives in a highly ornate golden model of the Matthias Church, which a 100Ft coin will illuminate. When Stephen was canonized, his tomb was opened, and the corpse's right hand was found to be missing. It was found in the manor of the keeper of the royal tombs. An abbey was designed to contain the hand, but not for long: it made a mini-world tour before it wound up in its new gilded home. The custom has been revived of parading it through the streets every 20th August in a procession celebrating the anniversary of the king's 1083 canonization.

A tiny room contains the few items of the **Treasury**. The best items are monstrances, gifts from abroad. More worthwhile is the panorama from the top (*adm*): this vantage point offers excellent views, including the best view of the roof of the former Post Office Savings Bank. You can get a lift part of the way, but 146 more steps remain. You don't get to see the inside of the church, but the space between the inner and outer domes is a curious spectacle.

Before leaving Szent Istvan tér, check out the wonderful green-tile Art Nouveau façade of the building at No.13.

Szabadság Tér (Liberty Square)

Flanked by stretches of glorious green that are home to a wide range of tree species, with a great playground at its southern end, Budapest's largest, most important square would almost resemble a park, were it not for the intrusive fencing and frequently high police presence. Scattered throughout this almost innocuous space are objects of great nationalist and political import, and around its edges stand some huge, imposing buildings, most of them banks. The biggest is now the home of Magyar TV, though its original function as a stock exchange suits it better. Built in 1905, incorporating touches of Greek and Assyrian temple architecture, it occupies the whole of the square's western side and would be terribly intimidating were it not for the cheap and nasty MTV Televízió sign above the door. It was on these steps that tens of thousands of people assembled on 15 March 1989, when the air was thick with long-awaited political change, to hear actor György Cserhalmi announce the 15 points of the newly formed opposition parties.

In the park in front is the **Memorial to the Martyrs of the New Building**, a modest monument to a tragic piece of history. The New Building (Újépület) stood here, an enormous Habsburg barracks in which countless Hungarians were imprisoned and executed. Among them were the country's should-be leaders, including, killed on 6 October 1849, its first independent prime minister, Count Lajos Batthyány. Loathed even more than the Citadella, the New Building's destruction in 1897 gave the square its name of Liberty. Across from here is a rather dull statue of Harry Hill Bandholtz. He was a US general present when Romanian troops tried to make off with the treasures of the National Museum, which he saved by blocking the doors with censorship seals.

The façades of the four similar grand buildings on the sqaure's northern end curve gently in a semi-circle that faces the fenced-in **Soviet Army Memorial**, a large white obelisk topped with a gold star, its base covered in reliefs that depict Red Army soldiers 'liberating' Budapest in 1945. From 1928 till then, a flag stood on this spot, permanently at half-mast, over a mound of soil from territories lost in the 1910 Trianon Treaty, which gave away two-thirds of Hungary's lands and a third of its population. It was accompanied by a quotation from British press baron Lord Rothermere, who campaigned against the unfair treaty, gaining such gratitude that he was even offered the Hungarian Crown. The Soviets removed the flag, and four statues called North, East, South and West, which also symbolised the lost territories. Why this ugly Soviet memorial has been allowed to remain in this symbolically charged location when all the others have been removed is puzzling, but may explain those fences.

Ironically, it stands close to the former HQ of the Fascist Arrow Cross and right in front of the **US Embassy**. This 1901 building, decorated in a Viennese Art Nouveau style, is where Cardinal Mindszenty, Hungary's Catholic Primate, was sheltered for 15 years following the 1956 Uprising. The situation, exacerbated by Mindszenty's uncompromising attitude and the coverage it received around the world, became embarrassing for the USA and the Vatican, which eventually persuaded him to leave for Austria in 1971. Most of this eastern side is taken up by **Hungarian National Bank** buildings, of which the one on the southeast corner is the most impressive. Built in 1905, it shows an eclectic combination of historical styles. Two large bronze statues in front of the tympanum symbolize agriculture and industry, while a series of limestone reliefs at the first-floor level depict mainly crafts and trades – the means by which the majority made money. This potentially corny idea works thanks to the sympathetic treatment of the subjects, each imbued with an air of nobility. Note also the carved faces representing the many nations of the world.

The Post Office Savings Bank

On Hold utca, behind the National Bank and now belonging to it, sits one of Budapest's architectural highlights, the former Post Office Savings Bank. Ödön

Lechner combined Art Nouveau with Hungarian folk art to forge a new nationalist architecture. 'Hungarian style has no past,' he said, 'but it does have a future.' The **façade** is all curves and gentle colours, simple motifs so delicate and playful that it's hard to do them justice. A wealth of small, lovingly conceived details adds up to a whole much greater than the sum of its parts. If you have children with you, this is one building they will also like. Note the ceramic bees climbing up the gable walls towards the hives on the roofs. The accepted interpretation is that these symbolize savers accumulating their wealth, but anyone familiar with the works of Gaudí, with whom Lechner has much in common, may remember the great Spaniard's interest in the architectural prowess of bees, whose constructions and techniques he was keen to study. These hives and the yellow majolica curlicues are the only hints from below of the extraordinary roof that is the building's finest feature. Here, multicoloured hexagonal tiles from the Zsolnay factory are ornamented with flowers, dragon tails, angel wings and Turkish turbans, a world of fairytale folk imagery. When asked who would enjoy such details, Lechner answered, 'The birds.' The best view of the roof is from the top of the Basilica with binoculars. Even the façade is difficult to see owing to a lack of vantage points and the many plane trees.

Over the road is one of Budapest's still-functioning **produce markets** (Vásárcsarnok), startlingly clean and orderly inside. On the way to the Parliament, where Hold u. meets Báthory u., an **Eternal Flame** inside a giant lantern commemorates the execution of Count Lajos Batthyány on this spot (then inside the New Building) on 6 October 1849. He was a conservative patriot, not a revolutionary, who had attempted to find a compromise with Austria and later headed a failed peace delegation. From here it's not far to **No.3 Honvéd u.**, which has one of the nicest, most original façades you'll see: very Art Nouveau, very playful (another one for the kids). Note the balconies, each utterly distinctive, and the use of glazed ceramics. There are roses, sunflowers, fruit, and more comparisons to be made with Gaudí.

Imre Nagy Monument

In Vértanuk tere (Martyrs' Square) is the monument to Imre Nagy. After Stalin's death in 1953, the strong-arm dictator Rákosi fell from grace with Moscow, partly because of his personality cult, which surpassed locally even that of Stalin. When Imre Nagy replaced him as prime minister, a period known as 'the thaw' began. Investment policies were implemented encouraging a healthier economic structure; forced collectivization was abandoned and peasants allowed to leave their co-operatives; the ideological atmosphere was relaxed, and silenced writers and poets allowed to re-enter the literary scene. The reign of terror had come to an end. When Nagy's protector in Moscow was dismissed, however, he too was removed from power (after just two years), and his changes criticised and reversed. Though a Communist, he had become much loved, so that, during the 1956 Uprising, the people called for him to speak. Eventually persuaded to address the crowds, he simply urged them to go home. Nevertheless, he accepted the position of prime minister for the 11 or so days when the Uprising seemed to have been successful, and attempted to appease both the revolutionaries and the Soviets.

In the end, the broader political picture sealed the country's fate, the Russians deciding they could not allow Hungary independent rule, and the Western powers agreeing not to interfere. So the Russian tanks appeared, and Nagy sought amnesty in the Yugoslavian embassy. After accepting an armistice, he was imprisoned for two years in Romania, then secretly tried in the spring of 1958 and executed on 16 June. During the trial he could have saved his own life by co-operating, but refused to revise his opinions. Though he never stopped being a Communist, Nagy really believed in the people, their freedom and independence, and he was not prepared to compromise those beliefs in the name of Moscow's policies. This spiritual defection is symbolized by his statue's position on a bridge, his back to the Soviet Army Memorial, looking towards Parliament. Nagy himself is not romanticized, but treated as an imperfect, very human individual, who lived a difficult destiny.

Kossuth Lajos Tér

This is another square that really wants to be a park. Either side of the gargantuan Parliament building are grassy tree-filled areas that could be joined were it not for a car park the size of a football pitch. On the square's southwest corner is a **statue of Attila József**, the popular working-class poet. Despite left-wing tendencies, he was too interested in life's bigger questions and the tragically fragile beauty of the human condition ever to conform to any ideology, and was not as popular with politicians as with ordinary people. Sculpted with tremendous empathy, the statue captures all this. The face is forlorn and troubled, too sensitive, too intelligent. Just as much is said about his state of mind by the way he's holding his hat, the coat thrown in a heap beside him. He is one of the greats, and he bears his nation's woes to a degree his fellows will never understand. He committed suicide in 1937, aged 32.

Right in front of Parliament is a far less enjoyable **statue of Ferenc Rákóczi II**, a prince of Transylvania who led the 1703–11 struggle for independence against the Habsburgs. Latin inscriptions on the plinth read 'For Country and Liberty' and 'The wounds of the noble Hungarian nation burst open'. The sentiment is echoed on the other side of the car park by an odd Modernist block carrying an **Eternal Flame** in memory of those who died here during the Uprising of 1956, particularly on 25 October, when Soviet snipers started taking pot-shots at the peaceful demonstrators below, who were socializing with Soviet tank crews at the time. The shots came from the roof of the Ministry of Agriculture, the nicely proportioned neoclassical building behind Rákóczi fronted by a massive Corinthian colonnade. Outside stand unmarked statues of noble peasant types. The Reaper Lad seems to be eyeing Parliament with numbed bewilderment, while the Female Agronomist looks stubbornly away.

The neo-Renaissance palace next door was built to house the Supreme Court and Public Prosecutor's Office, hence the fresco on the ceiling of the vast and ornately decorated main hall, which depicts Justitia, Goddess of Justice, surrounded by allegorical representations of Justice and Peace on the right, Sin and Revenge on the left. By Károly Lotz, it outshines his fresco in the Parliament. The palace is now the **Ethnographical Museum** (*open May–Oct daily 10–6; Nov–April daily 10–5; adm*), worth visiting as much for the building as for its contents. On the first floor, starting on the left, 13 rooms contain the permanent exhibition 'Folk Culture of the Hungarians'. By the 18th century the population of ethnic groups equalled that of Hungarians, so there is a wealth of diversity to be covered. Enlarged old black and white photos are often more interesting than the exhibits themselves and give a flavour of how life really was. The temporary exhibitions held here are also invariably excellent.

In the park outside the museum is a **statue of Lajos Kossuth**, the most powerful figure from the struggles of the 1840s. A brilliant writer and speaker, he revolution-ized the Hungarian media with his newspaper *Pesti Hírlap*, which he used, along with inflammatory speeches in Parliament, to rouse the people to demand separation from Austria. He was a contrast to the likes of Széchenyi and Batthyány, whose moderate stance he opposed. Széchenyi understood that Kossuth's insistence on revolution threatened to enrage the Austrians and destroy all the progress made by the more subtle path of reform, and history proved him right. When the inevitable war with Austria began, Batthyány stepped down, and Kossuth took up the prime minister's reins. He travelled the country rousing the people to arms, which is the subject of this statue, the six figures around him supposedly typical citizens. Unfortunately, the ensemble looks rather silly, like seven ham actors striking poses. Maybe the original statue was better. It depicted the gloom after the war with Austria was lost. The Soviets had it replaced with the present offering presumably because it was too downbeat, or maybe because Kossuth was surrounded by his aristocratic ministers such as Batthyány, Széchenyi and Eszterházy.

Just northwest of here is another little square, which contains a **statue of Mihály Károlyi**, a.k.a. the 'Red Baron'. He wasn't a fighter pilot but a wealthy landowner who became a radical liberal politician and in 1919 Hungary's first president. This was a very difficult time, at the end of the First World War when the Allied powers were preparing to confiscate two-thirds of Hungary's territory, and the people were swinging ever further to the left. Eventually forced to resign in favour of Béla Kún's Communist party, he went through two separate periods of exile. In this statue by Imre Varga he looks old and sad but stubbornly dignified, standing under two halves of an arch that do not meet.

Parliament (Országház)

t 441 4038. Tours in English leave at 10, 12, 2 and 6, on days when Parliament is not in session. Tickets (1,300Ft) can be bought at Gate X from 8am.

Occupying 880ft of the Danube embankment, there is no ignoring Budapest's most famous building, now gloriously free of scaffolding except for one small section on the Danube side. Based on – and reminiscent of – the House of Commons in London, it's a magnificently bold feat of virtuosity, so extravagant and pompous that the temptation is to belittle it. The 20th-century poet Gyula Illyés called it 'no more than a Turkish bath crossed with a Gothic chapel', drawing attention, even in this put-down, to the eclecticism so integral to Hungarian architecture. The ground plan is Baroque, but the façade is a fusion of neo-Gothic and neo-Renaissance. Designer Imre Steindl wanted 'to combine this splendid medieval style with national and personal features'. Tharaud spoke in 1899 of 'those Hungarian architects, with their bizarre passion for medievalism, without reason'. But there was a reason, which can be understood by comparing this structure with the frigid Baroque Royal Palace on the other side of the water: the Gothic harks back to better days, when Hungary was free to choose its own buildings. Whatever your reactions to the result, awe will be among them. As Patrick Leigh Fermor put it in 1934, 'Architectural dash could scarcely go further.' Upon completion, it was the largest parliament building in the world. The plan is one of perfect symmetry centred on the magnificent dome. The two wings are mirror images down to even the smallest details, one originally holding the House of Commons and the other the House of Lords.

It was in 1843 that the Hungarian Diet (Parliament) decided to build a permanent 'House of the Motherland'. For centuries before, they had met wherever they could. A competition was held which Steindl won. The second- and third-place designs were also used, the former now housing the Ethnological Museum, the latter the Ministry of Agriculture. Work began in 1885 and involved an average of a thousand people every day for 17 years, by which time it was six years too late for the millenary celebrations it was meant to crown, and Steindl was a sick old man giving directions from a chair. He died five weeks before it was completed.

Inside there are 20km of stairways and 691 rooms. Much of the trimming is painted with 22 or 23 carat gold, 60kg of it. On the guided tour you will only see a fraction of what is there. Just inside the main entrance on Kossuth Lajos tér is a model of Parliament made from 30,000 matchsticks. The 96 steps of the ceremonial staircase, with ceiling frescoes by Károly Lotz, lead to the 16-sided hall below the 96m-high dome. As in St Stephen's Basilica, these numbers allude to AD 896, when the Magyars arrived in the Carpathian Basin. The dome is the building's finest feature both outside and in, where it is decorated with intricate gilding leading the eye to an exquisite chandelier. Round the giant pillars that support the dome are statues of some of Hungary's rulers. All are staring straight ahead except Árpád, who is looking to his right, as if saying, 'What are those Habsburgs doing here?' Below the dome is the latest resting place of Hungary's crown jewels.

In the old Upper House, the colour scheme is blue, representing the blood of the lords. Outside the Lords' Chamber, used for conferences since their discontinuation, you'll see the brass ashtrays, numbered so that each member could retrieve his own cigar on returning from hearing the speaker who had lured him away from it. The length of cigar turned to ashes was an indication of the speaker's quality. These days, only the offices of the president, prime minister and speaker are here. All other MPs work in the White House, an ugly modern building farther north, which for 32 years was the power base of Communist dictator János Kádár.

North to the Nagykörút

The northern chunk of Lipótváros is a paradise for lovers of big buildings. Many of the modern ones are just as impressive as the old stalwarts which they are clearly designed to complement. For a first-class selection of both, try this suggested circuit, remembering that not all of the best buildings are on the route, though they are visible from it. From Kossuth Lajos tér walk down Alkotmány u., turn left on to Bihari

János u., then left on to Markó u. which crosses Nagy Ignac u. This last and Bihari János retain their quality up to the Nagykörút. If you feel like going this far, turn right for the beautiful **Nyugati Station** building. Constructed by the famous Eiffel company in Paris, it was the largest station in Europe until 1880. Known as the Western Railway Station, this was the site of the first such building in Hungary, from where the first train ran in 1846. Behind it on Váci út (not to be confused with the famous Váci utca in Belváros) is the postmodern **West End City Centre** shopping mall, from whose roof a moored hot air balloon called the **Budapest Eye** (Kilató; *t 238 7623, www.budapest kilato.hu; adm exp*) hoists passengers to stupendous views.

To the west the Nagykörút heads past the delightful **Vígszínház** (Comedy Theatre) to **Margaret Bridge** – with its own fantastic views, especially at night – and Margaret Island (*see* below). A path beside the Danube leads back south to the Chain Bridge.

Margaret Island (Margit-sziget)

Trams 4 and 6, or bus 26 from Nyugati station.

Margaret Bridge (Margit híd) is the northernmost bridge you are likely to encounter. It is easily recognizable by the 'elbow' in its middle, a 150° angle which allows it to continue the line of the outer ring road (Nagykörút) of which it is a part. At this elbow, a third section leads to Margaret Island. Essentially one big park, Margit-sziget is greatly appreciated by Budapesters, offering as it does a slice of tranquillity minutes from the city centre.

Named the 'Isle of Rabbits' in the Middle Ages, the island was used by the Árpáds as a royal game reserve. From the 12th century onwards various monastic orders replaced the hunters: Premonstratensions, Franciscans and the Order of St John. Béla IV had a convent built for the Dominican nuns, of which his daughter Margaret was the best-known inmate. Tradition has it that, during the Mongol invasion of 1242–4, Béla vowed that if Hungary survived he would have her brought up as a nun. In 1252, aged nine, she was confined to the convent, where she died 19 years later after many holy acts, which won her canonization (in 1943) and a place of honour in the Hungarian pantheon. In a change of pace, the Turks destroyed most of the island's holy buildings and used it for a harem. Open to the public since 1869, the park's popularity with lovers generated the saying, 'Love begins and ends on Margaret Island.'

The island is primarily attractive as a park, especially for children. There are plenty of open areas for games and sports, playgrounds, and much natural beauty. At either end, facilities can be rented including roller-skates, bikes, two-seater pedal-cars and electric cars. Choice and prices are greater at the northern end. Along the road, which runs down the western side, are the **Alfréd Hajós Swimming Pools**, designed by and named for the gold-medal-winner of the 100m and 1,200m swimming races at the first modern Olympics in 1896. More fun, and extremely popular in summer, is the **Palatinus Strand bathing complex**, 300m farther on. There are seven open-air thermal pools, a water chute, wave machine, segregated terraces for nude sunbathing (a gay favourite), and a 100m pool, one of the longest in Europe.

East of here is the oval-shaped **rose garden**; southwest the scant remains of a 13th–14th-century **Franciscan church**. East of the rose garden is a small **wildlife reserve** with goats, donkeys, peacocks and cranes. North is the park's most prominent feature, the 57m **water tower**. A pioneering structure when built in 1911, it now houses exhibitions in the summer, and is next to an **open-air theatre** that hosts operas, rock operas and plays. To the southeast stand the ruins of the **Dominican church and convent**, a series of low walls (*currently being renovated*). A marble shrine within marks Margaret's original burial place. Farther north stands the 1931 reconstruction of a 12th-century **Premonstratension chapel** in the Romanesque style. The bell hanging in the tower was made by master craftsman Hans Strous, lost for centuries, then found in the roots of a tree torn out during a storm in 1914.

Two giant hotels stand sentinel over the northern end of the island. The **Danubius Grand** is one of Budapest's classic hotels, built as a sanatorium in 1873 by Miklós Ybl. The baths to which it was attached are contained within the ugly **Thermal Hotel** next door. To the west is a **rock garden** whose warm-water ponds contain tropical fish, bullrushes, sculptures and lilies of varied colour. A network of small canals and bridges links the ponds and paths. What with the artificial waterfall and a small gazebo, this is one of the most attractive areas in the park.

Public toilets can be found between here and the hotels, or at the water tower.

Belváros: The Inner City

The Kiskörút (Little Boulevard) runs along the line of medieval Pest's walls, containing the city centre known as Belváros. Not much remains to identify this as the site of historic Pest: the town was razed when the Turks were driven out in 1686. What can be seen today is mainly a result of the massive expansion at the end of the 19th century. There are a few sights but the thing to do here is stroll – along the Dunakorzó, whose whole waterfront stretch has been declared a UNESCO World Heritage site, or around the lively hubs of Vörösmarty tér and Váci utca.

Deák Tér

Sitting on the Kiskörút at the junction of Pest's four inner districts and all three metro lines, Deák tér is undeniably the city's main hub, a busy and until quite recently rather sleazy spot. Its landmark is the squat, spireless **Lutheran Church** with its gently curving green roof. The inside is simple, and can only be seen during services or via the **museum** (*open Tues–Sun 10–6, closed Mon; adm*) next door, whose exhibits include a facsimile of Martin Luther's will and a copy of the first book printed in Hungary, a 1541 *New Testament*. The more attractive **Lutheran School** a couple of buildings west is a candidate for the best school of all time. As well as György Lukács, the Marxist philosopher who survived his country's changing politics relatively unscathed, and Sándor Petőfi, who didn't, three Nobel Prize-winners were educated here, plus pioneer scientists John von Neumann and Edward Teller. The best thing on this square is the neo-Gothic **VW building** at No.3, its corner topped by a turret. Across the main road, the giant mustard-yellow **Anker Palace** continues to crumble.

In the metro is the tiny **Underground Railway Museum** (*open Tues–Sun 10–6; closed Mon; adm a transport ticket*). The line (now M1) underneath Andrássy út, inaugurated in 1896, was mainland Europe's first metro, and the world's second after London's Metropolitan line. The exhibits are two refurbished carriages on a stretch of track.

The wide open space north, where Deák and Erzsébet squares collide, was proposed by Budapest's mayor as the site for a new National Theatre, until political wranglings from the FIDESZ government moved the theatre to a far less appropriate spot way south by Lágymányosi Bridge, leaving this potential plaza as an ugly building site. Attempts have now been made to use the space: a vast expanse of shallow water, with a glass case full of growing crystal floating around on top, is surrounded by park-benches and modern sculptures, with a broad stairway leading down to a club/music venue. **Erzsébet tér** to the west is a giant square of tree-lined paths converging on the **Danubius Fountain**. The male figure on top symbolizes the Danube, while the women on the lower basin represent tributaries, the Tisza, Dráva and Száva. The original, whose basin was carved from a single 100-tonne rock, was destroyed in the war.

Vörösmarty Tér

Free from traffic and lined by the terraces of cafés and restaurants, dotted with graceful iron lamp-posts and dominated by half a dozen giant trees, Vörösmarty tér is a focus of social activity – or inactivity, for it is a nice place to just hang out and watch (though the building site currently occupying its whole west side taints the atmosphere). At the centre is a **statue of Mihály Vörösmarty**, romantic reform writer and giant of 19th-century Hungarian poetry. On the front of the monument are the famous opening words of his *Szózat* (*Appeal*), which became a second national anthem: 'To thy Fatherland be unshakeably true, oh Magyar!' The black spot above this is supposedly the coin donated by a beggar towards the monument's cost. Festivals sometimes take over for a day, or a week, and street musicians and artists perform in the summer. Alive and atmospheric, the square never feels busy, tacky or sleazy. This is partly due to the hallowed institution on the north side, the **Pâtisserie Gerbeaud**. This 1861 building has been a café-confectioner's since 1870. Emil Gerbeaud bought it in 1884 and turned it into a landmark, famous as a meeting-spot as well as for its cakes. The three vast rooms that face the square resemble an English palace, exquisitely decorated with turn-of-the-20th-century furniture. The marvellous building with turret-like corners on the square's south side is the **Bank Palace**, housing the Budapest Stock Exchange, which reopened in 1990, 42 years after the Communists closed it down. Ignác Alpár, who designed the Magyar TV and National Bank buildings in Szabadság tér, considered it his major work.

To the north is **József Nádor tér**, flanked by fantastic buildings: the Romantic **Postabank** building on the south side, its façade alive with detail; **Credit Lyonnais** on the corner, lovingly restored; the **Ministry of Finance** on the west side, another Alpác construction, its top ledge boasting a statue of Mercury holding a model of the building on which he stands; the **OTP** (also Postabank) **building** on the east with an arcade running through the middle. Overlooking the square from József Attila u. is the **Merkantil Bank** building with an Art Nouveau façade. The statue in the square's centre is of the archduke whose name it carries. Habsburg Palatine from 1796 to 1847, he was a friend to Hungary. In 1808 he helped establish the Embellishment Commission for the restoration and development of Pest (an ongoing process). The Commission's leading supporter was architect János Hild, whose son József built the neoclassical **Gross House**, No.1 on this square, next to the Ministry of Finance.

Vigadó Tér to Petőfí Tér

West from Vörösmarty tér is a small square named after the Romantic **Vigadó Concert Hall**, whose name approximates to 'making merry'. It was so badly damaged in the Second World War that reconstruction wasn't completed until 1980. Underused and neglected, with a tacky bar at ground level, it is still a beautiful building. The symmetrical façade is richly embellished, with a ledge running like a frieze along its top, bearing the heads of Hungarian rulers and celebrities, and the old coat of arms at its centre. The columns carry reliefs of dancers, and statues of musicians line the first-floor ledge in front of the five arched windows. The foyer (*open from 12pm to sell tickets*), while grand enough, is a mere prelude to the Great Hall's dazzlingly rich colour scheme. Unfortunately this can only be viewed by audiences, and the awful acoustics make this an undesirable place to see a concert. On the square's railings, look out for a bronze statue, the *Little Princess* (1990). Prince Charles has a copy and invited the sculptor, László Marton, to exhibit his work in London.

The **Dunakorzó** has wonderful views of the Buda panorama, especially at night when lights dance on the water and the air is suffused with romance. In the 1900s this area was surrounded by fancy hotels, and the promenade was *the* place to stroll, to see and be seen. They are trying to recapture that atmosphere, and the tramlines keep the traffic at a distance.

Petőfi tér contains a giant Celtic tombstone, and the statue of Sandor Petőfi. More maybe than any other national hero, he stirs patriotism in the Magyar soul, thus his statue – despite making him look slightly silly – is a popular site for political demonstrations. Behind him is the Baroque **Greek Orthodox church** (*closed exc for services*).

Inner City Parish Church (Belvárosi Plébániatemplom)

Open daily 6.30am–9pm; Mass Mon–Sat 6.30am and 6pm,
Sun 9, 10 (Latin), 12 and 6.

Petőfi tér runs into Március 15 tér and Pest's oldest building, the Inner City Parish Church. From the outside it's nothing special. The plaster is crumbling in places and the paint peeling, the niches are empty and the Holy Trinity above the door look sadly decrepit. Even Christ's cross is rusting. Yet this is Budapest's only building east of the Danube to reflect anything like the history encountered on the other side. Sources disagree over how old it is. Some say that a church was founded here as a burial site for the martyred St Gellért in 1046. Others speak of a triple-aisled Romanesque church built at the end of the 12th century. Certainly the first occupant of this site was the 3rd-century Roman fortress Contra Aquincum, whose remains can be seen in the square beside the church. The original was razed during the Mongol invasions, though a single Romanesque arch survives in the southern tower. The 14th-century

Gothic replacement provided the basis of what you see today. The Turks converted it into a mosque and then returned it so that for a while it was the only Christian church in Pest. When they were kicked out it was damaged, then in 1723 it burned down. Reconstruction in a Baroque style saw the addition of today's twin towers and façade, resulting in a hybrid curious even by Budapest's eclectic standards: the back is Gothic, the front Baroque. After all that, the church was inevitably war-torn and then almost pulled down when the Elisabeth Bridge was built.

Inside, the historical mish-mash, as well as the grandeur, is much more apparent. The **nave** features a barrel-vaulted Baroque ceiling and is simple, with little use of gold and few paintings or figures. The **chancel** is much more ornate, its complex vaulted ceiling-arches edged with geometric shapes. On the right side are five **chapels**. The first three are Baroque; the fourth contains a beautiful Renaissance tabernacle of red marble and white limestone, its pedestal holding the crest of the Pest city council who commissioned it in 1507; the fifth is Gothic. The original **high altar** was destroyed during the war; this one dates from 1948 and is the work of sculptor Károly Antal and painter Pál C. Molnár. Behind the altar are Gothic **sedilias** and to the right is a souvenir from the church's time as a mosque, a **prayer-niche** (*mihrab*). You can only get a close look at these after Latin Mass on a Sunday. The fine wooden **pulpit** is neo-Gothic, from 1808. On the chancel's left side is a reconstructed Gothic tabernacle. The chapel before the chancel contains the remains of the church's frescoes. The last chapel holds the extravagant neoclassical tomb of a newspaper editor, constructed in 1835 by István Ferenczy.

Váci Utca

Váci utca runs the length of this district and was once Pest's main road. For the last 150 years it has held Budapest's premier boutiques, where rich ladies would seek the latest fashions, stroll among the gentry and enjoy the sophisticated café terraces. Over 30 years ago the northern half of the street, still considered by natives to be 'the' Váci utca, was pedestrianized, leading to a return of the boom times. It has become increasingly Westernized, tacky even, so you won't be very surprised by anything you see (unless you look up above the shop fronts). You will end up here anyway. It is gloriously traffic-free and humming with action, a place to watch the locals (who are probably there to watch the tourists). Its lively atmosphere is particularly worth seeking out at night. The southern half of Váci utca, only pedestrianized in 1997, is calmer and feels less like a tourist trap.

Szervita Tér

Walking north on Váci utca, before you get to Vörösmarty tér, a little square over-flowing with terrace tables opens up on the right. This is **Kristóf tér**, and at its centre is a statue of a *Fisher-Girl* which originally belonged at a fish-market nearby on the embankment, and apparently caused a stir due to the girl's skimpy attire: strange, given the number of naked classical statues everywhere. It leads into **Szervita tér**, centred on a copy of a 1729 **Immaculata column** with figures of Joseph, Anne and Joaquim at the base. The square is named after the run-down 1732 Baroque **Servite**

Church, whose most interesting feature is the large bas-relief to the right of the entrance, with Christ cradling a dying hero. This 1930 monument is dedicated to the VIIth Wilhelm Hussar Regiment who gave their lives in the First World War. Inside, the church is excessively lavish, with winged or haloed figures everywhere, lots of gold, and a pastel pink and blue ceiling covered with frescoes.

The real reason for visiting this square may elude you until you look up to the west. The building known as the **Turkish Bank House** (which it used to contain) looks at ground level like any other shop. Follow it up and things get more interesting. The whole façade is covered with vast arched windows. At the top in the playfully curved gable is Miksa Róth's masterpiece, an Art Nouveau mosaic entitled *Glory to Hungary*. Angels, shepherds, and heroes such as István Széchenyi, Lajos Kossuth and Ferenc Rákóczi, pay homage to a bethroned *Patrona Hungariae* (Our Lady, Patron of Hungary).

Two doors to the left, **Rózsavölgyi House** is interesting for its distinctions between retail, office and residential levels, a typical trait of the father of Hungarian Modernism, Béla Lajta, one of Ödön Lechner's students. The upper storeys' ceramic decoration reveals his earlier links with the Romantic school, while the whole antici-pates the avant-garde.

Ferenciek Tere

This is the main route for east–west traffic and very busy, which may blind you to its charms. As ever the key is to look up. Stand where the bridge stretches away before you and you will notice that two near-identical buildings, the **Klotild Palaces**, flank the road like mirror images, creating a gateway for the bridge. This 'gateway' is different but equally impressive coming the other way. Beneath the bridge in the subway is a collection of enlarged black and white photos taken by György Klösz which show details of this area before and after the building of the bridge. Opposite are modern photos of the same region.

On the north-facing wall of the **Franciscan church** which gives Ferenciek tere its name is a large memorial relief recalling the catastrophic flood of 1838 when the whole Inner City was under water and over 400 people died. It depicts Count Miklós Wesselényi, who rescued many in his boat.

Over the main road, the corner building smothered with gold-leaf mosaics, iron-work, busts and reliefs is the Párizsi Udvar or **Paris Arcade**. Note the naked figures striking poses either side of the clock (stopped at 12), and the fancy carving around the roof-line and towers. Above the third storey, naked figures appear from the waist up, as if plunging out of the wall. Such details met with disapproval when the building was erected as the Inner City Savings Bank. More in keeping was the theme of bees and the guardian archangel Gabriel on the relief below the gable. Have a closer look at the mosaic inside this porch. Theatrical masks, swirling patterns and gorgons' heads are all the more striking for the colours: gold and an amazing range of blues, greens and reds. Inside it is gloomy and contains nothing worthwhile but a bookshop, but the décor is astounding, full of sculpted wood, wrought iron, Art Nouveau mosaics and stained glass, of which the apotheosis is Miksa Róth's neglected glass dome.

Southern Belváros

In the calm of these narrow back streets you can catch a whiff of the past and the true spirit of the present. There is little sightseeing to be done. At Károlyi Mihály u. 16 is the neoclassical **Károlyi Palace**, mostly built 1832-41. Recently reopened, it contains the **Petőfi Museum of Hungarian Literature** (*t 317 3611; open Tues–Sat 10–6; adm for temporary exhibitions only*), which has little to interest foreigners beyond the chance of seeing the building's interior. Right behind it, off Magyar u., are the **Károlyi Gardens**, a green oasis popular with playing children and smooching couples. **Kálvin tér** to the southwest contains the **Calvinist church**, worth a quick look. Plain but elegant on the outside, the interior possesses its own grandeur. Decoration is almost non-existent, as befits the denomination, but the ceiling is enlivened with brass reliefs of floral motifs, particularly effective on the dome. The combination of the church's many curved planes particularly pleases the eye, drawing it back to the centre, in this case the altar, without so much as a cross.

Raday u. shoots south from here, Budapest's most exciting up-and-coming street, pedestrianized and lined with trendy bars and restaurants.

National Museum (Nemzeti Múzeum)

*Múzeum krt. 14–16, **t** 338 2122. Open June–Oct Tues–Sun 10–6; Nov–May Tues–Sun 10–5; adm for temporary exhibitions only.*

This grand neoclassical edifice is just off Kálvin tér. The huge central portico consists of eight Corinthian columns supporting a large tympanum filled with statues, chief among them Pannonia, the name of the ancient Roman province that occupied western Hungary. Opened in 1848, when it was far from the centre of town, it soon played host to one of Hungarian legend's most important scenes. A huge crowd gathered on 15 March 1848 to listen to the leaders of the young revolutionaries, and heard the popular poet Sándor Petőfi recite his now famous *National Song*, marking in a sense the beginning of the revolution. 'Choose! Now is the time! Shall we be slaves or shall we be free?' he cried, and the people chose.

As with the National Library, the National Museum was the inspiration of the great Count Ferenc Széchenyi, father of István. The count's extensive collection of manuscripts, prints, coins, coats of arms and maps was the basis of the museum's collection. Today the exhibits tell the story of Hungary's history in two halves: from the foundation of the state to its reconquest from the Turks, and from the end of the Turkish wars to the 1990s. Its two great treasures are **St Stephen's Sword** and the **Coronation Mantle**, both on the first floor. In the basement is a **Lapidarium** with a collection of Roman remains, mainly tombstones.

The permanent exhibitions are upstairs. On the ceilings and walls above the grand staircase are a series of frescoes completed in 1873 by Than Mór and Károly Lotz. The main images are symbolic representations of abstracts like Imagination, Inspiration and Enthusiasm for Beauty, while a frieze all round the top of the walls has scenes from Hungarian history, from St Stephen's conversion to Christianity up to the founding of the museum, a helpful prelude to the coming history lesson. A look at the family tree in Room 1 may help you with the convoluted dynasty of Hungary's early kings. It all begins with the turul-bird. You will probably get more out of the museum if you brush up on your Hungarian history beforehand (*see* pp.194–200), although there are explanations in English. The notes on individual exhibits are not given in English, on the other hand. On the positive side, dotted around are touch-screen information panels on 'History', 'Economy and Social Struggle', 'Science and Technological Development', 'Culture and Arts', and 'Who's Who in Hungarian History'. There is so much here of quality that it seems almost invidious to pick out individual examples of what is on show. It begins with a lot of weapons and religious relics and ends rather poignantly with a collection of Communist-flavoured street-signs, such as Leninváros, with red paint slashes across them.

Museum of Applied Arts (Iparművészeti Múzeum)

Üllöi út 33–7, t 456 5100. Open daily 10–6; adm for temporary exhibitions only.

East of Kálvin tér on Üllöi út is one of Budapest's most interesting museums, worth visiting as much for the building as for the exhibitions. Designed by Ödön Lechner and Gyula Pártos, it is a significant example of Lechner's blending of traditional folk art with more eclectic elements and Art Nouveau to forge a national architecture. It features a wonderfully colourful patterned roof trimmed with yellow majolica, which also enlivens the beautiful dome. Tiles on the façade create flower and foliage patterns, markedly around the rose window above the porch. The steps up to the door are flanked by banisters of yellow ceramic curlicues. Inside, all white, it resembles the Taj Mahal. Originally it was highly decorated with colourful Hungarian folk motifs. The main permanent exhibition, 'Arts and Crafts', is a disappointment. The works are housed in unaesthetic, outdated cases, and nothing is labelled in English, though laminated sheets (available in English) explain the techniques used in each type of craft. However, the main attraction of the museum is its consistently superb temporary exhibitions, of which there are normally three or four. Chief among them, and due to remain for the foreseeable future, is the excellent Art Nouveau exhibition. Exhibits are labelled in English, and a sophisticated booklet gives an introduction to the genre. There are many fine pieces from all over Europe.

Central Market Hall (Vamház)

Farther round the Kiskörút to the west of Kálvin tér is the magnificent Central Market Hall, resembling a grand old railway station, an impression maintained inside by the height of the ceiling and the iron staircases and walkways. Outside it is a particularly attractive, striking building with a fancy iron gate, lots of arches and a funky yellow, green and red roof. Inside it is incredibly clean and ordered, to the extent that one could almost think it existed just to impress tourists, yet thousands of Budapestians buy their groceries here every day. It is definitely worth looking inside, if only for the sausage stalls, where lumps of pork fat are sold by the kilo. Upstairs is food (including a good, rustic-style restaurant), souvenirs and lots of linen.

Next door is another notable building, the neo-Renaissance **University of Economic Sciences**, originally the Main Customs Office. The façade overlooking the river has 10 allegorical statues. It is worth going through the river-facing main entrance to check out the inner courtyard, once a customs hall, now an atrium, which contains a large bronze statue of Karl Marx. A bridge arches over the courtyard, commonly known as the 'Bridge of Sighs'.

Andrássy Út to City Park

Starting at one of Budapest's busiest junctions just north of Deák tér, Andrássy út runs northwest in a straight line for 2.5km, the central axis of Terézváros (Theresa Town), better known as District VI. In 2002, the street and its historical environs were granted UNESCO World Heritage status. It is worth a stroll along this most august of Budapest's boulevards just to admire the grandeur of the buildings, amongst them the State Opera House. But the main reason for coming here is the nightlife: the area around Andrássy út is easily the city's most lively quarter. The boulevard culminates in Heroes' Square (Hősök tere), a site of prime national importance flanked by two imposing edifices, including the excellent Museum of Fine Arts. Beyond lies City Park, a must for anyone with children, containing the fairytale Vajdahunyad Castle, the zoo, circus, amusement park and the most family-friendly spa complex in town.

Andrássy Út

Roads that just evolve rarely run straight, and sure enough Andrássy út was rigidly planned. Following the 1867 Compromise with Austria and birth of the Dual Monarchy, Budapest was reinvented as an imperial capital and for once had the luxury of wealth and peace with which to realize mighty ambitions. Heavily influenced by Haussmann's redevelopment of Paris, Andrássy út was conceived as a grand boulevard in the style of the Champs-Elysées. Inaugurated in 1884, the rather pompous result of these grandiose plans has carried a variety of names. First it was Sugár út (Radial Avenue), then it was named after the 19th-century statesman Count Gyula Andrássy, a name which natives upheld through the Communist designations Sztàlin út (1949–56) and the catchy Népköztársaság (Avenue of the People's Republic), and which officially returned in 1990.

The first part of Andrássy út as far as Oktogon is by far the liveliest, and should definitely be visited, preferably at night. The triangle bounded by Király út (south of Andrássy), Bajcsy-Zsilinsky and Teréz körút is a maze of small streets buzzing with restaurants, bars, cafés and clubs. This section is lined with closely built, eclectic but mainly neo-Renaissance buildings, as well as shops, offices and cafés.

State Opera House (Állami Operaház)

Andrássy út 22, t 331 2550; guided tour 3 and 4pm daily, adm;
box office open Tues–Sat 10–7, Sun 10–1.

One of the most sumptuous buildings in Budapest, its interior is even more impressive than its outside, making a night at the opera a grand occasion at a comparatively good price. This neo-Renaissance building was the crowning achievement of Miklós Ybl, who designed the Basilica. He spent nine years overseeing the Opera House's construction and is said to have checked every cartload of bricks. Its first musical director was the acclaimed father of Hungarian opera Ferenc Erkel, who also took up the conductor's baton for the grand opening in 1884. Liszt had written a work for the occasion but it contained elements of the Hungarian rebel melody Rákóczi March, and so was not performed. After all, the Compromise had been reached, and the building's funding came mainly from Habsburg Emperor Franz Josef. Gustav Mahler and Otto Klemperer have been musical directors here, and Puccini directed two of his operas. During the siege of Budapest in the winter of 1944–5, the vast cellars gave shelter to thousands, and the building survived relatively unscathed. In 1981 major renovations began and it reopened on its 100th anniversary on 27 October 1984 as brilliantly sparkling as new.

Either side of the entrance are statues of Liszt (right) and Erkel by Alajos Stróbl. Niches at the corners of the first floor contain statues of the four muses of opera, Terpsichore, Erato, Thalia and Melpomene (dance, love poetry, comedy and tragedy). On the stone balustrade around the second-floor terrace stand statues of the greatest opera composers (with the notable exception of Puccini). At the front (left to right): Rossini, Donizetti, Glinka, Wagner, Verdi, Gounod, Bizet. On the left side: Monteverdi, Alessandro, Scarlatti, Gluck, Mozart, Beethoven. On the right side: Mussorgsky, Tchaikovsky, Moniuszko, Smetana. There is also an Egyptian motif, with the 'needles' on the corners of the balustrade and the sphinxes to left and right.

Even without buying a ticket or taking the tour, you can go into the lobby. The gilded vaulted ceiling is covered with wonderful murals by Bertalan Székely and Mór Than. The marble columns, mosaic floor and chandeliers are upstaged by the sweeping main staircase. Even this, however, is just a prelude to the bits you won't see, the auditorium where a bronze chandelier weighing three tons illuminates the 23-carat gold leaf and the fresco of *The Greek Gods on Mount Olympus* by the genre's master, Károly Lotz. The royal box in the centre of the circle has sculptures representing the four operatic voices: soprano, alto, tenor and bass.

Up Andrássy Út to Oktogon

The neo-Renaissance building opposite that so complements the Opera House is the **State Ballet Institute**. Behind it on Paulay Ede u. is one of Budapest's best buildings, the **New Theatre** (Új Színház), undoubted masterpiece of Béla Lajta (*see* Szervita tér, p.239). Designed in 1908–1909 to house a music hall, its extraordinay façade combines elements of Art Nouveau, modernism, even Art Deco, which it predates by some 15 years. Note the little monkeys above the 1950s-style doors, forlornly holding blue ceramic globes; the brass Egyptian-style figures lining the roof; and the chintzy blue letters carrying the theatre's name. Redesigned many times, it was mercifully returned to its original form in 1990.

A block over at Nagymező 8 is the **Ernst Museum** (*t 413 1310; open Tues–Sun 11–7; adm*), with avant-garde and small temporary international exhibitions. Inside are benches and banisters by Ödön Lechner and a wonderful 1911 post-Impressionist stained-glass window by József Rippl-Rónai. Nearby is **Terézváros Parish Church**, with a graceful tapering tower that draws one's attention to the cross at its pinnacle.

The simple, elegant interior has some good paintings and a fine neoclassical high altar but is usually locked. On the corner diagonally opposite is a run-down but still superb Romantic-Gothic building, **Pekáry House**. **Nagymező utca** north of Andrássy has been dubiously dubbed 'the Broadway of Pest'. It does contain a few theatres and clubs, such as the **Operetta**, **Moulin Rouge** and the beautiful **Thália Theatre**.

A little farther up Andrássy út, scrutinising the traffic that passes it, is a **statue of romantic novelist Mór Jókai** on the square that bears his name. On the other side of the road is **Liszt Ferenc tér**, the most happening square in town. Pedestrianized, full of trees, benches, statues and terrace tables, it feels utterly Mediterranean and civilized. One statue is of journalist and poet Endre Ady, but the eye-catching one is the **statue of Ferenc (or Franz) Liszt**. Even sitting he looks like a crazed, dangerous maniac, which, if you listen to his music, is probably what he was. Erected to commemorate the centenary of his death, it contains a cameo of the sculptor (the bald man on Liszt's lapel). At the far end of the square is the **Franz Liszt Music Academy** (Ferenc Liszt Zeneakadémia), an extraordinary Art Nouveau building. A wealth of features adorn the façade, including a statue of Liszt, many strange mythological faces and musical motifs, and reliefs of children playing instruments. The interior is far grander. In the centre is a beautiful mosaic, while the walls above the entrances to the main auditorium carry a fresco by Hungarian Pre-Raphaelite Aladár Körösfői Kriesch entitled *Hungarian Wedding Procession in the 14th Century*.

Where the Nagykörút meets Andrássy út is **Oktogon**. Four enormous, very similar-looking buildings constructed in an eclectic mix of styles in 1873–4 face off against one another, their façades and the roads between them making a perfect octogon. Though it's surrounded by fast-food outlets and all-night restaurants, the effect is still quite impressive. This area never sleeps, largely because buses service the Nagykörút 24 hours a day. Like the boulevard on which it stands, Oktogon maintained its name while being officially subjected to others. It was Mussolini tér under the Horthy regime and November 7 tér, recalling the date of the Bolshevik Revolution so important to Hungarians, under the Communists.

Oktogon to Heroes' Square

The section of Andrássy út running to Kodály körönd is noticably wider, the thoroughfare flanked by secondary local-traffic roads separated off by pavements lined with trees, traditional lamp-posts and park benches. Though still close together, the buildings here are not so given over to commercial usage, so their self-important demeanour is more apparent.

Among them is the **Franz Liszt Museum** at Vörösmarty u. 35 (*open Mon–Fri 10–6, Sat 9–5; closed Sun; adm*). A couple of rooms of the composer's former house lovingly display his belongings right down to nutcrackers and handkerchiefs. There are pianos and organs, portraits and busts of the master, and notes about his life that mainly focus on his friendships with Augusz and Zichy, not even touching upon his rampant womanizing. You'd have to be a real enthusiast to get much out of it. Close by is the **Academy of Fine Arts** containing the child-friendly **Budapest Puppet Theatre** at No.69 (*t 321 5200; shows winter Mon–Thurs 3pm, Fri and Sat 10.30 and 4; closed summer; adm*).

The building at **No.60** has a notorious past. During the Horthy era, the ultra-right-wing regime made it their secret police headquarters, where they locked up, beat and tortured Communists. During the Second World War the Arrow Cross used it for the same purposes, the victims this time mainly Jews. After the war, the Communists kept the tradition alive, their secret police doing a fair amount of 'persuading' here, especially in the brutal 'dark 50s'. They probably used many of the same implements, though the legendary giant meat-grinder for disposing of bodies was never found. Today the building fittingly houses the new **House of Terror Museum** (*t 374 2600, www.terrorhaza.hu; open Tues–Fri 10–6, Sat and Sun 10–8; adm*), where photos, artefacts and daunting commentaries recall the victims of those two bitter pills so hard for the Hungarians to swallow: the Nazi Holocaust, and the Communist dictatorship.

Kodály körönd, like Oktogon, is defined by four massive buildings, but is much more sedate and elegant, and generally considered one of Budapest's most beautiful squares. The symmetrical neo-Renaissance edifices are near identical, though No.1 is better preserved and covered in attractive gilt sgraffitos. It was once the home of composer, researcher and teacher Zoltán Kodály, who incorporated traditional folk melodies into his work and travelled the country to collect and preserve them. Now it houses his archives and the **Kodály Memorial Museum** (*open Wed 10–4, Thurs–Sat 1–6, Sun 10–2; closed Mon and Tues; adm*). The house is in its original state, with furniture, manuscripts, and the composer's collection of folk art. At one point the square was named Hitler tér, which prompted Bartók to state that he didn't want his body to be buried in Hungary so long as anywhere was named after Hitler or Mussolini.

The boulevard gets more stately as it heads towards Heroes' Square, the buildings now detached mansions and villas, many containing embassies. Building buffs can veer left down **Bajza u.** for a look at Nos.42 and 44, then cut through to the parallel road **Munkácsy Mihály u.**, where Art Nouveau façades abound, particularly at Nos.19b, 21, 23 and 26. That Andrássy út was designed as a grand driveway leading to the Millenary Monument becomes clearer the closer you get. However, it is a long walk. The M1 metro runs beneath the road, and the no.4 bus follows the same route.

Heroes' Square (Hősök Tere)

In concept akin to the Arc de Triomphe, in execution more like London's Trafalgar Square, this vast paved arena is distinct in one significant way: being far from the city centre, it is rarely full of people. Even the odd tourist bus makes hardly a dent on the acres of space. In the evening this emptiness, together with the smooth surface, makes it a paradise for skaters of all kinds, performing tricks and weaving past each other, oblivious of the stony faces of ancient ancestors. The square and its contents, like the boulevard that leads to them, represent a conscious act of Magyar nationalism, born of a short-lived era of prosperity. Coming at the end of the 19th century, it happened to coincide roughly with the millennial anniversary of the Magyars' conquest of the Carpathian Basin. Though nobody knew exactly when this occurred, a date for celebrations was fixed at 1895, then changed to 1896 when it became clear not everything would be ready. The date has been official ever since and dictated such details as the height of the Basilica and Parliament domes.

Approaching the square, the centre of attention is the **Millenary Monument**, with the Archangel Gabriel atop an imposing 120ft column. Legend has it that Gabriel appeared to King Stephen in a dream, instructing him to convert the pagan Magyars to Christianity and offering him the crown of Hungary, shortly after which a crown arrived from Pope Sylvester II. To augment the symbolism, the archangel is standing on a globe holding the Hungarian crown and an apostolic cross. Despite the setting back of celebrations, the column and statue were still a year late, and were deemed unstable. While a reinforced column was prepared, the statue was sent to the 1900 World Exhibition in Paris where it won the Grand Prix. At the column's base are equestrian statues of Prince Árpád and the chieftains who led the Magyar tribes into the region. In front is a block of stone traditionally used for wreath-laying ceremonies. This Heroes' Monument carries the inscription: 'To the memory of the heroes who have sacrificed their lives for the freedom of our people and national independence.'

At a respectful distance behind the column is a two-part semi-circular **colonnade**. On the top, four groups of symbolic figures represent, from left to right, Work and Wealth, War, Peace, and Knowledge and Glory. Between the columns are statues of Hungary's most important rulers, from King Stephen to Kossuth. The Transylvanian princes were only added after the Second World War, when they replaced statues of Habsburg rulers. Below, reliefs contain legendary scenes from their lives, though most of them are battle scenes. During the short-lived Council Republic period of 1919, the revolutionary Soviets had the whole square draped in red and the column covered by a huge red obelisk bearing a relief of Marx. Focal point of fervent sentiments that it is, many important gatherings have taken place here, most recently the ceremonial reburial on 16 June 1989 of Imre Nagy, which symbolized the beginning of a new democratic era. His coffin was accompanied by five others, four representing other leaders executed after 1956, the fifth representing unknown victims of the time.

The composition of the square is best taken as a whole, the column and Magyar chieftains flanked by the colonnades and, pulling back the focus, the colossal **galleries** on either side of the square. To the right is the neoclassical red brick **Palace of Arts** (Műcsarnok), whose steps were used for Nagy's reburial ceremony. The colourful mosaic that fills the tympanum represents St Stephen as patron of the arts. Behind the portico's six massive Corinthian columns, a three-part fresco depicts *The Beginning of Sculpture*, represented by figures of Vulcan and Athene, *The Source of Arts*, with Apollo and the Muses, and *The Origins of Painting*, with images from ancient mythology. Two smaller frescoes in between depict allegorical figures of Painting and Sculpture. Inside, the largest **gallery** in the country (*t 363 2671; open Tues–Sun 10–6; adm*) houses temporary exhibitions of chiefly modern art.

Museum of Fine Arts (Szépművészeti Múzeum)

t 469 7100; open Tues–Sun 10–5.30; adm for temporary exhibitions only.

On the north side of the square a neoclassical building with Italian-Renaissance, Romanesque and Baroque-revival influences is an appropriate building for the excellent Museum of Fine Arts, the European equivalent of the National Gallery. Eight gigantic Corinthian columns support a portico whose tympanum bears a relief with a completed copy of a fragment on the Temple of Zeus at Olympia, depicting the *Battle of the Centaurs and Lapiths*. The exhibitions have been made to conform to the gallery rather than vice versa, so the interior is just as grand, particularly the sweeping staircases and the Grand Hall. Most exhibits are labelled in English.

The **Egyptian collection** is interesting enough if you haven't been to a better one. Highlights include some good painted sarcophagi, the head of a statue of a New Kingdom young man, a young lady bearing the standard of Hathor, some Late Period bronze sculptures of Harpocrates, Osiris, a raven and a cat.

The **19th-century collection** focuses on French artists of that period. Here are all the big names: Monet, Manet, Renoir, Delacroix. There are some familiar works such as Cézanne's *The Cupboard*, Toulouse-Lautrec's *These Ladies in the Refectory* and Courbet's vast and wonderful *The Wrestlers*. With a few notable exceptions like Monet's *Plum Trees in Blossom*, Pissarro's *Le Pont Neuf* and Gauguin's exotic *Black Pigs*, however, the works of these famous artists are not their best, and the better art on display is the work of lesser names: Dagnan-Bouveret's *Landscape with Trees*, for instance, or Carriere's ethereal *Maternity*. There are some fine sculptures also, such as Carpeaux's *Laughing Girl with Roses* and Clésinger's *Lucretia*. Highlight of the collection though, and on their own ample justification for a visit to this museum, are five sculptures by Rodin, including *Eternal Springtime* and *The Kiss*.

The **Old Masters Permanent Gallery** is the real *raison d'être* of the museum. The core of the collection was purchased from Count Miklós Eszterházy in 1871. Comprising 70 works, the **Spanish collection**, clustered around El Greco and his school, is probably the finest in the world outside Spain. It offers some vivid altarpieces, seven El Grecos, including *The Agony in the Garden* and *The Penitent Magdalene*, and five Goyas including two of the portrayals of common, humble folk for which he is famous, *The Knife-Grinder* and *The Water-Carrier*. There are also some excellent works such as Cerezo's powerful *Ecce Homo*, Ribera's plaintive *Martyrdom of St Andrew* and Velázquez' *Peasants at Table*. In the smaller **German collection** are Hans Baldung Grien's long, sumptuous, wonderfully stylized portraits, *Adam* and *Eve*. The three portraits by Christian Seybold are worthy of scrutiny, one of himself, one of his daughter, and the irrepressible *Laughing Man with Brawn*. Look out also for Dürer's *Portrait of a Young Man*, whose cheer is of a far subtler nature; the elder Jörg Breu's *Elevation of the Cross*; two works by Maulbertsch, *Scene with a Young Man* and *Christ on the Cross*; and Holbein's interesting *Dormition of the Virgin*. The **Italian collection** is more impressive and contains many stars, such as Raphael's so-called *Eszterházy Madonna* and Titian's *Portrait of the Doge Loredan*. Other first-class portraits include Giorgione's *Self-portrait* and *Young Girl*, and Bronzino's *Young Lady*. The latter was a favourite of late Canadian author Robertson Davies, who would have seen great depths in his allegorical *Venus, Cupid and Jealousy*. Other key players in the Italian dream-team are Tintoretto's *Supper at Emmaus*, Veronese's *The Crucifixion*, Bassano's **The Road to Calvary**, and Tiepolo's **St James Conquers the Moors**.

The **Dutch collection** is dominated by Brueghels. The younger Pieter provides the marvellous *Blind Hurdy-Gurdy Player* and *Affray between Peasants and Soldiers*, whereas the elder Pieter's quite different *St John the Baptist's Sermon* has the preacher addressing a group of Flanders peasants. The elder Jan's *Paradise Landscape* is another major work. Look out also for Rubens' *Mucius Scaevola before Porsenna*, and Sebastien Vrancx's *Outdoor Banquet*. Other exhibits include the **English collection**, a let-down: a few mediocre portraits by Hogarth, Reynolds and Gainsborough.

There is also some mainly very bad modern art, a selection of historical paintings, and some medieval Italian works. The **collection of antiquities** consists mostly of Greek ceramics that didn't fit in other collections, although there are some decent 5th-century BC Attic red-figure vases.

The museum also holds temporary exhibitions of 20th-century art, usually featuring major artists. The **shop** sells a decent selection of postcards, framed prints, posters, books, ceramics and jewellery. The **café** behind it is a good place to recover from sensory overload afterwards.

City Park (Városliget)

Heroes' Square is the gateway to the City Park, also created as part of the 1896 millenary celebrations. Over 200 halls and pavilions were erected here, displaying the agricultural, industrial and commercial life of the country. A bridge runs from the square over a lake that in winter is transformed into Europe's finest skating-rink, a marvellous scene when floodlit at night. Originally, skaters used the lake's frozen surface but an artificial surface was added in 1926 that unfortunately uglifies this whole section of the water. The clubhouse down below operates a café and plays host to various events like live music or sporting competitions.

Across the water, hanging there like a fairytale mirage, is the picturesque **Vajdahunyad Castle** (*t 343 1345; open April–mid-Nov Tues–Fri 10–5, Sat and Sun 10–6; mid-Nov–Mar Tues–Fri 10–4, Sat and Sun 10–5; closed Mon; adm*). It is not an authentic castle but was designed by Ignác Alpár especially for the 1896 celebrations, intended to illustrate in one cohesive building all the different architectural styles found throughout Hungary. Erected as a temporary structure, it was so popular with the public that Alpár rebuilt it in more permanent brick. On the road to the castle is a statue of the architect dressed as a medieval guild-master. The building is arranged in chronological order, most of the sections using details copied from some of Hungary's most significant historic structures, or inspired more loosely by the work of a particular architect whose style reflects his age.

To the left of the gate are towers copied from former castles in Upper Hungary, now Slovakia. To the right is a copy of the tower of Segesvár in today's Romania. The courtyard on the left contains the Romanesque wing, including a copy of the still-standing 1214 Benedictine Chapel of Ják in western Hungary. The portal, which is its finest feature, is also the part most true to the original, carrying statues of the 12 apostles. To the left is a chapel incorporating elements from the 11th to 13th centuries. Opposite, to the right, the palace section mixes elements of the Romanesque and Gothic, while to the left the section based on the 15th-century Transylvanian Vajdahunyad Castle is pure Gothic. This is the finest part and most visible from across the lake. Farther left, Renaissance style is represented by a small building with a balcony based on Sárospatak Castle in eastern Hungary. Next door, the large yellow

Baroque section is inspired by details from various 18th-century mansions. This part contains the **Agricultural Museum** (*same hours as castle; adm*), which traces the history of hunting and farming in Hungary, including the development of tools and some interesting varieties of livestock. Facing the entrance is the very popular **statue of Anonymous**, the first Hungarian chronicler, from whom much information about the Middle Ages has reached us. The words on the pedestal are those with which he signed his work, and translate as 'the notary of the most glorious King Béla'. Since there were four kings bearing that name in that era, the chronicler's identity remains a matter of speculation, thus the name Anonymous and the hood which shrouds the figure in wonderfully Gothic mystery. Behind him, a small lake surrounded by board-walks and willows is a pleasant place for a picnic or a daydream.

The bulk of the park stretches off to the south and west, encompassing the **Transport Museum** (*open Tues–Fri 10–5, Sat and Sun 10–6; closed Mon; adm*) and the **Petőfi Hall**, both of which might hold some interest, especially for kids. The museum explains how transport expanded and flourished around the turn of the 20th century, and features vintage locomotives, scale models of trains, cars and steamboats, and posters and regalia covering a period of 100 years. The Petőfi Hall is a major venue for rock and pop events, as well as an informal youth centre that hosts films, theatre, parties and a roller-skating club for children, a decent weekend flea-market and occasional raves. Behind the building a stairway leads to the **Aviation and Space Flight Exhibition** (*open mid-April–Sept Tues–Fri 10–5, Sat and Sun 10–6; Oct–mid-April Tues–Fri 10–4, Sat and Sun 10–5; closed Mon; adm*), with a collection of old aeroplanes.

To the north, on the other side of the busy road that bisects the park, stands a grandiose yellow neo-Baroque building containing not an embassy or summer palace but the **Széchenyi Baths** (*XIV. Állatkerti körút 11, t 321 0310; open April–Sept daily 6am–7pm; Oct–Mar Mon–Sat 6am–5pm, Sun 6am–4pm; adm*). At the entrance a statue depicts geologist Vilmos Zsigmond, who struck upon the hot spring while drilling a well in 1879. Apparently the water comes from deeper within the Earth's crust than any of the other baths, thus reaching the surface at a higher temperature (74–5°C). Inside the grand entrance hall is a series of mosaics, centred on the central dome, of a quality to rival anything in Budapest, plus an extraordinary fountain. This is one of the nicest of the baths, and certainly the most accessible. Everything is here: indoor pools of different temperatures, steam room, sauna, a heated outdoor pool where bathers play chess on floating boards, a swimming pool and a children's pool with water jets and waves, plus plenty of room for sunbathing, and a restaurant. The masseurs here are recommended. The inside looks like a run-down Victorian sanatorium, though more atmospheric than ugly.

North of the baths, along Állatkerti körút, you'll find from east to west an amusement park, a circus and a zoo. The **amusement park** (Vidámpark; *t 343 0996; open April–Oct daily 10–8; Nov–Mar daily 10–6*) is not likely to impress you or your kids: the rides are old-fashioned and shabby, while the rickety roller-coaster is frightening for the wrong reasons and the ghost train not at all. There are a few newer, scarier rides, and you may find the lack of sophistication endearing. The gilded merry-go-round, dating from the park's opening before the war, is certainly appealing and a reminder of the fact that this was the setting for Ferenc Molnár's play *Liliom*, on which the musical *Carousel* was based. Next door is a funfair for toddlers. The **Municipal Circus** (Fővárosi Nagycirkusz; *t 343 8300*) next door has been housing shows year-round since it was built in 1971, but there has been a circus on the site since 70 years before that. Acts involving the exploitation of animals are still a major feature.

Budapest's **Zoo** (Állat-és Növénykert; *t 343 6075, www.zoobudapest.hu*) is an altogether more venerable establishment. Dating back to 1866, an initiative of the Academy of Sciences, it contains, as well as all the usual animals, some important examples of Art Nouveau. The very gateway, covered with fakirs and animals, is a good introduction. The same architect, Kornél Neuschloss-Knüsli, is responsible for the Elephant House, which resembles a large Moorish mosque decorated with majolica and ceramic animals. The Bird House designed by Károly Kós in a National Romantic style allows the birds to fly freely. There are also two greenhouses full of exotic plants and a garden of bonsai trees recently donated by the Japanese ambassador. For all that, it still retains the unpleasant flavour of an old-style zoo in which the comfort of the animals was never the highest priority; but renovations are under way to rectify that and to make it a more child-friendly environment, including the opening last year of a new children's playground. All the best animals are found around the big mountain to the right of the entrance.

The Old Jewish Quarter

District VII, or Erzsébetváros, is the slice of Budapest's pie south of the Andrássy út area. The old Jewish Quarter covers the innermost part of this district, traditionally located between the two circular roads, with Király to the north and Dohány to the south. From the outset it has been a testament to anti-Semitism, its very foundation dating from the 18th century when Jews were still prohibited from living within the city walls. Ironically, as a 3rd-century AD gravestone inscribed with a menorah proves, there were Jews living here at least six centuries before the Magyar founding fathers arrived. When the city outgrew its walls, new laws prevented Jews from buying property. The second half of the 19th century brought a relaxing of these property laws, leading to a rapid rise in the Jewish population in this quarter. In 1867 Jews gained formal emancipation, partly as a reward for enthusiastic support of Kossuth during the revolution. Jewish rights and assimilation crested towards the end of the century, some even rising to the ranks of nobility or gaining seats in the Chamber of Deputies. By 1939 there were about 200,000 Jews in Budapest, many of them living here in a thriving community that had its own kosher shops, restaurants, places of worship and clubs, while striving to assimilate itself and achieve acceptance in a city where anti-Semitism never really stopped being an issue (Mahler complained about it when he was director of the Opera House).

A community, yes, but the area was never a ghetto until 1944. Before that, the Hungarian government had avoided putting all the Jews in one place for fear that this would encourage the Allied forces to bomb the rest of the city. Such considerations were eventually abandoned when the Nazis and Fascist Arrow Cross walled off the whole area and herded the remaining Jews inside as a prelude to deportation. Since the men had already been taken away to do forced labour, which literally worked them to death, the 70,000 crammed into this small area were mainly women, children and pensioners. Owing to disease, malnutrition, random killings and the cold, many of them never made it through the winter (though they fared better than those outside the city, 90 per cent of whom perished in the Holocaust).

Today the city's remnant of 80,000 still constitutes the largest Jewish community in Central Europe. Despite Communist attempts to homogenise the area and a tendency of younger, wealthier Jews to move to quieter, more attractive districts, a sense of cultural identity has survived, fuelled by a resurgent interest in roots and religion, as well as increased contacts with the international Jewish community. You can get a taste of this spirit by wandering around the shabby, decaying and bullet-pocked streets, but there's little to see apart from the magnificent Great Synagogue on Dohány út, which was one of the two entrances to the ghetto of 1944.

Great Synagogue

Open Mon–Thurs 10–5, Fri 10–3, Sun 10–2, closed Sat (service 9–12)
and at Passover; adm.

Situated on the edge of the Jewish Quarter, this enormous building is tucked discreetly up a side road off the Kiskörút so that, despite its size, you won't see it until the last moment. Before even arriving here, the corner building where Dohány u. meets the Kiskörút (No.3a) is worth attention. Its flattened corner holds a relief of a classical couple flanking an angel whose hands they hold, backed by a golden mosaic. Opposite this on the Kiskörút side is a fabulous Gothic building with much decoration, right-angled balconies jutting out point first, a central dome, and four gilded Art Nouveau mosaics across the fourth floor.

These are mere trifles, however, next to the Great Synagogue. Europe's largest synagogue, and the second largest in the world after Temple Emmanuel in New York, it can hold almost 3,000 people and has to be closed in winter because it's too big to heat. In the last decade, $40 million has been spent on its restoration, footed by the Hungarian State and an assortment of Jewish associations in the USA, chief among them the Emmanuel Foundation, fronted by Tony Curtis (né Bernard Schwartz), whose father was a Hungarian emigrant. It was money well spent, for this is truly one of Budapest's most outstanding constructions.

Built in a Romantic style in 1854–9 by Viennese architect Ludwig Förster, it incorporates many obvious Byzantine and particularly Moorish qualities. The patterns in the brickwork were inspired by ancient ruins in the Middle East, while the colours – yellow, red and blue – are representative of the Budapest coat of arms. This reflects other indications that the 19th-century Jews wished to assimilate with rather than distance themselves from their Gentile fellows. The twin towers, for instance, are reminiscent of church steeples, and the presence of an organ (which was played on many occasions by Liszt and Saint-Saëns) is not a very Jewish feature and was opposed by more Orthodox adherents. Its congregation was not and is not strictly Orthodox, espousing also certain Reformist elements in a uniquely Hungarian synthesis called Neolog. Thus the presence of the Ark of the Torah (*bemah*) is at one end rather than central, which is Reformist, but men and women sit separately (men on the ground floor, women in the gallery), which is Orthodox.

The outside of the synagogue avoids the brick-building trap of excessive squareness through its arched colonnade, doors and windows, the latter richly decorated with grilles and surrounds. Star-shaped motifs and curlicues abound, along with ceramic friezes at three levels. Two octagonal towers topped with gold-trimmed onion domes loom above a large rose window, below which a Hebrew inscription from the Book of Exodus reads, 'Make me a sanctuary and I will dwell among them.' (25:8). The interior, designed by Vigadó architect Frigyes Feszl, is just as grand and clearly Eastern in its influences. The floor is inset with eight-pointed stars, the balconies surmounted by gilded arches, and the ceiling adorned with arabesques and Stars of David. Outside in the courtyard, a collection of humble headstones marks the mass grave of those 2,281 Jews who died here during that bitter winter of 1944. Part of the brick wall that surrounded the ghetto can still be seen, with a plaque commemorating its liberation by the Soviets on 18 January 1945.

The staircase up to the **Jewish Museum** (*open April–Oct Mon–Fri 10–3, Sun 10–2;, closed Sat; adm*) bears a relief of Tivadar (Theodore) Herzl, the founder of the Zionist movement, who was born and educated here. It seems particularly appropriate that he should hail from a community continually struggling for emancipation within a country that has always faced the same struggle. The museum's foyer contains that highly significant 3rd-century AD gravestone inscribed with a menorah (seven-branched candlestick). The exhibition displays items from Hungary and abroad, mainly from the 18th and 19th centuries but some dating back to the Middle Ages, arranged according to the festival for which they were used. This includes some exquisitely crafted objects and books such as the Chevra book from Nagykanizsa, dating from 1792. The last room documents, through photos, clippings and examples of anti-Semitic propaganda, the nightmare of the Holocaust in Hungary.

Monuments and Memorials

Behind the courtyard is the **Heroes' Temple**, a squat, square building resembling a Moghul tomb, erected in 1931 to pay tribute to the 10,000 Jewish soldiers who died fighting for Hungary during the First World War. Since it is a working synagogue, it is not open to the public. Beyond it, farther down Wesselényi utca, a garden contains Imre Varga's 1991 **Holocaust Memorial**, which channels all that pain and sorrow into the poignant form of a metallic weeping willow in the shape of an inverted menorah. Each leaf bears the name of a family lost in the Holocaust. The broken marble slab in front contains the single word 'Remember'. The inscription from the Talmud on the plaque closer to the railings reads, 'Whose pain can be greater than mine?'

The **garden** is named in honour of Raoul Wallenberg, a Swedish consul who is believed to have saved as many as 20,000 Jews by placing them in safe houses or even rescuing them from Auschwitz-bound trains. The day before the liberating Red Army arrived, he went forward to meet them and was never seen again. After years of silence, a Soviet official announced in 1957 that Wallenberg had died in a Moscow prison 10 years earlier; they had believed him to be a spy. The Hungarian authorities were wary of the case. In April 1949, a sculpture of the hero depicting a male figure struggling with a snake disappeared on the eve of its unveiling and emerged years later, used for a different function, outside a factory in East Hungary. A copy appeared and remains in front of the Radiology Clinic on Üllői út, but was only acknowledged as Wallenberg in 1989. Even in 1987, a statue by Imre Varga (commissioned by the US Ambassador) was shoved miles away on an arterial road in Buda (at the junction of Szilágyi Erzsébet fasor with Nagyajtai u., four stops on tram 56 from Moszkva tér). So the naming of this garden could be seen as a conscious political act on the part of the Jewish community, who begin their plaque, 'May this park commemorate as an exclamation mark for the post-Holocaust generations the name of the Swedish diplomat Raoul Wallenberg.'

From here, walk down Rumbach to Dob u. and look right. Opposite No.11 is a **memorial to Carl Lutz**, the Swiss diplomat who helped many Jews to survive by issuing them with Swiss or Swedish papers, a ploy later adopted by his colleague Wallenberg. A gold figure attached to the wall seems to be throwing down a sheet to a woman wrapped in bandages lying on the floor below. Locals know it as 'the figure jumping out of a window'. A quote from the Talmud on the easily missed plaque reads, 'He who has saved one life, it's as if he had saved the whole world.'.

The 'Ghetto'

At the Dob/Rumbach junction are a few decent Art Nouveau buildings, while at No.11 Rumbach Sebestyén is a **synagogue** of the same name, built for worshippers of a more conservative persuasion. One of the only works in Hungary of Viennese architect Otto Wagner, its Moorish façade is similar to that of the Great Synagogue, with many fine features. Owned by the state, it is currently closed, decaying, and up for sale. The same is true of the amazing **Gozsdu Udvar**, a passageway linking seven courtyards between Dob u. 16 with Király u. 11. Abandoned and crumbling, this series of inelegant but enigmatic concrete squares with a dog-leg in the middle is eerie and atmospheric. Stand in the middle and look back towards the entrance and what you will see is a series of squares alternating light and shade, growing in size with perspective, thus illustrating what the Greeks called 'gnomonic expansion'. These days it is locked at the Király u. end, presumably for safety purposes. Run-down as it is, not much effort is required to imagine how it was at the beginning of the 20th century when this was the bustling heart of Jewish Budapest, filled with shops, artisans and immigrants. As a short building-lover's detour, Síp u. 11 is worth seeing for its Gothic arches, gargoyles and statue of a knight, and the Art Nouveau building on the corner of Síp and Dohány is wonderfully strange.

These days the community's central focus is on Kazinczy utca, a little farther down Dob u., shortly after Hungary's only kosher *pâtisserie*, **Fröhlich Cukrászda**, whose appearance doesn't live up to its reputation. To the left of Dob u., some decaying buildings at the Király end of Kazinczy have a certain nostalgic charm, especially No.51. Király u. 34 also has an interesting façade with Art Nouveau influences. The **Orthodox synagogue** is here, its Art Nouveau façade elegantly following the curve of the street. It is a plain building apart from the very top, whose undulating curves could be of Polynesian origin. Below this, amidst Stars of David and leaf patterns, big Hebrew letters read, 'This place is none other than the house of God and the gate to Heaven.' For Gentiles, entrance through the gate is unfortunately not allowed, but it's worth going through the doorway to the right, where a courtyard contains the back of the synagogue and an Orthodox complex including a Jewish school and the kosher Hanna restaurant. The buildings between here and Wesselényi u. are interesting if only for the radically differing architectural approaches they display. Note particularly the Wesselényi side of the corner building, with two giant topless angels spreading their wings. The building opposite is also worth a look, as is Wesselényi 17, which has nice Art Nouveau mosaics. There is also a beautiful Art Nouveau building farther down Dob u. at No.53.

If Kazinczy holds the local focus, the heart of activity is still centred on **Klauzál tér**, a block farther down Dob u. It was the heart of the 1944–5 ghetto as well, when – as Wallenberg bravely complained to the Germans – 50,000 people were crammed into living space intended for 15,000. Nowadays, it is given over to one big playground, and the scene of so much suffering now echoes with the sound of children's laughter.

Outside the Centre

The Buda Hills

Forested countryside stretches to the west of Buda, perfect for walking and cycling. There are established trails with signs indicating distance, or duration in minutes (p) and hours (ó). Budapesters like to get back to nature too, so the tranquillity factor is reduced at weekends. Particularly popular, especially with children, are the Children's Railway and the Chairlift, which can be combined with the Cogwheel Railway to form a circuit.

The **Cogwheel Railway** starts in the Városmajor Park, opposite the cylindrical Budapest Hotel (*a couple of stops west of Moszkva tér by buses 22, 56 and 156, or trams 18 and 56; trains leave every 15mins daily 5am–11.30pm, normal ticket required*). The terminus at Széchenyi-hegy is a short walk from the start of the **Children's Railway**. This narrow-gauge railway (760mm) covers 11.1km in about 45mins, mostly through dense woodlands. Built by youth brigades in 1948, it is run by uniformed 10–14-year-olds (except the engineer), giving the whole experience a slightly magical feel (*trains run Mon–Fri every hour 8–5, Sat and Sun every 30–45mins 8.45–5; Sept–May closed Mon; adm*). To visit the **Budakeszi Game Park**, alight at Szépjuhászné from the Children's Railway, catch the 22 bus and ask the driver for the Vadaspark. The entrance is a 15min walk past the Hotel Tanne. Apart from the animals in enclosures (wild boar, deer, etc.), you're likely to see little but butterflies and flowers. It is a beautiful place to wander, however, and usually empty. A wooden lookout tower offers a nice view of the hills, forest and village. The terminus of the Children's Railway, **Hűvösvölgy**, is a large meadow equally good for tranquil meandering. Buses run from here day and night back to Moszkva tér. It is also worth leaving the Children's Railway at János-hegy and following the trail across to the **Chairlift** (*runs May–Sept 9.30–6; Oct–April 9.30–5, closed alternate Mon; adm*). From here it is a short but steep walk up to the four-tiered neo-Romanesque **Erzsébet Lookout Tower**, designed by Frigyes Schulek, who built the Matthias Church. On the highest spot in the Buda Hills, it offers superb views. The Chairlift descends 235m in its 1km journey, taking about 15mins. Its Hungarian name, Libegő, means 'floater', and this is exactly what it does, about 8m above the ground, enough to bother those scared of heights and excite children who relish gentle doses of danger. Bus 158 runs from Zugliget at the bottom back to Moszkva tér.

Caves in the Buda Hills

Since Buda's caves were created by the action of hot thermal waters from below rather than cold rainwater from above, their appearance is unique, consisting of strangely beautiful rock sculptures. The two that are open to visitors are in the Buda Hills not far from Óbuda. They are reached from **Kolosy tér** (itself reached by bus 86 from Batthyány tér, M2 or Flórián tér in Óbuda, or bus 6 from Nyugati station, M3).

The larger and more impressive is **Pál-Völgyi** (*II. Szépvölgyi u. 162, t 388 9537; bus 65 from Kolosy tér; open Tues–Sun 10–4, closed Mon; adm*). This is the longest labyrinth discovered in the Buda Hills. The 30-minute tour involves narrow passages, steep climbs and some 600 steps. The stalagmites and stalactites are awesome, and many formations protruding from the rock face resemble animals.

About a 10-minute walk away is the **Szemlő-hegy Cave** (*II. Pusztaszeri u. 35, t 315 8849; bus 29 from Kolosy tér; open Mon and Wed–Fri 10–3, Sat–Sun 10–4, closed Tues; adm*). Not as big, impressive or convoluted, this system is maybe more striking. Instead of stalactites the walls are covered with bulbous, cauliflower-like mineral formations called 'cave pearls'. The air is so clean and pure that the lowest level (*not on the 25min tour*) contains a therapy centre for respiratory illnesses. A small museum displays cave finds from all over Hungary.

Béla Bartók Memorial House (Bartók Béla Emlékház)

II. Csalán u. 29 (bus 5 from Moszkva tér); t 394 2100, bartok-1981@matav.hu; open Tues–Sun 10–5, closed Mon; adm.

Set in beautiful grounds, this Art Nouveau villa was Bartók's last Hungarian home before he left in disgust at the country's increasing Fascism. The concert hall, often used for chamber concerts on Fridays, features the painted wooden panels of a 1740 church, plus many works of art often depicting the man himself. His study, personal objects and folklore collection are all displayed, along with the Edison phonograph he used for collecting old folk tunes.

Ludwig Museum of Contemporary Art (Kortárs Müvészeti)

ludwig@c3.hu; open Tues–Sun 10–6, closed Mon; adm.

Way south on the Pest embankment by Lágymányosi Bridge is the unlikely site chosen by the former FIDESZ government for a new Millenary City Centre, planned to emulate London's South Bank. Recently constructed are the National Theatre, and the Palace of Culture (Művészetek Palotája), home to the National Philharmonic Orchestra and the Ludwig Museum of Contemporary Art. Much of the stuff here is really modern, so much so that no accepted views of what to think of it have yet been laid down. The core of the collection was donated by the German billionaire and art patron Peter Ludwig, who is reputed to have bought at least one painting every day, largely according to his own enthusiasm rather than for investment purposes. Here you will find works of famous 1960s and 70s pop-artists such as Warhol, Lichtenstein, Rauschenberg, Hockney, Jasper Johns and Claes Oldenburg, as well as some lesser-known Europeans and even the odd Hungarian such as Miklós Erdély (*War Secrets*).

Cemeteries

Kerepesi Cemetery, next to Keleti station (*M2*), was declared a 'decorative' cemetery in 1885, meaning it is where the establishment of each age buried those it chose to honour, be they poets, politicians, artists, architects or war heroes. It thus provides an interesting perspective from which to view Hungary's turbulent recent history. All the big names are here, often easily reached by the wide avenues that criss-cross the vast orderly area. The main mausoleums, placed at key junctions, are those of Kossuth (by Alajos Stróbl), Batthyány and Deák, but look out also for the particularly beautiful tomb of popular singer Lujza Blaha.

Farkasréti Cemetery on Németvölgyi u. (*tram 59 from Moszkva tér*) in the Buda Hills is mainly visited for the extraordinary Mortuary Chapel built by Imre Makovecz, situated just to the right of the main entrance. A prime example of his 'organic architecture', the whole wooden structure resembles a giant oesophagus of some exotic creature. Another delightful spot for a stroll, the cemetery is overcrowded with graves and trees, and contains a rich and varied assortment of tombstones, some of them bearing famous names. Béla Bartók is buried here, with Georg Solti alongside him. Visit the information building to the left of the main gate for a map showing the locations of the cemetery's inmates.

One grave in particular attracts people – almost exclusively Hungarians – to the other major burial ground, **Újköztemető Cemetery**, way out at the edge of District X at Kozma u. 8–10 (*trams 28 or 37*). It is here that Imre Nagy was secretly buried in 1958, along with other key figures from the 1956 Uprising, and a large number of civilians dumped in a mass grave. After the ceremonial funeral of 1989 in Heroes' Square, they were reburied in the same plot (301), which is right in the farthest corner, about 30 minutes' walk from the main gate – not far enough to stop Hungarians from secretly placing flowers on the anonymous grave before 1989, which were duly removed by Soviet policemen. At the beginning of one of the paths leading into plot 300, which contains the mass graves, is a Transylvanian Gate inscribed with the words, 'Only a Hungarian soul may pass through this gate.' In the middle of the plot stands a wooden campanile, a type of decoration traditionally found in old Hungarian cemeteries, in front of panels listing the names of over 400 victims of the Uprising. Adjacent to Nagy's simple grave is György Jovánovics' *Monument to the Martyrs of the 1956 Revolution*, which could be seen as a 'deconstructed' early Christian basilica or as a symbolic passage through Purgatory.

Alongside this cemetery lies Hungary's largest **Jewish burial ground**. There are many grand tombs here, but the most striking, not far from the entrance, to the right of the main path, is that of the Schmidel family designed by Ödön Lechner and Béla Lajta. A central mosaic in green and gold tiles, representing the Tree of Life, is surrounded by flamboyant turquoise ceramics and floral motifs.

Statue Park (Szoborpark)

XXII. Balatoni út., t 227 7446, www.szoborpark.hu. Take red-numbered bus 7 from Ferenciek tere (M3) to its terminus at Etele tér, then the yellow Volán bus from gate 7 or 8 to Diósd-Érd (not included on a Budapest Card). Or take a direct bus from Deák tér, 2,450Ft including park entrance. Leaves Mar–Oct 11am and 3pm, July and Aug 10am and 4pm. Open daily 10–dusk; adm.

After the fall of Communism in 1989, instead of destroying all those Socialist monuments the Hungarians consigned them to a kind of retirement home on the edge of the city, far from impressionable young eyes and tormented older eyes, but close enough so that Hungarians can visit them and jeer, laugh or curse in catharsis. It's also a pretty unique tourist attraction. Here you will find all the old favourites like Marx, Lenin and Engels, plus idealized happy workers, victorious soldiers, and martyrs galore. Many of them are frighteningly massive, like the Red Army soldier that stood at the foot of the Liberty Statue on Gellért Hill. Aesthetically most interesting are Imre Varga's statue of Béla Kún, and the giant charging sailor based on a 1919 call-to-arms poster. Each of the 43 monuments represents a facet of Hungarian history. You're given most of the information you need with the ticket, but for those with a special interest the guide book is a worthy investment. The half-hearted should be warned, however, that it's a long way to go and many people find the site small.

Day Trips and Overnighters from Budapest

Óbuda

Situated on the Buda side, level with the northern tip of Margaret Island, today's suburb of Óbuda was actually the first settlement of any significance in this area. Using the Danube as the northern boundary of their province Pannonia, the Romans established a legionary camp and fortifications here as defence against the barbarians beyond. By the 2nd century BC a thriving civilian settlement had grown around the camp, centred on Aquincum 3km to the north. In the Middle Ages, Árpád and his successors built their royal residence here and the town flourished, but when Béla IV moved the royal seat to the more strategic location of Castle Hill, this original Buda (the ancient Hungarian word Ó means old) lost its importance along with its name. After the Turkish occupation, it enjoyed a renaissance as a market town, producer of wines, and somewhat bohemian gastronomic centre. Today's Óbuda, plagued by an ugly rash of tower blocks and housing estates, is the sort of area many people go on

Getting There

HÉV train to Árpád híd from Batthyány tér.
Bus 6 from Nyugati station, or 86 from any stop on the Buda promenade.

Eating Out

Óbuda t (01) –

Kéhli, III. Mókus u. 22, t 250 4241, *www.kehli.hu* (*expensive*). First-class home-made food based on traditional 19th-century cuisine, served in an authentic space with a plain country feel. Their classic dish is the hotpot with marrow-bone. *Closed Mon–Fri lunch.*

Kisbuda Gyöngye, III. Kenyeres u. 34, t 368 9246 (*expensive*). An intimate little place with a plush, old-style interior and an excellent reputation. Expertly prepared cuisine. Attentive service, and a fine selection of wine, whisky and *pálinka. Closed Sun.*

Uj Sipos halászkert, Fő tér 6, t 388 8745 (*moderate*). Elegant interior resembling a country manor, and outdoor tables in a round cobbled courtyard. The menu is old-style traditional.

Gigler, III. Föld u. 50c, t 368 6078 (*inexpensive*). The cheap and cheerful option. The interior and courtyard are basic but the food is authentic home-cooked Hungarian, tasty, plentiful and cheap. *Closed Sun eve and Mon.*

holiday to get away from, but its main attractions – mostly galleries and Roman ruins – can be seen simply and easily, and make a well-rounded day-trip when combined with Szentendre (*see* pp.260–61).

Opposite the HÉV exit on Szentlélek tér, a splendid old white building contains the **Vasarely Museum** (*open Tues–Sun 10–5, closed Mon; adm*), with an exhaustive collection of Op Art by one of the fathers of the genre, Victor Vasarely, endlessly exploring spatial distortions and optical illusions with geometric patterns. It's a bit tedious if you're not a fan. In the square to the left stands a fine **Holy Trinity column**. On the right, where Szentlélek and Fő squares merge, the Baroque Zichy mansion (Zichy Kúria) holds the **Kassák Museum** (*open Mar–Sept Tues–Sun 10–6; Oct–Feb Tues–Sun 10–4; closed Mon; adm*) and a local history exhibition. Lajos Kassák was a radical constructionist and publisher whose left-wing but anti-authoritarian stance led him into conflict with almost everyone. The museum contains works of avant-garde painting, sculpture, literature and typography.

Literally meaning Main Square, **Fő tér** remains to this day the focal point of the town. With its pedestrianized cobbled streets, old buildings like the lovely **theatre** (Városháza), antique lamp-posts, and traditional restaurants that still make a living from Óbuda's *bon-vivant* reputation, it almost single-handedly retains the fragile ambience of a medieval village. The 18th-century Copf-style house at No.4 contains the **Zsigmond Kun Folk Art Museum** (*open Tues–Fri 2–6, Sat and Sun 10–6; closed Mon; adm*), a collection of mainly 19th-century folk art: pottery, textiles, carvings and furniture, presented in the former home of this connoisseur who gathered them from all over greater (pre-Trianon) Hungary.

At the northeast corner of the square is the strange sight of three metallic and miserable-looking women beneath umbrellas. This is the start of Laktanya u., and the statue composition a prelude to Óbuda's only essential attraction, the **Imre Varga Gallery** at No.7 (*open Tues–Sun 10–6; closed Mon; adm*). Within is a substantial collection by this striking and versatile artist, who is responsible for the Holocaust Monument and the statue of Károlyi Mihály close to Parliament. As well as copies and photos of these and other major works, such as his *St Stephen* and composition of *Our Lady of Hungary* which stand in the Hungarian Chapel of St Peter's in Rome, there are many excellent sculptures.

A number of **Roman ruins** pay testament to Óbuda's ancient history, but you have to be a real aficionado to find them worth seeking out. **Flórián tér**, Óbuda's largest square and an unpleasant junction of major roads and flyovers, was built over the nucleus of the Roman military camp. Various remains, including some elegant columns, stand in the grassy centre, while the underpass is dotted with display cabinets and relics, and holds the **Roman Baths Museum**, a series of badly reconstructed low walls. South from here on Pacsirtamező u., the limited remains of a large **amphitheatre** (*at the junction with Nagyszombat u., a 30min walk*), are still quite impressive. Built in the 2nd century AD with an arena larger than that of the Colosseum in Rome, it could seat up to 15,000 spectators.

North of Flórián tér (northwest up Vörösvári u. then right on Vihar u. as far as Meggyfa u.) is the **Hercules Villa** (*open mid–end April and Oct Tues–Sun 10–5; May–Sept Tues–Sun 10–6; closed Mon and Nov–14 April; adm*). A series of mosaics are preserved where they were found. Under the first canopy an almost complete mosaic portrays Hercules shooting the centaur Nessos. The third canopy contains a mosaic of Alexandrian origin once composed of 60,000 stones and depicting Hercules about to vomit at a wine festival. It would be spectacular if complete, but sadly the three central figures are cut off just above the waist.

About 1km southwest of Flórián tér on a forested hilltop at Kiscelli u.108, and well worth the walk, is the **Kiscelli Museum** (*t 388 8560, www.btmfk.iif.hu; open April–Oct Tues–Sun 10–6; Nov–Mar Tues–Sun 10–4; closed Mon; adm*). This 1745 Baroque Trinitarian monastery contains a selection of major Hungarian artworks from about 1880 to 1990, including Rippl-Rónai's *My Parents After 40 Years of Marriage* and János Kmetty's Cubist *Városliget*. There are some fine 18th–19th-century engravings of Budapest, with the brand-new Chain Bridge and the Great Synagogue. The bombed-out shell of a Gothic church is now an eerie gallery, providing a striking setting for spectacles such as operas and fashion shows, permanent exhibitions of the urban history and fne art collections of Budapest, and temporary exhibitions of contemporary art. From here you're not far from the caves in the Buda Hills (*see p.255*).

Aquincum

HÉV to Aquincum from Óbuda's Árpád híd, or buses 34, 42 and 106. Open May–Sept Tues–Sun 9–6; Oct–Nov Tues–Sun 9–5; closed Dec–April; adm.

Roughly 3km north of Óbuda is Budapest's major Roman ruins, the former town of Aquincum. Starting life as a military camp and growing to become provincial capital of Pannonia Inferior, Aquincum was a buzzing civilian town of 40,000 inhabitants. No buildings survive, but the arrangement of the foundation walls and the underground piping give a fair idea of the scale and layout of the town, including the remains of a public baths, houses, a market place, a forum, law courts, an old Christian church, and a shrine to the Persian sun-god Mithras. The neoclassical **Aquincum Museum** contains locally found relics such as statues, pottery, tools, mosaics and jewellery, as well as a reconstructed 3rd-century Roman water organ. Across the road by the side of the HÉV station are the ruins of the civilian town **amphitheatre**, which could seat 8,000, considerably smaller than the military one in Óbuda. No ticket required, just walk around the surrounding bank peering through the vegetation.

Szentendre

Situated just 20km north of Budapest, the picturesque town of Szentendre is easily the most rewarding day trip from Budapest thanks to two very different types of historical migration. At the end of the 17th century, a mixture of Slav ethnic groups including Bulgarians and Dalmatians, but predominantly Greek Orthodox Serbians, arrived here in several waves, fleeing from the advancing Turks. Hard workers in trade and viniculture, they soon began building grand houses and churches with a characteristically Balkan flavour. Over two centuries later, after a series of floods and epidemics had all but emptied the town, this marvellous architecture, combined with the bucolic ambience and Danube setting, began to attract a stream of artists, whose numbers have swollen ever since, filling the streets with galleries and studios. Today this combination of art and history, together with the undeniably quaint cobblestoned streets, has led to a third wave of visitors: the tourists whose excessive volume represent Szentendre's only down side.

Following Kossuth Lajos utca north from the HÉV station, the first site is **Pozharevachka Church**, with the oldest iconostasis in town. Stop to pick up a map at the TOURINFORM office, then head to the focal **Fő tér**, a picturesque cobblestoned square centred on a memorial cross and lined with restaurant terraces. To its west on **Városház tér** is **Art'éria**, Hungary's first private, post-Communist gallery; on its east side is the **Art Gallery of Szentendre**; at No. 20 is **Erdész Gáleria**, a commercial gallery

Getting There

HÉV from Óbuda's Árpád híd or Budapest's Batthyány tér (*45mins*). **Boat** from Budapest's Vigadó tér (*summer only*). The first leaves Budapest at 9, the last leaves Szentendre 5.15.

Tourist Information

Szentendre TOURINFORM, Dumtsa Jenő u. 22, t (26) 317 965, *www.szentendre.hu*. Open Nov–Feb Mon–Fri 9–4.30; Mar–Oct also Sat and Sun 10–2.

Eating Out

Szentendre t (26) –
Aranysarkány, Alkotmány u.1a (*expensive*). Probably the best restaurant in town, with an interesting menu that includes sour cherry soup, and trout fillets with Campari.

Labirintus Etterem, Bogdányi 10, t 317 054 (*expensive*). Situated in the Wine Museum, with an interesting, extensive menu of traditional Hungarian cuisine such as larded venison with cranberries.

Chez Nicolas, Kígyó u. 10, t 311 288 (*moderate*). Less crowded than those down the hill. Good if predictable food at reasonable prices. Small terrace upstairs.

Szentendrei Corner Kisvendéglő, Duna Korzó 4, t 300 027 (*moderate*). The usual menu, but with some Serbian specialities also. Small courtyard, but no views.

Városháza Étterem, Rákóczi Ferenc u. 1, t 505 755 (*moderate*). Smart and elegant turn-of-the-century interior with a beautiful garden courtyard. The food is standard Hungarian fare.

with an impressive collection of 20th-century masters; to the north is **Blagovestenska Church** (*adm*) with a dark, atmospheric incense-scented interior and a wonderful iconostasis. Round the corner is the **Museum of Margit Kovács** (*Vastagh György u.1, t (26) 310790; open daily 10–6; adm*), which contains an extensive collection from this prolific, much-beloved ceramic artist. Frequently dismissed as mere kitsch, the beguiling simplicity and naïveté of her work draws attention away from the intense and complex emotions it often captures and evokes.

Heading north, **Bogdányi utca**, too quaint for its own good, is lined with restaurants, souvenir stalls, and a few more worthwhile galleries, including the **Museum of Painters Anna Margit and Amos Imre**, and the **Art Mill** (No.32, *t (26) 301 701; adm*). This ruined sawmill, featuring a dramatic half-empty shell used for festivals and shows, exhibits works by Hungarian and international artists, as well as the local community.

The best thing to do from here is to wander the maze of cobbled streets that range over the hillside above, lined with handsome, colourful, well-preserved houses and churches. You can't miss the large and impressive terracotta-colour **Serbian Orthodox cathedral**, whose grounds also contain the **Serbian Orthodox Art Museum** (*Pátriáka u.; open May–Sept Tues–Sun 10–6; Oct–April Tues–Sun 10–4; adm, including church*). Nearby is a **museum** (*Hunyadi u.1; adm*) dedicated to pre-war surrealist painter Vajda Lajos. Further south is Szentendre's oldest structure, the **Roman Catholic parish church**, constructed between 1241–80. The nave, chancel and sacristy are original, but most of it was rebuilt in the early 14th century. There are nice views from up here of church spires, the town's red-tile roofs, and the Danube.

Open Air Village Museum (Szabadtéri Néprajzi Múzeum/Skanzen)

Skanzen bus from stand 7, Szentendre, every 40mins–1hr, t (26) 312 304.
Open April–Oct Tues–Sun 9–5; closed Mon; adm, free Tues and Wed.

Covering an area of 115 acres, 5km north of Szentendre, this museum's goal is to represent traditional types of settlement and architecture from 10 regions considered to be Hungary's most characteristic. The buildings and their interiors elaborately recreate those inhabited by the various social strata and groups in villages and market towns from the late 18th –mid-20th centuries. Though only four have been completed, with another under way, this is still an impressive exhibition, and could easily fill half a day. From Thursday to Sunday, handicraft masters perform traditional labours in a working environment: the baker makes bread, the farmer tends his animals, etc. You can play traditional games, eat traditional food, see ancient breeds of livestock, and so on. Every second Sunday, craft workshops are held, offering the visitor hands-on experience of such skills as basket-weaving or pottery, and festivals are celebrated with dancing and other folkloric merry-making.

Esztergom

A further 20km north of Szentendre on the scenic 'Danube Bend' is Esztergom, Hungary's second most historically important town. Another former Roman

Getting There

Buses from Budapest's Árpad híd station run every half-hour. Those via Dorog take 75mins. The **train** from Nyugati Stn leaves up to 13 times daily and takes 90 mins. The last one returns at 10.10pm. **Boats** from Vigadó tér run 2–3 times daily June–Sept. The first boat leaves at 7.30am; the last boat returns at 4pm. 1 speedy **hydrofoil** runs daily June–Aug, leaving at 9.30am, returning at 3.30 pm.

Tourist Information

There is no official tourist office, nor a decent website. Ask at Budapest TOURINFORM before leaving, or try **Gran Tours** at Széchenyi tér 25, t 417 052, *open Mon–Fri 8–6, Sat 9–12*.

Eating Out

Esztergom t (33) –

Anonim, Berényi Zsigmond u. 4, t 411 880 (*moderate*). Perfectly prepared Hungarian dishes served in a historic town house close to the river in Víziváros.

Hotel Esztergom Restaurant, Prímás sziget, t 412 555, *info@hotel-esztergom.hu* (*inexpensive*). European style cuisine in surroundings that are striving to be upmarket.

Primas Pince Restaurant, Szent István tér 4, t 313 495 (*inexpensive*). A great location and a pleasant, relaxed patio. Typical Hungarian food. Very popular.

Csülök Csárda, Batthyány Lajos u. 9, t 312 420 (*inexpensive*). Large helpings of good home-cooked food, also very popular with locals.

settlement, where Marcus Aurelius wrote his *Meditations*, this was Hungary's first real capital, home of Prince Géza and reputed birthplace of his son Vajk, who was crowned here by the Pope on Christmas Day AD 1000 to become Hungary's first king, István I (Stephen). Stephen executed the pagan rebel Koppány here and hung his quartered remains on the city walls. He built a royal palace (excavated in 1934) that his descendants retained as royal seat and centre of the Hungarian Church until the Tatar Invasion of 1241, after which King Béla IV moved his capital to Buda and gave the castle to the archbishopric. It was razed again in 1543 by Sultan Suleiman II, and most of the town's remaining medieval buildings were destroyed 50 years later when the Habsburgs took it back. In 1761 the archbishopric recovered the castle and set about planning the biggest cathedral in the country.

Completed in the 1860s on the site of a destroyed 12th-century church, **Esztergom Basilica** (*t (33) 411 895; open daily 7–6*) took three architects and 40 years to complete. Situated high up on Castle Hill, surrounded by manicured grounds and extensive fortifications, and fronted by a pompous set of mighty pillars and portico, it really is a monumental example of neoclassical architecture. Ferenc Liszt composed his famous *Esztergom Mass* (1856) for its consecration. The marble-heavy interior focuses on an impressive cupola that rises 71.5m above the floor, but its real highlight is the red marble **Bakócz Chapel**, originally built in 1510 by Florentine craftsmen, then dismantled during the Turkish occupation, and reassembled in 1823. The **treasury** (*open Mar–Oct daily 9–4.30; Nov–Feb daily 11–3.30; adm*) contains an impressive collection of priceless ecclesistical artefacts, including the 13th-century Hungarian coronation cross. The large **crypt** (*open daily 9–5; adm*) is best known for the tomb of controversial Cardinal Mindszenty (*see* Szabadság tér, p.229). The lookout point at the top of the cupola offers magnificent views over the attractive Baroque townscape. South of the cathedral is the **Castle Museum** (*t (33) 415 986; open Tues–Sun 9–4.30; adm*), displaying remnants of the medieval royal palace and other local finds.

The town below is a regular, nitty-gritty place, barely affected by tourism, but full of Baroque and neoclassical buildings dating chiefly from the 18th century. Stretching along the banks of the Little Danube southwest of Castle Hill is the attractive Víziváros district centred on the pretty white **Víziváros parish church** (1738) on Mindszenty tere. The nearby **Primate's Palace** contains a **Christian Museum** (*Berényi Zsigmond u. 2, t (33) 413 880; open Tues–Sun 10–6; adm*) that holds Hungary's finest collection of medieval religious art. South of here, **Maria Valeria Bridge** connects with the city of Štúrovo in Slovakia.

Eger

Hungarians revere Eger as the site of one of their history's most glorious events. During a siege in 1552, a group of some 2,000 Magyars led by Istvan Dobó kept an army of 10,000 Turks at bay here for over a month. Legends abound: apparently, Dobó

Getting There

Train depart from Keleti station, 15 daily, taking 2hrs. The last intercity returns 7.10pm.

Tourist Information

Eger TOURINFORM, Dobó tér 2, t (36) 517715. *Open June–Sept Mon–Fri 9–8, Sat and Sun 9–5; April and Oct Mon–Fri 9–5, Sat 9–1.* A useful website is *www.egeronline.com.*

Where to Stay

Eger t (36) –

★★★Hotel Korona, Tündérpart u. 5, t 313 670, *www.koronahotel.hu* (*inexpensive*). A large, well-equipped hotel with decent rooms, a pool, Jacuzzi, sauna, fitness room and its own wine cellar. The hotel has a spectacular cellar restaurant and a lovely garden terrace. Breakfast included.

★★★Hotel Senator House, Dobó tér 11, t 320 466, *senator@ohb.hu* (*inexpensive*). A handsome 18th-century townhouse right on the main square, very comfortable and popular. Breakfast included.

★★★Hotel Villa Volgy, Tulipánkert u. 5, t 321 664, *villavolgy@dpg.hu* (*inexpensive*). A lovely new big building in Szépasszonyvölgy, next to a park. Some rooms have balconies.

★★★Panorama Panzió, Joó János u. 9, t 420531, *www.panoramapanzio.hu* (*inexpensive*). A

beautiful building with bright, attractive common areas, and rooms equipped with antique furniture. Sauna, Jacuzzi, and a delightful garden. Breakfast included.

★★★Hotel Romantik, Csíky Sándor u. 26, t 310 456, *www.romantikhotel.hu* (*inexpensive*). A charming little place close to the centre, with bright, pleasant rooms and a garden.

Eating Out

Eger t (36) –

Two of the best places to eat are the Hotel Korona and Hotel Senator House (*see* above).

Arany Oroszlán étterem (Golden Lion), Dobó tér 5, t 311 005 (*moderate*). A decent, central spot for Hungarian classics.

Imola Udvarház, Dózsa Gy. tér, t 516 180 (*moderate*). A little more fancy, but with the emphasis still on home-cooked food.

Fehérszarvas Vadásztanya (White Deer Hunter's Camp), Klapka u. 8, t 411 129 (*inexpensive*). Close to Dobó tér, but with the feel of a country lodge, decked out with silly hunting regalia. The hearty fare features wild game. It's very popular with locals, with live music most evenings.

There are a number of places to eat scattered among the wine cellars of Szépasszony-völgy. Two of the best are **Talizmán étterem** in the lovely Tulip Garden (Tulipánkert), t 412 533; and **Kulacs Csárda és Borozó** ('Canteen' Inn and Tavern), t 311 375.

opened the wine caskets so that his men would greet their attackers with red liquid dripping from their mouths. These days, the wine itself is what the town is more famous for, in particular the red blend Egri Bikavér, better known abroad as Bull's Blood. For the casual visitor, however, Eger is simply a gorgeous little town full of attractive Baroque buildings, that represents the most satisfying overnight trip from Budapest, 128km away.

The **castle** itself is Eger's most obvious sight, but there hasn't been too much to see since the Habsburgs blew it up in 1702. Within its rebuilt 15th-century Gothic Palace, however, is the **Castle Museum** (*t (36) 312 744; open 8–8; shorter hours off-season; adm*) with exhibitions on the history of castle and city, and tours of the underground fortress (Kazamaták). In the southeastern part of the castle is the **tomb of Géza Gárdonyi**, whose novel about that famous siege, *Egri csillagok* (*Stars of Eger*), remains a perennial favourite. Characters from the book can be seen in the museum's waxworks display. More enticing is a walk along the **castle walls** for great views of Eger's picturesque townscape.

A lovely place for aimless strolling, the pedestrianized centre revolves around **Dobó tér**, which contains a **Minorite Church** from 1771. Towering over nearby **Eszterházy tér** is Hungary's second biggest church, **Eger Basilica**, designed by József Hild, also responsible for the one in Budapest. Its impressive façade is topped by statues of Faith, Hope and Charity by Italian sculptor Marco Casagrande, who also produced the statues of kings and apostles that line the lengthy flight of stairs down to the square. Opposite, the **Lyceum** contains an **astronomical museum** (*t (36) 520 400; open Tues–Sun 9.30–3; closed Mon; adm*) full of 18th-century instruments, including a *camera obscura* (the 'Eye of Eger') which projects a view of the whole town. At the corner of Knézich and Markó Ferenc streets is a Turkish **minaret** from 1596 (*open April–Nov Tues–Sun 10–6; adm*) believed to be the northernmost in Europe. There are great views from the top, if you can stand the claustrophobia-inducing ascent.

A mere 25-minute walk from town is the horseshoe-shaped **Szépasszonyvölgy**, or 'Valley of Beautiful Women', the perfect place to sample local wines. Dozens of small, private wine cellars cater to the revellers who come to sample their cheap wares, eat, dance, listen to the spontaneous musical happenings, and make exceeding merry. Many places are closed by evening, so arrive early.

Language

German/Austrian

German is a complex language. There are three, rather than two, genders; nouns and adjectives decline; it is full of irregular verbs and deceptive conjugations; and the syntax is ornate, and often littered with parentheses. The verb often comes only at the end. But there are some advantages. Nouns are capitalized and easy to spot. Spelling is phonetic, so once you have grasped the basics of pronunciation there are few surprises.

Austrians speak German with a softer accent and many of their own colloquialisms; the most important to remember is that the usual greeting is not *Guten Tag* but *Grüss Gott* – which you should use whenever you encounter someone, to be polite.

Pronunciation

Consonants

Most are the same as in English. There are no silent letters. **G**s are hard, as in English 'good', but **ch** is a guttural sound, as in the Scottish 'loch'—though **sch** is said as 'sh'. **S** is also pronounced 'sh', when it appears before a consonant (especially at the beginning of a word), as in *stein*, pronounced 'shtine'. Otherwise the sound is closer to 'z'. **Z** is pronounced 'ts' and **d** at the end of the word becomes 't'. **R**s are rolled at the back of the throat, as in French. **V** is pronounced somewhere between the English 'f' and 'v', and **w** is said as the English 'v'.

Vowels

A can be long (as in 'father') or short, like the 'u' in 'hut'. Similarly **u** can be short, as in 'put', or long, as in 'boot'. **E** is pronounced at the end of words, and is slightly longer than in English. Say **er** as in 'hair' and **ee** as in 'hay'. Say **ai** as in 'pie'; **au** as in 'house'; **ie** as in 'glee'; **ei** like 'eye' and **eu** as in 'oil'.

An **umlaut** (¨) changes the pronunciation of a word. Say **ä** like the 'e' in 'bet', or like the 'a' in 'label'. Say **ö** like the vowel sound in 'fur'. **ü** is a very short version of the vowel sound in 'true'. Sometimes an umlaut is replaced by an e after the vowel. The printed symbol **ß** is sometimes seen instead of **ss**, though this guide uses 'ss'.

Useful Words and Phrases

yes/no/maybe	*ja/nein/vielleicht*
excuse me	*entschuldigung, bitte*
I am sorry	*es tut mir leid*
please	*bitte*
thank you	*danke (schön)*
it's a pleasure	*bitte (schön)*
hello	*guten Tag; hallo; Grüss Gott (in Austria)*
goodbye; bye	*auf Wiedersehen; tschüss*
good morning	*guten Morgen*
good evening	*guten Abend*
goodnight	*guten Nacht*
how are you?(formal)	*wie geht es Ihnen?*
(informal)	*wie geht es Dir?* or *wie geht's?*
I'm very well	*mir geht's gut*
I don't speak German	*ich spreche kein Deutsch*
do you speak English?	*sprechen Sie Englisch?*
I don't know	*ich weiss nicht*
I don't understand	*ich verstehe nicht*
my name is...	*mein Name ist... ; ich heisse...*
I am English (m)	*ich bin Engländer*
I am English (f)	*ich bin Engländerin*
American	*Amerikaner(in)*
leave me alone	*lass mich in Ruhe*
with/without	*mit/ohne*
and/but	*und/aber*
I would like...	*ich möchte...*
a little bit	*a bissel (Austria)*
how much is this?	*wieviel kostet dies?*
where is/are...?	*wo ist/sind...?*
how far is it to...	*wie weit ist es nach...*

near/far	nah/weit
left/right/straight on	links/rechts/gerade aus
can you help me?	konnen Sie mir bitte helfen?
I am lost	ich weiss nicht wo ich bin

Notices and Signs

open/closed	geöffnet/geschlossen
no entry	eingang verboten
(emergency) exit	(Not) ausgang
entrance	Eingang
toilet	Toilette
Ladies/Gents	Damen/Herren
push/pull	drücken/ziehen
bank	Bank
police	Polizei
rural police	Gendarmerie (Austria)
hospital	Krankenhaus
pharmacy	Apotheke
post office	Post
airport	Flughafen
railway station	Bahnhof
train	Zug
platform	Gleis
reserved	besetzt

Days and Months

Monday	Montag
Tuesday	Dienstag
Wednesday	Mittwoch
Thursday	Donnerstag
Friday	Freitag
Saturday	Samstag
Sunday	Sonntag

January	Januar; Jännar (Austria)
February	Februar; Feber (Austria)
March	März
April	April
May	Mai
June	Juni
July	Juli
August	August
September	September
October	Oktober
November	November
December	Dezember

Numbers

one/two/three	eins/zwei/drei
four/five/six	vier/fünf/sechs
seven/eight	sieben/acht
nine/ten	neun/zehn
eleven	elf
twelve	zwölf
thirteen	dreizehn
fourteen	vierzehn
seventeen	siebzehn
twenty	zwanzig
twenty-one	einundzwanzig
thirty	dreissig
forty	vierzig
fifty	fünfzig
sixty	sechszig
seventy	siebzig
eighty	achtzig
ninety	neunzig
hundred	hundert
two hundred	zweihundert
thousand	tausend
three thousand	dreitausend
million	eine Million

Time

morning	Morgen; Vormittag
in the morning	in der Früh (Austria)
afternoon	Nachmittag
evening	Abend
night	Nacht
week	Woche
month	Monat
year	Jahr
today/yesterday/ tomorrow	heute/gestern/ morgen

Food and Drink

the menu please	die Speisekarte bitte
the bill please	die Rechnung bitte
I am vegetarian	ich bin vegetarier
breakfast	Frühstuck; Brotzeit
lunch	Mittagessen
dinner	Abendessen
supper	Abendbrot
snack	Jause (Austria)
menu	Speisekarte
cup	Tasse
pot (e.g. of coffee)	Kännchen

glass	*Glas*
bottle	*Flasche*
salt/pepper	*Salz/Pfeffer*
milk/sugar	*Milch/Zucker*
bread/butter	*Brot/Butter*
boiled	*gekocht*
steamed	*gedämpft*
baked	*gebacken*
roasted	*gebraten*
smoked	*geräuchert*
stuffed	*gefüllt*
starters	*Vorspeise*
main course	*Hauptgericht*

Meat and Poultry *Fleisch und Geflügel*

roast beef	*Beiried (Austria)*
meatball	*Boulette*
duck	*Ente*
minced meat	*Hackfleisch*
chicken	*Huhn; Hähnchen*
goose	*Gans*
veal	*Kalbfleisch*
chop	*Kottelett; Schnitzel*
lamb	*Lammfleisch*
liver	*Leber*
oxtail	*Ochsenschwanz*
beef	*Rindfleisch*
ham	*Schinken*
pork	*Schweinefleisch*
bacon	*Speck*
steak	*Steak*
turkey	*Truthahn; Puter*
sausage	*Wurst*

Fish *Fische*

trout	*Forelle*
prawns	*Garnalen*
herring	*Hering; Matjes*
cod	*Kabeljau*
salmon	*Lachs*
haddock	*Schellfisch*
plaice	*Scholle*
sole	*Seezunge*
tuna	*Thunfisch*
squid	*Tintenfisch*

Vegetables *Gemüse*

aubergine	*Aubergine; Melanzini (Austria)*
beans	*Bohnen*
cauliflower	*Blumenkohl; Karfiol (Austria)*
peas	*Erbsen*

potato	*Erdäpfel (Austria)*
green beans	*Fisolen (Austria)*
cucumber	*Gurke*
garlic	*Knoblauch*
cabbage/red cabbage	*Kohl/Rotkohl*
leeks	*Lauch*
maize	*Mais; Kukuruz (Austria)*
noodles	*Nockerl (Austria)*
peppers/capsicums	*Paprika*
mushrooms	*Pilzen; Champignons; Schwarrmerl (Austria)*
asparagus	*Spargel*
spinach	*Spinat*
tomato	*Tomate; Paradeiser (Austria)*
onions	*Zwiebeln*

Fruit *Obst*

pineapple	*Ananas*
apple	*Apfel*
orange	*Apfelsine, Orange*
banana	*Banane*
pear	*Birne*
strawberry	*Erdbeere*
raspberry	*Himbeere*
cherry	*Kirsche*
apricot	*Marille (Austria)*
grapefruit	*Pampelmuse*
peach	*Pfirsich*
grapes	*Trauben*
sour cherries	*Weichseln (Austria)*
lemon	*Zitrone*

Dessert/Cheese *Nachtisch/Käse*

ice-cream	*Eis*
almonds	*Mandeln*
jam	*Marmelade (Austria)*
nuts	*Nüsse*
(whipped) cream	*Sahne/Schlagsahne; Obers (Austria)*
chocolate	*Schokolade*
cheese	*Käse*
curd cheese	*Topfen (Austria)*
tart/cake	*Torte/Kuchen*
sweets	*Zuckerl (Austria)*

Drinks *Getränke*

(mineral) water	*(Mineral) wasser*
fruit juice	*Saft*
tea (with milk)	*Tee (mit Milch)*
coffee	*Kaffee*
beer	*Bier*
red wine/white wine	*Rotwein/Weisswein*

Czech

It is difficult to imagine how Czech could be more alien to English-speakers. The language is Slavonic, with Latin influences, and in its modern form it dates from the 19th century, when, after 200 years of Germanization, it was re-established by scholars, with the help of peasants, a few old texts, and Polish, Serbo-Croat, Bulgarian and Russian dictionaries.

If you try to speak a few word of Czech it's appreciated by most people. Until the 1989 revolution German was the city's second language, but it has now been firmly over-taken by English. That linguistic shift – which seemed far from inevitable even ten years ago – has reasonable claim to be the most signifi-cant cultural change to hit Prague since the Thirty Years' War. Two entire generations were forced to learn Russian; it's widely understood, but almost universally reviled.

Pronunciation

Czech is a phonetic language (pronounced consistently according to its spelling) with none of the shenanigans of silent letters and the like. That's simple enough – the problem is learning how to pronounce the letters. If the language of the English southern middle class is used as a benchmark, the main differences are that **c** is spoken as 'ts', **j** is a vowel sound like the English 'y', and **r** is rolled at the front of the mouth. **Ch** is a consonant in itself – it's pronounced as in the Scottish 'loch', and you'll find it after 'h' in the dictionary.

A háček (ˇ) above a consonant softens it: thus **č** is pronounced 'ch' as in 'chill', **š** is 'sh', and **ž** is the 'zh' sound in 'pleasure'. With **ř**, you venture into territory uncharted by the English language, and every other known language in the world. Even Czech children have to be taught how to say it; the closest you're likely to get is by rolling an 'r' behind your teeth and then expelling a rapid 'zh'.

Vowels are less complicated – **a** is the 'u' in 'up', **e** is as in 'met', **i** and **y** are both as in 'sip', **o** as in 'hot', and **u** as in 'pull'. The sounds are lengthened if the vowel is topped with an accent (´) (or in the case of 'u', also the symbol °) – they're pronounced like the vowels in, respectively, 'bar', 'bear', 'feed', 'poor', and

'oooooh!'. The letter **ě** is pronounced as though it were 'ye' as in 'yet' and softens the consonant that comes before it. Accents affect only the sound of a vowel; and when pronouncing a word, it's always the first syllable that's stressed.

You don't use a subject (I, you, etc.) with a verb, since the ending in itself makes it clear who's doing the deed. The English pronoun 'you' has two forms, as in many European languages: 'vy' is polite and is used in most everyday situations (and where more than one person is being addressed); 'ty' is widespread among young people, and can be used to address anyone whom you could call your friend (you can also use it to be contemptuous to someone you've never met before). Beware also of the bewildering number of endings any ordinary word can have, depending on which of the seven cases, three-and-a-half genders and two categories it belongs to; if you're looking something up in a dictionary, plump for whatever looks closest. Finally, be alert to the fact that Czechs generally say 'no' or 'ano', when they're agreeing to something that's in doubt.

Useful Words and Phrases

yes/no	*ano/ne*
I don't understand	*nerozumím*
I don't know	*nevím*
Do you speak English?	*mluvíte anglicky?*
I am English	*jsem angličan(ka)*
Please	*prosím*
Please speak slowly	*mluvte prosím pomalu*
Thanks (very much)	*děkuji (moc)*
You're welcome	*prosím*
Not at all	*není zač*
I'm sorry	*promiňte*
Good morning	*dobré ráno*
Good day	*dobrý den*
Good evening	*dobrý večer*
Goodbye	*na shledanou*
My name is...	*jmenuji se...*
Pleased to meet you	*těší mě, že vás*
Call a doctor	*zavolejte lékaře*
Let me through	*puštte mě*
Who?	*kdo?*
What?	*co?*
Where (is)?	*kde (je)?*
When?	*kdy?*

How much/many?	kolik?
Do you have...?	máte...?
post office	poyta
stamp	námka
How are you?	jak se máte?
When are you open?	jak máte otevřeno?

Travel

How can I get to ... ?	jak se dostanu na...?
Where is ... ?	kde je...?
Let me out	puštte mě ven
airport	letigtě
bus- or tram-stop	zastávka
metro station	stanice
(railway) station	nádraží
taxi-rank	stanoviště taxi
aeroplane	letadlo
bus	autobus
tram	tramvaj
train	vlak
ticket	lístek

Days and Months

Monday	pondělí
Tuesday	úterý
Wednesday	středa
Thursday	čtvrtek
Friday	pátek
Saturday	sobota
Sunday	neděle

January	leden
February	únor
March	březen
April	duben
May	květen
June	červen
July	červenec
August	srpen
September	září
October	říjen
November	listopad
December	prosinec

Numbers

zero	nula
one	jedna
two	dva

three	tři
four	čtyři
five	pět
six	šest
seven	sedm
eight	osm
nine	devět
ten	deset
eleven	jedenáct
twelve	dvanáct
thirteen	třináct
fourteen	čtrnáct
fifteen	patnáct
sixteen	šestnáct
seventeen	sedmnáct
eighteen	osmnáct
nineteen	devatenáct
twenty	dvacet
twenty-one	dvacet-jedna
twenty-two	dvacet-dva
thirty	třicet
thirty-one	třicet-jedna
forty	čtyřicet
fifty	padesát
sixty	šedesát
seventy	sedmdesát
eighty	osmdesát
ninety	devadesát
one hundred	sto
one hundred and one	sto-jedna
two hundred	dvě stě
three hundred	tři sta
four hundred	čtyři sta
five hundred	pět set
six hundred	šest set
one thousand	tisíc
two thousand	dva tisíce
million	milión

Time

What time is it?	kolik je hodin?
morning	ráno, dopoledne
afternoon	odpoledne
evening	večer
night	noc
minute	minuta
hour	hodina
(to)day	dnes
week	týden
tomorrow	zítra
yesterday	včera

Food and Drink

Do you have a table?	*máte volný stůl?*
vegetarian	*vegetarián*
Do you have vegetarian dishes?	*máte bezmasé jídlo?*
Enjoy your meal	*dobrou chuť!*
breakfast	*snídaně*
lunch	*oběd*
dinner	*večeře*
soup	*polévka*
appetizer	*předkrm*
braised	*dušené*
grilled	*na rožni*
roast	*pečené*
fried	*smažené*
boiled	*vařené*
pasta	*těstoviny*

Meat/Poultry — *Maso/Drůbež*

pheasant	*bažant*
steak	*biftek*
wild boar (also used to mean potent man)	*divočák*
ham	*gunka*
beef	*hovězí*
goose	*husa*
liver	*játra*
stag	*jelení*
duck	*kachna*
sausage	*klobás(a)*
rabbit	*králík*
turkey	*krocan*
chicken	*kuře*
kidneys	*ledvinka*
stewed meat (beef)	*rogtěná*
minced meat	*sekaná*
kebab	*špíz*
venison	*srnčí*
sirloin	*svíčková*
veal	*telecí*
sausage	*uzeniny*
pork	*vepřové*

Fish — *Ryby*

perch	*candát*
carp	*kapr*
crab	*krab*
lobster	*humr*
plaice	*platýz*
trout	*pstruh*
anchovy	*sardelka*
sardine	*sardinka*
pike	*štika*
tuna	*tuňák*
eel	*úhoř*
whale	*velryba*
shark	*žralok*

Fruit/Vegetables — *Ovoce/Zelenina*

pineapple	*ananas*
banana	*banán*
potatoes	*brambory*
peach	*broskev*
pear	*hruška*
apple	*jablko*
strawberry	*jahoda*
apricot	*meruňka*
nuts	*ořechy*
orange	*pomeranč*
cherries	*třešně*
garlic	*česnek*
asparagus	*chřest*
onion	*cibule*
mushrooms	*houby*
french fries	*hranolky*
carrots	*mrkev*
cucumber	*okurka*
tomato	*rajčata*
rice	*rýže*
salad	*salát*
mushroom	*žampion*
cabbage	*zelí*

Dessert/Cheese — *Moučnicky/Sýr*

cake	*koláč*
pancake	*palačinka*
ice-cream sundae	*pohár*
whipped cream	*glehačka*
cream	*smetana*
ice cream	*zmrzlina*
sheep cheese	*ovči sýr*

Drinks — *Napoje*

coffee	*káva*
tea	*čaj*
with lemon	*s citrónem*
with milk	*s mlékem*
without milk	*bez mléka*
milk	*mléko*
juice	*džus*
mineral water	*minerálka*
beer	*pivo*
wine (white, red)	*víno (bílé, červené)*

Hungarian

No other language that uses Latin script is as baffling as Hungarian. Normally in a European country you would expect to be able to understand a few written words – the basics, the essentials. Come to Hungary with such expectations and they are soon dashed against the harsh rocks of impossible letter combinations, absurdly long words, and endless accents. The easy explanation for this is that Hungarian is one of the few languages in Europe that is not of Indo-European origin. During the course of trying to work out where the Magyars originally came from, linguistics experts were called upon, and found that the core vocabulary of Hungarian, the basic words that have descended through millennia, is related to languages in the Finno-Ugric family, though far too distantly for Finns and Hungarians to understand one another. This places Hungarians' origins in Western Siberia and the northern part of the Ural mountains.

The problem is compounded by the fact that the Hungarians, who have managed to avoid the usual fate of small countries surrounded by large predatory empires – that of having their language carefully eradicated – love their language and are reluctant to learn anybody else's. In tourist situations like hotels and restaurants, there is usually someone who speaks some English, but in shops, museums or at the baths, even rudimentary communication has to be conducted in sign language. If they do have a few words of something, it is likely to be German. Latin languages will gain no glimmer of recognition. In desperate circumstances, seek out a young person.

There's no point trying to learn to speak the language, whose grammar is as difficult as its vocabulary. What follows is a glossary of words and expressions that might make life easier for you and the Hungarians you encounter. If you do make the effort, they may find it hard to hide their amusement at your pronunciation, but they will love you for it.

Pronunciation

Hungarian pronunciation is fairly straightforward and consistent. Letters and combinations are always pronounced in the same way; there is no nonsense with silent letters and the like. The stress pattern is regular, with the first syllable slightly emphasized and each following syllable clearly and evenly pronounced. Accents denote a longer vowel (except for é and á). Double consonants are pronounced longer.

In dictionaries and listings, words beginning with ö and ő count as separate letters, with their own listings after 'o'. Sz also counts as a separate consonant.

a	like *o* in hot	á	like *a* in far
e	like *e* in send	é	like *a* in day
i	like *i* in hit	í	like *ee* in feet
o	like *o* in open	ó	same but longer
ö	the sound that starts earth		
ő	like the *u* in fur	u	like *u* in put
ú	like *u* in rule	ü	like *u* in French *tu*
ű	the same but longer		
c	like *ts* in hats	s	like *sh* in cash
cs	like *ch* in touch	sz	like *s* in sit
zs	like *s* in pleasure		
j	like *y* in yes	ly	like *y* in yes
gy	like *d* at the start of dune		
ny	like *n* in new	ty	like *t* in tulip

Useful Words and Phrases

yes/no/maybe	*igen/nem/talán*
please	*kérem*
thank you/thanks	*köszönöm/kösz*
OK/very good	*jó/nagyon jó*
good/nice	*szép*
bad/ugly	*csúnya*
hello (to one person)	*szervusz*
hello (more than one)	*szervusztok*
hello (familiar)	*szia*
goodbye/bye	*viszontlátásra/viszlát*
excuse me (to get past)	*szabad?*
excuse me (for attention)	*bocsánat, uram*
I beg your pardon?	*Tessék?*
Can you help me?	*Kérhetem a segítségét?*
Do you speak English	*Beszél angolul?*
I am English /American	*Angol/amerikai vagyok*
I don't speak Hungarian	*Nem beszélek Magyarul*
I (don't) understand	*(Nem) értem*
What is your name?	*Mi a neve?*
My name is...	*A nevem...*

Nice to meet you	Örvendek
police	rendőrség
doctor	orvos
ambulance	mentőautó
I feel ill	Rosszul vagyok
I would like...	Kérek...
How much is this?	Ez mennyibe kerül?
expensive/cheap	drága/olcsó
big/small	nagy/kicsi
open/closed	nyitva/zárva
entrance/exit	bejárat/kijárat
this one/that one	ez/az
push/pull	tolni/húzni
men's/women's	férfi/női
bookshop	könyvesbolt
chemist	patika/gyógyszertár
department store	aruház
market	piac
post office	postahivatal
art gallery	képcsarnok
bridge	híd
castle	vár
cinema	mozi
hill	hegy or domb
palace	palota
tower	torony
wood or park	liget
left/right/straight on	bal/jobb/egyenesen
where	hol
Where is the...?	Hol van a...?
How far is...?	Milyen messze van...?
address	cím
floor	emelet
street/avenue	utca/út
square	tér/tere
boulevard	körút
walk or promenade	sétány
bus	autóbusz
tram	villamos
trolleybus	troli(busz)
train	vonat
underground	metró
bus stop	buszmegálló
railway station	pályaudvar
station	állomás
platform	vágány
boat	hajó
aeroplane	repülőgép
airport	repülőtér
departure	indulás
arrival	érkezés
ticket	jegy
seat (place)	hely

Days and Months

Monday	hétfő
Tuesday	kedd
Wednesday	szerda
Thursday	csütörtök
Friday	péntek
Saturday	szombat
Sunday	vasárnap

January	január
February	február
March	március
April	április
May	május
June	június
July	július
August	augusztus
September	szeptember
October	október
November	november
December	december

Numbers

one	egy
two	kettő/két
three	három
four	négy
five	öt
six	hat
seven	hét
eight	nyolc
nine	kilenc
ten	tíz
eleven	tizenegy
twelve	tizenkettő
twenty	húsz
twenty-one	huszonegy
thirty	harminc
forty	negyven
fifty	ötven
sixty	hatvan
seventy	hetven
eighty	nyolcvan
ninety	kilencven
one hundred	száz
one hundred and ten	száztíz
two hundred	kétszáz
one thousand	ezer
one million	millió

Time

minute	*perc*
hour/half an hour	*óra/félóra*
day/week	*nap/hét*
month/year	*hónap/év*
morning/afternoon	*reggel/délután*
evening	*este*
today/tomorrow	*ma/holnap*
yesterday	*tegnap*
now	*most*

Food and Drink

I'd like...	*Szeretnék egy...*
I am a vegetarian	*Vegetáriánus vagyok*
The bill please	*Számla, kérem*
menu	*étlap*
wine list	*itallap*
breakfast	*reggeli*
lunch	*ebéd*
dinner	*vacsora*
restaurant	*étterem/vendéglő*
salt	*só*
pepper	*bors*
glass	*pohár*
bottle	*üveg*
cheers	*egészségedre*
starters	*előételek*
main courses	*főételek*
vegetables	*zöldség*
desserts	*édességek*
soup	*leves*
egg	*tojás*

Meat / Hús

lamb	*bárány*
chicken	*csirke*
sausage	*kolbász*
beef	*marha*
liver	*máj*
pork	*sertéshúst*

Fish / Halételek

trout	*pisztráng*
carp	*ponty*
pike-perch	*süllő*

Vegetables / Zöldségek

beans	*bab*
boiled potatoes	*főttburgonya*
mushroom	*gomba*

onion	*hagyma*
chips/fries	*hasábbburgonya*
cabbage	*káposta*
tomato	*paradicsom*
rice	*rizs*
peas	*zölborsó*
dumplings	*zsemlegombóc*

Fruit / Gyümölcsök

apple	*alma*
banana	*banán*
lemon	*citrom*
orange	*narancs*
plum	*szilva*
strawberry	*eper*

Drinks / Italok

mineral water	*ásvány-víz*
fruit juice	*gyümölcslé*
coffee	*kávé*
tea	*tea*
sugar	*cukor*
milk	*tej*
red wine	*vörösbor*
white wine	*fehérbor*
beer	*sör*

Hungarian Dishes

jókai bableves bean soup with vegetables, smoked pork and small dumplings

libamáj zsirjában roast goose liver

hortobágyi palacsinta pancakes stuffed with minced pork, covered with sauce made from pork gravy, mushrooms and sour cream

bakonyi sertéshús pork in mushroom and sour cream sauce

kacsasült roast duck

töltött paprika stuffed peppers

pörkölt stew, usually meat

paprikás pörkölt with sour cream

paprikás csirke paprika chicken

halászlé hot and sour fish soup

gombafejek rántva breaded and fried mushrooms

saláta salad (often pickled cabbage, gherkin or pepper)

rántott sajt cheese fried in batter

rétes (almás/cseresznyés/túrós) (apple/cherry/curd cheese) strudels

túrógombóc curd cheese balls

Gundel palacsinta pancakes stuffed with walnuts and topped with chocolate sauce

Index

Main page references are in **bold**. Page references to maps are in *italics*.
V = Vienna. **P** = Prague. **B** = Budapest.

Budapest: Metro and HÉV

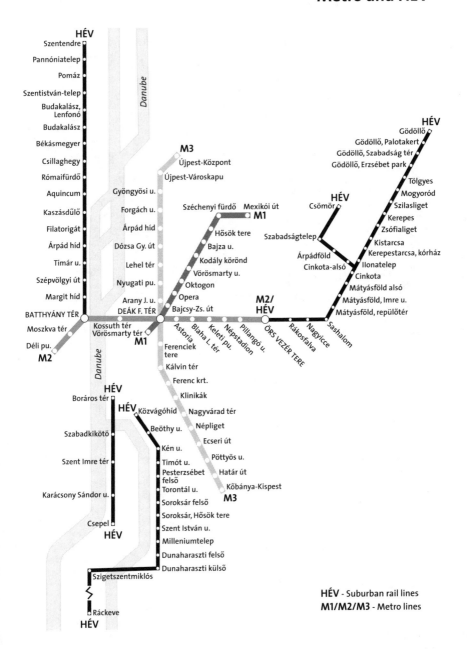

HÉV - Suburban rail lines
M1/M2/M3 - Metro lines

Vienna: U-Bahn